W9-CIG-671

HOUSTON PUBLIC LIBRARY
HOUSTON, TEXAS

GIFT OF

EDNA JOSEPH FUND

The Cambridge Companion to Beethoven

Cambridge Companions to Music

Composers

The Cambridge Companion to Bach
Edited by John Butt
0 521 45350 X (hardback)
0 521 58780 8 (paperback)

The Cambridge Companion to Beethoven
Edited by Glenn Stanley
0 521 58074 9 (hardback)
0 521 58934 7 (paperback)

The Cambridge Companion to Berg
Edited by Anthony Pople
0 521 56374 7 (hardback)
0 521 56489 1 (paperback)

The Cambridge Companion to Brahms
Edited by Michael Musgrave
0 521 48129 5 (hardback)
0 521 48581 9 (paperback)

The Cambridge Companion to Benjamin Britten
Edited by Mervyn Cooke
0 521 57384 X (hardback)
0 521 57476 5 (paperback)

The Cambridge Companion to Chopin
Edited by Jim Samson
0 521 47752 2 (paperback)

The Cambridge Companion to Handel
Edited by Donald Burrows
0 521 45425 5 (hardback)
0 521 45613 4 (paperback)

The Cambridge Companion to Schubert
Edited by Christopher Gibbs
0 521 48229 1 (hardback)
0 521 48424 3 (paperback)

The Cambridge Companion to

BEETHOVEN

EDITED BY
Glenn Stanley

CAMBRIDGE
UNIVERSITY PRESS

HOUSTON PUBLIC LIBRARY

R01120 45786

PUBLISHED BY THE PRESS SYNDICATE OF THE UNIVERSITY OF CAMBRIDGE
The Pitt Building, Trumpington Street, Cambridge CB2 1RP, United Kingdom

CAMBRIDGE UNIVERSITY PRESS
The Edinburgh Building, Cambridge CB2 2RU, UK http://www.cup.cam.ac.uk
40 West 20th Street, New York, NY 10011–4211, USA http://www.cup.org
10 Stamford Road, Oakleigh, Melbourne 3166, Australia

© Cambridge University Press 2000

This book is in copyright. Subject to statutory exception and to the provisions
of relevant collective licensing agreements, no reproduction of any part may
take place without the written permission of Cambridge University Press.

First published 2000

Printed in the United Kingdom at the University Press, Cambridge

Typeset in Adobe Minion 10.75/14 pt, in QuarkXpress™ [SE]

A catalogue record for this book is available from the British Library

Library of Congress cataloguing in publication data

The Cambridge Companion to Beethoven / edited by Glenn Stanley.
       p.   cm. – (Cambridge companions to music)
Includes bibliographical references and index.
ISBN 0 521 58074 9 (hardback) – ISBN 0 521 58934 7 (paperback)
1. Beethoven, Ludwig van, 1770–1827 – Criticism and interpretation.
I. Stanley, Glenn.   II. Series.
ML410.B4C24   1999
780'.92–dc21   98–42732   CIP

ISBN 0 521 58074 9 hardback
ISBN 0 521 58934 7 paperback

Contents

Illustrations

between pages 300 and 301

Contributors

Leon Botstein is the President of Bard College and the Leon Levy Professor of the Arts and Humanities. He is the director of the American Symphony Orchestra and the American-Russian Youth Orchestra and the editor of *The Musical Quarterly*. He has edited the *Compleat Brahms* (1999).

Scott Burnham is Associate Professor of Music at Princeton University. He is the author of *Beethoven Hero* (1995) and translator of *Musical Form in the Age of Beethoven* (1997), a selection of music theoretical writings by A. B. Marx. Currently he is pondering issues of subjectivity in the instrumental music of Mozart and Schubert.

Barry Cooper is a Senior Lecturer at the University of Manchester. His books include *Beethoven and the Creative Process* (1990) and *Beethoven's Folksong Settings* (1994), and he is General Editor of *The Beethoven Compendium* (1991), a standard reference work that has been translated into five other languages. He has also written over thirty articles on Beethoven and other subjects, and completed a version of the first movement of Beethoven's unfinished Tenth Symphony.

John Daverio is Professor of Music and Chairman of the Musicology Department at Boston University. He is the author of *Nineteenth-Century Music and the German Romantic Ideology* (1993), *Robert Schumann: Herald of a "New Poetic Age"* (1997), and numerous articles on the music of Schumann, Brahms, and Wagner.

David B. Dennis is Associate Professor of History at Loyola University, Chicago. He is the author of *Beethoven and German Politics, 1870–1989* (1996).

Alain Frogley is Associate Professor at the University of Connecticut, Storrs. He is the editor of *Vaughan Williams Studies* (1996). He has published articles on Beethoven in the *Musical Times* and *Beethoven Forum*, and has also written extensively on twentieth-century British music. He is a frequent contributor to *BBC Music Magazine*.

Amanda Glauert is a Senior Lecturer at the Royal Academy of Music in London, and has contributed articles to *19th-Century Music*, the *New Grove Dictionary of Opera*, and *Wagner in Performance*. She is the author of *Hugo Wolf and the Wagnerian Inheritance* (1999).

Roger Kamien holds the Zubin Mehta Chair in Musicology at the Hebrew University of Jerusalem. He is the author of *Music: An Appreciation* and articles dealing with Haydn, Mozart, and Beethoven. He has recently completed a book on Beethoven's piano sonatas.

Mark Kaplan, a violinist, brings to his chapter on the instrumental works with piano the sensitivity and authority of his international experience as a concert artist and teacher. As a violinist, Kaplan has appeared as soloist with

every major symphony orchestra in Europe and North America, and is a
founder of the celebrated Golub–Kaplan–Carr Trio. He is Professor and Chair
of the String Department at the University of California, Los Angeles, and
continues to perform regularly with orchestras and major chamber music
festivals.

William Kinderman is Professor of Music at the University of Victoria, British
Columbia, and has taught extensively at the Hochschule der Künste, Berlin. He
is the author of *Beethoven's Diabelli Variations, Beethoven,* and editor of
Beethoven's Compositional Process and *The Second Practice of Nineteenth-
Century Tonality.* He is currently working on an edition of Beethoven's
sketchbook Artaria 195. As pianist, he often presents concerts and lecture
recitals and has recorded Beethoven's last sonatas and Diabelli Variations.

Birgit Lodes teaches at the University of Munich and is author of *Das Gloria in
Beethovens Missa solemnis* (1997). She has recently published chapters on the
Mass, the Requiem, and the Motet in the nineteenth century in the
Handbuch der musikalischen Gattungen, vol. 9: *Messe und Motette* (1998). She
is currently working on a book about music and musical life in Augsburg
1490–1530.

Nicholas Marston is Reader in Music at the University of Oxford, and Fellow and
Tutor of St. Peter's College. His research interests center on Beethoven sketch
studies and Schenkerian analysis. In addition to *Beethoven's Piano Sonata in E,
Op. 109* (1995) and *Schumann: Fantasie, Op. 17* (1992) he has published widely
in leading academic journals. He currently serves on the editorial boards of
Beethoven Forum, Music Analysis, and *The Journal of the Royal Musical
Association.*

Margaret Notley has published articles about Brahms, Schubert, Bruckner, and
Viennese musical life in *19th-Century Music,* the *Journal of the American
Musicological Society,* and a number of anthologies. She is currently writing a
book about late Brahms.

Elaine Sisman is Professor of Music at Columbia University. The author of *Haydn
and the Classical Variation, Mozart: The "Jupiter" Symphony* (Cambridge Music
Handbook), and editor of *Haydn and His World,* she specializes in music and
aesthetics of the eighteenth and nineteenth centuries, and has written on such
topics as Beethoven and the meaning of *pathètique* and *fantasia,* Haydn's
theater symphonies, the sublime in Mozart's music, and Brahms's variations.
She is an editor of *Beethoven Forum* and associate editor of *19th-Century
Music.*

Glenn Stanley is Associate Professor of Music at the University of Connecticut,
Storrs. He has edited volumes 3 and 6 of *Beethoven Forum,* of which he is an
associate editor. Stanley has published articles on Mendelssohn, Schubert,
Wagner, and Mozart; written on the early keyboard variations of Beethoven
and the aesthetics of the keyboard sonata in the Classical-Romantic period;
and contributed articles on historiography and German music criticism to the
revised *New Grove Dictionary.* He is currently working on a study of Arnold
Schering's hermeneutics and his theory of musical symbolism in the music of
Bach and Beethoven.

Michael C. Tusa is Professor of Music at the University of Texas at Austin. He has published a number of studies on Carl Maria von Weber and Ludwig van Beethoven, including essays on *Fidelio* in the *Journal of the American Musicological Society*, *Beethoven Forum*, and the Cambridge Opera Handbook *Fidelio*, ed. Paul Robinson.

Preface and acknowledgments

The *Cambridge Companion to Beethoven* is principally about Beethoven's music and its reception. The music is placed in its historical contexts in chapters presenting a chronology and some thoughts about biography, a look at Beethoven's musical "thinking and doing" when not composing, and a discussion of the compositional process as revealed in sketches and autographs. These chapters are followed by a cross-genre examination of stylistic and structural questions, including a consideration of Beethoven's stylistic debts to (and independence from) the legacy of Haydn and Mozart – a discussion that also helps to establish historical context.

I asked the authors of the genre chapters to define for themselves problems specific to their genre as the basis for their thinking. They posed and solved the problems in various ways – with an emphasis on problems of ensemble (chamber music with piano, symphony), genre aesthetics (string quartet and *Lied*), the place of the genre within Beethoven's career and with respect to music in other genres (piano music, sacred music, and opera) – all of which further emphasize the importance of context to the understanding of Beethoven's achievement. Context also plays a role in the chapters on reception, a role that may be described as dialectical. The way that composers, performers, theorists, and participants in general culture have interpreted Beethoven's music has established the parameters for successive generations' views of his music and, it has been argued, all of music. At the same time, their approach has been influenced by currents in the musical life and in the broader cultural arena, as they developed during and after Beethoven's life. Our book takes its place within this process, reflecting traditional emphases in Beethoven studies and incorporating some of the most recent developments in musicology and theory that have served to broaden the perspectives of the field.

I owe thanks to many people. Alain Frogley and Peter Kaminsky, my colleagues at the University of Connecticut, helped me in the process of soliciting authors. I repeatedly turned to Alain Frogley and to Christopher Gibbs for advice in technical details. Barry Cooper, Alain Frogley, Christopher Hatch, Birgit Lodes, and Margaret Notley all made valuable comments on my chapter, while my assistant Sandra Binder helped me to prepare the chronology and the selected further reading. I would also like to thank the Research Foundation at the University of Connecticut for providing generous support for my work on this project. Finally a note of thanks to all the authors; this was a joint effort; it is our book, not mine.

Glenn Stanley

Abbreviations

Literature

Anderson   Emily Anderson, ed. and tr., *The Letters of Beethoven*, 3 vols. (London, 1961; rpt. New York, 1985)

BS I, BS II, BS III   *Beethoven Studies*, ed. Alan Tyson, vol. I (New York: Norton, 1973), vol. II (Oxford, 1977), vol. III (Cambridge, 1982)

BG   *Ludwig van Beethoven: Briefwechsel Gesamtausgabe*, ed. Sieghard Brandenburg, 8 vols. (Munich, 1997–98)

CB   Karl-Heinz Köhler, Grita Herre, and Dagmar Beck, eds., *Ludwig van Beethovens Konversationshefte* (=Conversation Books), 8 vols. (Leipzig, 1968–93)

GA   *Beethovens Werke: vollständige, kritisch durchgesehene Gesamtausgabe*, 25 vols. (Leipzig, 1862–65, 1888)

Hess   Willy Hess, *Verzeichnis der nicht in der Gesamtausgabe veröffentlichten Werke Ludwig van Beethovens* (Wiesbaden, 1957)

JTW   Douglas Johnson, Alan Tyson, and Robert Winter, *The Beethoven Sketchbooks: History, Reconstruction, Inventory*, ed. Douglas Johnson (Berkeley and Los Angeles, 1985)

Kinsky-Halm   George Kinsky, *Das Werk Beethovens: thematisch-bibliographisches Verzeichnis seiner sämtlichen vollendeten Kompositionen*, completed and ed. Hans Halm (Munich and Duisburg, 1955)

Klein   Hans-Gunter Klein, *Ludwig van Beethoven: Autographe und Abschriften, SPK, Kataloge der Musikabteilung*, ed. Rudolf Elvers, Erste Reihe: Handschriften, vol. II (Berlin, 1975)

N I   Gustav Nottebohm, *Beethoveniana* (Leipzig and Winterthur, 1872)

N II   Gustav Nottebohm, *Zweite Beethoveniana: nachgelassene Aufsätze* (Leipzig, 1887)

N 1865   Gustav Nottebohm, *Ein Skizzenbuch von Beethoven* (Leipzig, 1865); English trans. in *Two Beethoven Sketchbooks*, tr. Jonathon Katz (London, 1979), pp. 3–43

N 1880   Gustav Nottebohm, *Ein Skizzenbuch von Beethoven aus dem Jahre 1803* (Leipzig, 1880); English trans. in *Two Beethoven Sketchbooks*, tr. Jonathon Katz (London, 1979), pp. 47–125

New Grove   *The New Grove Dictionary of Music and Musicians*, ed. Stanley Sadie, 20 vols. (London, 1980)

Schindler (1840)   Anton Schindler, *Biographie von Ludwig van Beethoven* (Münster, 1840); trs. into English as *The Life of Beethoven*, ed. I. Moscheles, 2 vols. (London, 1841)

Schindler (1860)   Anton Schindler, *Biographie von Ludwig van Beethoven*, 2 vols. (3rd edn., Münster, 1860)

Schindler–MacArdle   Anton Schindler, *Beethoven as I Knew Him*, ed. Donald W. MacArdle, tr. Constance S. Jolly (Chapel Hill, 1966)

SBH   Hans Schmidt. "Die Beethoven Handschriften des Beethovenhauses in Bonn," BJ 7 (1971), vii–xxiv, 1–443

SG   Joseph Schmidt-Görg, "Wasserzeichen in Beethoven-Briefen," BJ 5 (1966), 7–74

SV   Hans Schmidt, "Verzeichnis der Skizzen Beethovens," BJ 6 (1969), 7–128

TDR, I–V   Alexander Wheelock Thayer, *Ludwig van Beethovens Leben*, vol. I (rev.) continued by Hermann Deiters (Berlin, 1901); vols. IV–V completed by Hugo Riemann (Leipzig, 1907, 1908); vols. II–III, rev. Riemann (Leipzig, 1910, 1911); Deiters's 1901 edn. of vol. I rev. Riemann (Leipzig, 1917); vols. II–V reissued (Leipzig, 1922–23)

Thayer I, II, III   Alexander Wheelock Thayer, *Ludwig van Beethoven's Leben*, 3 vols. (Berlin, 1866–79)

Thayer–Forbes   *Thayer's Life of Beethoven*, rev. and ed. Elliot Forbes, 2 vols. (Princeton, NJ, 1964)

Thayer–Krehbiel   Alexander Wheelock Thayer, *The Life of Ludwig van Beethoven*, tr. into English and ed. Henry Edward Krehbiel, 3 vols. (New York, 1921)

Thayer, Verzeichniss   Alexander Wheelock Thayer, *Chronologisches Verzeichniss der Werke Ludwig van Beethoven's* (Berlin, 1865)

Wegeler–Ries   Franz Gerhard Wegeler and Ferdinand Ries, *Biographische Notizen über Ludwig van Beethoven* (Coblenz, 1838), suppl. Franz Gerhard Wegeler (Coblenz, 1845)

Journals

Acta   *Acta Musicologica*

AfMW   *Archiv für Musikwissenschaft*

AmZ   *Allgemeine musikalische Zeitung*

BF   *Beethoven Forum*

BJ   *Beethoven-Jahrbuch* (1908–09) and *Beethoven-Jahrbuch*, Zweite Reihe (1953–)

JAMS   *Journal of the American Musicological Society*

JM   *The Journal of Musicology*

JMT   *Journal of Music Theory*

ML   *Music and Letters*

MQ   *The Musical Quarterly*

NBJ   *Neues Beethoven-Jahrbuch*

19CM   *19th-Century Music*

Libraries

BL   British Library, London

BN   Bibliothèque Nationale, Paris

DSB   Deutsche Staatsbibliothek, Berlin

GdM   Gesellschaft der Musikfreunde, Vienna

PrStB   former Preußische Staatsbibliothek, Berlin

SBB   Staatsbibliothek zu Berlin – Preußischer Kulturbesitz, Berlin

SPK   Staatsbibliothek Preußischer Kulturbesitz, Berlin

PART I

A professional portrait

1 Some thoughts on biography and a chronology of Beethoven's life and music

GLENN STANLEY

The three style periods

The idea that Beethoven's music and his career as a composer fall into three periods was first proposed in rudimentary form by an anonymous French author in 1818 – at the very beginning of what we now consider the third period and almost ten years before his death in 1827. It was advanced again in 1828, and taken up by some of the most influential biographers and authors of life-and-works studies in the nineteenth century, among them A. Schindler (*Biographie von Ludwig van Beethoven*, 1840), and W. Lenz (*Beethoven et ses trois styles*, 1852). Yet almost from the start objections were raised to its usefulness, and it did not figure prominently in the seminal biography by A. W. Thayer (first published in Germany in three volumes, 1866, 1872, 1879), which includes little discussion of the music. And there was little agreement among those authors subscribing to the idea about the criterion for and the chronological limits of the "style periods." But the necessity of imposing some kind of narrative structure was self-evident, and, while some twentieth-century authors have advanced four-part and even five-part divisions, the original ternary one has proved to be remarkably strong.[1]

As ever more details of Beethoven's life became known, it was recognized that "the breaks between the periods correspond with the major turning-points in Beethoven's biography."[2] This certainly increased the attractiveness of the basic idea, regardless of the number of periods proposed, because with the new biographical underpinning, such divisions provided a (superficially) persuasive answer to the question of the connections between the artist and his art. The new periods are precipitated by personal crises that help trigger artistic ones; the new style is the result of Beethoven's overcoming or surmounting both personal and creative problems.

The following discussion of the three periods represents an amalgam and critique of various traditional tri-partite divisions that differ in details but are in basic agreement about general contours.

1. A relatively untroubled "formative" or "early" first period runs until 1802, in which Beethoven masters the "Classical" style and establishes himself as a virtuoso composer for piano. In addition to the obvious flaw

that ignores the personal and musical importance of Beethoven's move to Vienna in 1792, this periodization does not acknowledge several small-scale crises that affected his productivity, the significance of Beethoven's turn to string quartet and symphony c. 1798, or the "new path" identified by Beethoven himself in 1801. A separate Bonn period has been suggested, and the first decade in Vienna has been subdivided into spans preceding and following 1799–1800.[3]

2. The devastating episode of the "Heiligenstadt Testament"(October 1802) – a letter written, but not sent, to his brothers when Beethoven, in despair about the hearing losses that had begun some three years earlier, considers and then rejects taking his life – ushers in the second, or middle period. It runs from the *Eroica* Symphony (1803–04) through 1813–14 and is sometimes poeticized as the "heroic decade." Now, having assimilated the Classical style, Beethoven forges his own more dramatic and monumental one, while concentrating more on the symphony and concerto, and large scale choral and dramatic works. Even the works for piano and chamber ensemble reflect the new expressive and structural emphases. A shortcoming in this division lies in its over-identification with the style of the Third and Fifth Symphonies and other "heroic" works, and its failure to acknowledge first-period precedents for them, e.g. the *Pathétique* Sonata for Piano op. 13 (1798). It also denies the non-heroic character of the Seventh and Eighth Symphonies, the Fourth Piano Concerto, and the Violin Concerto, and ignores the importance of a number of lyrical works for piano and for chamber ensemble composed from 1809 onwards, which has led some recent authors to sub-divide this second decade around that year.

3. The third or "late" period begins with several relatively fallow years in which Beethoven is preoccupied with a whole host of personal calamities: the catastrophe of the "Immortal Beloved" (a love affair with a married woman whose identity cannot be established with complete certainty – Antonie Brentano is the current leading candidate; Josephina Deym-Brunsvik has also been suggested – that was broken off in 1812), and as a result the abandonment of any hopes to marry and establish a family; the deep disappointment about the political restoration after the defeat of France in 1813 and the bitterness about the political conditions in Vienna; the death of Beethoven's brother Caspar Carl in 1815, and the ensuing five-year struggle with his sister-in-law Johanna over the guardianship of her son Karl; the ever-worsening deafness that forces Beethoven to renounce completely public performance as a pianist and contributes to his feelings of social isolation. This period is marked by intense formal and stylistic innovation and an increasing emphasis on personal subjectivity in contrast to the more objective character of the

heroic music. Just where this period really begins has been the subject of extended debate. Works as early as the 1814 final version of *Fidelio* and the Piano Sonata op. 90 have been viewed as important transitional music, yet as late a composition as the "Hammerklavier" Piano Sonata of 1818 has been suggested as the crucible for the third-period style. A. Oulibicheff (*Beethoven, ses critiques et ses glossateurs*, 1857) sets the beginning of the third period even later, with the composition of the last string quartets and the *Grosse Fuge* after the completion of the *Missa solemnis* and Ninth Symphony (1823–24). This suggestion has not been influential, although P. Bekker (*Beethoven*, 1911) and more recently W. Kinderman (*Beethoven*, 1995) have adopted it for a sub-division of the third period. In either form, a new beginning with the quartets de-emphasizes important ties between them and the last three piano sonatas, the most clear of which are the revolutionary experiments with the number, order, and weighting of movements.

These experiments actually began in earnest with the Piano Sonata op. 101 (1816) and the Two Cello Sonatas op. 102 (1817), which I believe should be viewed as full-fledged members of the late group. Moreover, Beethoven's efforts to seek alternatives to conventional three- and four-movement designs (which, however, were not as monolithic as the style-critical literature on the Classical period often suggests) began already in the first style period. The continuity suggested herein can be extended to include many other stylistic features. The refined lyricism of many late works is often related back to the second phase of the second period, while the third-period pre-occupation with fugue and variations that is often stressed in the literature represents nothing new, but rather the culmination of interests in these forms that had always been strong.

Such continuities counter at least partially the image of a progressive stylistic development that has been viewed positively and negatively. There has been little disagreement about the relation of the second to the first periods; progress and mastery sum it up. (The least refined view has the "real" Beethoven emerging only at this time.) The third period represents either further progress or, as critics during Beethoven's lifetime and authors such as Fétis and Lenz have suggested, evidence of decline. This latter view has virtually no influence today; it is agreed that Beethoven makes progress, but that progress is neither inevitable, nor constant. The periods are not seen as steps in Beethoven's personal and artistic *Gradus ad Parnassum*; they represent a cautiously advanced idea of progress that avoids sweeping value judgments. For example, Maynard Solomon has suggested an objective, style-critical approach that grafts Classical, high-Classical, post-Classical, and Romantic phases onto four life-and-works periods (Bonn is the first) that include sub-periods of transition and consolidation.[4] On the other hand he stresses the psychological factors in this process; Beethoven's search for new styles stems in large part from his attempt to come to terms with personal crises. Style-critical and aesthetic criteria have also served arguments that stress the playing-out of opposing tendencies over the entire course of Beethoven's career. In these less-established schemes, which have much to offer in conjunction with the periods, such dualities as sonata vs. symphonic style, private vs. public genre and character, Classical vs. Romantic, and experimental vs. traditional define the parameters of Beethoven's continuous search for the technical and expressive solutions to the creative problems of the day.

One measure of the significance of the style periods for Beethoven research can be seen in the fact that periodization itself has been the subject of recent scholarship; as numerous articles and three conferences, one per style period, all held in the United States in the 1990s show.[5] Despite the limitations of this approach, the periods have become virtually axiomatic for our understanding of Beethoven's personal and artistic history. They are recommended – *cum grano salis*.

The inner Beethoven; Beethoven in context

In the above discussion and the chronology, and in my chapter on Beethoven's professional life, I try to provide some sense of the biographical circumstances that impacted on his work. But space does not allow more than a sketch, and I am particularly aware of the limitations of my hints and suggestions about his psychological make-up, his often tortured relations with family, friends, and associates, his romantic involvements and his sexual nature and attitudes, and his responses to the crises and misfortunes that impacted so heavily on his life and undoubtedly influenced his music. On these topics there is an abundant literature – much of it is popularizing, myth-perpetuating, and lacking in critical reflection and empirical underpinning – which by its very nature is speculative (I do not use the word in a negative sense) and interpretative and, therefore, controversial. Solomon's psychologically oriented biography, *Beethoven* (1977, 2nd edition, 1998) and the pertinent chapters in his *Essays* (1988) enjoy deserved – though not unchallenged – authority that rests in part on the basis of the author's scrupulous consideration of documentary evidence in support of his arguments. Readers interested in these crucial aspects of Beethoven's biography are advised to begin with Solomon's work and then read further. I also tried to provide some idea of the context – social, cultural, and political – in which Beethoven worked, yet here too, I could do little more than broadly sketch the situation in

Vienna, in Austria, and in greater Europe. Again there is a plenitude of literature; again the relevant chapters in Solomon's biography and in his *Essays* have shaped contemporary thinking on these subjects. Other recent contributions include Tia De Nora's controversial study of patronage and the establishment of Beethoven's reputation, *Beethoven and the Construction of Genius: Musical Politics in Vienna, 1792–1803* (Berkeley, Los Angeles, and London, 1995), and Leon Botstein's essay "The Patrons and Publics of the [String] Quartets: Music, Culture, and Society in Beethoven's Vienna," in *The Beethoven Quartet Companion,* ed. Robert Winter and Robert Martin (Berkeley, Los Angeles, and London, 1994) as well as portions of his "Franz Schubert and Vienna," *in The Cambridge Companion to Schubert,* ed. Christopher Gibbs (Cambridge, 1997). This list could, of course, be greatly expanded; a monographic study of Beethoven's life and work from the perspective of social and cultural history would, if of sufficient merit, be an invaluable contribution to Beethoven studies.

Any consideration of biographical literature on Beethoven most include the most comprehensive non-interpretative biography, Thayer's *Life of Beethoven* in the edition that was edited and revised by Elliot Forbes in 1967. Although a new revision of this classic is certainly needed, it remains an indispensable source for scholars and lay readers.

Chronology[6]

Bonn

1770	16 December (?): Born in Bonn, second child of Maria Magdalena and Johann van Beethoven, court singer. An older brother, Ludwig Maria, had died six days after his birth on 2 April 1769. Five younger children are born into the family. Caspar Anton Carl (April 1774) and Nikolaus Johann (October 1776) survive and come to Austria in the 1790s, where their lives closely intersect with Beethoven's. Three children born later also died as infants: Anna Maria Franziska in 1779, four days after her birth in February, Franz Georg, two years old, in 1783, and Maria Margaretha Josepha, born in 1786, who died in 1787.
c. 1775	Beethoven begins music lessons with his father, a severe and cruel teacher, who is said to have often beaten his son.
1778	Piano recital in Cologne, but Beethoven does not establish himself as a child prodigy.
1779	Composition lessons with Christian Gottlob Neefe.
1782	Unsalaried assistant court organist under Neefe (c. 1781–82: Beethoven leaves school). First published composition: "Dressler" Variations for Piano WoO 63.

1783	Journey to Holland with his mother. Beethoven plays harpsichord in court orchestra. Publication of three "Kurfürst" Piano Sonatas WoO 47. Neefe praises Beethoven in Cramer's *Magazin der Musik*.
1784	Appointed deputy court organist (salaried).
1785	Composition of three Piano Quartets WoO 36, nos. 1–3 (published 1828)
1787	March–May: Beethoven travels to Vienna and possibly plays for Mozart. July: Beethoven's mother dies. Father's long-standing drinking problems deteriorate into incapacitating alcoholism.
1788	Count Ferdinand Waldstein in Bonn, one of Beethoven's important early patrons; he later helps arrange Beethoven's study with Haydn in Vienna.
1789	Matriculation at the University of Bonn; no evidence of serious study. One half of father's salary paid to Beethoven, who is responsible for family. Beethoven plays viola in court theater orchestra. The repertory includes Mozart's *Die Entführung aus dem Serail*, and in the second season (1790) *Le Nozze di Figaro* and *Don Giovanni*.
1790	Composition of Funeral and Elevation Cantatas (WoO 87 and 88) on the occasion of the death of Emperor Joseph II and the elevation of Leopold II (neither performed).
1791	Publication of "Righini" Variations for Piano WoO 65.
1792	October: French troops in the Rhineland. November: Beethoven leaves for Vienna to study with Haydn. Before he departs friends give him a "Stammbuch" expressing best wishes and including literary citations. Beethoven formed several life-long (although intermittent) friendships in Bonn, among them with the Wegeler and von Breuning families. Expected to return to Bonn. December: death of father.

In Bonn Beethoven composed numerous songs, three piano sonatas, piano variations, chamber music for various ensembles, several concertos, and the cantatas.

Vienna

1793–94	Beethoven is sponsored by leading members of the Viennese nobility – Lobkowitz, Lichnowsky, et al. – and he achieves early success as a piano virtuoso and composer of solo and ensemble piano music. Early in 1794: Haydn leaves for London and returns in 1795. In his absence Beethoven studies with Albrechtsberger and, later, with other teachers. Compositions: 1794, Three Trios for Piano, Violin, and Cello op. 1 (pub. 1795). Trio no. 1 probably originated in Bonn.
1795	First Public Concert in Vienna; performance of First or Second Piano Concerto. Brother Johann arrives in Vienna. Compositions: Three Piano Sonatas op. 2 (pub. 1796); Piano Sonata op. 10 no. 1 (?). Work on a symphony in C major begins and is broken off.
1796	February–July: Beethoven travels to Prague, Dresden, Leipzig, and Berlin on his only extended concert tour. Compositions: Two Cello Sonatas op. 5, for J. L. Duport in Berlin (pub.

1797); Quintet for Piano and Winds op. 16 (pub. 1801). Concert Aria, *Ah! perfido* op. 65 (pub. 1805). Work on Piano Sonata op. 10 no. 1. Publication of String Trio op. 3 (fin. before 1794?, autograph 1795).

1797   Summer: little information about Beethoven; possibility of serious illness.

Compositions: Piano Sonata op. 7 (pub. 1797). Work begins on Three Violin Sonatas op. 12 (finished in 1798, pub. 1799). Work continues on Three Piano Sonatas op. 10 (fin. and pub. in 1798). Publication of *Adelaide* op. 46 (fin. 1794–95?).

1798   Beethoven performs First (op. 15) and Second (op. 19) Piano Concertos (revised version of no. 2) in Prague. First use of bound sketchbooks instead of single leaves. Circa 1798 lessons with Salieri in vocal and dramatic composition.

Compositions: Piano Sonata op. 13, *Pathétique* (pub. 1799); Piano Sonata op. 14 no. 1 (pub. 1799); Three String Trios op. 9 (pub. 1799); Clarinet Trio op. 11 (pub. 1798). Intermittent work on String Quartets op. 18.

1799   Compositions: Piano Sonata op. 14 no. 2 (pub. 1799); Septet op. 20 (premiere 1799, pub. 1802); First Symphony op. 21 (fin. 1800, prem. April 1800, pub. 1801); first version of op. 18 no. 1 given as farewell present to Karl Amenda.

1800   April: first concert in his own benefit in the Court Theater, First Symphony, First Piano Concerto, Septet, and other works: Beethoven's public reputation enhanced. Increasing tension between Haydn and Beethoven.

Compositions: Horn Sonata op. 17 (pub. 1801); String Quartets op. 18 (pub. 1801); Piano Sonata op. 22 (pub. 1802); Violin Sonatas opp. 23 and 24, "Spring" (fin. 1801; both pub. 1801); Piano Sonatas opp. 26 and 27 no. 1 (fin. 1801, pub. 1802); work on Third Piano Concerto op. 37 (? see 1803); Ballet, *Die Geschöpfe des Prometheus* op. 43 (prem. 1801, pub. 1801).

1801   June: Beethoven writes of hearing loss to Wegeler in Bonn. Ferdinand Ries and Carl Czerny are students; they remain long-term associates of Beethoven. Successful performances of *Prometheus*.

Compositions: Second Symphony op. 36 (fin. 1802, prem. April 1803, pub. 1804); Piano Sonatas opp. 27 no. 2, "Moonlight," and 28 (both pub. 1802); String Quintet op. 29 (pub. 1802); Three Violin Sonatas op. 30 (fin. 1802, pub. 1803); Bagatelles for Piano op. 33 (fin. 1802, pub. 1803); "Gellert" Songs op. 48 (fin. 1802, pub. 1803). Publication of First and Second Piano Concertos op. 15 (comp. 1795, rev. 1800), and op. 19 (begun 1785?, revised twice in Vienna), Six String Quartets op. 18 (Quartet no. 1 was revised and Beethoven asked Amenda [in Courland] to not show anyone the first version, "for only now have I learned to write quartets . . ."

1802   October: "Heiligenstadt" Testament, Beethoven's draft of a letter to his brothers while presumably contemplating suicide.

Compositions: Piano Sonatas op. 31 nos. 1 and 2 (pub. 1803) and no. 3 (pub. 1804). These sonatas mark the beginning of Beethoven's "new path"; Beethoven supposedly expressed dissatisfaction with his previous compositions; Variations for Piano opp. 34 and 35, "Eroica" Variations, (both pub. 1803); Violin Sonata op. 47, "Kreutzer" (fin. 1803, premiere with George Bridgetower in May 1803, pub. 1805).

1803   April: Performance of First and Second Symphonies; premiere of Third Piano Concerto op. 37 (begun in 1800?, pub. 1803) and Oratorio *Christus am Ölberge* op. 85 (rev. 1804 and 1811, pub. 1811). Beethoven plans a trip to Paris and considers leaving Vienna permanently.
Compositions: Symphony no. 3 op. 55, *Eroica* (private prem. 1804, public prem. 1805, pub. 1806); Piano Sonata op. 53, "Waldstein" (fin. 1804, pub. 1805); the original second movement is published separately as the *Andante favori* WoO 57 (pub. 1805); Triple Concerto op. 56 (fin. 1804, prem. May 1808, pub. 1807).

1804   May: Napoleon crowns himself Emperor in Rome; Beethoven destroys the title page with a dedication to Napoleon of the manuscript score of Third Symphony with the title ("Sinfonia Buonaparte"); title of first edition: "Sinfonia Eroica," with a subtitle, "composed to celebrate the memory of a great man." Late Fall/Jan. 1805: Close relationship with Countess Josephine Deym (née Brunsvik) through 1807. (Beethoven more ardent than Josephine.)
Compositions: work begins on *Fidelio* (Beethoven's preferred title was *Leonore*); Piano Sonatas opp. 54 (pub. 1806), and 57, "Appassionata" (fin. 1805, pub. 1807). Intermittent work – sketching – begins on Fourth Piano Concerto op. 58 (fin. 1806/7, prem. March 1807, pub. 1808) and Symphony no. 5 op. 67.

1805   November: Unsuccessful premiere of *Fidelio* (French troops in Vienna, Viennese aristocrats flee city). Count Andreas Razumovsky commissions three string quartets (op. 59). Beethoven meets Luigi Cherubini, whose music he admires greatly. Publication of Two Piano Sonatas op. 49 (composed 1795–97?).

1806   Birth of nephew Karl in September. March–April: performances of second version of *Fidelio*.
Compositions: Three String Quartets op. 59 (pub. 1808); Fourth Symphony op. 60 (prem. March 1807, pub. 1808); Violin Concerto op. 61 (prem. Dec. 1806, pub. 1808); Thirty-two Variations for Piano WoO 80 (pub. 1807).

1807   Prince Nikolaus Esterházy commissions a mass (Mass in C op. 86). Beethoven meets Muzio Clementi, who agrees to publish String Quartets op. 59, the Fourth Symphony, and other works and commissions three piano sonatas (opp. 78, 79, and 81a). Unsuccessful petition to Court Theater in Vienna for appointment as composer.
Compositions: intensive work through 1808 on Fifth Symphony (prem. Dec. 1808, pub. 1809); *Coriolan* Overture op. 62 (prem. March 1807, pub. 1808); Cello Sonata op. 69 (fin. 1808, pub. 1809, pub. 1809); Mass in C op. 86 (prem. at Esterházy palace in September 1807, pub. 1812).

1808	Beethoven offered a position as Kapellmeister in Kassel (capital city of French-dominated Westphalia). Brother Johann moves from Vienna to Linz. Several important concerts, in December premiere of Fifth and Sixth Symphonies and other important works in a landmark concert lasting over four hours.

Compositions: Sixth Symphony, *Pastoral* (pub. 1809); Two Piano Trios op. 70 (pub. 1809); Choral Fantasia op. 80 (prem. Dec. 1808, rev. 1809, pub. 1810).

1809   Annuity established for Beethoven by Austrian aristocratic patrons guarantees lifelong income; Beethoven declines position in Kassel. Death of Haydn. May: French bombardment of Vienna; Beethoven suffers great physical and psychological distress. Archduke Rudolph begins composition lessons and remains a student, patron, and close friend into the 1820s.

Compositions: Fifth Piano Concerto op. 73 (prem. Nov. 1811, pub. 1810); String Quartet op. 74 (pub. 1810); Piano Sonatas opp. 78 and 79 (pub. 1810); Piano Sonata *Das Lebewohl* op. 81a (fin. 1810, pub. 1811); Fantasia for Piano op. 77 (pub. 1810); Overture and Incidental Music to *Egmont* op. 84 (prem. June 1810, overture pub. 1810, incidental music pub. posth.).

1810   Beethoven befriends Bettina Brentano von Arnim, and her brother and his wife Franz and Antonie Brentano in Vienna; Bettina writes to Goethe about Beethoven, preparing for their encounter in 1812. Publication of Fifth Symphony op. 67; review by E. T. A. Hoffmann in AmZ.

Compositions: String Quartet op. 95 (revised 1814?, pub. 1816); Piano Trio op. 97, "Archduke" (fin. 1811, rev. 1814–15?, pub. 1816).

1811   Close friendship with Antonie Brentano (probable "immortal beloved" of 1812). Devaluation of Austrian currency reduces value of annuity income. Exchange of letters with Goethe.

Compositions: Symphony no. 7 op. 92 (fin. 1812, prem. December 1813, pub. 1816).

1812   Diary ("Tagebuch") kept by Beethoven until 1818. Travel to Bohemian spas in summer; letter to the "immortal beloved" suggesting that Beethoven is breaking off his relationship with her; Beethoven abandons hopes of marriage. Meets with Goethe: mutual ambivalence.

Compositions: Eighth Symphony op. 93 (prem. February 1814, pub. 1817); Violin Sonata op. 96 (rev. 1814–15?, pub. 1816).

1813   Successful public performances of Seventh Symphony and *Wellington's Victory* before and during the Congress of Vienna (1814). Brother Carl ill, names Beethoven as guardian of Karl after his death. Hoffmann reviews op. 70 Trios for the AmZ.

1814   Congress of Vienna: Beethoven gives numerous successful public concerts and the final version of *Fidelio* is performed by Beethoven. Patriotic works often include *Wellington's Victory* op. 91 (comp. 1813, pub. 1816), and Cantata *Der glorreiche Augenblick* op. 136 (pub. posth.). Beethoven plays the piano part of the "Archduke" Trio op. 97 in a public performance in April; Spohr critical of his playing.

Compositions: Piano Sonata op. 90 (pub. 1815); Cantata *Meeresstille und glückliche Fahrt* op. 112 (fin. 1815, pub. 1822); *Elegischer Gesang* op. 118 (pub. 1826).

1815   Last public appearance as pianist. Charles Neate brings to Vienna a commission from the Philharmonic Society of London for three overtures (opp. 113, 115, and 117). Gesellschaft der Musikfreunde in Vienna commissions an oratorio; Beethoven accepts contingent on suitable text, but the commission remains unfulfilled. Before his death in November, Carl appoints his wife Johanna as co-guardian with Beethoven of Karl. Legal struggles between them over Karl continue until 1820.
Compositions: Song-Cycle *An die ferne Geliebte* op. 98 (fin. 1816, pub. 1816); Two Cello Sonatas op. 102 (pub. 1817). Work on a piano concerto begins and is broken off.

1816   Karl in Beethoven's care; Beethoven appointed legal guardian. Carl Czerny teaches Karl piano.
Compositions: Piano Sonata op. 101 (pub. 1817). Work (sketching) on an unfinished piano trio.

1817   Illness. Invitation from Philharmonic Society of London to visit London and compose two symphonies. Beethoven requests a loud piano from the piano maker Streicher in Vienna.
Compositions: Piano Sonata op. 106, "Hammerklavier" (fin. 1818, pub. 1819). Intermittent work on first movement of Ninth Symphony op. 125 (fin. 1824, prem. May 1824, pub. 1826).

1818   Illness. Trip to London cancelled. Legal and personal problems with Karl and Johanna continue; Beethoven unable to prove his aristocratic lineage; case heard in lower court. Beethoven receives a new Broadwood piano from the English manufacturer. Beethoven begins to use conversation books, deafness complete.
Compositions: Folksong settings op. 108, published by Thomson in Edinburgh. Some work on Ninth Symphony.

1819   Beethoven ordered to give up guardianship of Karl, who returns to Johanna. Beethoven conducts Seventh Symphony in a concert in January. Brother Johann purchases a large estate; Beethoven's attempt to buy a house fails.
Compositions: work begins on "Diabelli" Variations op. 120, interrupted by composition of *Missa solemnis* op. 123, 1819–23.

1820   March: Elevation of Rudolph as Bishop, *Missa solemnis* not finished in time for the ceremony. April: Beethoven awarded custody of Karl, who soon moves in with him. Three piano sonatas (opp. 109–11) accepted for publication by A. Schlesinger.
Compositions: Piano Sonata op. 109 (pub. 1821). Work continues on *Missa solemnis*.

1821   Prolonged illness.
Compositions: Piano Sonatas op. 110 (fin. 1822, pub. 1822) and op. 111 (fin. 1822, pub. 1823). Completion of Five Bagatelles for Piano (later op. 119, nos. 7–11) for Friedrich Starke's *Wiener Pianoforte-Schule*.

1822   Meetings with Friedrich Rochlitz (?) and Rossini in Vienna. Letter to Goethe with copy of the cantata *Meeresstille und glückliche Fahrt* op. 112 on Goethe's poem; Goethe does not reply. Schubert reputedly brings to Beethoven's residence a copy of his Piano Variations op. 10, dedicated to Beethoven. Negotiations with publishers for *Missa solemnis*. Prince Nikolaus Galitzin (St. Petersburg) commissions three string quartets. Compositions: Bagatelles nos. 1–6 of op. 119, complete set of eleven pub. 1823. Work resumes on "Diabelli" Variations; work continues on Ninth Symphony.

1823   Successful revival of *Fidelio*. Beethoven seeks, unsuccessfully, an opera libretto. Meets with and hears Liszt play (?). Invitations throughout Europe to royalty and other notables for deluxe subscription edition of *Missa solemnis*.
        Compositions: completion of "Diabelli" Variations op. 120 (pub. 1823). Intensive work on Ninth Symphony until Spring 1824.

1824   April: Premiere of *Missa solemnis*, St. Petersburg. May: Premiere of Ninth Symphony, Vienna. Invitation to London from Philharmonic Society. Compositions: Bagatelles for Piano op. 126 (pub. 1825). Work begun on String Quartet op. 127 (fin. 1825, pub. 1826), first of three quartets for Galitzin. Work on last quartets (three for Galitzin plus two more) continues until 1826.

1825   Unrealized plans for a complete edition of Beethoven's music with Schott. April: first London performance of Ninth Symphony, Finale sung in Italian. First performance (Vienna) of String Quartets op. 127 and op. 132.
        Compositions: String Quartet op. 132 (pub. 1827); String Quartet op. 130 (first version with *Grosse Fuge* fin. January 1826, substitute finale fin. November 1826, pub. 1827). *Grosse Fuge* published as op. 133, 1827. String Quartet op. 131 (fin. 1826, pub. 1827).

1826   July: Karl attempts suicide. Fall: Beethoven suffers continuous worsening illness – dropsy, pneumonia. December: first of three operations. Compositions: String Quartet op. 135 (fin. Oct., pub. 1827). In November Beethoven begins but does not complete his last major work, String Quintet WoO 62. His last finished work is a puzzle canon composed in December for Karl Holz: "Wir irren allesamt" ("we all make mistakes").

1827   January: Karl begins military service. January–March: Two more operations. Possible reconciliation with Johanna. 26 March: death of Beethoven. 29 March: large public funeral service in Vienna. April–May: Publication of *Missa solemnis*, String Quartets opp. 131, 132, 135, and *Grosse Fuge* op. 133.

2 Beethoven at work: musical activist and thinker

GLENN STANLEY

Beethoven's professional life in Vienna was largely defined by his lack of institutional employment. Only his deafness had an equal impact on his career. In Bonn he had served the electoral court, playing organ and viola, and was expected to resume his duties after a period of study with Haydn that began in 1792. But the cessation of his salary in 1794 (perhaps for misleading the Elector Max Franz about his progress and refusing to return home) and the collapse of the electoral court in the French-controlled Rhineland later in that year did not bode well for his prospects in Bonn, and the freedom and opportunities he enjoyed in the imperial city outweighed the strength of long friendships and familial obligations he had left behind.[1] His concerted attempt to secure an appointment, with the Vienna Court Theater in December 1806, not surprisingly failed: after the problems and acrimony surrounding the performance of the first two versions of *Leonore* (Beethoven's original title of *Fidelio*) in 1805 and 1806, the directors apparently did not even respond to his multi-year offer to compose one opera and a smaller dramatic or choral work per annum. Beethoven sought the position, which would have allowed him ample time to compose instrumental music of his own choosing, despite continuing material and social support from a group of Viennese aristocrats who in the 1790s had eased his entry into Viennese cultural life. Led by Prince Karl Lichnowsky, they sponsored his first performances in their salons, took him along on tours to Prague, Berlin, and other musical centers, occasionally fed, clothed, and sheltered him, gave him books to read and refined manners to imitate or scorn. Their financial assistance culminated in the annuity set up in 1809 by Archduke Rudolph and the Princes Lobkowitz and Kinsky that helped persuade him to decline the appointment to the Napoleonic Court of Westphalia in Kassel that had been offered in the previous year.

Beethoven formed long-term friendships with several of his patrons; one notable for its endurance was with Baron Nikolaus Zmeskall von Domanovecz, who befriended Beethoven at the beginning of the century, participated as a cellist in chamber music readings, endured many sarcastic jokes (and enjoyed the distinction of the dedication of the Quartet in F minor op. 95), and, in ill health, attended the first performance of the Ninth Symphony in 1824. These friendships, and ones with non-aristocrats as well, had to withstand the intermittent conflicts and breaks triggered by Beethoven's rudeness and acute sensitivity to real and imagined affronts to his personal and artistic dignity. Whether bound by close personal or more formal ties, both Beethoven and his patrons had much to gain: his artistry enhanced their status and self-image; their social position added luster to Beethoven's reputation, which for many years he sought to enhance by allowing to flourish the myth that he was of Dutch aristocratic lineage on the basis of the *van* in his name.[2] However, Beethoven had decidedly mixed feelings about the aristocracy and its cultural influence. After his long anticipated meeting with Goethe in 1812 he remarked "Goethe delights far too much in the court atmosphere, far more than is becoming to a poet."[3] When in 1823 Archduke Rudolph, another long-standing patron and close friend, and other aristocratic supporters, among them Lichnowsky, wanted to help him secure his long coveted appointment as "Imperial and Royal Chamber Music Composer," they suggested he write a mass for the Emperor. Beethoven applied for the position but did not compose the mass, and, in the event, the position was eliminated. The group promoting Beethoven was, nevertheless, annoyed and embarrassed about Beethoven's failure to take their advice.[4] Perhaps he valued his independence, which he had always fought to maintain, more than an honorific title and some secure income. (His recently finished struggle with the *Missa solemnis* and his contract to write quartets for Prince Nikolaus Galitzin in St. Petersburg might also have been factors.) Toward the end of his life he moved much less frequently in aristocratic circles than in the heyday of his career as virtuoso.

Although Beethoven was essentially a free agent within the patronage system, he never suffered such acute financial hardships as experienced by Mozart in the last years of his life, but still worried constantly about money, especially after the inflation in the years following 1811 greatly eroded the value of the annuity, and his nephew Karl came into his care in 1816. Thus, not only purely artistic impulses, but also his concern to preserve his autonomy and to earn sufficient income obliged him to compose a steady stream of new compositions and, as long as his hearing allowed, to play and conduct them. He vigorously "marketed" his music (often before it was finished), composed on demand from continental and British publishers, and occasionally received commissions from private individuals. While the following chapters treat that music and the responses to it, this one is about the professional and intellectual activities surrounding the central one of composition. Viewing Beethoven in action, we will imagine him within a series of spheres encompassing individuals, institutions, and ideas – in Vienna and beyond. His many dwelling places – the epicenter of his world – were his most important workplaces, but we shall begin on the perimeter and then move inwards, taking a path that traces the long-range trajectory of his career from the colossus of the salon and the academy to the (relative) recluse of the final years.

The public man: playing and conducting

Beethoven established himself in Vienna in the semi-public sphere of the salon, as a virtuoso and composer for piano: solo works, concertos, and chamber music. Possessing a powerful technique, he reportedly did not like to practice; even before his hearing began to deteriorate, many witnesses to his playing were struck by its roughness; others emphasized its nobility of spirit. Carl Czerny, who studied briefly with Beethoven and remained associated with him until his death, praised his *cantabile* playing, which Beethoven himself contrasted with the prevailing "Mozartean" style. Around the turn of the century, he engaged in semi-formal competitions with Joseph Wölffl and Daniel Steibelt; although he did not emerge the clear favorite, the reports in local newspapers and in the *Allgemeine musikalische Zeitung* (published in Leipzig and read throughout German-speaking Europe) certainly helped his growing reputation.

Despite its importance for his career, Beethoven considered performance in the salons an onerous burden. His boyhood friend Franz Wegeler relates that in the years 1794–96 Beethoven "often came to me ... gloomy and out of sorts, complaining that they had made him play, even though his fingers ached and the blood under his nails burned."[5] After 1800 he increasingly delegated the playing of his music to associates. When forced to play, he preferred improvisation, which had an artistic status equal to, and perhaps higher than, playing finished works. In a conversation with the pianist Johann Wenzel Tomaschek in 1814 he supposedly railed against improvisers dependent on mechanistic formulae; improvisation must be "homogeneous, an entity," a "well thought-out work."[6] Celebrated for their technical skill and their depth of expression, his own improvisations were said to last as long as a half-hour and to include structured movement forms. His playing could have, to cite Czerny, "such an effect upon every hearer that frequently not an eye remained dry, while many would break out into loud sobs; for there was something wonderful in his expression in addition to the beauty and originality of his ideas and his spirited style of rendering them."[7]

When Beethoven began to play in public concerts in 1795, he offered music by Mozart and Haydn as well as his own. One of his first appearances took place at a concert organized by Haydn, and the first evening entirely devoted to his piano music occurred only in 1800. Beethoven did not often give public concerts, and they declined in frequency over the course of his career. His increasing deafness certainly contributed to this, but there were never many opportunities at the Court Theater, and perhaps he was discouraged by recurring disagreements with theater managers and musicians about financial and logistical details; while intrigues against him undoubtedly occurred, his overly suspicious nature only exacerbated problems. He played the piano publicly for the last time in 1815, but he conducted occasionally into the 1820s, in which years he also sometimes simply lent his presence to concerts of his music. Public performance yielded mixed artistic and financial results; contemporary accounts relate both his artistic powers and the deficiencies resulting from lack of adequate rehearsal time, from his eccentricities as a pianist and conductor, and, most importantly, from the extraordinary demands he placed on the listeners and on the performers of his music. (Beethoven was noted for his indifference to the problems he created for his players and singers and for his occasional fits of rage at their shortcomings.)[8]

One of Beethoven's most notable concerts (December 1808, with mixed reviews) featured the first performances of the Fifth and Sixth Symphonies in an evening of music that lasted four hours in the bitterly cold Burgtheater.[9] Concerts during the Congress of Vienna in 1814 marked the high point of Beethoven's fame; the greatest acclaim fell not to the first performances of the Seventh and Eighth Symphonies, but rather to the trivial depiction of a battle, *Wellington's Victory* op. 91 (1813). At the first performance of the Ninth Symphony in May 1824, for which the Kärntnertor Theater was full but for the vacant imperial box, the enthusiastic applause was as much for the person of the aging, deaf composer, who stood before the orchestra that had been instructed to disregard his conducting and had to be turned to face the audience, as for the music he had composed. The performance had not gone well.[10]

Beethoven's shortcomings as a performer long preceded the milestone year of 1818, from which time his complete deafness required his associates to write down their remarks in "conversation books."[11] If we accept as accurate the memory of Ignaz von Seyfried, concertmaster of the orchestra at the Theater an der Wien, eyewitness, and a good friend to Beethoven for more than three decades, then we must sympathize with the orchestral players performing under him in the years 1800–05. Seyfried wrote this graphic description in 1832:

> Our master cannot be presented as a model conductor, and the orchestra always
> had to be careful not be led astray by its mentor; for he had ears only for his
> composition and always attempted to indicate the intended expression through
> the most varied gesticulations. He often conducted a down beat for an accent on

a weak beat. He used to indicate a *diminuendo* by shrinking into himself, and for a *pianissimo* he would virtually crawl under the music desk. As the ensemble grew more massive, he seemed to arise from the depths, and when the entire orchestra had entered, make himself gigantic; balancing on his tiptoes and waving his arms, it looked as if he wanted to soar up into the clouds. His entire body was actively involved, not a single part of his body was at rest, the man was like a perpetuum mobile.[12]

The music historian and conductor Peter Gülke understands Beethoven's idiosyncrasies before an orchestra as manifestations of his uncompromising efforts to "realize" his musical "intentions": he refused to limit his role as conductor to that of the conventional "measure-beater"; his "subjective" conducting anticipated and perhaps helped usher in the tradition of virtuoso interpretation at the podium.[13] (The descriptions of Beethoven's conducting conjure up images of a nineteenth-century Leonard Bernstein. Bernstein, however, could rely on the great advances in orchestral training and discipline since Beethoven's time – his orchestras could keep the beat without him.) Seyfried himself recognized that Beethoven could inspire his orchestras and be inspired by them:

> But when he became aware of how his musicians accepted his ideas, how they played with increasing ardor, how they were possessed and inspired by the magic of his music, then joy would transfix his face, all his features radiated pleasure and satisfaction . . . and a thundering "Bravi tutti!" would reward the artistic success.[14]

Beethoven at home

In the last years of his life, Beethoven suffered complete deafness and frequent illnesses and endured (as before) breaks with or the death of family members, aristocratic patrons, and personal friends. His chronic mistrust of individuals intensified and he viewed with increasing bitterness a world that had dealt him harsh personal failures and mixed professional success. Perhaps he also realized that his appearance and behavior were perceived as ever more eccentric. No wonder that he withdrew, confining himself increasingly to his rooms and to his bed; his home was a haven at the end of his life. There and only there did he continue to play the piano long after he had retired from the salon and the concert hall. He even played for friends sometimes; his (self-imposed?) isolation and alienation were not complete: if he did not often venture out into the world, it came to him. He received visitors from Vienna and abroad with great regularity; the conversation books record his interest in his own fortunes and in events of the outside world; letters came frequently. Still capable of having a good time, he delighted in the musical and verbal jokes preserved in the conversation books and letters.[15] The young Gerhard von Breuning, a reliable witness to the last two years of Beethoven's life, even proclaimed that Beethoven had reconciled himself to his deafness, and would have had a "very pleasant life," had it not been for his troubles with his brother Johann and nephew Karl.[16]

Beethoven was fond of dubbing some of his closest associates with military names; he was, to be sure, the "Generalissimus," and the game suggests that Beethoven enjoyed viewing himself as the commander for whom loyal troops from "his private army" fought for high art against its adversaries.[17] And this fight had begun decades earlier – Beethoven's many dwelling places, whose very number can be interpreted as evidence of an inner existential instability,[18] were the base of operations, his primary work place and gathering point for the friends and relatives (they also frequented taverns and inns) who comprised a kind of substitute family for the life-long bachelor. At home, Beethoven wrote and played music (he also composed – with the use of pocket sketchbooks – on walks, especially during summer sojourns outside of Vienna), gave lessons (he also taught at aristocratic students' homes), corrected proofs of his music, studied scores by other composers, read reviews of his compositions and books on the most diverse subject matter, and wrote letters or had them written for him. These activities filled his long working days: with the crucial exceptions of composition and playing, they are not particularly exalted; even the creative activities were predicated on the hard work for which Beethoven was noted. This daily regimen of routine endeavor forms the background and the context for his music; without them our understanding of his life and work would be incomplete.

Teaching and learning music

Beethoven the teacher was Beethoven the eternal student, who took a critical view of his own music and the music of others, and continued to learn throughout his life. Without this perspective he might have found it difficult to achieve his avowed goals of originality and artistic progress. During the first decade in Vienna he gave piano lessons to a number of aristocratic women; some of them were gifted; some of them – like the sisters Brunsvik in 1804 – apparently mixed amorous pleasure with musical business. After 1805 he stopped giving piano lessons and taught composition only sporadically. Only Ferdinand Ries, who studied in the years 1801–05, and the Archduke Rudolph were formally acknowledged as pupils;[19] Rudolph continued with composition lessons for some twenty years until 1824. Asked in 1811 if he would accept students, Beethoven declined, reportedly describing teaching as "vexatious work" and complaining about Rudolph, "whom he would gladly get rid of if he could." [20] (Yet ten years later Beethoven wrote to the Archduke with warm words of encouragement and advice.) Musicians sometimes were able to play for Beethoven or show their music to him, but in the last decade of his life, visits by musicians like the young Liszt (1823) had more the character of a pilgrimage than a lesson, for he often showed little interest in their music.

Czerny and Ries are the most important witnesses regarding Beethoven as teacher. According to Czerny, Beethoven stressed the position of the hand and the fingers; Theresa von Brunsvik reports that his preference for a low hand and curved fingers departed entirely from her previous training. [21] The new style of *cantabile* playing that Czerny praised – and passed down, with other contemporary pianists – must certainly have figured in his piano pedagogy. [22] It may come as a surprise that Ries remarks on his patience, for reports to the contrary are more common. Beethoven gave him long lessons and had him repeat passages "ten times or even more often" in order to achieve correct expression and character as opposed to technical proficiency. Errors were accidents, insensitive playing "resulted from inadequate knowledge, feeling or attention." [23] Beethoven purportedly referred Ries to Johann Georg Albrechtsberger for lessons in counterpoint and figured bass, explaining, as Ries recalls, that it "required a particular gift to explain them with clearness and precision." [24] This self-critical view might also reflect the dissatisfaction he had felt studying with Haydn (1792–94), which led him to seek out Johann Schenk (1793), Albrechtsberger (1794–96), and Antonio Salieri (intermittently for vocal composition, 1792–1802). [25]

Beethoven was particularly interested in counterpoint. As a boy he played the *Well-Tempered Clavier* under his teacher Christian Gottlob Neefe and possibly knew Johann Philipp Kirnberger's *Kunst des reinen Satzes*, but in Bonn his study of counterpoint was neither systematic nor strict. [26] In Vienna he used Johann Joseph Fux's *Gradus ad Parnassum* under Haydn [27] and worked with Kirnberger's and Albrechtsberger's own materials for his studies with the latter; a large quantity of contrapuntal studies, modulating fugues, and other diverse exercises have been preserved in exercise and sketch books. He owned or was familiar with Johann Mattheson's *Der vollkommene Kapellmeister*, C. P. E. Bach's famous *Essay* (*Versuch über die wahre Art, das Clavier zu spielen*), and other important theoretical treatises, and he continued to study even after his formal instruction had come to an end. [28] The emphasis on counterpoint surfaces in a letter written in 1823 to Rudolph, in which Beethoven reminds the Archduke to work on the model of his teacher:

continue ... especially to practice quickly writing down your ideas (you need a small table next to the piano for this); not only will this strengthen your imagination, but it also will teach you to record the most abstract ideas; but it is also necessary to write without the piano ... [take] a simple melody sometimes – a chorale – and just develop it with different contrapuntal figures or freely.[29]

Beethoven's "genius" (in the romanticized sense of unreflected inspiration) did not suffer from his interest in the technical aspect of composition; indeed, as his many contrapuntal-structural sketches show, he depended on craftsmanship to solve problems of large-scale design and process.

Beethoven had strong views about piano methods; he used Bach's *Versuch* when he taught Czerny in the early 1800s; in 1826 he advised Stephan von Breuning against purchasing Czerny's own piano method for his son Gerhard (although Czerny was teaching Beethoven's nephew Karl at that time!), opposed his use of Ignaz Pleyel's didactic works, and sent him Clementi's *Vollständige Klavierschule* (the German edition of *Introduction à l'art de toucher le Pianoforte* op. 42, 1807).[30] Anton Schindler, Beethoven's assistant for several years in the 1820s, reports that he did not admire Hummel's method and intended to write his own. According to Schindler, Beethoven also planned to issue a complete edition of the piano sonatas with revisions of earlier works that would exploit the expanded range of newer instruments. This edition was also supposed to contain remarks about performance and programmatic explanations of their poetic content. Beethoven did indeed consider such a project in 1816, but the only extant letter about it mentions neither revisions nor commentary.[31] Why Beethoven preferred one method over another can be surmised: Clementi's sonatinas and sonatas are better music than the pedagogical compositions of Czerny and Pleyel – it has been argued that Clementi's piano music influenced the development of Beethoven's own style.[32] Beethoven once commented that he was "no friend" of virtuosic pieces, "because they only advance mechanical playing."[33]

Czerny describes another aspect of Beethoven's pedagogy, which also has important ramifications for his musical aesthetics:

Far more valuable (still) than his written remarks on theoretical matters were Beethoven's oral statements about musical matters of every sort, about other composers, etc. whom he always judged with great assurance, pertinent, often caustic, wit and invariably from the high standpoint which his genius allocated to him and from which he surveyed the whole of Art. For that reason, his assessment, even of classical names, was always a strict one and was uttered in the manner of one who feels himself to be their equal.[34]

In 1815, during one of the worst of the personal and artistic crises that punctuated his life and career, Beethoven wrote into his diary, "Portraits of Handel, Bach, Gluck, Mozart, and Haydn in my room. They can promote my capacity for endurance."[35] These composers had also formed the backbone of his musical education. In Bonn and Vienna he avidly attended concerts and the opera as long as his hearing permitted, and throughout his life petitioned publishers and friends to send him scores of music he did not already own. Beethoven congratulated Franz Anton Hoffmeister in 1801 for his project to publish keyboard music of Johann Sebastian Bach, whom he described as the "progenitor of harmony," and in 1810 he asked the Leipzig publishers Breitkopf & Härtel for music by both J. S. and C. P. E. Bach.[36] At this time he wrote out the bass line for the Crucifixus from the B Minor Mass both in a sketchbook and in a letter to the publishers; and other books contain excerpts copied from Mozart, Haydn, and Handel.[37]

By 1817, after having received an English edition of Handel's works, Beethoven placed Handel above Mozart as the greatest composer in the musical pantheon.[38] This preference for older music was symptomatic: in the years after the Congress of Vienna, as his own concert-hall fortunes were in relative decline, Beethoven's attitude toward contemporary composers became ever more critical. He admired Carl Maria von Weber's *Der Freischütz*, and praised Cherubini as the greatest living composer to the English composer and pianist Cipriano Potter in 1817, but more typical was his annoyed reaction to Potter's remark about Ignaz Moscheles being the premier pianist in Vienna: "Don't ever speak again of such passage players."[39] His comment about Rossini to Louis Spohr in 1823 also reveals his love of puns, as well as his critique of Viennese taste and his feelings about his falling popularity: "I cannot tell you much about what is happening here, except that there is a rich harvest of raisins [*Rosinen*] (dried, pressed-out grapes)."[40] Yet we should not conclude that Beethoven saw a wholesale return to the past as an antidote to contemporary bad style; imitations of an historical style are rare in his music, despite the lessons he learned from Renaissance (Palestrina) and Baroque masters, and his ambivalence about early music emerges in a letter of 1819 to Rudolph about the craft of composing: in the music of "older composers . . . there is generally real artistic value," but "among them, of course, only the *German Händel* and *Sebastian Bach* possessed genius" (emphasis in the original).[41]

Letter writing

Remarks about music and composers are found throughout Beethoven's correspondence, and he often wrote, especially to childhood friends, about his personal fortunes, but he did not enjoy writing letters and did not use them *primarily* as a medium to express his views about art, or to hold forth about politics (a dangerous undertaking at a time of political turbulence and zealous censorship), or to discuss details of his life. The great majority of his letters concerned practical matters; a great many of these went to publishers of his music, but he sometimes fired off scolding missives to the editors and publishers of musical journals in which his music was negatively reviewed, and wrote ingratiatingly and sometimes obsequiously to prominent cultural and political figures (Goethe, the King of Prussia) to whom he sent or wanted to sell music. He also corresponded with prospective authors of texts for songs and operas (among them Franz Grillparzer, the most distinguished Austrian author in the first half of the nineteenth century), with the directors of theaters and concert institutions about performances, and with relatives (his brothers and his nephew Karl), friends, and associates acting as personal agents in Vienna and in cities across the continent and in England.

The letters reveal Beethoven as a sharp, sometimes unscrupulous businessman, not above misleading publishers about his progress on compositions and his negotiations with other publishers. Beethoven accepted in 1820 an advance on the *Missa solemnis* from Simrock in Bonn while offering it to Peters in Leipzig and Artaria in Vienna at the same time. In 1822 he received money from Peters for the Mass and for other works, but the Mass was first published by Schott in 1827, long after Beethoven had issued a limited edition by subscription.[42] Beethoven must be condemned for such dishonesty, which contrasts sharply with his avowed ethical idealism, yet it must be acknowledged that this behavior had a context – the lack of copyright protection that often resulted in pirate editions for which he received nothing, and his contempt for publishers who paid him less than he deserved and cared little about the accuracy of their editions. In the case of the *Missa solemnis*, moreover, Beethoven was at the time under financial pressure; he had loans to repay, some of which had been advanced by publishers themselves, and was forced to sell off some bank shares. He did return the money to Peters.

Real or imagined financial exigencies sometimes led Beethoven to take a very dispassionate view of his music. In 1823 he tried to sell a subscription copy of the *Missa solemnis* to Carl Zelter, the leader of the Berlin *Singakademie* (a chorus devoted to the performance of historical music), by calling it an oratorio that could be performed with organ accompaniment only. And in the same year, when he sent the eleven bagatelles of op. 119 to Ries, his instructions were to "dispose of them as favorably as you can ... I need the money."[43] The letter identified the pieces as being in two parts (the latter six were composed in 1820–22; the first five were reworkings of older material); the English original edition (Clementi, 1823) and subsequent continental editions retained the sequence but did not differentiate between the two groups, which, however, apparently did not bother the composer. This willingness to compromise occasionally what we regard as the integrity of great works seems to contradict the Herculean efforts that went into their composition. It is balanced by his opposition to arrangements of his works (particularly if they were not authorized by him) and his insistence on editions of his music that preserve his intentions.

Many of Beethoven's letters to publishers contained lists of mistakes he had found in proofs or first editions. Sometimes he vented his anger about them by indulging his capacity for brutal jokes, as in this remark to Gottfried Härtel in 1811: "Mistakes, mistakes, you yourself are just one whole mistake," and then developed the one-word theme throughout the letter.[44] Just two weeks later, however, after learning of the death of Härtel's wife, Beethoven consoled him, showing feelings and expressing human interest with a genuineness that belies opportunism. And wit often softened the hard edges of his business and personal conduct; his delight in jokes both sophisticated and naive could be disarming.

Reading and thinking: literature and music

Contradictions like these make it difficult to discover regular patterns in Beethoven's professional behavior and modes of thought. If any consistencies can be discerned, they are a vehement unwillingness to compromise in the pursuit of his professional and artistic goals, even if they sometimes seem to be at odds, and a passionate engagement with the literary, philosophical-aesthetic, ethical, religious, and political ideas of his time. Of paramount importance for his personal and artistic journey, these tendencies and interests, which themselves led to contradictions, characterized a mind for which life, thought, and art formed an indissoluble unity. Reading and thinking, even just feeling, Beethoven was still "in action," still "at work."

In the summer and fall of 1809, when Beethoven suffered physical distress and mental anguish from the French bombardment and occupation of Vienna and the temporary collapse of his cultural and social world, he seems to have been possessed by a great need for artistic and intellectual sustenance. Repeatedly pressing Breitkopf & Härtel for scores and literary works, he can't get enough: J. S. and Emanuel Bach, Handel's *Messiah*, Mozart's *Requiem*, Haydn's Masses – no, everything by Mozart and Haydn, Goethe and Schiller – all that can be had, Wieland, Ossian, Euripides. Beethoven made such requests throughout his life, though rarely with such breathless intensity. One of these letters is as self-reflective as it is self-aggrandizing:

> You will not easily find an essay that is too learned *for me*; although I don't claim to be genuinely learned, I have tried since I was a child, to grasp *the spirit of the best and wisest* [minds] of every age. Shame on the artist who does not consider it his duty to achieve at least so much.[45]

Indeed Beethoven had little formal education. A "backward student,"[46] he did not attend Gymnasium, although he occasionally sat in on university lectures. He wrote French badly, and because he had no Greek or non-liturgical Latin, no Italian or English, he had to rely on translations of Shakespeare, Homer, Plato and Aristotle, Plutarch and other classical poets and historians.[47] His written German was flawed, as Sieghard Brandenburg notes, "It was difficult for him to formulate his thoughts precisely . . . his vocabulary was small and his sentence structure not seldom grammatically incorrect."[48] Despite his devotion to Goethe and Schiller, and his reading of Herder, Klopstock, Kant, and other contemporary German literature and philosophy (he had no apparent interest in the English, French, or Italian thought of his day), his ability to comprehend the most abstract aspects of the literature was surely limited. His understanding of Kant, for example, was drawn from secondary sources (journals) and elevated conversation – he was in "contact with the most distinguished minds in Bonn" in the late 1780s. That his grasp of Kant was "superficial"[49] says nothing, however, about his intellectual integrity; the sketchbook entry of 1820, "The moral law in us, and the starry sky above – Kant!!!," is testimony to the personal meaning that the categorical imperative had for him. Beethoven was very stimulated by his reading and by the "world-historical spirit" (Hegel) and dramatic events of the revolutionary age in which he lived, all of which helped shape his views about life and the meaning and function of music.

At the broadest level, the authors in Beethoven's pantheon provided a model for cultural greatness and aesthetic significance that at the end of the eighteenth century was still reserved for men of letters and literature. Calling himself "Tondichter" (poet in sound), he succeeded in achieving a similar status for himself and for his art. In a letter to Wegeler in 1801, Beethoven proclaims his greatness and reconciles his personal ambition

with his sense of morality, the perfectibility of man, and social obliga-
tion:

> All I can tell you is that you will only see me again as a truly great man. Not only
> shall you find me greater as an artist, but better, more nearly perfect as a man.
> And if the prosperity of our country improves, my art shall be exhibited only in
> the service of the poor.[50]

Artistic greatness was defined not only in purely aesthetic terms, but also
in the role assumed by the artist in culture. Beethoven concluded the critique of Goethe cited earlier with the assertion that "poets . . . should be
regarded as the leading teachers of the nation": Goethe disqualified
himself with his social pretension.

A later remark (1812), apparently in response to a young girl pianist in
Hamburg, expresses the views of a more mature, less self-involved thinker
about the nature of art:

> Continue, but do not just practice your art, rather also penetrate its inner
> meaning; it merits this, because only art and science can raise men to the
> level of the Gods.[51]

Lofty stuff for a twelve-year-old! Well past its prime, the Enlightenment,
in the idealist German form he had learned in Bonn, speaks through
Beethoven in these remarks. Concepts central to the *Aufklärung*, such as
"humanity and human dignity, tolerance, and freedom" in moral philosophy, and aesthetic "nobility and sublimity," appear repeatedly in letters
and in memoranda to himself in sketchbooks and his diary. "The Empress
Reason" was a favorite catchphrase.[52]

At the end of the eighteenth century, the primary exponent of the
belief that art and artistic endeavor are not solely matters of pleasure and
ends unto themselves was Schiller, who in the early 1790s authored a
series of *Letters on the aesthetic education of mankind*. And it is Schiller
who is generally recognized as having most profoundly influenced
Beethoven's views. William Kinderman finds a close link between
Beethoven's aesthetics and Schiller's interest in the "synthesis of the sensuous and rational" in art, and also sees a Schillerian outlook in the composer's belief that "'freedom and progress are the main objectives" in art
and in life.[53] Maynard Solomon emphasizes a common life-affirming uto-
pianism with a strong ethical and religious dimension drawing on classical antiquity as well as Christianity. The most perfect embodiment of
these qualities is the Finale of the Ninth Symphony, based on fragments of
Schiller's ode "An die Freude."[54] In the 1790s Beethoven had planned to
set the entire poem; and, in the face of the crushing personal and political
disappointments he experienced over the next two decades, his dedica-

tion to its sentiments bespeaks an impressive intellectual tenacity and unvanquished optimism – or self-delusion. (Schiller distanced himself from the poem before his death in 1804.) Elaine Sisman associates the Piano Sonata op. 13, *Pathétique* (1799), with Schiller's emphases on pathos and the sublime as aesthetic categories.[55] Whether Beethoven ever read Schiller's essays cannot be determined, but the argument that "moral resistance to suffering" in art must replace the mere representation of that suffering was a leading ethical and aesthetic idea for the composer and finds expression in the music of his entire career.

Music was Beethoven's primary weapon of resistance; the creative urge gave him the stoic inner strength to endure, day in and day out, in times of the greatest personal crisis and psychological stress.[56] The theme of salvation through art sounds again and again in letters and in the diary used by Beethoven in the years 1812–18; the Heiligenstadt Testament of 1802 offers one of its earliest and most powerful statements. Despairingly describing incidents of his failing hearing, he confesses:

> a little more of that and I would have ended my life – it was only my art that held me back. Ah, it seemed to me impossible to leave the world until I had brought forth all that I felt was within me.[57]

Solomon has described the Heiligenstadt Testament, which was written at the cusp of the first period and the "heroic decade," as the "literary prototype of the *Eroica* Symphony," composed in the years 1803–04. The remark can help us understand the connections – and their limits – between Beethoven's literary explorations and his music. Heroes were certainly available to Beethoven in the dramatic works of Schiller and Goethe; the composition of incidental music to the latter's *Egmont* op. 84 (1810), was as much a labor of belief as the fulfillment of a commission. And his choice of *Leonore*, after the rejection of several opera libretti in preceding years, was as much a matter of the heart and mind as the awareness that rescue operas were a popular success. To these heroic subjects can be added Prometheus (the ballet *Creatures of Prometheus* op. 43, of 1801), whom Beethoven also associated with the so-called "Eroica" Variations for Piano op. 35 (1802) that share thematic material with the dance music and were intended by Beethoven to have the subtitle "Prometheus." Beethoven's conception of heroic greatness must, however, derive in great measure from two real-life sources: his veneration for Napoleon, the "Prometheus" of his age and the original "subject" of the Third Symphony, and his own self-image. Perhaps the latter was more important: all the literary-historical heroes in Beethoven's works – to whom we may add the person of Jesus in the oratorio *Christ on the Mount of Olives* op. 85 (1803–04) – suffer or die, and their heroism emerges as a consequence of their ordeal and fate. (Among these figures, who are all male, only one, Florestan, does not perish, and he survives only because a woman-hero who dresses and acts as if she were a man is able to save him.) It seems likely that Beethoven identified closely with these suffering heroes; his artistic voice expressed his own person, not just an aesthetic persona, and in the Heiligenstadt Testament it is the artist in Beethoven who saves the man.

Except for the oratorio, the works in this group, along with the *Coriolan* Overture op. 62 (1807) and the Ninth Symphony, have been interpreted – justifiably – as manifestations of Beethoven's sympathies for political and social alternatives to the remnants of feudalism and unenlightened absolutism that he loathed in his own Austria. He glimpsed such alternatives in the republican strivings of the French Revolution, but also in the constitutional monarchy of England; the young democracy of the United States of America does not seem to have had any significant impact on his views. For all the strength of his political convictions, we must remember that they were those of a man in the street. There is little indication that he read social theory; we search in vain for evidence that he knew the work of a Locke or Rousseau. On the other hand, he did possess a copy of a polemical essay against the nobility by August von Kotzebue,[58] and we can safely assume that he was exposed to subversive political ideas in conversation and literature in Bonn and in Vienna. Whatever its sources, Beethoven's republicanism was not so firmly anchored that he was unwilling to compromise it, at least externally. Patriotic works composed before and during the Congress of Vienna – *Wellington's Victory* is the most notorious – have been read both as sincere expressions of German nationalism in the face of French aggression (yet Beethoven met with members of the French military and diplomatic corps during the occupation of Vienna in 1809), or as opportunistic products of careerism. The haste with which he dispatched these uninspired occasional works has also supported the view that Beethoven had a private, bitter laugh, thumbing his nose at "Vienna, Queen of Cities" (from *Der glorreiche Augenblick* op. 136, the patriotic cantata composed for the Congress that celebrates imperial Austria and the political restoration), while deriving social and material gain by associating himself with her victory. In the years thereafter Beethoven often expressed his contempt for Metternichean Vienna and pondered leaving the city.

Apart from direct links to specific works, how can we assess the impact of Beethoven's political views on his art? In view of his republicanism and his ideas about the artist in service to his nation, we might expect a concern for intelligibility and popularity, so that his music could speak to a large segment of the society. Yet neither of these attributes marks the early reception of Beethoven's music, and despite a few statements by him about the need for simplicity and writing beautifully for a large public, Beethoven, who had little use for the "common" people, was not interested in popularizing; the handful of exceptions prove the rule. As E. T. A. Hoffmann realized, the "multitude is oblivious to Beethoven's depths."[59] While there is little reason to doubt the sincerity of the evocation of a unified "Humanity" in *Fidelio*, the "Choral" Fantasy (op. 80, 1807), and the Ninth Symphony, Beethoven, like his contemporaries in music and the other arts, created his great works for an intellectual elite that included the enlightened segment of the aristocracy and the well-educated middle classes of the German-speaking *Bildungsbürgertum*. Within this small socio-cultural group, a few symphonies achieved real popularity on the virtue of their sweep and power; they were claimed by both the political right and the left and understood as both elite and popular.

Beethoven's opinions about opera libretti provide one of the clearest indications of the "aristocratic" nature of his art, to be understood not as a matter of class association but rather aesthetic elitism and serious high-mindedness. He rejected the licentiousness of the subject matter of Mozart's Italian comic operas, admiring only *The Magic Flute* (and, we can conjecture, primarily those parts that treat enlightened Masonic ideas). In 1823, in the wake of the success of *Der Freischütz* and the rising popularity of romantic operas on supernatural themes, he thought about setting libretti by Grillparzer on "Drahomira," a semi-diabolical story drawn from Bohemian legend, and on the water nymph Melusine, yet never worked seriously on either. Most of the many libretti considered by Beethoven over the course of his career were based on epic themes from biblical or classical history, or were reworkings of serious dramatic masterworks – histories or tragedies – by authors such as Shakespeare and Schiller.[60] It is hard to imagine Beethoven composing a fairy opera or a comic opera, even a *Magic Flute*, with its Papageno and Papagena.

Yet his instrumental music is full of humor, and this important aspect of his art seems at odds with his self-image as an artist and the literary-philosophical basis of his aesthetics. What are its sources? We have noted his propensity for verbal puns and jokes that are virtually devoid of the Mozart family's ribaldry but reminiscent of its less-than-highbrow humor. The humor in Beethoven's music seems to result from direct experience, rather than from literature; it is the musical distillation of telling jokes, not reading them. This differs from the context for his tragic-heroic music and all the different kinds of music – suffering, pleading, yearning, sentimental – that has origins not only experiential and psychological but also issues from intellectual activity, from his engagement with literature and philosophy. Attempts to ground Beethoven's musical humor in a broader intellectual context have established affinities to Laurence Sterne or Friedrich Schlegel but not direct debts; they cannot demonstrate that he knew their work. On the other hand, musical sources were readily available, for example in Mozart's genius at comic characterization and unfolding and in the wit of Haydn's instrumental style.

The concept of "romantic irony" has gained currency in some recent discussions of Beethoven's music, which have extended beyond discussions of his humor to the question of Beethoven's distancing himself from his art.[61] Especially in the late music, it has been acutely argued, paradox and contradiction, fragmentation and interruption, ambiguity and openness, permeate the musical discourse and force us to acknowledge an ambivalence and self-doubting in the composer, which are projected in serious, aesthetically compelling ways. Such arguments have sought "hard" biographical evidence in the nature of Beethoven's non-musical irony and sense of humor, which he sometimes turned on himself but other times used as a weapon of resistance. On his death bed, he found in classical Latin comedy the source for ironic self-deprecation, "Applaud, friends, the comedy is over."[62] Yet a question remains – would he have said it to himself, or was he attempting to help his friends overcome their grief and prevent a scene of unbearable pathos? Verbal irony was a subcurrent in Beethoven's world view and musical irony a subcurrent of his art. They are neither a foil nor a negation, but rather an expression of a subjectivity that had not abandoned the hope for certainty.

There is little humor in his diary (1812–18), written for himself alone, which not only records personal struggles (and unsparing remarks about his views towards individuals and society at large),[63] but also contains the most revealing account of his cast of mind at a crucial and crisis-filled time in his life and career, which witnessed the deeply disappointing Congress of Vienna, the drama of the "Immortal Beloved," the painful struggle over Karl, and the difficult and slow working out of a new musical style. The diary documents the composer's unflagging devotion to the literature and philosophy of his early maturity, but reveals new (or at least previously unmentioned) interests in the work of Herder and more recent German and Italian literature. More importantly, it records his increasing preoccupation with religious, metaphysical, and mystical ideas. Beethoven wrote out excerpts from the Rig-Veda, the Bhagavad-Gita, and German literature on Indian subjects, as well as passages from Kant's early essay on cosmology, "A General Natural History and the Theory of the Heavens." The image of the stars as the gateway to heaven fascinated Beethoven over long periods of his life (and in the Finale of the Ninth Symphony inspired some of his most sublime music).[64]

The *Missa solemnis*, Ninth Symphony, and "Heiliger Dankgesang" of

the String Quartet in A minor op. 132 are the best-known musical manifestations of Beethoven's religious sentiments in his later life. Some of the
late songs are also "saturated with religious imagery and sentiment."[65]
And Beethoven had plans to write more masses, including a Requiem, and
accepted, without fulfilling, a commission to compose a sacred oratorio.
Moreover, evidence for his "new ability to call for help, to pray, to give
thanks, to reveal weakness, and even provisionally to accept his dependence upon an immaterial and unknowable deity"[66] extends to compositions without specific religious connotations, as the spiritual quality of,
for example, the variation finales of the Piano Sonatas opp. 109 and 111
eloquently attest.

Conclusion

This music is not abstract but rather personal and subjective, not a declar-
ation of absolute faith in things revealed but the expression of human
engagement with metaphysical problems and the (sometimes tortured)
existential process of that engagement. In this respect Beethoven's late
spirituality – which itself has much earlier roots – differs little from earlier
intellectual preoccupations. They all provided strong impulses to
compose; equally strong, perhaps stronger still, were the stirrings of his
heart and soul – as his emotional life might well have been characterized
in his own time – and his "pure" engagement with music itself, if such a
thing is possible. While Beethoven's emotional life, his non-musical intellectual interests, and his musical pursuits are separate aspects of his life
and career, they form an ultimate unity in the creative process; music was
the medium in which he sought his own answers to the existential and
conceptual problems that confronted him. When asked to contribute to
the musical journal *Cäcilia* in the 1820s, he declined – and did so at a time
when ever more musicians felt compelled to express themselves through
verbal language. A diary entry, a citation, suggests that music could
encompass all of life for Beethoven: "Life is like the quivering tones and
Man the lyre."[67] And in the letter to Rudolph about composition,
Beethoven eloquently expresses what music can provide – the path to self-
discovery and realization: working at music "won't give his imperial
majesty a headache, yes, it will rather provide great pleasure, when one
perceives oneself within art."[68]

3 The compositional act: sketches and autographs

BARRY COOPER

One of the best-known features of Beethoven's composing activity is his enormous efforts and struggle to produce his great masterpieces, in contrast to Mozart, who is reputed to have composed with great facility, working everything out in his head. Abundant evidence for Beethoven's struggles comes from his numerous sketchbooks, which were sufficiently prominent and unusual to draw forth comment from several eye-witnesses who wrote accounts of him. For example, Ignaz von Seyfried reported: "He was never found on the street without a small note-book in which he was wont to record his passing ideas."[1] Although Beethoven is not the only composer to have used sketchbooks, he seems to have been the first to have done so in any kind of systematic way, and almost no other composer has devoted such a large proportion of his time to refining his initial ideas through sketching processes.

Beethoven's propensity for making rough drafts and sketches for his works began almost as soon as he started composing as a boy. Moreover, one of his first published works – a set of three piano sonatas of 1783 (WoO 47) – contains a number of handwritten amendments in the printed score he owned, which are not merely corrections but subtle refinement of such things as articulation marks.[2] Such close attention to detail, and an incessant desire to seek improvement on his existing ideas, were elements that remained with him throughout his life, and gave the impetus to increasingly elaborate methods of sketching. By the time he left Bonn for Vienna in 1792 he had made many pages of sketches and unfinished drafts, and he valued these sufficiently to take a sizeable portfolio of them with him. In Vienna, he continued making sketches on loose sheets of paper for the next few years, and in most cases more than one work can be found on a single page, giving a very jumbled appearance.[3]

By 1798, as the number of pages of sketches increased rapidly and threatened to get out of hand, Beethoven decided he needed a better way of storing his sketches, and turned to using actual manuscript books prepared specially for the purpose. So began a series of sketchbooks that eventually amounted to over seventy altogether.[4] One reason why he made the change to sketchbooks in 1798 may have been that he began to write his first string quartet (op. 18 no. 3) at that time. He seems to have regarded string quartets as a particularly elevated form of composition, and so perhaps he felt the need for the increased space and coherence that a proper sketchbook would provide. At all events, the main work sketched in the first half of his first sketchbook was op. 18 no. 3, although the jumbled nature of his earlier sketches persisted, with other works appearing on some of these pages.

Beethoven's first sketchbook, known as Grasnick 1, lasted from mid-1798 until early 1799, and subsequent sketchbooks of similar size generally lasted a roughly similar length of time. Their size varied considerably, however, some having nearly 200 pages while others have fewer than 50; sixteen staves was the most common number per page, laid out in oblong format. Virtually all the surviving sketches from the early period were written in ink. If he sketched out of doors in pencil, as he did later, these sketches have disappeared. Loose sketchleaves were not entirely abandoned with the arrival of sketchbooks, but their use was confined mainly to periods between the end of one sketchbook and the start of the next. Although his first two sketchbooks were acquired ready-made, in subsequent years he often prepared his own by sewing together left-over (or newly acquired) manuscript paper to create home-made sketchbooks, such as Landsberg 7 of 1800–01. In such cases, their make-up was generally irregular, with the number of staves sometimes varying between different sections of the book.

During the 1800s Beethoven's sketching gradually became increasingly elaborate, with larger numbers of drafts and sketches being made for later works, although the increase was erratic rather than steady. He also began to show a preference for doing some of his composing out of doors, during the long walks that he liked to take at all times of the year. Since it was impracticable to carry large sketchbooks, pen, and inkwell with him, he took to carrying in his pocket loose sheets of manuscript paper and a pencil, in order to jot down ideas that occurred to him while he was out. The best of these would then sometimes be transferred to his sketchbook when he reached home. Thus these were effectively sketches for sketches, and were rarely incorporated direct into a finished score. Some sheets were also evidently used partly at home and partly out of doors, for they contain a mixture of pencil and ink sketches; in some cases this was because he used the pencil while at home, but where the leaf has a fold down the middle this suggests that it was at one time folded for putting in his pocket to carry around.

Inevitably, as the sketching process grew more complex, he eventually found that loose leaves were inadequate, as they had been in 1798 for his main sketching, and he began using "pocket sketchbooks" as they have become known. Each of these consisted of a batch of single sheets of oblong manuscript paper, which were folded down the center by

Beethoven and stitched together to create a little booklet in upright format (height greater than breadth) – again usually with sixteen staves per page. Sometimes he did not bother to stitch the leaves together, and so where the total number of pages is very small, it becomes debatable whether one can refer to it as a sketchbook at all, rather than just a couple of bifolios folded together. Almost every pocket sketchbook has well under fifty pages, and so each tended to be used up much quicker than a desk sketchbook.

The earliest known pocket sketchbook dates from 1811, and contains sketches for *Die Ruinen von Athen*, but all the rest date from 1815 or later, forming a more or less continuous sequence that runs parallel to the main sequence of desk sketchbooks. In both sequences there may be a substantial gap between one sketchbook and the next, but there is virtually never any overlap. It has been suggested there is an overlap between the Kessler and Wielhorsky sketchbooks of 1802–03, and between Mendelssohn 6 and the sketchbook containing *Meeresstille*, but in the former case the evidence for the overlap is far from compelling, while in the latter the *Meeresstille* sketchbook probably dates from about March 1813 to early 1814 (earlier than was once thought), in which case it wholly precedes Mendelssohn 6 of 1814–15.[5] A more persuasive case for an overlap occurs in a sketchbook of 1810–11, where some sketches for the last two movements of the Quartet op. 95 clearly predate some in the preceding sketchbook (Landsberg 11). There are also occasionally situations where Beethoven created a home-made sketchbook using paper that had already been partly filled (as may have happened with the one of 1810–11), giving an apparent, but not real, overlap. In addition, there is a curious case where a sketchbook of 1801 (Landsberg 7) contains a group of sketches for *Egmont* that clearly could not have been inserted before 1810. But such instances are rare, and the sketchbooks can by and large be seen as a kind of calendar of Beethoven's composing activity.

A further type of sketch format comes into prominence in connection with Beethoven's late quartets (1824 onwards). This consists of individual bifolios containing sections of string quartet written in full score.[6] Previously, his sketches had normally occupied only one or two staves for each bar, but now he started regularly using four staves per bar, in what have become known as score sketches. Only rarely are all four staves completely filled, but the extra space that became available enabled him to develop what he himself called a new kind of partwriting, in which all four instruments are allocated important melodic lines in a sort of polyphonic harmony. His earlier sketches, by contrast, tend to imply that only one or at most two melodic strands are important at any one time, even though this was of course not always the case. There are occasional instances of sketching in score amongst his earlier sketches, and his numerous folksong settings (1809–20) were sketched almost exclusively in this way, virtually none appearing in his sketchbooks. Only in 1824, however, did he adopt score sketching as a regular procedure alongside his other sketching methods. Thus in his last three years four possible formats were available: loose leaves, pocket sketchbooks, desk sketchbooks, and score sketches. One might expect there to be a sense of progression from pocket sketchbook to desk sketchbook to score sketch to final score for each passage, but this is rarely the case: the score sketches might contain early ideas, or the pocket sketchbooks might contain ideas for late revisions, and so anyone studying the genesis of these quartets has an exceedingly difficult task trying to follow the sequence of sketches from different formats.

In addition to the actual sketches, other types of material can be found associated with the composing process. A few works were abandoned after being begun in full score. This applies to several early piano works and, most notably, to a piano concerto of 1815 that would have been Beethoven's last. Here the score begins confidently, but peters out during the orchestral exposition.[7] More commonly encountered are abandoned pages of an autograph score. Sometimes, after writing out his final score, he made further corrections that necessitated inserting new leaves in place of existing ones, which were discarded but might still survive.[8] On other occasions, after he had begun a score, the work in question was set aside for some time, with the pages left incomplete. Then a new score would be written out, with the blank spaces of the incomplete score perhaps being used for sketches for some other work. There are, for example, several pages of an early score for the *Namensfeier* Overture (op. 115) in which only the first violin part has been entered, with the remaining staves used for sketches for another work. Occasionally the final score for a whole movement or work became so messy with corrections that Beethoven was forced to write it out again, as with the finale of the Piano Sonata in A♭ op. 110, but normally he ensured there was only one autograph score.

Throughout his life Beethoven carefully preserved his earlier sketches and clearly valued them, though how often he actually consulted them is uncertain – probably not very often. Despite changing his lodgings in Vienna frequently, and moving to a different residence in the country almost every summer, he managed to preserve his sketchbooks more or less intact right up to his death. After his death, however, the picture deteriorated rapidly. His musical effects were sold by auction on 5 November 1827, and his sketches were sold off as individual books or small lots to the highest bidders. Thus they were immediately dispersed, and the dispersal widened throughout the nineteenth century. Some buyers sold books on still intact to various collectors, while others sold individual pages or gave them away to friends as souvenirs of Beethoven's handwriting (the sketches themselves were regarded at this stage as more or less indecipherable and of no consequence). In due course several collectors owned most of the books, which eventually found their way into various public libraries – mainly the Gesellschaft der Musikfreunde in Vienna, the Beethoven-Archiv in Bonn, and especially the Prussian State Library in Berlin (now the Staatsbibliothek zu Berlin, Preußischer Kulturbesitz). But by this time nearly all had a few pages missing, while one from 1801 (containing the "Moonlight" Sonata amongst other works) had been systematically dismembered by Ignaz Sauer, who had bought the sketchbook at the original auction and sold off its pages individually at a profit. Most of the missing pages from the sketchbooks do still survive, but they have inevitably become scattered round the world, as have some of the loose sketchleaves that never formed part of a book. Now, however, scholars have managed to identify which of the dismembered pages belong in which books, by using some ingenious pieces of evidence such as matching up watermarks, sketch content, stave-rulings, stitch holes and even ink blots![9] This has enabled the sketches themselves to be studied more successfully than would otherwise have been possible. Meanwhile some of the missing leaves have still not been located, and there are even a few whole sketchbooks missing. One, the Boldrini pocket sketchbook, has not been seen since the late nineteenth century, and one or two others probably disappeared during Beethoven's lifetime or immediately afterwards: his Septet, First Symphony, and Quartet op. 18 no. 4 were all composed within a short space of time in 1799–1800, and yet virtually no sketches survive for any of them, so that the obvious inference is that a single sketchbook has been lost, rather than large numbers of loose leaves. (Still more improbable is any suggestion that Beethoven wrote these works without any sketching. He made sketches for the simplest and most minor works, and so it is inconceivable that he made none for such large and complex works as these.)

Altogether over 8,000 pages of sketches still survive – such a large number that a great many of them have still not been studied in detail, although the works on each have nearly all been identified. From the sketches that have been examined closely, many conclusions have been drawn about Beethoven's composing methods. The pioneer in this study was Gustav Nottebohm, who published extensive descriptions and extracts of most of the main sketchbooks during the latter part of the nineteenth century.[10] After him, little further original work was done for

Example 3.1 Sketches for a symphony in C minor, Bonn, Beethoven-Archiv, Mh 59, fol. 61v

nearly a hundred years, although there are some notable exceptions. Since the 1960s, however, study of Beethoven's sketches and autograph scores has blossomed, with important contributions from at least a dozen writers, enabling a much fuller, though still somewhat provisional, account of his composing methods.[11]

Beethoven's methods varied considerably, since no two works posed exactly the same problems and so were not composed in exactly the same way, and his sketching processes became increasingly complex during his lifetime, as indicated earlier. Some broad strategies, however, can be found fairly consistently throughout his entire output. Often the genre of a new work would be determined by some commission he received from a patron or publisher. On other occasions he chose a particular genre of his own volition. Once the genre was chosen, a few brief ideas would be jotted down, fixing the key and something of the character of the work. The key signature normally appeared with the initial sketch, since this helped to define the work, but it was usually omitted from subsequent sketches once the key was established firmly in his mind. These preliminary sketches are generally referred to as "concept sketches," although there is no precise definition of this term and it sometimes embraces any short new idea. Very many concept sketches can be found for works that never got off the ground – Nottebohm once estimated that Beethoven had begun at least fifty symphonies, most of which never progressed beyond the title and the first few bars, as in Example 3.1 (Bonn, Beethoven-Archiv, Mh 59, fol. 61v), an idea for a C minor symphony to follow no. 8 in 1812. Once the initial concepts were down on paper, Beethoven turned his attention to the form of the work or movement. If the movement was to have a regular form such as sonata form, there is generally no indication in the early stages, except perhaps for a word such as "Rondo" or "Minuet." If he was planning some innovative form, however, as in the finale of the *Eroica*, he usually sketched a kind of synopsis of either the movement or the work (or sometimes a group of movements) at an early stage.[12] This synopsis would often include a mixture of themes and words, the words including references to such things as keys, tempi, and formal or structural procedures. In a few cases he made more than one synopsis sketch for a single

Example 3.2 Sketches for the *Egmont* Overture, Vienna, Gesellschaft der Musikfreunde, A 42, p. 3

work or movement – there are several for the Quartet in C♯ minor op. 131.[13]

If the work was to have several movements, Beethoven worked intensively on each one in turn – almost always in numerical order except that, if the work was to have an overture, this was always composed last. Once he had established the broad outline of a movement, he moved on to making longer drafts for it, covering a substantial section or even the whole of a very short work such as a strophic song. These sketches have become known as continuity drafts, since he appears here to have been trying to establish the overall flow of the music, and a sense of the proportions between one passage and the next. Such drafts are normally written with the texture compressed on to a single stave – whether the work was a symphony or a piano sonata – with only the main melodic outline shown. In some bars the bass line may be shown instead, perhaps with some indication of harmony in the form of figured-bass numerals. These features are illustrated in Example 3.2 (Vienna, Gesellschaft der Musikfreunde, A 42, p. 3), which shows part of a draft for the *Egmont* Overture (cf. mm. 207–28). In a few drafts, particularly for vocal works, two staves are used instead of one, although one or other might be left largely blank; and in the late quartets the score sketches generally fulfilled the role of the continuity drafts, which appear only rarely in the relevant sketchbooks. In Beethoven's early period, one or two continuity drafts often sufficed, but in his later works ten or a dozen can sometimes be found for a single section. In such cases, each successive draft tends to be closer to the final version than its predecessors, but there is some backtracking, with ideas from early drafts disappearing, only to reappear at a late stage.

Short drafts of fifteen to thirty bars are relatively uncommon, and when they do appear they can often be found to link up with another section on an adjacent page to form a longer draft. Alongside the longer drafts, however, Beethoven often made what might be termed "variant sketches," when one or more alternatives to short passages would be jotted down. These might then be incorporated into a subsequent draft, thereby providing a valuable indication about their sequence. Normally he proceeded from the top of a page to the bottom, and from the beginning of a book to the end. Sometimes, however, he left blank spaces, which might later be filled in with further sketches, either for the same work or even a different one altogether. Moreover, initial concept sketches were often entered at the top of a blank page, in which case the rest of the page might well be filled with some completely unrelated material. This jumbled appearance, coupled with difficulties in reading the sketches (the pitches of noteheads are often unclear, there are numerous alterations and crossings out, and words are often badly written), makes the sketches seem extremely daunting at first sight, and is one reason why they were studied so little in the decades after Beethoven's death.

Another reason for neglect of the sketches was their incomplete and uncertain nature. Although the above description gives a fair indication of Beethoven's normal progress, it is somewhat idealized; usually some sketches are missing, so that it is rarely possible to trace the precise growth of a work from initial conception to final version. Sometimes, too, he composed with the aid of the piano – especially in his earlier years before his hearing deteriorated – in which case fewer written sketches would be needed. It also happens that all sketches are open to more than one interpretation, with regard to both their content and their layout; thus although it is often possible to deduce what probably happened, both in terms of Beethoven's concept of the work and of how he set about putting the sketches on paper, relatively little can be concluded with scientific certainty.

When Beethoven had more or less finished sketching a work, he began writing out the autograph score, and the final continuity draft is often extraordinarily similar to this, with most bars matching exactly. The autograph score itself, however, was sometimes amended extensively. The changes made at this stage were rarely of structural matters or phrase lengths, but generally of texture or layout.[14] In some autograph scores it can be seen that he began writing them out a little too early, so that although the first page has barely a single correction, subsequent pages become increasingly messy. Occasionally whole pages became so bad that they had to be replaced, as mentioned earlier.

Even after the final score was ready for the publishers, changes sometimes continued to be made. In most cases a copyist used to prepare a fair copy of the work, either for performers or the publisher, and some of these fair copies show last-minute alterations. There are also some famous cases of still later alterations. The prolongation of the second

Example 3.3 Piano Sonata op. 106, "Hammerklavier," mvt. 2, addition of first measure, letter to Ferdinand Ries 19 April 1819 (BG IV, no. 1295; Anderson II, no. 993)

pause in the Fifth Symphony was one of a number of small changes to this and the Sixth Symphony that were made "during" the first performance (according to Beethoven), after copies of the music had already been sent to the publishers, who had to be sent a list of these late changes. The first bar of the slow movement of the "Hammerklavier" Sonata was also added at a similar stage, as indicated in a letter to Ferdinand Ries (see Example 3.3).[15] And in the Second Piano Concerto, which had been repeatedly revised between about 1788 and 1798, Beethoven's final thoughts of 1801 came too late to be incorporated into the published version at all. The same applies to his final ideas for the Fourth Piano Concerto, which were evidently inserted into a copyist's score after the work had been published.[16]

What clearly emerges, then, is that the works do not exist in some "ideal" form where perfection has been achieved and nothing could be altered. In some works, notably the last piano sonata, op. 111, Beethoven's final intentions are not always clear in the sources, which contradict each other in places.[17] Even where his intentions do seem clear, he might well have thought of further modifications if he had returned to the work later. With *Fidelio*, his 1814 revisions to the earlier version were very substantial;[18] and he indicated that he would have liked to revise many of his earlier works. Perhaps the imperfections in his works help to enhance their character. Many of his works evoke a sense of struggle, and striving for the unreachable – a quality rarely evident in Mozart's work. The view that Beethoven found composition more of a struggle than Mozart did is partly correct but is misleading in several ways. Beethoven could compose as quickly as Mozart, for his numerous improvisations – instant compositions – were admired by all. Mozart's music is generally simpler in texture than Beethoven's, and would therefore need less sketching; moreover, Mozart did not hoard any sketches he made, so that where he encountered difficulties – as in his six quartets dedicated to Haydn – evidence for his struggle is largely lost. Nevertheless, the desire to strive for the highest

Example 3.4 Sketch for main theme of *Eroica* Symphony, Moscow, Glinka Museum, Wielhorksy, Sketchbook, p. 44

possible achievements, even those beyond grasp, is an integral part of Beethoven's character, and the abundance of sketches is a reflection of that desire.

Beethoven's sketches, then, function as both musical and biographical documents, and they form the strongest link between his life and his output, which are all too often considered separately. At the most basic level, study of the sketches has enabled many works to be dated with far greater precision than would otherwise be possible, even though the sketches themselves hardly ever bear any dates, and it has often led to substantial revision of a work's supposed period of composition. For example, the "First" *Leonore* Overture was composed after nos. 2 and 3, in 1807, not before them as some used to believe.[19] And Beethoven's pupil Czerny claimed that the last three piano sonatas (opp. 109–11), though completed in the 1820s, originated before 1817,[20] whereas the sketches show that none were begun before 1820. The sketches also furnish evidence about Beethoven's composing habits and how these changed over the years, as well as how systematic (or unsystematic) he was in organizing his compositions on a practical level. They also prove that his unprecedentedly complex compositions were achieved as a result of extremely hard work, as well as pure genius. Thus the sketches indicate much about his life and character.

They are equally significant, however, on a purely musical level. They provide extensive clues as to why certain notes are where they are, and why works turned out as they did, as well as giving some indication of how else they might have turned out. Study of the sketches helps one to see, and therefore hear, the music from the same angle as Beethoven saw it, thereby aiding communication between the composer and the listener, and understanding of the music itself. They sometimes reveal previously overlooked motivic relationships between different ideas in a movement, or confirm one's suspicions that such a relationship is significant and was planned by the composer. For example, it has been claimed that the opening theme of the *Eroica* is an elaboration of the first four notes from the bass line of the finale (this bass line having been composed earlier). The sketches confirm that Beethoven devised the opening theme in this way, for his earliest sketch for it (Example 3.4) is an almost exact quotation of those four notes. Although this discovery does not affect the existence of the abstract relationship between the two themes, it is reassuring that Beethoven was clearly aware of it and approached the first-movement theme from this angle. Conversely, sketch study can refute an analytical hypothesis. In the Quartet op. 130, which originally concluded with the *Grosse Fuge* as finale, it has been suggested that the whole quartet is founded on this fugue theme. Yet the sketches show that most of the quartet had been written before Beethoven first considered the *Grosse Fuge* for the finale, by which time he had sketched about a dozen other possible finale themes. Thus the themes in the earlier movements are not dependent in any way on the *Grosse Fuge*.

With such striking biographical and musical revelations, it is no accident that sketch study has proved to be one of the most fruitful fields of Beethoven research in the past thirty years. Yet the majority of the sketchbooks have still not been published in facsimile and transcription – an essential step toward their better understanding.[21] So many sketches still remain to be examined in detail that significant information about both Beethoven's life and the musical content of his works is likely to emanate from such studies for many years.

PART II

Style and structure

4 "The spirit of Mozart from Haydn's hands": Beethoven's musical inheritance

ELAINE SISMAN

Open any textbook in music history or music appreciation and the problem of Beethoven's relation to music historiography becomes immediately apparent: is he Classical or Romantic or both or neither? Is he part of the Canonical Three of the Viennese Classical Style – Haydn, Mozart, Beethoven – or is he a chapter unto himself, as the One destined to inherit and transform, even liberate, the achievements of the Classical Duo? As Charles Rosen astutely pointed out, "it would appear as if our modern conception of the great triumvirate had been planned in advance by history": Count Waldstein's entry in Beethoven's album, written in 1792 as the young composer left Bonn for Vienna, famously assured him that "You will receive the spirit of Mozart from the hands of Haydn."[1] This attractive phrase refers to the sense of lineage both conceptual and practical that places Beethoven in a musical culture already fully fledged in its genres and expressive possibilities. Mozart's premature death and the position of Haydn as Beethoven's teacher in Vienna left Beethoven perfectly placed to come into his inheritance. This chapter will examine some of the dominant elements in European music in the last few decades of the eighteenth century, and explore some of his methods of appropriating and personalizing the expressive language of Haydn and Mozart.[2]

Oppositions

By 1790, observers of the musical scene could classify the genres and structures of music according to shared assumptions about their place in musical life and the level of sophistication of their audience. About Vienna we read of a broad division of the musical public into the more and less knowledgeable: audience members, including patrons, comprised "connoisseurs" and "amateurs," while performers might be classed as "virtuosi" or "dilettanti" according to their skill.[3] Music was performed in a range of venues from the grand and costly public theaters associated with courts (for example, Vienna's Burgtheater) to the salons of the aristocracy and wealthier middle classes, from open-air gardens and coffee-houses to private homes. The composer-about-town needed to assess the intended audience for concerts or publications. C. P. E. Bach published collection after collection of piano pieces for "Kenner und Liebhaber"; Mozart's often-cited letter to his father at the end of 1782 about the piano concertos he was about to publish included the significant clause, "here and there connoisseurs alone can derive satisfaction; the non-connoisseurs cannot fail to be pleased, though without knowing why."[4]

Understanding the audience as a two-tiered target for composers enables us to confront the other sets of "oppositions," some of them actually rather fluid, that informed musical life toward the end of the eighteenth century. The distinction between the public and private realms of music-making meant that some genres were always associated with larger public, festive venues – symphonies and operas, for example – while others, including most of what we now know as "chamber music," were inveterately private – piano sonatas, trios, and songs. (Even Beethoven's piano sonatas were not performed in public during his lifetime, with but a single exception.[5]) Still others straddled both, depending on the city: string quartets, for example, were performed at Haydn's grand London concerts in the 1790s but served as more private fare in Vienna.[6] The distinction may be further complicated by considering that pieces like variations for piano, published with an eye to the expanding market for home music-making, may have originated in improvisations by virtuosos at public concerts (e.g. Mozart during his benefit concert at the Burgtheater in March 1783) or at aristocratic salons (e.g. Beethoven throughout the 1790s in Vienna).

Critical writings and books on musical style toward the end of the century seemed to recognize a fundamental difference in approach between the vigorous rhythms, thick textures, and generalized melodies of the more public style, which they referred to for convenience as a "symphony style," and the more nuanced, delicately individualized, and expressive gestures of the private realm exemplified by the "sonata style," a distinction that sometimes transcended genre when symphonic gestures appeared in works for keyboard. Other oppositions can similarly be shown to be related to qualities of style between and within genres, such as difficult vs. accessible, galant vs. learned, elevated vs. plain, serious vs. popular, and tragic vs. comic. These ideas lead to the rich field of rhetoric, which guided speakers and writers – and, in the eighteenth century, composers and artists as well – toward choosing a stylistic "level" commensurate with occasion and audience, finding "topics," that is, subjects and arguments, and enhancing persuasive power of the whole with appropriate figures.[7]

Mozart, whose works were often found to be too difficult or "highly spiced" by his contemporaries, offered a negative view of the world of opposition he was forced to inhabit. In the same letter of 1782 cited above, he remarked that "the mean [or middle ground], truth in all things, is known and valued no longer; to receive approval one has to write something so easy to understand that a coachman can sing it right off, or so incomprehensible that it pleases precisely because no rational person can understand it." In several works, such as the finales of the "Jupiter" Symphony (no. 41 in C K. 551) and G major String Quartet K. 387, and the overture and Armed Men scene of *Die Zauberflöte*, he almost revels in the disparity between the accessible galant style of simple textures and clearly phrased melodies and the difficult learned style of fugues and intricate counterpoint. Haydn, too, was a master of works that both juxtaposed and united opposites: the finale of his Symphony no. 101 ("Clock") is on one level a typical combination of rondo with sonata form, but when its main theme returns the first time it is decorated with melodic variations, and then at its second reappearance is transformed into a fugue.

Genres

What would a young composer make of the generic and individual musical styles current in the late eighteenth century? Would he instinctively grasp the nature of such "oppositional" thinking and seek to participate in it? What would an audience member, whether connoisseur or amateur, expect of the various kinds of music he or she would hear performed during the same period? Were the rhetorical modes of stylistic "levels" and musical "topics" consciously understood by listeners? Was musical form intelligible? How was musical meaning conveyed?

Let us consider first the "idea" of the multimovement work. Rooted in almost biological necessity when interest was to be sustained over a lengthy timespan, variety in tempo allowed instrumental genres to develop a kind of "plot" based on the association of "character" with particular tempos, meters, and keys. An Andante in 6/8 was an altogether different affair from an Andante in 4/4; Andante itself had a different character from Adagio; G minor was altogether different from E♭ major as the choice of slow-movement key in a piece in B♭ major; a piece with a minuet had a different effect from one without. The development of symphonies into the genre with the least "allowable" variation in external form – four movements in fast (sonata form, perhaps with slow introduction)–slow–minuet/trio–fast order – was offset by the much more flexible "private" genres for keyboard – sonatas and trios in two or three movements in virtually any order of tempi, without the necessity of sonata form up front, and with the possibility that movements may run into one another with a half-cadence and *attacca*. Neal Zaslaw describes the characters embodied in Mozart's symphonies from the 1760s and 1770s as follows:

> The first movements represent the heroic, frequently with martial character; many early- and mid-eighteenth-century sinfonia movements were limited to this character, but later ones (all of Mozart's included) contain contrasting lyrical ideas. Appropriately, given the origins of the sinfonia in the opera pit, the two sorts of ideas – lyrical and martial – may be seen as comparable to the persistent themes of opera seria itself: love vs. honour. The andantes deal with the pastoral . . . The minuets stand for the courtly side of eighteenth-century life . . . The trios, on the other hand, often deal with the antic, thus standing in relation to the minuet as the anti-masque to the masque . . . The finales are generally based on rustic or popular dances: gavottes, *contredanses*, jigs, or quick-steps. Taken together, the heroic, the amorous, the pastoral, the courtly, the antic, and the rustic or popular, represent the themes found most often in eighteenth-century prose, poetry, plays, and paintings. Only the religious is not regularly treated . . . Hence, the symphony may be considered a stylized conspectus of the eighteenth century's favourite subject-matter.[8]

This list is a good first step toward assessing the psychological profile, as it were, of a multimovement work in general, but it needs broadening to include other character types that appear in Haydn's and also Mozart's symphonies of that era and of the 1780s and 90s, as well as music (and the other arts, especially literature) to which the terms "sensibility" and "irony" apply. Its usefulness to genres other than the symphony also needs to be assessed. Symphonic opening movements, for example, may go beyond the martial and lyrical to reflect passionate, agitato styles sometimes referred to as "Sturm und Drang." Some of their opening gestures, without being literally martial, put one in mind of the grand style of rhetoric for which "the symphony is most excellently suited" with its "expression of grandeur, passion, and the sublime."[9] Dance-like topics may even appear in a first movement, especially those in "danceable" meters like 3/4: the opening of Haydn's Symphony no. 82 ("Bear," 1785) moves rapidly from grand style to stylized minuet gesture before a lengthy fanfare leads to a half cadence. The Allegro of Mozart's Symphony no. 38 ("Prague," K. 504, 1786) covers so many topics after the grand style of its slow introduction that its topical variety is virtually a topic in its own right, in stark contrast to the "controlling" topics of its pastoral Andante and buffa Presto.[10] About the opening movements of quartets, sonatas, and trios, one can say only that grand style is sometimes in evidence – think only of Haydn's "big" E♭ major Sonata Hob. XVI:52 – but that it is often amalgamated with the more intimate gestures and expressive nuances befitting the "sonata" style.

That slow movements offer a "respite" in some sense from the length and complexity of the first is suggested by the term "pastoral," but the pastoral as a musical topic is generally more specific than "mere" respite: it applies to those movements that employ some combination of the compound meter, a melody with dotted rhythms (especially the dotted rhythms of the siciliana) or trochees in thirds and sixths, and prominent passages of drone bass. Just as a pastoral literary topos could include real-world pain in contrast to idyllic bliss, there may be substantial disruption in the musical pastoral.[11] Two problematic issues immediately arise. First, what is one to make of slow movements that do not exhibit any of the time-honored pastoral techniques? The slow movement of Haydn's Symphony no. 88 in G (1787), with an idyllic first theme and passages of almost "pure" disruption without thematic content, is a Largo in 3/4 without any "overt" pastoral features but certainly reflects a pastoral "spirit" if not its literal topos. And second, what of movements that exhibit these traits but are not in slow-movement position? The first movement of Haydn's Sonata in G Hob. XVI:40 (1784), for example, is an Allegretto in 6/8 whose first theme is certainly a pastoral "type"; the second-movement Minuet of the Sonata in B minor Hob. XVI:32 (1776) is entirely an idyll in contrast to the stress-laden perpetuum mobile of the Trio, and in fact stands in for a slow movement in middle position. Thus, we cannot pigeonhole topic and character too narrowly.

As for minuets being "courtly" and trios "antic," these very broad categories cannot do justice to the range of expression in Haydn's minuets and trios, although to be sure there is a greater variety in string quartets than in symphonies. Calling them scherzos, marking them Allegro, filling them with hemiolas, pregnant silences, and skewed phrase structures (e.g. op. 33 no. 5, op. 77 no. 2), Haydn did much to liberate his minuets from their courtly origin. Yet he must have felt beleaguered by the evident necessity of including minuets in everything, for he told his biographer Griesinger some time during the last decade of his life, "I wish someone would write a really *new* minuet."[12] Although Haydn did not mention them, Beethoven's scherzos are usually considered to be the consummation of Haydn's wish. One wishes for a specific date for that remark; otherwise, it seems that Haydn was either unaware of the *Eroica* and the op. 59 string quartets or else thought Beethoven's piano-sonata scherzos of the 1790s not quite the innovation he had hoped for.

It is in the finales that some of the greatest stylistic oppositions met and mingled, the racy comedy of rapid-fire dance tunes brought up short by learned counterpoint (Mozart's F major Piano Concerto K. 459; the movements in the quartet K. 387 and Haydn's Symphony no. 101 mentioned above) or the stormy minor-key mood suddenly transformed by an incongruously lighthearted tune (Haydn's quartet op. 76 no. 1). The extra weight afforded to many first movements by slow introductions made the finale sound more disposable, but this balance often changed, as in those pieces with a slow introduction to their finales (Mozart's G minor String Quintet K. 516) or finales with an exceptional density of polyphony ("Jupiter" Symphony). While it is a commonplace to find in Beethoven the first seriously "teleological" approach – that is, finale-weighted and end-driven – to the multimovement cycle, with the "Jupiter" as the Great Precursor, the long history of rhetorically mixed finales proves fruitful for Beethoven as well, in such pieces as the String Quartets in B♭ op. 18 no. 6 and in C op. 59 no. 3.

Thus, genre-types and movement-types were complex, multifarious, and sophisticated entities at the end of the eighteenth century, offering an extraordinary range of expressive and formal possibilities. Moreover, the traditional meanings of such time-honored topoi as "pastoral" and "learned" were increasingly stretched and recontextualized. "Pastoral" went, in effect, from being a melodic type with a sweetly abstract sense of respite (however internally opposed) to a subject for an entire piece: the D major Sonata op. 28, with its full array of the associated techniques already in the first movement, was quickly nicknamed "Pastorale" (though not by Beethoven) and it is the title of Beethoven's most famous "characteristic" symphony, even if its composer sought to distinguish the "expression of feelings" from "[mere] tone-painting."[13] New topics were also developed: in Haydn's Quartet in D op. 76 no. 5 (1797), and Beethoven's piano sonata in D op. 10 no. 3 (1797–98), the slow movements are marked both Largo (the most "serious" slow-movement tempo) and "mesto" ("melancholy"). Haydn's is serene (it is also marked "cantabile"), resigned, poignant, and in the unusual key of F♯ major; Beethoven's is dark, and filled with "pathetic accents," as in the series of ascending diminished seventh chords, mm. 23–25 and 62–65.[14] With such a broad field to play in, how would a composer choose his path?

Modeling

Although Waldstein's comment linking Beethoven with Mozart and Haydn has already been deconstructed by Tia DeNora – she explores the extent to which the "'Haydn's hands' narrative" created a self-fulfilling prophecy in which both pupil and teacher colluded each to enhance his own reputation – it is worth considering for a moment the entire passage in relation to the musico-cultural situation in Germany and Austria.

> Dear Beethoven. You are going to Vienna in fulfillment of your long-frustrated wishes. The Genius of Mozart is still mourning and weeping the death of her pupil. She found a refuge but no occupation with the inexhaustible Haydn; through him she wishes to form a union with another. With the help of assiduous labor you shall receive *the spirit of Mozart from Haydn's hands.* Your true friend, Waldstein.[15]

Usually interpreted as slighting if not actually insulting Haydn, and thus as a way to ensure Beethoven's reputation as Mozart's heir but Haydn's superior, this flight of eloquence ought instead to be understood as emblematic of generational identification. Count Waldstein was born in 1762, six years Mozart's junior and eight and a half years Beethoven's senior. He saw Haydn, already sixty, as simply not in need of "Mozart's genius" because he had his own. He was already the patriarch of the musical world: as productive as he could possibly be and too old to complete Mozart's work for him. Someone was needed to carry on in the future.

Significant also is the use of the term genius as Muse, in an era when "genius" increasingly referred to the whole person rather than to a talent or spiritual quality of the person.[16] DeNora emphasizes that in the "first extant telling of the Haydn–Beethoven story offered by a Viennese observer to Viennese recipients" in 1796, Schönfeld's *Yearbook of Music in Vienna and Prague* describes Beethoven as "a musical genius."[17] She stresses that Schönfeld devotes more than four times as much space to Beethoven as to any other musician but Haydn, who is first. But this is simply incorrect: Schönfeld gives sixty-six lines to Haydn, who is described as a "great genius" and twenty-four lines to Beethoven, but sixty-one to Kozeluch (demonstrably no genius), more than twenty-four to various nonentities also described as "geniuses," and twenty to Hummel, "a pleasant youth of fifteen" who is "a born genius."[18] What is in fact significant, however, is the strongly worded statement in the Beethoven entry that "Much can be expected when such a genius entrusts himself to the most excellent master."

Lineage and tutelage went hand in hand, although there was a certain uncertainty in what the genius was, precisely, to learn from the master. Was one to imitate him or to follow rules that he imparted? The tension between imitation and genius had long been recognized in the eighteenth century. As Edward Young wrote in 1759,

> An *Original* ... rises spontaneously from the vital root of Genius; it *grows*, it is not *made*: *Imitations* are often a sort of *manufacture* wrought up by those *Mechanics*, *Art*, and *Labour*, out of preexistent materials not their own ... Learning is borrowed knowledge; Genius is knowledge innate.[19]

Young's book became wildly popular in Germany, where it appeared in two translations within a year of its original publication. Continuing on this path was Lessing, who in 1769 declared "O you manufacturers of rules, how little do you understand art, and how little do you possess of genius which creates the ideal . . ."[20] Haydn virtually announced himself the enemy of rules: "Art is free and will be limited by no artisan's fetters."[21] He even allowed that rules of strict counterpoint could be broken, and yet he was to teach Beethoven counterpoint. Surely he did not expect Beethoven to imitate him. Indeed, some aspects of Haydn's evidently imitable style created a fraught situation, as the article "Modest Questions put to modern Composers and Virtuosi" made clear in the inaugural volume of the *Allgemeine musikalische Zeitung* in 1798: the author, probably Zelter, decried the current fashion for slavishly imitating every innovation of Haydn until "we are used to them, they make no more effect . . . these things have been spoiled by the imitators."[22] This may perhaps have affected Haydn's sensitivity about his pupils publicly identifying themselves as such; he always referred to Pleyel as his pupil when the latter was his rival in London, and he wanted Beethoven to identify himself as "pupil of Haydn" on the title page of his first "official" publication, the op. 1 piano trios. Beethoven, for his part, jealously guarded his innovations from imitators, writing to Eleonore von Breuning in 1794 of the necessity to publish his piano variations before imitators made off with his trademarks.[23]

Several recent studies deal with specific aspects of Beethoven's modeling procedures, in which he based some of his pieces on works by Haydn and Mozart, choosing the ordering of movements, their keys and formal types, and details of texture, harmonic planning, and even melodic contour, as templates.[24] These studies join a considerable number of earlier essays in which Beethoven's relationship to tradition has been extensively explored.[25] Beethoven's debts to Haydn are more often considered to involve particular structures, processes, and strategies, rather than entire works as models. But the reader will find one essay declaring a piece to be based clearly on Mozartean procedures, while another will assert the same piece to be based on Haydn.[26] How does one tell? What are the general and specific features of style upon which Beethoven drew? And are the pieces by Beethoven that reveal "modeling" necessarily early? Beethoven copied out works by older masters throughout his life, from J. S. Bach and Handel to C. P. E. Bach to Haydn and Mozart, whenever he needed them.[27]

Beethoven's reasons for making a score copy in 1794 of Haydn's Quartet in E♭ major op. 20 no. 1 (1772) have not been ascertained, since he wrote no quartets at that time and his first essay in string-trio writing,

Example 4.1
(a) Haydn, String Quartet in E♭ op. 20 no. 1, finale, mm. 1–5

(b) Beethoven, String Trio in E♭ op. 3, finale, mm. 1–7

op. 3 (written in 1794), was modeled at least in its outward plan of six movements (Allegro con brio–Andante–Menuetto–Adagio–Menuetto–Finale) on Mozart's Divertimento K. 563 (with the Adagio in A♭ major and Andante in B♭ major reversed).[28] The finale in both is a very relaxed sonata-rondo. Yet a comparison of the finales of Beethoven's trio with Haydn's quartet suggests that Haydn's movement was the source for thematic and harmonic details despite the strikingly smaller dimensions of the latter (160 measures compared to Beethoven's 457!). Not only are the opening themes similar in contour, but Beethoven makes more explicit Haydn's off-tonic opening (Example 4.1). Haydn compresses considerable harmonic activity into the passage of syncopation emerging from the theme (mm. 11–32), while Beethoven turns his into a big three-part sequence (I–vi–V, mm. 25–53), with figuration moving from violin to viola to cello. Both second themes ascend from f^1 to c^3 as a goal, then make their way back down. Beethoven's lengthy closing section returns to the three-fold presentation of his bridge, reversing the order of instruments and opting for repetition rather than sequence. Each exposition descends to $B♭^2$, slurring it over the barline to B♮, a mini-retransition to a partial return of the main theme, a sonata-rondo inflection. The harmonic goal of each development section is C minor, which Beethoven reaches immediately because of the looseness of the sonata-rondo format. Haydn moves first to F minor and sequences the main theme in a polyphonic passage more metrically sophisticated than anything in Beethoven's square-cut finale. From C minor each continues with a harmonically dense passage moving successively from a dominant or diminished seventh to its tonic in related keys. Haydn moves to a full retransition on a dominant pedal, and a reiteration of the B♭–B♮ fillip. In Beethoven's final statement of the theme, he expands that little transition to four full measures.

Beethoven's later appropriations contained more conscious and inevitable attempts at distancing. For example the first movement of his First Symphony (op. 21, 1800) relates to the first (and to a much lesser extent the last) movements of the last symphony by Mozart (K. 551, the "Jupiter," 1788) and the last C major symphony by Haydn (no. 97, 1791).[29] Here we see, I believe, a clear example of Beethoven choosing models for his symphonic debut with the purpose of homage, of placing himself within a tradition, laced with one-upmanship, and casting the result in the most brilliantly conventional and instantly recognizable of eighteenth-century symphonic modes: the "C major symphony" tradition with its trumpets and drums and "ceremonial flourishes."[30] (I will refer to these pieces as the First, the 97th, and the "Jupiter," and trust that their composers can be ascertained therefrom.) This canny choice of a festive mode to please the public drives the striking similarities among the three grand-style opening Allegro themes: each is based on an "annunciatory" ascending fourth with a dotted rhythm, the "Jupiter's" filled in, the 97th's hollow, the First's nearly hollow but inflected by the leading tone (Example 4.2). Beethoven's conflates the unison opening/harmonized sequel phrase structure of the "Jupiter" with another C major theme structure, that of a piano opening phrase restated on the supertonic, as in Haydn's String Quartet op. 33 no. 3 (1781).[31] He does this with a quiet opening in the strings switching to wind chords which antiphonally cue the next statement, first toward the supertonic, then toward the dominant. The expansion of the antiphonal winds passage in the recapitulation into complete chromatic ascent comes from the dissonant chromatic recasting of the opening theme in the "Jupiter" finale; the wind transition into both development and recapitulation comes from the "Jupiter" first movement.

Only one other significant element is triggered by the "Jupiter," I believe, beyond the harmonic plan of the development section, convincingly demonstrated by Carl Schachter:[32] the minor episode which interrupts what appears to be a closing tutti after the second theme (mm. 77–87). Mozart signifies the end of the second theme and beginning of the closing group with a "doubting" passage whose questioning chords trickle out in a five-beat grand pause, then a "minor shock," a sudden tutti C minor chord.[33] The rhetorical effect of this sequence of events is a powerful emotional charge, delivered by first breaking off and then virtually collaring the listener with a forceful direct address (Example 4.3a). Moreover, in the finale of the "Jupiter," a C minor "swerve" sets up a

Example 4.2 Three first-movement themes
(a) Mozart, "Jupiter" Symphony, mm. 1–8

(b) Haydn, Symphony no. 97, mm. 1–11

(c) Beethoven, Symphony no. 1, mm. 1–8

preview of the conventional "Mannheim" cadence before the final close (Example 4.3b). Beethoven's turn to minor provides virtually the opposite effect: from a cheerful wind-dominated second theme to a conventional vigorous tutti, we suddenly enter a mysterious shadow world in the low strings (mm. 77ff.), the *ombra* topic of supernatural operatic scenes (Example 4.3c). Wind intervention and the conventional "Mannheim" cadence (mm. 85–88, found also in the "Jupiter" finale, mm. 145–51) are needed before the "true" closing theme can begin. Functioning as an antipode to the "C-major symphony style," the *ombra* is an expressive device of some sophistication.

But it is from the 97th that Beethoven derives the most striking effects of his first movement: the off-tonic opening of the slow introduction, the use of a chord progression in the introduction that returns later in the movement, and the idea of a slow introduction propelling itself into the

Example 4.3
(a) Mozart, "Jupiter" Symphony, mvt. 1, minor "shock," mm. 77–82

(b) "Jupiter' Symphony, mvt. 4, minor "swerve," mm. 125–29

(c) Beethoven, Symphony no. 1, mvt. 1, *ombra* episode beginning m. 77

(d) episode ending with "Mannheim" cadence, mm. 85–88

Allegro without a cadential chord and fermata. Haydn's 97th is the only one of his slow introductions to use the beginning of the Allegro as the resolution of its final chord progression. That this chord progression has also been heard at the beginning of the introduction is especially significant because it means that the potentially static idea of "symmetry" is used as an agent of propulsion; moreover, this progression, which begins with a diminished seventh chord (the vii^7 of V), appears in the closing groups of both exposition and recapitulation (Example 4.4a). Beethoven simply lops off the opening unison-tonic measure of 97 in order to begin, notoriously, on the dominant of the subdominant. The passage does not provide a root-position tonic chord until m. 8, the appearance of which triggers a six-measure cadential chord progression propelling itself into the Allegro (Example 4.4b). Beethoven then saves this progression until the very end of the piece, bringing it back over and over in mm. 271–77 of the coda whereupon it leads to the most brilliant fanfare sound of the entire movement.

Thus the earliest example of Beethoven's harmonic long-range plan-

Example 4.4

(a) Haydn, Symphony no. 97, mvt. 1, mm. 2–4, chord progression in slow introduction

(b) Beethoven, Symphony no. 1, mvt. 1, mm. 8–11, chord progression in slow introduction

ning – a virtual signature in symphonies from the *Eroica* on – can be revealed as very likely inspired by Haydn. But the wholesale recurrence of slow introductions in the original tempo – the *Pathétique* Sonata op. 13 and *La Malinconia* in the finale of the quartet op. 18 no. 6 are the earliest of these – probably owe their existence to Mozart's D major String Quintet K. 593 (1790), in which the Larghetto introduction returns during the coda, as well as the dramatic stroke whereby the opening – drumroll and all – of the "Drumroll" Symphony, no. 103, returns in the recapitulation. (The latter has a quite different effect from the "disguised" thematic incorporation of the slow introduction melody into the Allegro itself.) Thematic reminiscence of the slow introduction in its original tempo is entirely different from the recall of a harmonic progression for closural effect.

Mozart's influence on Beethoven's treatment of minor keys, especially C minor, has been noted in detail by Michael Tusa and Joseph Kerman.[34] Mozart's C minor Piano Concerto no. 24 K. 491 is especially important in this respect; Beethoven must have known it before he heard it at the Augarten in 1799, exclaiming to the composer J. B. Cramer after the performance, "Cramer, Cramer! We shall never be able to do anything like that!"[35] Tusa points out the similarities between the first movements of K. 491 and Beethoven's C minor Piano Trio op. 1 no. 3, beyond their triple meter and unison opening: their "main theme (triple meter, downbeat start on $\hat{1}$, arpeggiated melody, melodic emphasis on $\hat{6}$, soft dynamics) and in the specific treatment of the beginning of the recapitulation" (figuration passage over dominant pedal leading to forte recasting of the theme).[36] There is another structural similarity: the two second themes in the solo exposition of K. 491, each with its own closing figuration and trill cadence, may be the source of the large dimensions and thematic

Example 4.5 Mozart, Piano Concerto no. 24 in C minor K. 491, mvt. 1
(a) main tutti theme, mm. 1–6

(b) theme 2a, mm. 148–51

(c) theme 2b, mm. 201–04

multiplicity of Beethoven's exposition, although the dimensions of the trio are closer to the recapitulation of the concerto. (Example 4.5 gives the principal themes of the Mozart.) Beethoven's first theme is divided into the arresting unison gesture described by Tusa and a more motivically repetitive sequel that recurs in the bridge and at the end of the closing section. Moreover, the second theme is divided as well into a more rhythmically active and a more contemplative theme, the first in E♭ and the second in A♭; a third contemplative "interlude" appears in the closing section. When Mozart's "first second theme" appears in the recapitulation, its reiteration by the piano is in the subdominant. (Example 4.6 shows each of the Beethoven themes.) While Beethoven's works for piano of the 1790s are routinely called "symphonic" because of their size and especially because of their four-movement plans, the mere fact that the concerto is in three movements ought not to disqualify it as a model.

The evocative qualities and intrinsic characteristics of the different keys, an essential part of eighteenth-century thinking, are powerfully displayed in the idea of a composer choosing his models from among pieces in the same key.[37] Thus one looks immediately to Mozart's "Prague" Symphony in assessing the existence of a structural or expressive or textural "source" for Beethoven's Second – and indeed it is to be found, in both the slow introduction and main theme. In cases of direct thematic quotations or allusions, however, the key of the original seems less an issue. For example, Beethoven quotes the famously beautiful G major melody of the slow movement of Haydn's Symphony no. 88 in the Allegretto ma non troppo movement of his Piano Trio in E♭ op. 70 no. 2, in A♭ major.[38] But Beethoven certainly didn't come to terms with his forebears only through

Example 4.6 Beethoven, Piano Trio in C minor op. 1 no. 3, mvt. 1
(a) theme 1a, mm. 1–7

(b) theme 1b, mm. 10–14

(c) theme 2a, mm. 59–63

(d) theme 2b, mm. 76–79

(e) theme 3 (within closing), mm. 110–18

quotation and modeling, on the one hand, or through assessment and expansion of contemporary expectations of topics and structures of the principal genres, on the other. He also transformed the decorum of conventional or characteristic formal designs in ways that asserted "difficulty" as an aesthetic principle.[39]

Decorum

A single example can suffice to reveal Beethoven's transformation of decorum in a type of piece utterly familiar to his contemporaries: the variation form as a movement in a larger work.[40] The rhetorical concept of decorum, or propriety, is clearly outlined by Cicero, in *Orator*. The orator must consider "what to say, in what order, and in what manner and style to say it." As for the latter,

> In an oration, as in life, nothing is harder than to determine what is appropriate. The Greeks called it prépon; let us call it decorum or "propriety" ... This depends on the subject under discussion, and on the character of both the speaker and the audience ... Moreover, in all cases the question must be "How far?" For although the limits of propriety differ for each subject, yet in general too much is more offensive than too little ... [41]

In works by Haydn and Mozart, the decorum of a variation movement – its traditional and hence normative technical and expressive limits – depended upon its position in the work, upon genre, and upon the nature of the theme. In general, its implicit code included several different proprieties: a "propriety of ordering," in which simpler textures appeared early in a set while imitative polyphony never did, a "propriety of performance style," in which extremes of instrumentation and dynamics would be introduced for local contrasts, rarely as the topic of an entire variation, and "propriety of contrast and return," in which distantly related or contrasting material would be followed by returns of the theme melody. Finally, the theme itself would observe a certain propriety, not only in its two-reprise (binary) structure with clearly delineated phrases, but also in the degree of repetition and contrast in its melodic segments, rhythms, and textures.[42]

All of these proprieties devolve upon the concept of familiarity and recognition – without which, Koch said, "[the variations] give the impression of a group of arbitrarily related pieces which have nothing in common with each other, and for whose existence and ordering one can imagine no basis."[43] Michaelis's evocative account of variation form, in an article of 1803 on repetition and variation, asserts that

> if the basic theme, the main melody, appears clothed in a new manner, under a delicate transparent cloak, so to speak, then the soul of the listener obtains pleasure, in that it can automatically look through the veil, finding the known in the unknown, and can see it develop without effort. Variation demonstrates freedom of fantasy in treatment of the subject, excites pleasant astonishment in recognizing again in new forms the beauty, charm, or sublimity already known, attractively fusing the new with the old without creating a fantastic mixture of heterogeneous figures ... Variation arouses admiration insofar as everything latent in the theme is gradually made manifest, and unfolds [into] the most attractive diversity.[44]

Michaelis stresses that the process of unfolding the secrets of the theme happens "gradually."

By the time Beethoven began work in 1799 on the fifth of his op. 18 string quartets, he had already written at least twenty sets of variations, including six movements in larger works, although none in as "serious" a genre as the quartet. I believe that this movement radically breaks with the

decorum of classical variation movements, and that this is clearest in precisely those areas in which Beethoven appropriates earlier techniques.
First, the "abstract construction" of the theme (Kerman's disparaging
term)[45] has a level of repetitiveness unusual in that it involves pitches as
well as rhythms (Example 4.7a); it thus differs from the repetitive rhythmic patterns underlying the themes of Haydn's String Quartet op. 76 no. 6
(first movement) and Symphony no. 75 (second movement), as well as
Mozart's B♭ major Piano Concerto K. 450 (second movement). The first
variation recasts the ordering of classical variations. Normally, a contrapuntal or fugal variation would be placed at or near the end of a set: here
the cello alone immediately sets out the terms of a gritty contrapuntal
buildup, with a crescendo to underscore the registral expansion and
offbeat sforzandos to deny a final coming together of the disparate voices
and registers (Example 4.7b). By virtue of its prominent position, this
variation becomes a manifesto, asserting control over the language of the
classical variation while challenging its decorum.

Variations 2 and 3 return to standard equipment – triplet-sixteenth
figuration in the first violin in the former and theme fragments accompanied by thirty-second notes in the latter. Yet the texture is again unusual:
the thirty-second note pattern consists of slurred appoggiaturas instead
of the customary broken-chord or scalar patterns, and the thematic fragments are themselves fragmented in instrumentation and register, ending
the first period with viola and cello joined at the octave in an odd feminine cadence. The fourth variation draws on the last one of Haydn's
"Emperor" Quartet variations, op. 76 no. 3, reharmonizing the theme, but
accomplishes this here by altering the melody itself in a strange borrowing of the melodic minor scale in B minor to end the first period in the
mediant. It hardly prepares for the fifth and last variation, in which the
high trill, offbeat accents, and jumping cello line both balance the first
variation and exceed the expressive limits of allowable contrast; indeed,
Kerman refers to its unprecedented driving orchestral style (Example
4.7c).[46]

These novelties are surpassed by the coda, which begins as a deceptive
cadence in ♭VI on the same disjunct cello figuration, Beethoven's only
literal appropriation from Mozart's K. 464. Beethoven wittily inverts the
theme in sixteenth notes as contrary-motion accompaniment to its original rhythm; each statement reassigns the theme and counterpoint, beginning with a theme/counterpoint pairing of second violin/viola (B♭), then
cello/first violin (D), then viola/second violin counterpoint (G)
(Example 4.7d). Moving the theme through the voices in this way seems
to be a reference to Haydn's cantus firmus technique in the quartets of op.
76 published in the same year. Contrary motion becomes the logical

Example 4.7 Beethoven, String Quartet op. 18 no. 5, second mvt.
(a) theme

(b) var. 1

development of the closing measures of the theme, while the sudden turn to B♭ at the beginning of the coda may correlate enharmonically with the single biggest earlier shock in the movement, the A♯ in the melody of variation 4.

Beethoven breaks Classical decorum by calling into question every one of the proprieties mentioned above. His most radical step is his first, for it is here in variation 1, in the sudden eradication of harmony and conventional register in favor of the cello subject, that he defamiliarizes the theme. In a variation movement of 1799 one might diverge very widely from the theme, but a general propriety of familiarity asserted that the

Example 4.7 (*cont.*)
(c) var. 5

(d) coda

beginning was not the place for such a technique. By "making strange" the beginning of a variation work, Beethoven effectively violated Michaelis's context of the intelligible environment in which the theme can be recognized. This is not to say, of course, that the listener of 1799 could not make sense of the relationship between variation and theme. But by inserting a new level of difficulty into a previously more accessible form, Beethoven was staking his claim to a new decorum. And he expanded his claim so far in subsequent years that some listeners still instinctively reject the presence of what Beethoven knew to be his inheritance.

5 Phrase, period, theme

ROGER KAMIEN

Perceptive musicians of the early nineteenth century, like many listeners today, admired the originality of Beethoven's musical ideas and his imaginative ways of developing them. For example, in an 1813 review of the Piano Trio in D major op. 70 no. 1, the writer, composer, and music critic E. T. A. Hoffmann wrote that the finale begins with "a short, original theme, that appears again and again throughout the movement in many changes and ingenious allusions, in alternation with various figures."[1] Hoffmann also singled out the way in which Beethoven's openings create tension and expectation. In a 1812 review of the *Coriolan* Overture, he observed that the "principal theme of the Allegro has a character of irresistible restlessness, of unquenchable longing . . . the transposition of this theme a tone lower is unexpected and increases the tension which was already felt in the opening measures . . . Everything combines . . . [to create] the highest pitch of expectation for that which the rise of the mysterious curtain will reveal."[2] Later in the nineteenth century, Beethoven's themes became models for students of composition. In the early 1890s, for example, Brahms advised his student Gustav Jenner "to make a diligent study of Beethoven's sonata themes and to observe their influence on the structure of the movement . . ."[3]

To provide a background for my discussion of Beethoven's themes, I begin with a brief introduction to Classical *phrase rhythm*, a term referring both to phrase structure and the metrical grouping of measures.[4] I discuss some of the ways in which phrases are paired to form periods, and how phrases are connected and expanded, using passages from Beethoven's works as examples.

Eighteenth-century theorists often made analogies between segmentation in language and music.[5] In 1771, Johann Philipp Kirnberger wrote that "just as a paragraph in speech consists of segments, phrases, and sentences that are marked by various punctuation symbols such as the comma (,), semicolon (;), colon (:), and period (.), the harmonic [equivalent of the paragraph] can also consist of several segments, phrases, and periods."[6] A phrase may be defined as a group of measures containing a tonal motion to a cadential goal.[7] Phrases of four or eight bars occur most frequently, but other phrase-lengths are also common (see, for example,

[64]

Example 5.1 Piano Sonata op. 53, "Waldstein," mvt. 1, mm. 35–43

the ten-bar phrases opening the Sonata for Piano and Violin in F major op. 24 ["Spring"] and the Piano Sonata in D major op. 28).

Two or more phrases can form a musical unit called a *period*. Often, the period includes two phrases, the second of which ends with a more conclusive cadence than the first. The second phrase of a period may be a varied repetition of the first or have a different motivic content. An important type of formal organization in Classical music is the *parallel period*, consisting of an antecedent phrase ending with a half cadence, and a *consequent* phrase beginning like the antecedent but ending with a full cadence. This full cadence resolves the tonal and melodic tension produced by the half cadence of the antecedent. Example 5.1 shows the eight-bar parallel period initiating the second theme group of the Allegro con brio from Beethoven's Piano Sonata in C major op. 53 ("Waldstein"). The pianist, composer, and theorist Carl Czerny, who had studied with Beethoven, described this theme in the early 1830s as "the beautiful choral-like middle subject in E major, which, *like so many of Beethoven's ideas*, derives its melody from the simple diatonic scale . . ."[8] Typically, each four-bar phrase of the period subdivides into two-bar units called *subphrases* (indicated by dotted slurs in Example 5.1). As Czerny observed, these subphrases are made up of segments of the E major scale.

In musical periods, alternate bars or groups of bars are often perceived as metrically strong and weak, analogous to beats within a measure. In

Example 5.2 Sonata for Piano and Violin op. 96, Scherzo, mm. 1–8 (piano only)

Example 5.1, mm. 1, 3, 5, and 7 are metrically stronger than 2, 4, 6, and 8. Therefore, mm. 1–2, 3–4, 5–6, and 7–8 form two-bar groups known as *hypermeasures*. Various verbal indications by Beethoven suggest his awareness of *hypermeter* – the presence of recurring groups of strong and weak bars. In the scores of several works, for example, he writes *ritmo di due battute*, *ritmo di tre battute* or *ritmo di quattro battute* ("rhythm of two beats [measures]," rhythm of three beats [measures]," or "rhythm of four beats [measures]").[9]

Many classical themes include a type of phrase known as a *sentence* (Example 5.2). The typical sentence is eight or sixteen bars in length and can be outlined as $(2 + 2) + (1 + 1 + 2)$ or $(4 + 4) + (2 + 2 + 4)$. As Rothstein has observed, "the distinguishing feature of a sentence is the immediate repetition, often transposed or otherwise varied, of the initial melodic segment. Thus, if the sentence is eight measures long, mm. 3–4 will be a repetition or closely related variant of mm. 1–2 (the initial segment), while mm. 5–8 contain more distantly related variants. These later variants tend to diminish progressively in length, as parts of the initial segment are omitted or compressed. This process of progressive shortening obviously produces an acceleration or 'drive to the cadence'..."[10] In Example 5.2, the opening two-bar segment on V is presented in a varied repetition in mm. 3–4 that moves from V to I. The second half of the sentence begins with a fragmentation of the opening segment into one-bar units (mm. 5 and 6) and concludes with a cadence to the minor V (D minor). Beethoven often creates momentum in such themes by this kind of progressive contraction or acceleration of motivic units, a process also referred to as motivic foreshortening.

Like Haydn and Mozart, Beethoven was a master at linking successive

Example 5.3 Symphony no. 2 op. 36, Finale, mm. 1–14

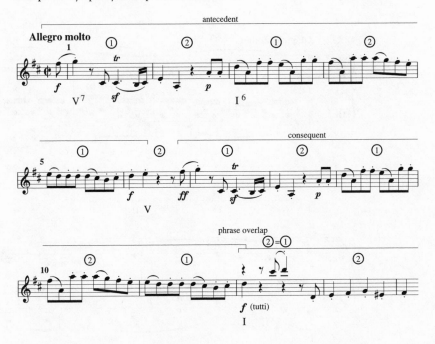

subphrases or phrases. His themes often have expansive melodic lines that call for performance as though they were sung on a single breath or played in a single bow. In these melodic lines, subtle links between successive subphrases or phrases achieve a feeling of almost unbroken flow.[11] To create continuity between successive subphrases or phrases Beethoven uses a wide range of techniques. For example, successive phrases can be linked by a *lead-in*, a continuous rhythmic motion in the melody or accompaniment. In Example 5.1, the antecedent and consequent phrases are linked by the lead-in B–A–G♯, from the inner voice of m. 38 to the top voice of m. 39. In m. 42, a lead-in of triplet eighths continues the stepwise ascent B–C♯–D♯–E of m. 41 and connects the end of this period with the following varied repetition.

Often, the end of one phrase overlaps with the beginning of the next, so that the ending note of one phrase simultaneously functions as the beginning note of the next. An instance of this technique appears in the finale of the Second Symphony, which begins with six-bar antecedent and consequent phrases (Example 5.3). Here the melodic pitch D and the tonic chord end the consequent on the downbeat of m. 12 and simultaneously initiate a new phrase. Such phrase overlap sometimes brings metrical reinterpretation as well. In Example 5.3, for instance, each phrase divides into three two-bar hypermeasures. Because of the sudden *forte* and downbeat motivic idea in m. 12., the listener reinterprets the "weak"

Example 5.4 Piano Sonata op. 13, *Pathétique*, mvt. 2, mm. 1–8

second bar of a hypermeasure as the "strong" first bar of a new hyper-measure. Such metrical reinterpretation results in the "stifling or suppression of a measure," in the words of the eighteenth-century theorist Heinrich Christoph Koch.[12] Koch explains that "the measure which now contains both the caesura of the first phrase and the beginning of the following phrase must be doubly taken into account with respect to the rhythmic relations of phrases: namely, one as the measure with which the first phrase ends, and secondly as the first measure with which the second phrase begins."[13]

Along with continuous rhythmic motion, phrase overlap, and metrical reinterpretation, Classical composers use weak and deceptive cadences, contrapuntal imitation, and harmonic, motivic, or voice-leading connections to link the end of one unit and the beginning of the next. The refrain of the Adagio cantabile of the Piano Sonata in C minor op. 13 illustrates Beethoven's mastery of phrase linkage (Example 5.4).

The extraordinarily lyrical theme of this rondo movement (mm. 1–8, repeated an octave higher in mm. 9–16) is a duet between the top voice and the bass with an accompaniment in steady sixteenth notes in the inner part. Though divided into two thematically differentiated phrases (mm.1–4, 5–8), the theme creates the effect of a seamless melodic flow spanning eight bars. Motivic and tonal links between the two phrases of the theme are integral to the continuity. For instance, the E♭ that ends the first segment of the melody (downbeat of m. 4) is connected to the beginning of the next segment by the slurs in the outer voices, by the continuous motion of the accompaniment, and by the chromatic passing tone E♮ in the top voice (last eighth note of m. 4). The E♮ functions as a lead-in to the F that begins the second subphrase.[14] What makes this passing tone so essential to the magic and rhythmic flow of the melody? In part, it parallels the rhythmic pattern of the chromatic ascent E♭–E♮–F of mm. 4–5 and that of the descent E♭–D♭–C of mm. 2–3. More importantly, the ascent E♭–E♮–F (m. 4) grows out of the preceding ascent A♭–B♭–C–D–E♭ in the "accompaniment" of mm. 3–4 (see the letter names in Example 5.4).

In the second phrase of the theme, the concealed inner-voice motion A♭–A♮–B♭ in mm. 6–7 subtly echoes the ascent E♭–E♮–F of mm. 4–5. The descending fifth B♭–E♭ in the top part of mm. 3–4 – an inversion of the ascending fourths B♭–E♭ and E♭–A♭ of mm. 1–3 (see the brackets in Example 5.4) – initiates another motivic link that bridges the first and second subphrases. This descending fifth generates no fewer than three descending fifths in mm. 5–7: F–B♭, E♭–A♮, D♭–G. In m. 7, the D♭–G is rhythmically expanded and varied by the descending arpeggiation D♭–B♭–G.

The descending motion of the bass line, which moves stepwise from the A♭ of the I in m. 3 to the B♭ of the II in m. 7, also contributes to the continuity between the two segments of the theme. The series of ascending and descending octave leaps which begins in m. 3 and extends through m. 5 reinforces this feeling of continuity in the bass. Notice also the progressive augmentation of rhythmic values in the pitch classes of the stepwise bass descent of mm. 3–7: from eighth notes (A♭–G, m. 3), to a quarter note (F, m. 3), to half notes (E♭–D♭–C–B♭, mm. 4–7). There is a beautiful augmentation in the top voice as well: the descending third progression F–E♭–D♭ of mm. 5–7 responds to the more rapid ascending third progression C–D♮–E♭ in mm. 3–4 (see the letter names above the staff in Example 5.4).

Like Haydn and Mozart, Beethoven uses a variety of techniques to expand phrases. He may introduce a phrase with a *prefix* or extend a phrase by means of a *suffix*. Prefixes and suffixes are highly variable in length, ranging from one to many bars. A brief prefix and several brief suffixes appear in the opening theme of the Adagio molto e cantabile of the Ninth Symphony, the beginning of which is shown in Example 5.5. Observe that the opening four notes of the prefix anticipate the countermelody in the second violins and violas, second half of m. 6 (see the letter

Example 5.5 Symphony no. 9 op. 125, mvt. 3, mm. 1–7

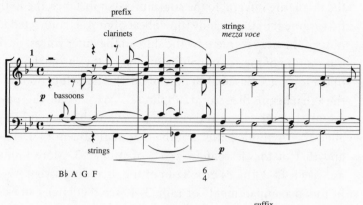

names in mm. 1 and 6). Beethoven blurs the boundary between the prefix and opening phrase with an anticipatory tonic 6/4 (last eighth note of m. 2), a characteristic procedure in his late works. The chorale-like texture of the opening phrase is typical of Beethoven slow-movement themes of all periods. Beethoven expands the opening phrase with a suffix in the winds (m. 7) that poignantly echoes the preceding half cadence in the strings.[15]

Classical composers also expand phrases from within by means of a variety of techniques including motivic repetition. An internal expansion by motivic repetition together with a large suffix appears in the opening theme of the String Quartet in F major op. 18 no. 1 (Example 5.6). The theme begins with a parallel period composed of an eight-bar antecedent and a twelve-bar consequent (mm. 9–20). The consequent is expanded internally by the sequential repetition of mm. 13–14. How much this expansion contributes to the tension of the consequent is demonstrated by the abridged recomposition shown in Example 5.7. The consequent is externally extended by a long suffix, a recomposed transposition of the second part of the consequent, in which the first violin line of mm. 13–18 appears in the second violin.

Haydn, Mozart, and Beethoven also extend phrases from within by lengthening one or more melodic tones or harmonies. Heinrich Schenker has pointed out the fermata-like nature of this technique, which is used at

Example 5.6 String Quartet op. 18 no. 1, mvt. 1, mm. 1–29

Example 5.7 Condensed recomposition of Example 5.6, mm. 13–20

the beginning, middle, or ending of phrases.[16] Sometimes a group of measures in which the tone or harmony is extended is perceived as a metrical expansion of an analogous measure in a preceding phrase. This procedure frequently heightens the tension before the final cadence of a period. A striking instance appears near the end of the second theme group of the finale of the Piano Sonata in C# minor op. 27 no. 2 (Example 5.8). The entire second theme group (mm. 21–43) falls into the following thematic units: a (mm. 21–24) a' (mm. 25–28) b (mm. 29–32) c (mm. 33–36) c' (mm. 37–43). Beginning in m. 21, Beethoven establishes four-bar hypermeasures as the norm for the second group. The deceptive cadence to VI ending unit c (m. 37) motivates unit c'. It is at this point that the established hypermetrical structure changes. The preceding four-bar group expands to six bars with the phrase closing on the downbeat of the seventh bar. The expansion (mm. 40–41) stretches the third bar of unit c (m. 35) to a length of three bars.

Having considered several techniques of Classical phrase rhythm, I now turn to characteristic features of Beethoven's themes, beginning with their individuality. As an initial illustration of this individuality, let us consider Beethoven's innovative approaches to one of the conventions of Classical style, the unison opening of a movement.[17] Typically, unison openings clearly establish the basic tonality and meter. They stress the tonic note and include the fifth and – usually – the third degrees of the tonic scale (think of the first movements of Haydn's Symphony no. 97 in C major, Mozart's *Eine kleine Nachtmusik* K. 525, or Beethoven's Piano Concerto no. 2 in B♭ major). Unison openings often include octave doubling in which each line is separated from its registral neighbor by the interval of a single octave.

Beethoven's unison openings sometimes deviate dramatically from these conventions. The jolting opening of the finale of the Second Symphony, for example, arpeggiates the dominant-seventh chord, not the tonic triad of D major (Example 5.3). Beethoven heightens the abruptness of this non-tonic beginning by the registral peak on G – the seventh of the V[7] – and by the rapid downward leap of a diminished twelfth to C#. This tonal instability is coupled with rhythmic tension, created by the *sf* on the second (weak) beat of m. 1 and the stressed off-beat (second

Example 5.8 Piano Sonata op. 27 no. 2, mvt. 3, mm. 33–43

quarter note) of m. 2. The unison opening of the Fifth Symphony generates even more power and aggression: its rapid repeated eighth notes G
and F contrast dramatically with the long E♭ and D, both extended by fermatas. Beethoven creates metrical ambiguity by means of the fermatas
and the eighth-note rests preceding the repeated eighth notes. The
opening conveys tonal ambiguity as well, because Beethoven omits the
tonic note C. For E. T. A. Hoffmann, up to the appearance of the bass tone
C in m. 7, "the key is still not well defined: the listener presumes E♭
major."[18] Heinrich Schenker hears the unison melodic line within V of C
minor, interpreting the E♭ as an appoggiatura resolving to D over an
implied G in the bass.[19] Through a distinctive texture or dynamic level,
Beethoven generates tension even within tonally stable unison openings.
The opening (mm. 1–2) of the Piano Sonata in F minor op. 57, for
example, sounds hollow and suspenseful because of the unusual *pp*

indication and because the right and left hand parts are two octaves apart, not one.

Beethoven's thematic statements often grow out of their initial musical idea, which appears repeatedly in diverse melodic and rhythmic transformations and in changing harmonic contexts. The initial idea itself is sometimes made up of smaller motivic elements that Beethoven subsequently develops. The motivic relationships between the initial idea and later parts of the theme are usually quite easily heard, as in the opening theme of the String Quartet in F major op. 18 no. 1 (Example 5.6), where the initial turn-motive appears in almost every bar. Even the decorative turn in m. 19 derives from this motive. Typically, the opening figure also recurs in later sections of the movement in many different transformations. Some of these transformations are shown in Example 5.9a–f. In addition to these melodic transformations Beethoven also includes expansions of striking harmonies in the theme. The two diminished seventh chords of mm. 14–15 and 16–17 give rise to an expansion of these harmonies in the development section (mm. 129–40).

Beethoven's themes often combine easily heard motivic connections with more subtle motivic transformations. A case in point is the lyrical opening of the Piano Trio in B♭ major op. 97 ("Archduke"), where mm. 5 and 6 introduce obvious motivic contractions of mm. 3–4 (Example 5.10). A more concealed motivic connection appears in mm. 7–8, when the melodic climax is approached by a rising sixth that rhythmically enlarges the ascending sixth of mm. 2–3, on a higher pitch level (see the upper brackets in Example 5.10).[20]

Central to many Beethoven themes are the techniques of registral expansion and gradual registral ascent. Perhaps even more consistently than Mozart or Haydn, Beethoven coordinates these procedures with other modes of intensification such as rhythmic acceleration, motivic foreshortening, crescendo, addition of voices, or arrival at a dissonant chord, all in the service of creating a particular expressive effect. For instance, registral expansion or gradual registral ascent in a theme often increases momentum toward a powerful goal or climax. The opening theme of op. 18 no. 1 (Example 5.6) expands registrally from one octave in the relatively soft opening bar to four octaves (F to f^3) at the powerful concluding cadence in m. 29. About seven years after op. 18 no. 1, Beethoven used the same registral expansion within the opening theme (mm. 1–19) of his next string quartet in F major, op. 59 no. 1.[21]

The intensity of Beethoven's themes results largely from their rhythmic momentum, subtlety, and complexity.[22] Contemporaries such as Anton Schindler – a violinist and Beethoven's unpaid secretary in the 1820s – singled out Beethoven's rhythm for special praise. In his biogra-

Example 5.9 Transformations of turn motive in String Quartet op. 18 no. 1, mvt. 1

phy of the composer, Schindler wrote that "as for the rhythm in general, it constitutes one of the particular attractions of Beethoven's music. What delightful handling of rhythm we find, for instance, in the first movement of the C minor symphony! What a wealth of variety in the rhythmic patterns throughout the whole work! And yet this variety is far surpassed in several of the sonatas for piano solo."[23] The piano music, observed Schindler, is characterized by the "rhetorical pause and caesura," which "have the effect of heightening the expressiveness of what follows."[24]

E. T. A. Hoffmann, in a review of the Fifth Symphony published in 1810, admired Beethoven's ability to connect different themes through

Example 5.10 Piano Trio op. 97, mvt. 1, mm. 1–8

common rhythmic ideas. Concerning the first movement, Hoffmann wrote that "with great admiration, one becomes aware that Beethoven knew how to relate all secondary ideas and all transition passages through the rhythm of that simple [opening] motive [mm. 1–2] . . ."[25] He also observed that though the phrases of the movement are short, their effect is not fragmentary, as one might expect. "Instead, it is precisely the ordering of the whole and the constant succession of the repetitions of short phrases and individual chords that holds the heart firmly in unspeakable longing."[26] Carl Czerny also praised the phrase rhythm of Beethoven's music in his *School of Practical Composition*, published in London around 1848. Czerny comments that composers who seek originality through asymmetrical phrase structure usually do so "at the expense of what is pleasing and intelligible. But that originality can exist within the bounds of regular [phrase] rhythm, has been proved by many great composers, and particularly by Beethoven."[27]

Gradual acceleration of note-values – also called rhythmic acceleration, or progressive diminution – is a basic technique of intensification in works of Haydn, Mozart, and Beethoven.[28] In a passage of increasing animation, each rhythm tends to be twice as fast as the preceding one, moving, for example, from quarter notes, to eighths to sixteenths. Charles Rosen points out that "the movement from one rhythm to another is felt as a transition not as a contrast."[29] The overall effect, then, is of gradually increasing tension to a climax.

Progressive diminution appears in virtually every type of music in the Classical era, and is particularly prominent in theme and variations movements, where the use of ever-shorter note values in successive variations contributes to a sense of directionality and larger formal organization. In theme and variations movements, Beethoven often created a unique sense of directionality by combining progressive diminution with other techniques of intensification such as registral ascent and syncopated rhythms. Surface rhythmic acceleration also occurs frequently in expositions of Classical sonata-form movements, where it helps to create momentum within the first theme and bridge, or within the second theme group.

In Beethoven's music, progressive rhythmic animation sometimes appears on a larger scale than in music of Haydn and Mozart. Moreover, he coordinates it even more consistently with other techniques of intensification such as crescendo, registral expansion, motivic foreshortening, and increased syncopation. A case in point is the second theme group of the first movement of the Sonata in C major op. 53 ("Waldstein"), where rhythmic acceleration, motivic foreshortening and syncopation combine to produce an extraordinary, gradual progression from serene lyricism to pulsating energy. The second theme group consists of two sections: (1) an eight-bar chorale-like parallel period (mm. 35–42, shown as Example 5.1) with a varied repetition (mm. 43–50), and (2) an enormously expanded phrase of twenty-five bars (mm. 50–74). The surface rhythmic motion of the second theme group accelerates from half notes and quarter notes in the opening chorale (mm. 35–42), to triplet eighths in the varied repetition of the chorale and the opening of the second section (mm. 43–57), to sixteenth notes in the remainder of this section (mm. 58–74) and finally to the unusually high left-hand trill (mm. 72–73) at the cadence.

Syncopation – produced by rhythmic stress on off-beats or weak beats – is crucial to the rhythmic vitality and energy of Beethoven's themes. Many bars in succession include one or more stressed weak beats or off-beats. Moreover, Beethoven often increases momentum by accelerating and intensifying the stresses on off-beats and weak beats. For example, a stressed weak beat will first appear every other bar and then in successive bars, as in the opening of the Sonata for Piano and Violin in G major op. 96 (Example 5.2, mm. 1–4 and 5–7). Typically, this acceleration of weak-beat stresses begins when Beethoven compresses the opening two-bar motive to a single bar.

Beethoven often heightens tension before a cadence by combining accelerated syncopations with metrical expansion. This procedure may be observed at the end of the second theme group of the finale of the Piano Sonata in C♯ minor op. 27 no. 2 (Example 5.8). The musical segment (mm. 33–36) preceding the metrical expansion is unsyncopated but includes a surface rhythmic acceleration in the left hand (a single attack in m. 33, two in 34, four in 35) that heightens the tension of the prolonged $\flat II^6$. The deceptive cadence to VI in m. 37 motivates the varied and expanded repetition (mm. 37–42) in which syncopations accelerate from one to four per bar (mm. 37–39). These exciting accelerated syncopations apparently resulted from Beethoven's revisions in the autograph manuscript. At one stage, m. 38 was simply a repetition of m. 34 an octave lower.[30]

Like stressed weak beats and off-beats, stressed weak measures – usually the second or fourth bar of a four-bar group – are an important feature of Beethoven's rhythmic style. This procedure is particularly important in scherzo or scherzo-like movements, where an entire bar is often felt as a beat. In such cases, Beethoven often progressively intensifies the stress on weak bars. This technique contributes to the growing intensity of the opening theme of the String Quartet in F major op. 18 no. 1, which divides into four-bar hypermeasures (Example 5.6). The C and D on the first beats of mm. 2 and 4 are stressed through length – essentially they last the whole bar – and by the eighth notes and leaps preceding them. In the lyrical transformation of the turn motive in mm. 5–6, the weak sixth bar is emphasized more strongly by the crescendo, half note and melodic peak. In the second part of the consequent, weak mm. 14 and 16 receive even greater stress because of diminished-seventh chords, dissonant appoggiaturas and $<>$ indications. In the varied repetition of the second part of the consequent, the metrically weak mm. 22 and 24 are emphasized still more strongly by *sf* indications and by the interjections of the turn motive in violin 1. This process culminates in mm. 26–27, when sequential repetition of the turn motive in the first violin causes the weak second bar of a hypermeasure (m. 26) to be metrically reinterpreted as the first bar of a new hypermeasure.

In Beethoven's music, stresses sometimes appear first on weak bars and then on weak beats. (Occasionally, the acceleration continues to a stress on an off-beat.)[31] Beethoven uses this procedure with great subtlety in the opening theme of the Piano Trio in B♭ major op. 97 in combination with intensified stresses on metrically weak bars (Example 5.10). A dotted half note emphasizes the beginning of m. 2 and the *sfp* and higher pitch (G) in the melody give an increased stress to the beginning of m. 4. In mm. 5 and 6 *sfp* indications and local melodic apexes highlight the second quarter note, while half notes stress the second half of the bar. Finally, Beethoven creates a climax in m. 8 with the melodic peak on f^2, the crescendo to *f*, and the arrival at V in root position. The hemiola (3×2 quarter notes) created by the rising sixth of mm. 7–8 heightens the stress on the climactic f^2.

Sometimes a succession of emphasized weak bars results in a "shadow" hypermetrical pattern that competes with the main one.[32] Such shadow

Example 5.11 Piano Sonata op. 27, no. 2, mvt. 2, mm. 1–8

hypermeters occur in many kinds of music but are particularly frequent and prominent in scherzo or scherzo-like movements made up of four-bar phrases subdivided 2 + 2. Typically, the basic four-bar hypermeter coincides with the four-bar melodic units. However, melodic apexes, chord changes, or cadences may emphasize even-numbered bars, sometimes creating a certain degree of ambiguity in the hypermetrical structure. The Allegretto of the Sonata in C♯ minor op. 27 no. 2 is a case in point (Example 5.11). According to Tovey, Beethoven composed metrical ambiguity into this movement because either odd bars or even bars can be perceived as strong. Tovey argues that "to play the movement in such a way as to compel the listener to recognize only one accentuation is to miss the point altogether. Beethoven chooses short bars in order to equalize the accents."[33] Rothstein agrees with Tovey that there is real ambiguity, but he decides in favor of strong odd-numbered bars in the main section because the trio opens with an unequivocally strong bar.[34]

In my view, the hypermeter of the main section is less ambiguous since even-numbered bars are not stressed quite as strongly as odd-numbered bars. For example, though the eb^2 of m. 2 (and analogous tones in the second bars of subsequent four-bar units) is indeed a melodic apex, it comes at the end of a slur, which normally indicates a light, unaccented release. In addition, the eb^2 is lightly supported by a 6/3 chord, whereas the c^2 of m. 1 is more strongly emphasized by a 6/4 chord. It is the dissonance of the 6/4 chord – specifically, the suspended fourth in the alto – that suggests metrical accents on mm. 1 and 5. (In mm. 3 and 7, the fourths are only implicitly prepared.) Consequently, in performance, I would gently highlight the hypermeter beginning with m. 1, a suggestion also made by Rothstein.[35]

Beethoven's opening themes frequently generate enormous tension and expectation. Of course, Haydn and Mozart also wrote opening themes that create rhythmic and tonal instability or ambiguity. Haydn, especially, often opened a movement with a "gesture of destabilization," as

James Webster has observed.[36] Yet, Beethoven's opening gestures tend to be more extreme in this respect. Beethoven often uses chromatic inflection to build instability, tension, or tentativeness directly into opening themes. For example, he introduces prominent chromatic tones such as the C♯ in m. 7 of the *Eroica* Symphony, the D♯ in m. 10 of the Violin Concerto, the F♮ in mm. 5–6 of the Piano Trio in D major op. 70 no. 1, and the C♯ in m. 17 of the finale of the Eighth Symphony. Starting in 1802, Beethoven also tonicizes such chromatic chords as ♭VII, ♭II, and III♯ within the opening theme. In three movements in major, for example, he sequentially repeats an opening unit in I a step lower in ♭VII (opening movements of Piano Sonatas in G major op. 31 no. 1 and C major op. 53 and the second movement of the String Quartet in F major op. 59 no. 1). As we have seen, E. T. A. Hoffmann singled out Beethoven's use of this procedure in a minor-mode movement as well, the *Coriolan* Overture. In four movements in minor, Beethoven sequentially repeats an opening unit in I a half-step higher in ♭II (the opening movement and finale of the Piano Sonata in F minor op. 57 and the opening movements of the String Quartets in E minor op. 59 no. 2 and F minor op. 95). A tonicized III♯ (B major) is introduced by the orchestra, playing *piano*, in the Piano Concerto no. 4 in G major as a magical reharmonization of the opening melodic tone, B. Another tonicized III♯ (F♯ major), in the finale of the Piano Trio in D major op. 70 no. 1, sounds like a comic intrusion.

In the diatonic context of an opening theme these chromatic events are "marked for memory" and are reflected in later themes of the exposition as well as in large-scale tonal motions or key successions.[37] Musical analysts have investigated the relationship between detail and large-scale plan in the works of many composers, including Haydn, Mozart, and Beethoven.[38] As Charles Rosen has observed, Haydn was a pioneer in "making us hear the directional force implicit in a musical idea." In his works, "the primary directional element is generally a dissonance which, strengthened and properly reinforced, leads to a modulation."[39]

The relationship between chromatic or motivic detail and tonal structure is particularly close in Beethoven's music. We have already seen how two diminished seventh chords in the opening theme of op. 18 no. 1 generate prolonged diminished sevenths in the development section. A better-known instance appears in the first movement of the *Eroica* Symphony, where the unexpected C♯ at the beginning of the exposition (m. 7) is enharmonically transformed into a D♭ that ushers in a tonicization of II (F major) at the beginning of the recapitulation (mm. 402–12). Because of the thematic parallelism between these passages, our recognition of this enharmonic transformation is not inhibited by the intervention of almost four hundred bars. Finally, at the beginning of the coda (mm. 555–76), D♭ leads down to a tonicization of VI (C major) that functions as a way station to II and V.

Beethoven also builds instability into the opening theme with an initial tonic harmony that is relatively unstable or fleeting, delaying the arrival of a strong, root-position chord. A well-known instance is the opening of the String Quartet in F major op. 59 no. 1, where the $^6_4$ position of the initial tonic harmony is emphasized in mm. 1–4 and a strongly articulated tonic chord is postponed until the end of the opening theme (m. 19).

Finally, Beethoven creates tension or tentativeness within the opening theme by means of non-tonic beginnings, as we have seen in the startling arpeggiation of V^7 that initiates the finale of the Second Symphony (Example 5.3). Other non-tonic opening harmonies include V, V^6, V^9, II, II^6_5 (or IV with added sixth), IV, VI, and augmented sixth, diminished seventh, and applied dominant chords.[40] The second movements of two piano sonatas begin with a four-bar phrase in V that is immediately repeated in I (Piano Sonatas in A♭ major op. 26, and C♯ minor op. 27 no. 2). In the fantasy-like opening theme of the Sonata in D minor op. 31 no. 2 ("Tempest"), Beethoven resolves the opening V^6 chord to a fleeting tonic, building a powerful momentum by postponing arrival points, delaying the fulfillment of expectations, and throwing the weight of resolution ever forward.[41] Initially, the opening twenty bars sound more like an improvised introduction than a first theme. The Largo arpeggiated V^6 chord (mm. 1–2) seems intended to introduce a recitative. Before the "singer" can begin, however, an Allegro phrase rushes breathlessly through the I of mm. 3–4, only to come up short against the Adagio of m. 6, which introduces a semicadence on V. Our expectation of the tonic is then frustrated by the return of the opening Largo, transposed to a startling C major chord (mm. 7–8). The subsequent Allegro seems to search for a way to the tonic and, after a long, agitated prolongation of V, cadences strongly on I (m. 21). Here, at last, seems a true beginning, as an assertive transformation of the Largo motive in the bass, appearing successively on I, V^4_3, and I^6 (mm. 21–30), reinforces the tonic. However, the accelerated ascent of the bass to the V of V minor (mm. 29–41) reveals that this section is in fact a bridge. In retrospect, the opening twenty-one measures constitute a first theme, but it is a theme so unstable in tonality and surface design that the weight of resolution is thrown forward into the bridge.

In Beethoven's sonata-form movements, the opening of the second theme group often introduces a lyrical contrast to vigorous, driving, or dramatic first theme. Carl Czerny recognized this when he wrote (around 1848) that a good second theme "is much more difficult to invent than the

Example 5.12 Bass of auxiliary cadence in second theme group
of Piano Sonata op. 31 no. 2, mvt. 1, mm. 41–63

commencement: for *first*, it must possess a new and more pleasing melody
than all which precedes; and *secondly*, it must be very different from the
foregoing, but yet, according to its character, so well suited thereto, that it
may appear like the object or result of all the preceding ideas, modulations or passages."[42]

However, Beethoven frequently departs from this pattern of thematic
contrast. For example, a cantabile opening theme may be followed by a
second theme that is assertive, dancelike or lyrical, as, respectively, in the
opening movements of the Sonata in F major for Violin and Piano op. 24,
the Piano Trio in B♭ major op. 97, and the Piano Sonata in F♯ major op. 78.
Moreover, Beethoven's second themes are sometimes developmental in
character. In the opening movements of the Piano Sonatas in A major op.
2 no. 2 and C minor op. 13, for example, the second theme group begins
with a minor-mode coloration, and includes sequential repetition, foreshortening, and the tonicization of several different tonal degrees including chromatic ones.

Particularly characteristic of Beethoven are second theme groups in
which a strong arrival at the goal key of the exposition is delayed, a procedure also fairly common in works by C. P. E. Bach and Haydn.[43] Typically,
such a second theme group begins with a prolongation of V of the
new key. There follows a unit articulating an "auxiliary cadence" to
the new key, one in which the harmonies preceding the strong entrance
of the new tonic in root position are subordinate to the preceding V of the
new key.[44] If, as is common, the auxiliary cadence is made up of the progression I⁶–V–I in the new key, the I⁶ is understood as an anticipation of
the goal harmony. An auxiliary cadence appears in our concluding illustration, the expansive second theme group (mm. 41–87) of the Piano
Sonata in D minor op. 31 no. 2, opening movement (Example 5.12). The
beginning of the second theme group overlaps with the V/V that concludes the bridge (m. 41). In this second theme group, Beethoven welds
together several distinct thematic ideas by delaying the conclusive arrival
of minor V. These thematic ideas will be referred to as units a (mm.

41–55), b (mm. 55–63), b′ (mm. 63–74), and c (mm. 75–87). An extended pedal point on V^7 of the goal key (unit a) is followed by an auxiliary cadence theme beginning with I^6 of the goal key (unit b). Even this auxiliary cadence theme does not lead to a strong cadence in the goal key. Instead, the closure of the cadence to minor V in m. 63 is weakened because there is no linear descent to Î (A) in the top voice and because unit b′ begins as a variation of unit b, with the melody shifted to the bass. A modal shift from A minor to A major – which almost sounds like the V of D minor – also weakens the tonal stability of unit b′. The fleeting tonicization of III of minor V (m. 70) and the extended V of A minor within unit c that is not completely resolved until m. 87 sustain the tonal tension until the closing measures of the exposition.

Beethoven used techniques of Classical phrase rhythm and motivic elaboration to forge thematic statements of striking individuality. His late works include themes that push beyond Classical norms in a number of ways. The openings of the String Quartets opp. 127, 130, and 132, for example, flexibly integrate highly contrasting adagio and allegro passages. The Adagio espressivo second theme (mm. 9–15) of the Vivace in the Piano Sonata in E major op. 109 creates the novel effect of a fantasy or improvisation by introducing a change of tempo and meter, cadenza-like arpeggation, and unexpected harmonic shifts. The Allegretto ma non troppo of the Piano Sonata in A Major op. 101 provides a final example of Beethoven's departures from convention in late works. The extraordinarily compressed opening theme (mm. 1–4) evokes a sense of yearning: it begins and ends on the V of the tonic key, A major, and does not include an emphasized tonic chord in root position. The absence of such a root-position tonic chord constitutes a major deviation from tonal norms in Classical opening themes. (One might object that a root-position A major harmony – decorated by a 6/4 chord – does in fact appear in the second half of m. 3. But the high register and relatively weak metrical position of the bottom vice A (m. 3) make this tone subordinate to the low C♯ that immediately follows on the downbeat of m. 4. The C♯ supports a I^6 harmony that has more structural weight than the preceeding A major 5/3 chord. In effect, the "bass" A of m. 3 functions as the tenor voice of the following I^6 harmony (m. 4).) Remarkably, a stable-root-position tonic triad does not appear in the Allegretto until near the end of the recapitulation (m. 77), possibly a unique instance in Beethoven's works. The enormous tension, instability, and excitement of the themes Beethoven composed throughout his career were to have a profound influence on composers of the Romantic period.

6 "The sense of an ending": goal-directedness in Beethoven's music

NICHOLAS MARSTON

What we call the beginning is often the end
And to make an end is to make a beginning.
The end is where we start from.

(T. S. ELIOT, *FOUR QUARTETS*, "LITTLE GIDDING," V, 1–3)

Why does a piece of music end? Or rather, why does it end where it does? Webern, during the composition of his Six Bagatelles for string quartet op. 9, felt driven to a particularly uncompromising answer: "Here I had the feeling, 'When all twelve notes have gone by, the piece is over.'"[1] He was, admittedly, recalling his path to twelve-note composition; yet Heinrich Schenker, concerned exclusively with the structure of tonal music – to him, Webern's was a "path" that led away from music altogether – was equally clear about endings. In *Free Composition* he claimed that "with the arrival of Î the work is at an end. Whatever follows this can only be a reinforcement of the close – a coda – no matter what its extent or purpose may be."[2] There will be more to say about codas in due course; but we need immediately to distinguish Schenker's construal of "coda" from the conventional one whereby, for example, the section of music that follows the end of a sonata-form recapitulation is denominated the "coda." A particularly clear Beethoven example is the coda to the finale of the "Appassionata" Sonata, beginning at m. 308: the double bar and new tempo indication articulate this coda especially strongly. Schenker's notion of ending is, like Webern's, bound up with his particular theoretical perspective, whereby any tonal composition is understood as the "composing-out" of a primordial contrapuntal construct (the *Ursatz*). The upper-voice component (the *Urlinie*) traces a stepwise descent through the triadic space $\hat{3}$–Î or $\hat{5}$–Î, while the bass articulates the large-scale progression I–V–I. The endpoint of the *Urlinie* – the arrival at the tonic note (Î) – may or may not coincide with the last note of the piece, or with some surface formal division. Thus it is entirely possible that the arrival at Î – Schenker's "ending" – might occur within or before a "formal" coda such as that at the end of the "Appassionata."

This brief excursus on the Schenkerian coda is intended to show how our initial question ("why does a piece of music end?") shades easily into another: *how* does a piece of music end? What accounts for that "sense of

[84]

an ending"[3] that music, and particularly tonal music, communicates so powerfully? This is to ask not so much about *ending* as about *closure*.

Closure is by no means exclusive to music; it is also a property of literary texts, both fictional and non-fictional, of film, and is a much-discussed topic in literary criticism. Don Fowler distinguishes "five senses in which the word 'closure' [is] used in modern criticism:

1. The concluding section of a literary work;
2. The process by which the reader of a work comes to see the end as satisfyingly final;
3. The degree to which an ending is satisfyingly final;
4. The degree to which the questions posed in the work are answered, tensions released, conflicts resolved;
5. The degree to which the work allows new critical readings."[4]

These definitions may serve equally for the study of musical works; we need only substitute "musical" for "literary" in no. 1, and (perhaps) "listener" for "reader" in no. 2. All five are pursued to varying degrees in the examples from Beethoven's music which follow; for as Fowler himself admits, while it is possible to distinguish these various senses of closure, "they are all intimately connected."[5]

Understanding a musical work in terms of questions posed and processes played out involves the notion of causation: the work is interpreted as a sequence of events with the potential to affect one another and to precipitate certain consequences. On this view, the end of a work is anything but arbitrary: it comes to seem a logical necessity, preordained and even "willed" from the outset. This interpretative mode is one that is powerfully associated with Beethoven's music, and above all with his so-called "heroic" style. Scott Burnham has made particularly strong claims about the stranglehold that this particular style, "to which only a handful of [Beethoven's] works can lay unequivocal claim," continues to exert on our experience of music:

> For nearly two centuries, a single style of a single composer has epitomized musical vitality, becoming the paradigm of Western compositional logic ...
> This conviction has proved so strong that it no longer acts as an overt part of our musical consciousness; it is now simply a condition of the way we tend to engage the musical experience. The values of Beethoven's heroic style have become the values of music.[6]

Burnham is clear as to the special quality of heroic-style endings, and in an absorbing account of the *Egmont* Overture he writes as follows of Beethoven's celebrated codas:

> they strongly narrate the form, not only culminating the movements to which they are attached but standing apart from them, adding "The End" to their

respective stories in such a way that one leaves the experience convinced that "The End" is more than some arbitrary cutoff point: it is actually present, in potentia, from bar 1. The process of narration and the story being told become one.[7]

"The end" is indeed where we start from.

The individual movement

A particularly clear example of an ending that responds directly to an initial premise occurs in a work that is itself a beginning of sorts: the first movement of the Piano Sonata op. 2 no. 1.[8] The first eight-bar phrase articulates an imperfect cadence (i–V) (Example 6.1). The arpeggios in mm. 1–2 and 3–4 establish the melodic highpoints ab^2 and bb^2, supported by f and e in the bass. Bars 5 and 6 then repeat these highpoints (note the *sforzando* emphasis); the sense of connection between them – that is, that ab^2 links up to bb^2 despite the intervening turn figures – is reinforced by the metrical "foreshortening" whereby the initial two-bar units (mm. 1–2 and 3–4) are condensed into one-bar units. This has the effect of an acceleration, driving the music onward to the climactic m. 7, where a new highpoint, c^3, is reached. That this defines a goal and a turning point in the music is variously marked: by the *fortissimo* marking, the unique rhythmic value (a full mimim) assigned to the c^3, and by the spread chord that, spanning c^2–c^3, may be understood as a development of the grace-note (c^2) embellishment of ab^2 and bb^2 in mm. 5 and 6. Thereafter the melodic line descends quickly to the cadential e^2 in m. 8. The bass, conversely, continues to rise; having ascended from f to g in mm. 5–6, it undergoes in m. 7 an acceleration equivalent to that in the top voice of mm. 5–6, so that m. 7 contains ab–bb, leading on to the cadential c in m. 8. All this is illustrated in Example 6.1, which makes one additional point: that the climactic c^3 is not obliterated by the succeeding descent but remains "active" over and beyond the cadential dominant in m. 8. (The sudden plunge in m. 9 into a hitherto unheard low bass register is vital to the sense that the c^3 is left hanging in musical space.)

Thus the first eight-bar phrase initiates a fragmentary melodic line in a specific register (ab^2–bb^2–c^3); one task for the movement will be to pick up this thread and find a satisfactory means of "knotting" it. The knot is tied only in the closing bars; but the sense of that ending is enriched by events at the outer extremes of the development section. After the conventional exposition modulation from the tonic minor to the relative major (Ab), the development begins by transposing the opening bars to that key, but with the important difference that the original two-bar units

Example 6.1 Piano Sonata op. 2 no. 1, 1st mvt., mm. 1–8

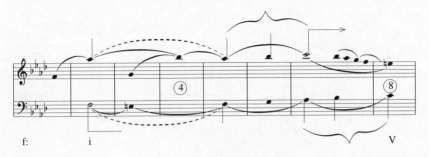

(mm. 1–2 and 3–4) are extended to three bars (mm. 49–51 and 52–54). The immediate melodic goal of the transposed mm. 1–2 is precisely the climactic c^3 of m. 7, but harmonized now in relation to A♭ major rather than F minor. The "extra" m. 51 provides a new element, $d♭^3$, representing a further ascent in the long line begun with $a♭^2$ in m. 2. This $d♭^3$ is reiterated in mm. 53–54, after which the upper voice returns to the register below c^3.[9]

The recapitulation is signalled already at m. 81, where a long dominant pedal commences. Following the textural reduction to an isolated, repeated middle C in mm. 93–94, the bass descends by step from there to f in m. 101, where the recapitulation begins. This stepwise bass motion c^1–f is the reverse of the ascending progression heard in mm. 5–8 and about to be repeated in mm. 105–08. And there is another reversal at work as the recapitulation approaches: $d♭^3$, reintroduced in m. 96, initiates a line descending to $a♭^2$ (m. 102), from which the exposition ascent to c^3 will be recapitulated. In their "undoing" of bars 1–8, these reversals in the outer voices change the sense of the $a♭^2$ in m. 102: this now sounds less as the origin of an ascent to c^3 than the goal of a descent therefrom (Example 6.2). What appears as straightforward repetition thus discloses a quite different meaning; and the heightened dynamic (*forte* rather than *piano*) also works to make of the recapitulation something paradoxically *new*, despite its otherwise repeating literally music heard at the beginning of the exposition.

Redefinition of the commencement of the recapitulation relative to the exposition can of course be made much more dramatic than in the case of op. 2 no. 1. The parallel moment in the first movement of the Ninth Symphony, for example, demonstrates the power of a simple modal inflection to promote a sense of forward motion as opposed to a circular return to the already-heard. By launching the recapitulation from an electrifying D major triad in $^6_3$ position, Beethoven ensures that F♯, the crucial defining element of the major mode, will be forced upon the listener's consciousness. Conversely, the *downplaying* of the double return

Example 6.2 Piano Sonata op. 2 no. 1, 1st mvt., mm. 93–102

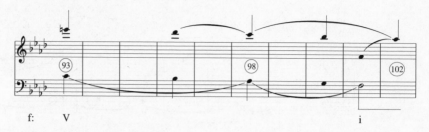

Example 6.3 op. 2 no. 1, 1st mvt., mm. 145–52

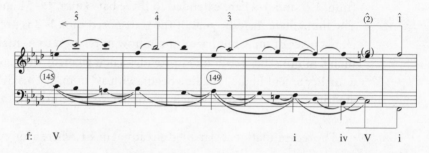

(thematic and tonal) at the recapitulation can itself contribute to goal-directedness by delaying the resolution of tension: with Beethoven, as is well known, the locus of such resolution is typically the much-extended coda. Good examples of a destabilized recapitulation occur in the first movements of the Eighth Symphony and the "Appassionata" Sonata: in each case unstable tonic $^6_4$ harmony replaces the expected root-position triad.[10]

To return to op. 2 no. 1, the immediate continuation of the recapitulation reintroduces the climactic c^3 in m. 107, so that the $a\flat^2$ of m. 102 should be regarded more precisely as having the sense both of an ending and a re-beginning, the conclusion to which is to be found in the last eight bars (145–52). It is easy to hear that c^3, sounding for the last time, *fortissimo*, in m. 146, ushers in a stepwise descent to the cadential f^2.[11] Meanwhile, the bass makes its way down through the fifth c^1–f once more before attaining a lower register to reinforce the close (Example 6.3). This is no arbitrary ending, but one predicated upon specific initial circumstances. To understand those circumstances and their consequences later in the movement is to understand why this particular ending makes sense.

The first movement of op. 2 no. 1 exemplifies clearly some typical features of Beethoven's goal-directed structures. The "goal" arises through the early establishment of a *lacuna* or gap, and one "purpose" of the movement is to fill that gap.[12] In the case of op. 2 no. 1 the gap is melodic and harmonic (the $\hat{3}$–$\hat{5}$ ascent $a\flat^2$–c^3 combined with an imperfect cadence,

I–V); it is also registral, in that Beethoven is careful to maintain the f^2–c^3 register as the site of melodic closure; closure is delayed until the very end of the movement; and the entire sequence of events is mapped on to a sonata-form structure. Sonata form, by its very tonal and thematic dynamic, lends itself particularly well to this kind of compositional thinking, and it is thus no accident that many of the movements discussed below are exemplars of that form. But this is not to say that the strategies employed in op. 2 no. 1 may not be transferred to other, broader, formal and generic contexts. The next two sections move beyond the single movement to consider goal-directedness across entire multisectional and multimovement works, beginning with works in variation form.

Variation form

Beethoven employed variation form both in individual movements of multimovement genres and in independent works. Compared to sonata form, Classical variation form might seem largely antithetical to the creation of goal-directed structures: the concatenation of a tonally closed theme with a series of similarly closed variations preserving its essential tonal structure and proportions, with minimal tonal development (typically, a modal shift in one variation from major to minor, or the reverse), threatens to produce circularity, even stasis.[13] There is theoretically no limit to the number of variations a composer might write on a given theme; why, we must ask, does the series stop where it does? And is the order of the variations significant, or might it be altered without detriment to the sense of the whole? Such questions are important in the analysis of variation sets.

The majority of Beethoven's independent variation sets, using either pre-existing or original themes, are represented by the piano variations he composed chiefly for his own performance prior to 1802;[14] variation-form movements in instrumental works are spread more widely, and it is often observed that Beethoven's later works show an increased interest in variation form.[15] Of special interest in the present context are those multimovement works with variation-form finales: examples are the "Harp" String Quartet op. 74, the Violin Sonata in G op. 96, and the late Piano Sonatas in E and C opp. 109 and 111. (The finale of the *Eroica* Symphony is a fascinating hybrid.[16]) Variation-form slow movements include those in the String Quartet in A op. 18 no. 5, the "Archduke" Trio op. 97, and the String Quartets in E♭, C♯ minor, and F opp. 127, 131, and 135;[17] the slow movements of the Ninth Symphony and the String Quartet in A minor op. 132 employ variation form, too, though as part of a broader scheme in which the theme and its variations are separated from one another by the intrusion of a sharply contrasting theme.[18] And not to be forgotten is the variation-form *first* movement of the Piano Sonata in A♭ op. 26.

A gradual increase in elaboration from one variation to the next was an accepted strategy for imparting a sense of direction. This was often coupled with proportional diminution of note values: the progressive increase in the surface rhythmic figuration created the effect of a gradual acceleration in tempo, and a real increase in the level of virtuosity, while the underlying harmonic rhythm remained constant. The variation movements of the "Archduke" Trio and the Piano Sonata op. 111 both employ this technique, a further effect of which is the sense of a gradual recession of the theme into the "distance" as it is left further and further behind by successive variations. But in some cases the "distance" between theme and variation is widened radically at the very outset, two examples being the first of the variations on "Rule, Britannia" WoO 79, and variation 1 in the finale of the Piano Sonata op. 109. The latter work is striking in that variation 2 immediately restores a sense of close proximity to the theme, almost as though it is the "true" first variation which has somehow become displaced.[19]

Departure implies return; and a valedictory reprise of the theme following its elaboration in a series of variations is a powerful means of creating closure in such works. Goal and origin are essentially identical in such cases, although all but one of Beethoven's reprises are characteristically non-literal, involving a degree of transformation or partial variation. Examples include the "Eroica" Variations op. 35 (mm. 132ff.), the finale to op. 111 (mm. 131ff.), and the slow movements of op. 127 (mm. 76ff.) and op. 131 (mm. 243ff.): in each case the melody of the theme returns more or less literally while variation persists in the accompanying parts.[20] Moreover, the reprise in opp. 111, 127, and 131 follows hard upon a tonal move flatward from the tonic to a submediant or mediant region. In op. 111, variation 4 is separated from variation 5 (the reprise-variation) by a brief transitional passage tonicizing E♭ major before returning to the tonic, C major, through a series of descending thirds; in op. 127, variation 3 (mm. 59ff.) is itself set in the enharmonically notated flat submediant (E = F♭), which then falls a semitone to E♭, the dominant of the tonic, in m. 77 in preparation for the ensuing reprise-variation; and in op. 131, the reprise-variation (which is not complete) forms part of a substantial coda that begins by stating the beginning of the theme in the flat mediant, C major. (A balancing statement in the flat submediant, F, appears on the other side of the partial reprise: see mm. 254–57.)

In coupling a thematic reprise with a return to the tonic following a tonal digression (which, moreover, may unfold outside the confines of a strict variation) Beethoven was drawing upon elements of sonata-form development and recapitulation.[21] The variation movements of opp. 111 and 127 are more unusual than that of op. 131 in this respect, since tonal digression from the tonic during the coda of a variation set, as in op. 131, was in fact a relatively common procedure. A fine example from Beethoven's works occurs in the Variations on "La stessa, la stessissima" WoO 73, where variation 10 merges with an extended and tonally "developmental" coda including, at m. 145, a partial reprise in the neapolitan key, B major, of the opening of variation 10 itself. WoO 73 also demonstrates the importance routinely accorded to the coda in creating goal-directedness and closure in variation works: uniquely independent of the tonal and proportional constraints of the theme, the coda could well serve as the locus of greatest dramatic weight in the composition. Thus the distinctively Beethovenian end-weighted sonata design – whether one thinks of the individual sonata-form movement, as discussed above, or the multimovement structures considered below – might be thought almost endemic to the variation genre. A further, related means of adding weight toward the end of a variation movement was likewise to depart from the strict variation chain by inserting a fugue: two examples are the "Eroica" Variations and the "Diabelli" Variations op. 120. In each case the fugue is followed by a reprise-variation and coda, and thus functions analogously to a sonata-form development within the total form, a function made even clearer in op. 120 since the fugue is set in the flat mediant, E♭ major, prior to the return of the tonic in the final variation and coda.[22]

While important in themselves as illustrations of Beethoven's concern to overcome the inherently static, non-directional nature of variation form, these various end-weighting strategies also serve to throw into relief his uniquely strict approach in the finale of the Piano Sonata op. 109. All six variations staunchly preserve the tonic key – not even a minor-mode digression here – and the proportions of the theme. And this is Beethoven's only variation work to end with a literal repeat of the theme, save for the omission of the repeats and a few grace notes, and some added octave doubling. If there is a sense to this ending, it surely lies beyond a mere homage to Bach's "Goldberg" Variations. Firstly, inasmuch as the theme "composes out" a progression from the initial $g\sharp^1$ to b^1 and back, the entire movement may be said to "compose out" that structure of departure and return. Secondly, inasmuch as the theme can be understood as a recomposition and completion of a first movement lacking unequivocal closure, it is itself powerfully imbued with the sense of an ending.[23]

The multimovement work

Rather than relying on issues of long-range linear completion, as do so many celebrated end-weighted movements of Beethoven's instrumental works, goal-directedness between the outer movements of a multimovement work may more typically concern relative weight or gesture. Here it is important to retain a sense of the conventional succession of forms and characters associated with the genres under discussion; and it is the typical casting of the first movement as the most complex and weighty that is chiefly at issue. First movements almost always employed sonata form, while less dynamic, more repetitive formal types such as rondo or variation form were considered appropriate to finales.[24]

In short, one might speak of a progressive easing of the demands made on the late eighteenth- or early nineteenth-century listener; the rondo finale of a mature Haydn symphony, with its frequently "popular" melodic style, might even be equated with the (equally) traditional operatic *lieto fine*.[25] Beethoven too subscribed to this aesthetic (compare, for example, the primary themes in the outer movements of his First Symphony op. 21); yet he seems from an early stage to have been interested also in subverting it, by writing finales that are not merely equal in weight to their respective first movements, but which actually overpower them. Minor-key works form a special class here. In op. 2 no. 1 and op. 10 no. 1, Beethoven chose sonata form for both outer movements; in the *Pathétique* Sonata op. 13, he resorted to the more conventional rondo finale, but without easing the tone of the music appreciably. Neither did he opt in any of these three works to lighten the ending of the finale by a turn to the major mode: the music remains implacably in the minor. Elsewhere, the powerful sense of resolution imparted by this simple modal inflection offered a means of suggesting closure either within an individual movement or between two movements: the *locus classicus* is of course the Fifth Symphony, its triumphant C major finale dispelling at a stroke the threatening gloom both of the first movement and of the third, with which it is continuous.[26] The finale of the Ninth also rehearses the yielding of minor to major, thereby elevating to the level of the entire work the strategy adopted in the first movement.[27]

Notwithstanding the potent sense of arrival at the finales of the Fifth and Ninth Symphonies, these movements can hardly be said to outweigh entirely their respective first movements, which are themselves of conventionally heavyweight build. In fact it is a measure of Beethoven's respect for generic convention that in his symphonies he never seriously departed from the norm of a big first movement. Things were different in the case of the sonata, where several decisively finale-weighted works may be identified. The earliest is the "Moonlight" Sonata op. 27 no. 2, the second of the two works that Beethoven published as "sonata quasi una fantasia." The description has as much to do with the *attacca* and *segue* instructions directing the linkage of the separate movements into connected, fantasia-like structures as it does with the unconventional movement-sequences themselves; nevertheless, it is this latter aspect that plays most powerfully to the end-weighting of the "Moonlight," in which Beethoven reserves a driving, "first-movement" sonata form for the finale. Two much later and important examples are the Piano Sonata in A op. 101, and its close neighbor, the Cello Sonata in C op. 102 no. 1. The first movement of op. 101 can be assimilated to sonata form only weakly, thanks to the avoidance of a strong tonic articulation before m. 77 where the recapitulation closing group begins. By placing the exposition first group on the dominant, which harmony is then almost imperceptibly tonicized at an early stage, Beethoven all but destroys the tonal polarization on which sonata form so vitally depends. This is just one of many features that contrive to make the first movement of op. 101 unconventionally muted.

This muting begins to make sense when an improvisatory flourish brings the third movement (*Langsam und sehnsuchtvoll*) to an early halt on a V/A triad, only to give way to a modified and fragmented version of the opening bars of the first movement. This recall itself soon yields to the finale, a full-scale sonata-form movement that provides unequivocal tonic definition at the outset (mm. 32–33). There is a strong sense that the right-hand falling third E–C♯ accompanying the initiatory V–I cadence is a "corrective" to the more feeble descending fourths e^2–b^1 in mm. 2 and 4 of the first movement, serving as they do merely to prolong the underlying dominant harmony.[28] The finale of the Ninth again comes to mind, even though in op. 101 no soloist is on hand to reject previously heard music with the peremptory injunction, "O Freunde, nicht diese Töne!"

The Cello Sonata op. 102 no. 1 makes essentially the same statement in an even more remarkable way. The work opens in C major with what might at first appear to be a slow introduction. But rather than ending poised on the dominant, as convention would demand, it closes in the tonic, only to be followed by a full-scale sonata-form "first" movement in the relative minor, A minor.[29] The precise status of the initial C major section is thus cast in doubt. An unexpected recall of this material again occurs partway through the slow movement – and as in op. 101, this has an improvisatory, fantasia-like cast – before all is swept away by the finale. "These tones, but not in the same order" might be the unspoken command here, for the opening of the sonata-form finale audibly reverses the descending fourth c^1–b–a–g intoned by the cello at the very outset. Both sonatas, then, effectively "narrate" their end-weighted movement sequence; and, to the extent that Beethoven's strategy relies powerfully on withholding until the finale the kind of strong tonic affirmation that would normally be expected at the beginning of a such a work, we see clearly here that "to make an end is to make a beginning".

Contra closure

Beethoven's tendency to alter the conventional dynamic of multimovement works, his main purpose usually being to shift the main dramatic weight from the beginning to the end of the sequence, is obvious enough. Works such as op. 101 and op. 102 no. 1 further illustrate not only his radical departure, above all in his later music, from the conventional number and sequence of movements but also his challenge to the autonomy of the individual movement itself. These tendencies become especially pronounced in the last three piano sonatas (opp. 109–11) and the five late string quartets (opp. 127, 130/133, 131, 132, 135). As Richard Kramer has put it,

> the aesthetics of Classical style dictate a work in which the individual movements make powerful claim to *Selbständigkeit*. But in the music of the 1820s, and nowhere more eloquently than in Beethoven's last quartets, the fragile networking of "fragmentary" pieces together into some work whose concept depends on the palpable ties between movements . . . can be said to renegotiate the terms by which the work claims to be a sum of its parts.[30]

Perhaps the best example (one quoted by Kramer himself) is the String Quartet in C♯ minor op. 131, whose seven movements flow into one another in such a way as to weaken their autonomy. The numbering of the movements from 1 to 7, a curious detail reminiscent of an operatic score, only reinforces the sense that these are not so much individual movements in the Classical sense but rather interdependent sections of a single long movement.[31] Beethoven makes op. 131 a strongly end-directed work by withholding a full-scale sonata-form movement until the finale. End and beginning are palpably connected in this quartet, in that the finale includes a prominent thematic transformation of the first four notes (G♯–B♯–C♯–A) of the fugue subject with which the quartet opens (Example 6.4).[32]

Yet the very end of the op. 131 finale casts doubt on the tonal closure of the whole work, since the concluding C♯ major triads portend both V/IV and I$^{\natural 3}$. In fact the music leans strongly towards F♯ minor (IV) from m. 349 onward; and this, too, links the finale with the first movement, where the sense of the ending is poised precariously between tonic and subdominant.

Example 6.4 String Quartet op. 131, 1st mvt., mm. 1–4; finale, mm. 22–25

In his survey of Beethoven's quartets, Joseph Kerman stresses the degree to which the late works are characterized by opposing tendencies towards *dissociation* and *integration*. To him, op. 131 represents Beethoven's most highly "integrated" work while the String Quartet in B♭ op. 130 counts as the most "dissociated."[33] Although a work that pushes dissociation to extremes need not entirely forfeit satisfactory closure, there can be no doubt that op. 130 forces a confrontation with closural issues that are more profound and troublesome than in any other Beethoven work. Simply put, the celebrated "finale-problem in Beethoven" reaches its apogee with this work. The substitution of a light-weight sonata-rondo movement for the original fugal finale, subsequently published as the *Grosse Fuge* op. 133, raises major aesthetic questions which (to anticipate my conclusion) cannot be definitively resolved, but which have nonetheless dogged a vast literature addressing whether Beethoven jumped or was pushed – whether his substitution of the new finale reflects a personal judgment that the fugal finale was a mistake, or whether he made the change unwillingly, at others' insistence – and whether one or the other version of the quartet is therefore *the* definitive one. Probably no one has argued more lengthily, passionately, and at times misguidedly, for the priority of Beethoven's original conception than Ivan Mahaim; though Klaus Kropfinger, a more recent apologist, has also con-cluded unequivocally that "only the original version [with the *Grosse Fuge* as finale] corresponds to Beethoven's [compositional] idea."[34]

For Kropfinger and others before him, Beethoven's sketches figure importantly in an argument favoring the fugue. The argument holds that a fugal finale, and even the theme of the *Grosse Fuge* itself, was part of Beethoven's earliest conception of the quartet. Kropfinger makes the point quite explicitly:

> The analysis of the sketches ... demonstrates, then, that the fugal finale of the B-flat quartet was not something arbitrary, but rather was the decisive *Schlußgestalt* of the cyclic configuration of the work: that is, one based on an original intention, confirmed, made fast, and developed through numerous decisions in the course of the compositional process, and then finally realized as a whole.[35]

But a diametrically opposite view can be found. Barry Cooper finds in the sketches evidence that "the *Grosse Fuge* was by no means Beethoven's first idea" for the finale, and concludes that it may in fact "be seen as something of an intrusion into the quartet, rather than the germ from which the work sprang."[36] On this reading, the eventual substitution of the new finale poses fewer aesthetic problems. Kerman is also disinclined to say that "the fugue 'must' have been central to [Beethoven's] conception from the start"; and he is in any case adamant that the answer to the aesthetic problem ("which finale?") is properly to be sought not in the sketches but in the work itself.[37]

Confrontation with the work itself raises the question of closure at two levels: firstly, closure within the *Grosse Fuge* itself, whether taken as the finale to the quartet or as an independent work; secondly, the closural role of the *Grosse Fuge* in relation to the quartet as a whole. Beethoven himself famously described the fugue as "tantôt libre, tantôt recherchée," and it is a critical commonplace that for long stretches it is hardly fugal at all. This is especially true of the second main section, the G♭ major Meno mosso e moderato (mm. 159ff.), and also of the ensuing jig-like Allegro molto e con brio (mm. 233–72). This latter section, indeed, seems in some sense decisive for the fugue as a whole: it is the only music treated to anything like a formal recapitulation (mm. 533–64), whereafter it sets the controlling "tone" for the rest of the movement. But how to take the concluding section, beginning at m. 662? A linear-contrapuntal approach might identify the passage from m. 716, where the preparation for the concluding cadence begins, as one that concludes a process begun at the beginning and end of the first main section. As Example 6.5a shows, the initial countersubject accompanying the "gapped" version of the main theme (mm. 30–35) contains a middleground $\hat{5}$–$\hat{4}$–$\hat{3}$ (f^2–$e\flat^2$–d^2) progression which turns back on itself (d^2–e^2–f^2, mm. 34–35) in order to meet the tonal requirements of the answer. The climactic entry of this countersubject in m. 153, now set one octave higher, falters on $e\flat^3$ (mm. 155–56), harmonized as $V^7/B\flat$; and this $e\flat^3$ falls not to d^3 but to $d\flat^3$ (m. 158) as the harmony is abruptly skewed upward to G♭ (♭VI/B♭), which becomes the local tonic of the following section (Example 6.5b). The music beginning at m. 716 relates both to the initial presentation of subject and countersubject and to the climactic entry of the latter in m. 153; but now the lines and previously syncopated metrics are smoothed out as the melodic descent continues beyond $e\flat^3$ to complete, at last, a large-scale $\hat{5}$–$\hat{1}$ descent (Example 6.5c).

As with the first movement of op. 2 no. 1, this ending makes sense as a long-delayed completion of processes interrupted in the early stages of the work. But with the *Grosse Fuge* there is also the extraordinary change

Example 6.5a *Grosse Fuge* op. 133, mm. 31–35

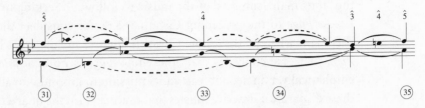

Example 6.5b op. 133, mm. 153–58

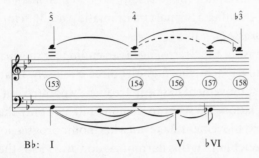

Example 6.5c op. 133, mm. 716–end

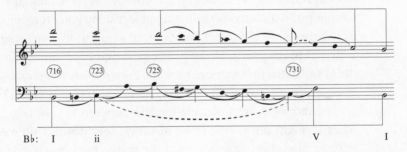

of "tone" to be considered. Far from merely completing the middle-ground linear processes begun with the initial combination of subject and countersubject, these concluding bars confirm the total transformation of the character of that material; the *Grosse Fuge* ends a world away from where it begins. Kerman notes the "incongruity of tone" set by the jig-like material of the Allegro molto e con brio, which he describes as a "vise for the form"; he also detects an ever-closer grappling with the theme that is important for the "over-all sense of the work."[38] But one might argue to the contrary, that the "over-all sense" is precisely one of the ultimate abandonment of contrapuntal rigor (albeit "tantôt libre . . ."), with all its connotations of seriousness, to a distinctly more homophonic texture (the combination of subject and countersubject in mm. 716ff. somehow does not sound "contrapuntal") connoting a lighter, even humorous vein. For Richard Kramer, the progression is one from obscurity to coherence, as hinted by the reverse presentation, at the outset, of the "premonitions" of the "four main 'subjects' of the music to follow."[39] Seeking to relate the *Grosse Fuge* to the preceding Cavatina, Kramer considers the operatic precedent whereby the "short Cavatina" figures in "the crisis before the *Lieto fine*." He concedes that "the *Große Fuge* is no *lieto fine*, but it *is* emphatically a finale, not least in its mission to ground – to absorb – all these disparate, refractive musics that precede it [in the quartet]."[40] Not a single, undifferentiated *lieto fine*, certainly; but the internal trajectory – from confusion or complication to resolution and *lieto fine* – of the *opera buffa* chain finale can offer a formal and dramatic paradigm for the "overall sense" of the *Grosse Fuge* itself.

What of the sense of the *Grosse Fuge* as an ending for the quartet? That the pitch configuration of the fugue subject is closely related to the opening of the first movement has been frequently pointed out. Kramer's analysis of this relationship seeks to demonstrate not only that the first four bars of the first movement stake out a harmonic progression implicit in the fugue subject, but that this harmonization also yields the underlying circle-of-fifths progression (G–C–F–B♭) in the *Overtura*.[41] Example 6.6 expresses the relationship differently, by revealing the two-part counterpoint underlying the fugue subject: a top voice moving chromatically between B♭ (implied) and G, over a neighbor-note progression B♭ (–B♮)–C–B♭ (implied). The upper-voice progression appears in octaves at the outset of the first movement, while the complete two-voice complex is easily distinguishable in the ensuing consequent phrase (mm. 2^3–4).

The fact of a thematic relationship between the outer movements, while it might promote a sense of unity, does not infallibly establish a sense of goal-directedness toward the finale (the same is true of the op. 131 relationship shown in Example 6.4). And even though Reti, Misch, Kerman, and others have demonstrated more pervasive networks of inter-movement relationships in op. 130, such relationships still might not form a processive sequence of which the finale is the felt culmination.[42] Nor should one neglect all that in op. 130 which resists the Forsterian imperative "only connect." Inter- and intramovement relationships in op. 130 stand in a dialectical relationship to the celebration of "dissociation" that Kerman finds central both to the individual movements and to the totality of the quartet: "in many ways the Quartet in B♭ is problematic, but the heart of the problem lies in the quite radical attitude it embodies toward the balance, confrontation, or sequence of the movements"; op. 130 seemingly shuns any "sense of a central action, in some sort of analogy with the drama"; "digressions," unanchored to any central action, then "assume a life of their own, and the life of the whole piece becomes the life of the 'digressions.'"[43] From this perspective, the

Example 6.6 The subject of the *Grosse Fuge* in op. 130, 1st mvt., mm. 1–4

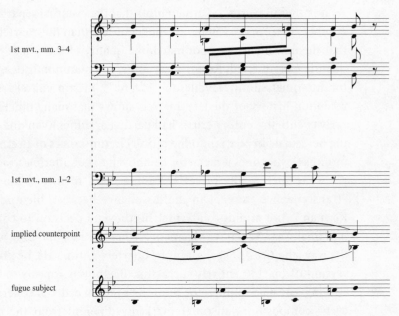

Grosse Fuge as quartet finale can hardly provide that sense of an ending whereby

> the finale [acts] in some sense to resume, or resolve, or reinterpret, or transfigure ... One would not even want to say that the Great Fugue transcends the early parts of the quartet: it wipes them out. There is a sense in which this Finale trivializes the journey which it means to terminate, and there is also a sense in which the Great Fugue orbits upon a private musical sphere of its own, needing no other sounds, needing no other universe.[44]

Beyond the ending

> Closure is a far more absolute condition in classical music than in most other arts. Literary narratives, for instance, often play with degrees of closure.
>
> ...
>
> By contrast, in most tonal music of the eighteenth and nineteenth centuries, nothing less will suffice for purposes of concluding pieces than complete resolution onto the [tonic] triad. Equivocal endings, not coincidentally, are few and far between.[45]

> When music ends, it ends absolutely, in the cessation of passing time and movement, in death.[46]

By stressing its autonomy and self-sufficiency ("needing no other sounds
. . . no other universe"), Kerman hints that the eventual separation of the
Grosse Fuge from op. 130 harms the fugue less than the quartet. The view
that the new finale does not match the quality of the *Grosse Fuge* is frequently encountered; Kerman, certainly, can summon little enthusiasm
for this "quiet, sunny, Haydnesque *Allegro.*"[47] Kristin Knittel's study of the
reception history of the late quartets shows that many nineteenth- and
early twentieth-century critics had particular difficulty in understanding
the new finale in relation to the pitiful circumstances of Beethoven's last
months ("what does it mean for Beethoven to be suffering so acutely, and
yet write such a silly piece?"), leading them to invoke the notion of
"transcendence" to explain the dissonance between life and art.[48] Yet
Kerman is not afraid to interpret Beethoven's decision to compose the
new finale "as an acknowledgement . . . that he saw something wrong with
the way [the *Grosse Fuge*] sat in the quartet." Ultimately, he finds neither
version of op. 130 entirely successful: Beethoven appears to have been
striving – unsuccessfully – for "some new idea of order or coherence in the
cyclic composition, an order markedly different from the traditional
psychological sequence."[49]

This last point is a reminder not to underestimate the consequences of
Beethoven's decision to write a new finale for op. 130, whatever his
reasons for doing so. He must have been well aware that the substitution
would have a profound effect on the quartet *as a whole.*[50] To tack on a new
ending while keeping the story unchanged was not an option: the new
ending would itself "rewrite" the entire story. The new finale affects the
overall sense of op. 130 most obviously through its redistribution of
"weight." Whereas the original version was massively end-orientated –
whatever the precise sense of that ending – "the centre of gravity in the
new version . . . is shifted from the end to somewhere else – just where, is
hard to say; the other movements seem a little lost without the Great
Fugue to dominate them. The Fugue runs the danger of trivializing the
experience of the other movements, but the new finale runs the danger of
seeming trivial itself."[51] Walter Riezler was able to find meaning in both
versions of the quartet:

> The present finale is not, as is often maintained, a mere make-shift, forced upon
> [Beethoven] by his publishers' opposition and lack of understanding on the part
> of the public. Two possibilities are inherent in the previous movements: to
> increase the tension to the limit of human endurance and shift the climax to the
> end of the whole work, or to relax it and finish in a mood of quietness and
> serenity, which often, to be sure, hardly conceals the "abysses of the world." Both
> endings are "organic," and both are in keeping with the "idea" of the work, for it
> is this that is open to the "world-background."[52]

Riezler's words conceal a timely admonition: the end is not necessarily "where we start from." Rather, musical material is fluid, possessing multiple tendencies and possibilities that are not directed towards a single inevitable *telos*. Moreover, we as listeners or "readers" are ineluctably complicit in creating the sense of an ending. Nor should we forget that the composer is his own reader, and never more so than in a case like this one. Figuring Beethoven as a reader of op. 130 when faced with the task of composing a new finale opens up suggestive parallels with literary texts, which not infrequently adumbrate endings beyond the point at which they literally stop.[53] Such "aftermaths," or endings beyond the ending, may be straightforwardly narrated at an earlier point in the text, or hinted at more obliquely; they may even derive from the reader's possession of knowledge external to the text itself. The effects of such aftermaths may be profound, sometimes entirely reversing the sense of the ending in the text itself. We might, then, profitably conceive the new finale in op. 130 not as an alternative but as the composer/reader's individually constructed aftermath to his original ending;[54] equally, circumstances allow us to read the *Grosse Fuge* as an external source that modifies our sense of the ending in the main text.[55]

These last remarks are intentionally suggestive – it is hoped, provocative – of new beginnings rather than endings. Having begun by documenting the very precise sense of the ending of the first movement of Beethoven's earliest piano sonata bearing an opus number, this study concludes with his last completed composition, one that casts naked light on the precariousness – the senselessness? – of our topic. How, then, to end? "Plaudite, amici, comoedia finita est!" Beethoven's reportedly "sarcastic-humorous" deathbed curtain-cue perhaps suggests that death, ineluctable but arbitrary, trivializes life: a sense of an ending, yet an ending without sense.[56] Or it may be read as "a gesture of defiance, reminding us that life, although transient, is necessarily more vivid than death."[57] *Finis coronat opus.*

PART III

Genres

7 The piano music: concertos, sonatas, variations, small forms

WILLIAM KINDERMAN

The piano represented a springboard for Beethoven's achievements and a primary vehicle for the pathbreaking innovations of his evolving musical style. His early reputation as a prodigy at Bonn rested on his playing of Bach's *Well-Tempered Clavier*, and his success at Vienna after 1792 was founded in no small measure on his ability to improvise at the keyboard. In assessing Beethoven's musical legacy for the piano, we should first consider the cultural context of his music and the relation of his works to his activities as a performing virtuoso. As some recent studies have emphasized, Beethoven's career coincided with and lent support to the rise of the notion of the autonomous musical artwork – the unique composition regarded as independent of specific conditions of performance.[1] The fulfillment of Count Waldstein's famous prophecy made at Bonn "you shall receive Mozart's spirit from Haydn's hands"[2] – as well as the fortification of Beethoven's style from earlier models, such as J. S. Bach,[3] reflected the high cultural ambitions of his art as an indispensable basis for his originality. The negative tone of some early reviews of Beethoven's works sprang from perceptions of their challenging character and their overturning of conventions – reasons why a more thorough acquaintance based on repeated hearings was appropriate.[4]

In evaluating this change in aesthetic reorientation, it is tempting but misleading to oppose the improvisatory tradition of Mozart and Beethoven as orators in tones with the growing recognition of autonomous works at the threshold of the nineteenth century.[5] Important musical forms and procedures such as sonata designs, fugue, rondo and variations were established vehicles for extemporized performance. The performance context in private aristocratic salons is poorly documented, and public concerts of solo piano works hardly existed; yet the evidence available indicates that published solo works were often formalized versions of music originally presented as improvisation or fresh composition. For instance, Mozart writes in a letter of 24 October 1777 from Mannheim to his father about improvising what became the Sonata in C major K. 309 (with a different slow movement): "I then played . . . all of a sudden a magnificent sonata in C major, out of my head, with a rondo at the end – full of din and sound."[6] Ferdinand Ries and Carl Czerny reported how Beethoven performed the "Waldstein" Sonata op. 53 in its original unpublished version from 1803–04 with the *Andante favori* WoO 57 as slow movement, and Czerny even explains the special title of the piece as arising out of this performance context: "Because of its popularity (for Beethoven played it frequently in society) he gave it the title 'Andante favori.'"[7] A decade later, in 1814, after he had given up performing on account of his deafness, Beethoven still insisted vehemently on the essential unity of performance and work in comments made to Johann Wenzel Tomaschek: "It has always been known that the greatest pianoforte players were also the greatest composers; but how did they play? Not like the pianists of to-day, who prance up and down the keyboard with passages which they have practised – *putsch, putsch, putsch*; – what does that mean? Nothing! When a true pianoforte virtuoso played it was always something homogeneous, an entity, if written down it would appear as a well thought-out work. That is pianoforte playing; the other thing is nothing!"[8]

Beethoven's musical thought was deeply rooted in the rhetorical art of the sonata style, whereby the notion of musical form as a process is tantamount: many theorists have regarded his piano sonatas as exemplifying an "organic" model of musical integration, in which motivic relations, harmonic and tonal factors, or melodic and voice-leading continuities can be given emphasis.[9] Such demonstrations of internal unity, however important, fail to adequately address issues of expressive character and dramatic meaning,[10] or the rich variety of musical textures. Like Mozart, Beethoven often assimilated into his keyboard works the textures of chamber music and orchestral and vocal idioms. The most specifically "pianistic" works are often those of a virtuosic cast, employing elaborate figuration, original pedal effects and a brilliant use of trills. One thinks in this regard especially of sonatas like op. 2 no. 3, op. 10 no. 3, and the "Appassionata," "Waldstein," and "Hammerklavier" Sonatas, as well as of the concertos and the variation sets, particularly the "Eroica" and "Diabelli" Variations.

The improvisational currents in Beethoven are thus balanced against his penchant for deterministic construction. He was a formidable musical architect, but typically filled out such structural mapping with imaginative and surprising expressive events, which strain the formal frameworks without quite breaking them. Paul Mies, in his 1970 study *The Crisis of the Concerto Cadenza in Beethoven*, identified a key element in the evolution of Beethoven's later style as the increasing incorporation of improvisatory elements into his style, culminating in works like the Quartet in C♯ minor op. 131.[11] The moment of enhanced stylistic internalization of the resources of extemporization came in 1809, the time when Beethoven, in

response to his increasing loss of hearing, retreated from the concert platform. At this point he wrote out solo cadenzas to his earlier concertos, and
incorporated the cadenzas to his Concerto in E♭ major op. 73 directly into
the score, thereby foreclosing the opportunity for other performers to
improvise. As his deafness became virtually complete by about 1818,
Beethoven invested ever more compositional labor in the form of written
sketches that often record improvisatory flights of fancy. The later sketchbooks provide a revealing window onto Beethoven's capacity to spontaneously generate new musical conceptions and rationally shape, refine,
and develop these ideas. The present survey of the piano works considers
both aspects, exploring issues of musical character no less than formal
unity and structural integration.

The concertos

For Beethoven, as for Mozart, the concerto for piano was an important
dramatic genre in which the composer himself assumed the role of
soloist. Between 1790 and 1809 Beethoven wrote five piano concertos, the
first two of which he revised repeatedly for his own performances. The
C major Concerto op. 15 was written mainly in two stages, in 1795 and
1800. The "second" concerto in B♭ major eventually published as op. 19
was actually the first of the concertos composed; in its original form
dating from the early 1790s at Bonn it probably had an entirely different
finale, the movement now known as the Rondo in B♭ major WoO 6.
Beethoven's perfectionistic struggle for compositional mastery and the
inevitable comparison with Mozart's great legacy of piano concertos are
reflected in the prolonged genesis of the B♭ Concerto. The rondo finale
WoO 6 was modeled on the finale of Mozart's Piano Concerto in E♭ K. 271,
a work whose influence also left traces in Beethoven's first movement. It
was the D minor and C minor concertos of Mozart, however, together
with the opening Allegro maestoso of the C major K. 503, that most
deeply impressed Beethoven.

   The composer himself expressed dissatisfaction with the concerto in
B♭ in his letter to Breitkopf & Härtel of 22 April 1801:

> I wish to add that one *of my first concertos* and therefore *not one of the best of my
> compositions*, is to be published by Hoffmeister, and that Mollo is to publish *a
> concerto which*, indeed, *was written later*, but which also does *not* rank among *the
> best of my works in this form*.[12]

Despite these reservations, the B♭ concerto is an attractive and subtle
work. The opening Allegro con brio opens with a dualistic gesture: an

assertion of the tonic chord *forte*, spelled out in energetic dotted rhythm, followed by lyrical legato phrases played *piano*. Beethoven develops both elements as the movement unfolds, with the lyrical impulse pervading the initial entry of the solo piano and the ethereal *pianissimo* passage heard in the remote key of D♭ major (G♭ major in the recapitulation) near the beginning of the second subject group, whereas the more assertive passages with dotted rhythms dominate other parts of the form, including much of the solo cadenza.

The reflective, hymn-like character of the Adagio harbors a surprising dramatic intensity, to which the pianist contributes with elaborate keyboard figuration and a compelling rhetorical expression. In their inward fervor, the soloistic passages marked "con gran espressione" near the end of the movement foreshadow the great slow movement of the Fourth Concerto. The rondo, in 6/8 time, is characterized by immense vitality and humorous wit – nowhere more than in the blustering central episode in minor keys, where Beethoven highlights the syncopated accents of the main subject. The rondo theme displays a contour similar to the opening of the first movement. In particular, it employs an initial motive descending a third to the tonic degree, paralleling the opening descending triadic gesture of the Allegro con brio, and these pitches are followed by the stepwise rising third A–C, which recalls the lyrical phrase in mm. 2–4 of the first movement. These thematic relations seem to parallel the motivic kinships between the outer movements of Mozart's D minor concerto, as Geoffrey Block has pointed out.[13]

In the C major Concerto op. 15, Beethoven retains the general formal outlines of the preceding work, with an opening Allegro con brio and a high-spirited rondo finale enclosing a thoughtful slow movement: a spacious, decorative, almost hymn-like Largo in A♭ major. In its brilliance and grandeur, the first movement is somewhat reminiscent of Mozart's Concerto K. 503, in the same key. In the orchestral ritornello, Beethoven sets off the lyrical second subject through a series of striking modulations, to E♭ major, F minor, and G minor – a sequence of ascending keys that also assumes importance in the development section.[14] As in the B♭ concerto, Beethoven's humor is most obvious in the finale, especially in the colorful subordinate theme in A minor, with its insistent accented turns and staccato bass. But perhaps the funniest idea in the entire concerto is found near the end of the longest of the three solo cadenzas for the first movement that Beethoven wrote out in 1809. He indulges here in a trick that he employed in his own solo performances. After twice sounding the trills that would normally signal the end of the cadenza and imminent reentrance of the orchestra, Beethoven mischievously continues with the lengthy cadenza. At last, after presumably exasperating conductor, orchestra, and audience with such delaying tactics, he interpolates another surprise – a soft, provocatively understated arpeggiated chord on the already much-emphasized dominant seventh chord, the doorstep to the cadence. This gesture prefaces the long-awaited – yet no longer predictable – return of the orchestra.[15]

Like the two earliest concertos, the Third Concerto had an extended compositional genesis. Its origins reach back to Beethoven's journey to Berlin in 1796, when he made the notation "To the Concerto in C minor kettledrum at the cadenza" – a remark which relates to a passage near the end of the first movement of the finished work. Beethoven may have originally intended to play this concerto at his benefit concert at Vienna on 2 April 1800, but the piece seems not to have been completed in time; he probably performed a revised version of the older C major Concerto op. 15. The C minor concerto was apparently played for the first time on 5 April 1803, with the composer at the piano.

The initial phrase of the first movement is anchored by a cadential figure in dotted rhythm – the same motive which is tapped out in the timpani at the end of the solo cadenza. This motive has a military flavor that harks back to Mozart's example;[16] in Beethoven's hands it becomes a prominent compositional element throughout the Allegro con brio. The opening orchestral ritornello is quite extended and embraces statements of a contrasting lyrical subject in E♭ major and C major before the main theme is powerfully reasserted in the minor, with an effect of pathos. The ensuing entrance of the solo piano is fortified by ascending scales leading to the principal subject boldly proclaimed in octaves. Later, in the development, Beethoven often reduces this thematic gesture to the martial cadential motive, which is exchanged between the piano, winds, and strings.

Beethoven's treatment of his main theme in the solo cadenza is especially original and displays a vast architectural logic. After the opening "lead-in," he dwells at length on the interval of a rising third from its first bar, as brilliant arpeggiations carry the music into distant tonal regions. Near the conclusion of the cadenza, Beethoven resumes this thread, developing the second bar of the theme in combination with an extended double trill. What remains are the following two bars with their striking dotted rhythm. These are played by the "kettledrum at the cadenza," with the effect heightened by the mysterious harmonic context and by the delay of the tonic resolution. Strictly considered, the cadenza embraces not only the solo but also the timpani statements, and ends only with the long-postponed C minor cadence, where a new dialogue between the piano and strings leads to the terse close of the movement.

The slow movement is a reflective Largo, whose expressive contrast to the pathos of the outer movements is heightened by the brighter tonal color of E major as the tonic key. This distant tonal relation motivates the emphasis, in the main theme of the rondo finale, on the semitone G–A♭: the prominent G♯ from the Largo is thereby reinterpreted as A♭ in the key of C minor. Beethoven's rondo design makes room for a dream-like recall of E major in the central section – a glimpse of the slow movement seen through the veil of the rondo theme. The Presto coda, on the other hand, offers a final resolution of the crucial A♭ as G♯, this time not in E major but in the major mode of the tonic, C. The expressive atmosphere of the coda is unmistakably that of the *opera buffa* finale; comic wit and jubilation crown the denouement of this drama in tones.

Beethoven completed his Fourth Concerto in 1806; it was first performed together with the Fourth Symphony at the palace of Prince Joseph Lobkowitz in March 1807. Like several other works from this period, this concerto displays a quality of spacious lyrical serenity. In the opening Allegro moderato, Beethoven gives special prominence to the dialogue between solo and tutti by beginning with a short piano passage, whose initial G major sonority is reinterpreted with wonderful sensitivity by the strings on a B major harmony, marked *pianissimo*. At the recapitulation, by contrast, this meditative opening by the soloist is recast as a more forceful gesture, while the ethereal inflection in B major is shared between the piano and orchestra.

According to a tradition stemming from Liszt and others, the Andante con moto is associated with Orpheus taming the Furies.[17] In this movement, the classical *topos* juxtaposing stark, unharmonized unisons and plaintive, harmonized lyricism is imposed on the relationship between tutti and soloist, investing the music with a mythic aura. Beethoven bases the movement on the principle of gradual transformation, whereby the soloist gradually gains primacy over the orchestra. After having subdued the antagonists, the soloist then exploits them as audience for an unforgettable climactic message – a cadenza featuring a loud, sustained trill. The searing intensity of this cadenza is the apex and turning-point of the entire concerto.

The vivacious rondo finale shows a special richness of thematic material. The main theme has a dance-like character and begins not in the tonic G major but in C major. The transitional and developmental passages emphasize a dramatic exchange between the piano and orchestra, whereas the focus of inward expression is a *dolce* subject in which the solo piano presents two contrapuntal lines with a vast gap in register, supported by a deep pedal point in the strings. The reinterpretation of this expressive *dolce* theme in different keys is a prominent feature of the recapitulation and cadenza. The transition to the coda is marked by that specialty of Beethoven's piano playing showcased in each movement of this great work – the triple trill – and the final Presto section resolves the main theme to the tonic G major with irresistible energy and compelling finality.

The so-called "Emperor" Concerto from 1809 represents a pinnacle of Beethoven's pianistic virtuosity and a major monument of his "heroic" style cast in the same key as the *Eroica* Symphony, E♭ major. Its outer movements assume a majestic character, with rhythmic figures evocative of military style. This Fifth Concerto stems from that point in Beethoven's career when the composer curtailed his own solo performances on account of his incurable deafness. Cadenzas are now no longer left open to possible extemporization; at the end of the first movement, Beethoven explicitly instructs performers not to play their own cadenza, but inserts the cadenza-like passage to be played right into the score. The opening Allegro actually begins with an impressive cadenza-like passage, which is reaffirmed at the outset of the recapitulation.

In the solo exposition of the opening Allegro, the pianist presents a transparent, *pianissimo* subject in B minor and C♭ major, thereby presaging the Adagio un poco mosso in B major, the enharmonic equivalent of C♭. In the overall design of the concerto this serene slow movement in B major acts as an immense parenthesis. Its mood of dream-like reflection is dissipated with wonderful sensitivity at the transition to the festive rondo finale, in which appearances of an energetic round-dance are interspersed with more playful, *dolce* subsidiary themes. As in the first movement, Beethoven employs here a wide range of contrast: the *dolce* second subject contains hesitating phrases and transparent textures, whereas in the coda, the music reaches a surprising still point as the music slows to Adagio. Even the piano seems to fall mute, as only the rhythmic ostinato is still heard softly in the timpani. Then the soloist caps the finale with an exciting chain of rapid rising scales, leading to the closing orchestral fanfares glorifying the rhythm of the dance.

The piano sonatas

Beethoven's legacy of sonatas is so vast and significant that a short chapter cannot possibly do it justice. We shall focus here on selected representative works, including the contrasted trilogy of works he published as Opus 2 in 1795, the two monumental sonatas from about a decade later – the "Waldstein" and "Appassionata" Sonatas – and the superbly integrated final sonata trilogy from 1820–22: opp. 109, 110, and 111. Each of the op. 2 sonatas is a highly profiled individual, and their resourceful treatment

Example 7.1 Piano Sonata op. 2 no. 1, mvt. 1, mm. 1–11

of form and texture demonstrates Beethoven's early mastery of the genre. The F minor Sonata op. 2 no. 1 shows a terse dramatic concentration, whereas the second sonata, in A major, is more expansive and radiant in character, and the C major Sonata op. 2 no. 3 is brilliant and virtuosic, studded with cadenzas in the outer movements.

The opening Allegro of the F minor sonata is dominated by Beethoven's favorite procedure of rhythmic foreshortening, under which phrases are divided into progressively smaller units.[18] Such foreshortening contributes to the inexorable drive of the music. The opening gesture – a rising staccato arpeggiation to a turn figure in the right hand, punctuated by syncopated chords in the left – is stated on the tonic and then on the dominant (Example 7.1). These two-measure units are then compressed to single bars, half-bars and single beats before the process dissolves into silence – a fermata in the eighth measure. At the same time, Beethoven emphasizes the melodic ascent from A♭ to B♭, highest tones in the right hand, reaching a climax at the broken chord with the highest tone C played *fortissimo* – a sonority that is itself a compression of the initial rising arpeggio. The opening salvo of Beethoven's very first sonata is a classic example of dynamic forward impulse shaped in sound.

The second movement is a spacious Adagio in F major, which indulges at times in ornate melodic decorations and an almost orchestral rhetoric. Beethoven drew motivic material for this slow movement from his Piano Quartet in C major WoO 36 no. 3, written a decade earlier at Bonn. In the third movement, a minuet in F minor, Beethoven plays tricks with a conventional cadence formula in a spirit of Haydnesque wit. The Prestissimo finale is in sonata form of a special type. In the exposition and recapitulation, the arpeggios from the opening Allegro become an agitated texture in triplets supporting powerful chords in the treble. In the development, by contrast, an expressive tune emerges in A♭ major that is adorned in melodic variations. The development thus becomes the sonata's last focus

Example 7.2 Piano Sonata op. 2 no. 2, mvt. 1, mm. 57–85

of lyricism before the music re-enters the turbulent dramatic idiom in F minor. The overall plan of this unusual movement distantly foreshadows Beethoven's only other sonata in F minor, the "Appassionata" op. 57.

Each of Beethoven's sonatas of op. 2 expands the conventional three-movement Classical design to four movements, with a Minuet and Trio in penultimate position.[19] The opening Allegro vivace of op. 2 no. 2 in A major also audaciously expands the sonata design itself. At the beginning of the second subject group, the music seemingly comes to rest in E minor, the dominant key. Instead of presenting a "theme" at this juncture, Beethoven offers modulating sequences on a chromatically rising bass. This pattern carries the music through the most remote keys, while the thematic material is gradually curtailed through a dramatic process of rhythmic foreshortening. The progression soon grinds to a halt, dwelling on the semitone E to D♯ (Example 7.2). Then, to fill the void, a motive drawn from the opening theme intrudes rambunctiously in the depths of the bass, with almost grotesque effect. Beethoven savors this paradoxical moment to the fullest by playfully reiterating the pivotal E–D♯ semitone in the high register, before the music finally bursts into the sought-after E major in a spirit of unbuttoned revelry.

The slow movement in D major, marked Largo appassionato, has a noble, hymn-like character. Beethoven effectively varies the chorale-like main theme, juxtaposing somber massiveness in the minor mode with a transparent, almost luminescent final variation that leads into a meditative coda. Like the first movement, the scherzo and rondo finale of op. 2 no. 2 feature motives based on rising arpeggios, which Beethoven develops here in a lightly sensuous, scintillating manner, quite unlike op. 2 no. 1. The trio of the scherzo and contrasting theme of the rondo take on a darker, stern character in A minor, laced with dissonance and chromaticism. The closing Grazioso movement of the A major sonata is the first great rondo finale in Beethoven's sonatas, a worthy forerunner of the gracious closing movements of op. 7, op. 22, and op. 90.

In composing the opening movement of his third sonata, Beethoven skillfully re-worked material from his early piano quartet, the same piece from which he had borrowed for the Adagio of op. 2 no. 1. The opening Allegro con brio of op. 2 no. 3 displays Beethoven's pianistic virtuosity: it abounds in chains of broken octaves, arpeggios, and trills. Beethoven begins with a measured double trill played on the tonic and then on the dominant; the interval of a third elaborated here resurfaces over and over in the brilliant ensuing passage-work. After this bravura beginning, the group of subsidiary themes offers a varied succession of instrumental colors – an oboe followed by a flute; and a brief orchestral tutti leading into a small string ensemble, before the virtuoso pianist reappears. The development offers a coy false recapitulation in D major that is overturned with almost violent energy, as the thirds are hammered out in syncopated octaves in both hands. The coda re-examines the material of the development, leading through a cadenza and reprise of the main theme to the emphatic close.

What follows is one of the most moving inspirations in early Beethoven. He places the ensuing Adagio in a distant key – E major. The contrast in tonal color casts a dream-like veil over the delicate lyricism of the slow theme. When Beethoven arrives at the cadence in m. 11, however, this aura vanishes; the theme is unable to sustain a resolution. Instead, Baroque-style figuration emerges in the minor, with deep bass octaves and expressive inflections in the high register. The transition is laden with tragic overtones. The scherzo of op. 2 no. 3 also juxtaposes conflicting perspectives, but with an entirely different result – one of Beethoven's first gems of comic music. This Allegro has a jocular character, but the gaiety of the opening music is soon pitted against mock bluster in the minor. At the climax, the music seems to be imprisoned within the minor, unable to find the door to C major that will open the ensuing reprise of the scherzo. The humor persists in Beethoven's coda, as the right hand insists on the major mode of C at the same time as the left persists in the minor, stressing A♭ to G, and then D♭ to C.[20]

The sonata-rondo finale restores the virtuosic tone of the opening movement. This Allegro assai sports a dazzling pianistic technique: the main theme begins with rapid parallel chords of the sixth, a configuration that is changed to octaves for acoustical reasons whenever the subject appears in the low register. The character is capriciously humorous; each new appearance of the principal theme is enriched by surprising new variants. Beethoven caps his finale with a coda beginning with the main theme played in the left hand, under an extended trill. The ensuing cadenza-like passages strive upward to reach a linear goal on F, a fourth higher. As first they fail: a triple trill fades into silence; groping attempts to reassert the head of the theme stumble into the "wrong" keys, A major and A minor. Does this passage recall the amusing search for the "door" in Beethoven's scherzo? The music at last seizes hold of the high F, unlocking the original tonality and tempo in its jubilant rush to the conclusion.

The most outstanding of Beethoven's other sonatas from the 1790s is perhaps the Sonata in D major op. 10 no. 3, and particularly its profound Largo e mesto, in D minor. Together with the *Sonate Pathétique* op. 13, this somber slow movement exemplifies the young Beethoven's impressive command of tragic expression in music. Friedrich Schiller, in his 1793 essay *Über das Pathetische*, offers a lucid discussion of tragic art whose conceptual framework applies well to Beethoven. Schiller stresses that the depiction of suffering *as such* is not the purpose of art; what must be conveyed is resistance to the inevitability of pain or despair, for in such resistance is lodged the principle of freedom. Such an existential conflict seems encoded in the rhetorical structure of the Largo e mesto, in sonata form. The opening theme develops a slow melodic turning figure that is weighed down by thick, dark chords in the bass. The ensuing theme contains vocal accents and inflections in the higher register. Yet this yearning personal expression is consistently contradicted in this Largo by emphatic dissonant chords and by a starkness that often signals the death-like void of silence. At the outset of the development, the music moves with hopefulness into F major before this brighter, optimistic tone is contradicted by accented dissonant sonorities. The following expressive treble figuration in thirty-second notes floats above long pedal points in the bass, whose seemingly inevitable resolution sounds like an unfolding of irreversible fate. Beethoven exploits here a wide registral gap between

Example 7.3 Piano Sonata op. 10 no. 3, mvt. 2, mm. 63–68

the plaintive figures in the treble and the low, thick sonorities rooted on D that will ground the imminent recapitulation. At the registral descent preceding the recapitulation, the sighing figures fade into a silence, which is broken only by the anguished gesture of a rising diminished seventh interval.

The climax of the narrative design of the Largo e mesto occurs in the weighty coda, beginning where the cadential progression in D minor is completed with a vast drop in register into the depths of the bass, with an accompaniment in undulating sextuplets in the right hand (Example 7.3). Here the turning figure gravitates downwards in sequence, reaching a harrowing low climax on G♭ before a chromatically ascending bass-line strives upward to reach the register that had been prepared already in m. 64. In completing the cadence into the bare octave D in m. 76, Beethoven subordinates and merges the continuity of plaintive vocal figures into the stark unharmonized unison followed by silence. The poignancy of this passage lies in its silencing of the implied human voice (Example 7.4). The movement ends with references to fragments from the opening theme and allusions to the registral disparities between its low chords and the extracted motive of a semitone in the highest register. Remarkably, the second and third notes of the turning motive – C♯ and D – are stifled into the evocative silence of m. 76, only to echo again in the last two measures. To the end, Beethoven maintains the expressive dialectic between the

Example 7.4 Piano Sonata op. 10 no. 3, mvt. 2, mm. 73–87

fragility of human expressivity and the immovable reality of termination. The full-voiced, accented diminished seventh chords with which the exposition and recapitulation peak (mm. 23–25; 62–64) are caught between these poles, laden with anguish and unfulfilled yearning. In Schiller's terms, resistance is manifest, although incapable here of transformation and hence doomed to melancholy resignation.

An attitude of resistance, even defiance, is more evident in the famous *Sonate Pathétique,* published in 1799. In the introductory Grave of the first movement, this resistance to suffering is implied in the contrast between an aspiring, upward melodic unfolding and the leaden weight of the C minor tonality, with its emphasis on dissonant diminished seventh chords. The rising contour and harmonic dissonances of the Grave are then transformed into forceful accents in the turbulent main theme of the ensuing Allegro di molto e con brio. Beethoven later recalls the Grave to preface the development and coda, underscoring the juxtaposition of tempi as a germinal idea of the movement.

A even more concentrated contrast of tempi launches the most celebrated of the sonatas from Beethoven's pivotal transitional period around 1802: the so-called "Tempest" Sonata in D minor op. 31 no. 2. Innovations also characterize the immediately preceding sonatas: in the Sonatas in A♭ major op. 26 and in E♭ major op. 27 no. 1, Beethoven dispenses with any movements in sonata form, whereas in the following Sonata in C♯ minor op. 27 no. 2 (mistitled "Moonlight"), he shapes the three movements into a directional sequence leading from a soft, improvisatory Adagio sostenuto to a turbulent Presto agitato finale, whose sonata design reinterprets the thematic substance of the opening movement. Both of the op. 27 sonatas are labeled "Sonata quasi una Fantasia." Their quality of extemporization also surfaces in op. 31 no. 2, which begins with a suspended, tonally ambiguous first-inversion dominant chord in Largo tempo, a gesture paired in turn with a driving passage in Allegro tempo. Only at the recapitulation does the Largo reveal its full expressive significance in giving rise to passages of recitative strongly anticipating the setting of "O Freunde, nicht diese Töne!" ("O friends, not these tones!") in the finale of the Ninth Symphony.

The two biggest sonatas of Beethoven's middle period – the "Waldstein" in C major op. 53, and "Appassionata" in F minor op. 57 – partake of the key symbolism of Beethoven's opera *Fidelio,* which in its original version dates from 1805. If Florestan's "God! – what darkness here!" might serve as commentary on the conclusion of the "Appassionata," the choral text "Hail to the day! Hail to the hour!" at the end of *Fidelio* might almost be the motto for the jubilant coda of the "Waldstein" finale. Another, more subtle link was signaled by Beethoven's replacement of the original decorative slow movement of the "Waldstein," the *Andante favori,* by a mysterious, searching *Introduzione,* which is related structurally to the music heard at the dungeon scene in the last act of the opera.[21] Donald Francis Tovey wrote that the "Appassionata" is Beethoven's only work to maintain "a tragic solemnity throughout all its movements,"[22] but the impression of the outer movements is far less solemn than forcefully dramatic. In a perceptive recent study, Gregory Karl has regarded the narrative unfolding of the first movement as "the internal experience of a persona in pursuit of an ideal destined to be crushed by an inscrutable and intractable antagonistic force."[23] The middle movement is an Andante con moto in Db major, whose unfolding variations take on a dream-like quality. As in the "Waldstein" Sonata, this slow middle movement is connected directly to the finale. The serenity of the music is shattered when Beethoven substitutes a dissonant diminished seventh harmony at the implied moment of closure: the moment of tragic reversal is marked by thirteen *fortissimo* chords that launch the closing Allegro, ma non troppo.

In the "Waldstein" and "Appassionata," the sonata has become a superbly integrated dramatic canvas on an imposing scale. Poised at the beginning of Beethoven's gradual withdrawal from active solo performing, this pair of sonatas raises the stakes for interpretation, distancing the music from established genre categories and conventions while encouraging the application of the autonomous work-concept – the notion of the artistic masterpiece lifted out of history. Like the *Eroica* among the symphonies, these two sonatas have taken on a canonical status, profoundly reshaping subsequent expectations about the genre of the Classical piano sonata.

During the ensuing decade, the piano sonata became less conspicuous in Beethoven's output. He produced another trio of works around 1809: op. 78 in F♯ major, op. 79 in G major, and op. 81a, the *Lebewohl* or "Farewell" Sonata. The *Lebewohl* bears the imprint of the turbulent political events of 1809, when Napoleon's armies invaded Austria and occupied Vienna after bombarding the city. Many of Beethoven's friends fled from Vienna, including his student and patron the Archduke Rudolph, to whom the sonata is dedicated. Beethoven entered the dates of the Archduke's departure and return into the score and allowed the emotional progression of "farewell–absence–return" ("Lebewohl–Abwesenheit–Wiedersehen") to determine the basic character of the three movements. Yet the *Lebewohl* is far from being a merely programmatic, illustrative work, in the manner of Beethoven's later "Battle Symphony," *Wellington's Victory* op. 91, from 1813. Its most impressive passages tend to do double duty, bending musical inspirations to symbolic ends. For instance, the harmonic boldness characteristic of this sonata is most of all evident in the coda of the opening movement, where the tonic and dominant are repeatedly sounded together. Here the imitations of the original "Lebewohl" motto seem to recede into the distance, implying that the departure has taken place.

Beethoven's next sonatas, the works in E minor op. 90, from 1814, and in A major op. 101, from 1816, are connected to his distinguished piano student Baroness Dorothea Ertmann. Ertmann was one of the first pianists to become known specifically for her interpretations of Beethoven; her intelligent and sensitive performances so delighted him that the appreciative composer once dubbed her his "dear, valued Dorothea-Cäcilia."[24] In a letter from 1810, Wilhelm Karl Rust commented about the performances of the Baroness: "She always makes music entirely as I imagine it. Either she plays me a Beethoven sonata that I select, or I play her favorite fugues by Handel and Bach."[25] Ertmann was especially recognized for her playing of op. 90, whose second, final movement is the most Schubertian movement in Beethoven, a luxurious rondo dominated by many appearances of a spacious cantabile theme. According to Anton Schindler, whose testimony can be trusted in this instance, "she nuanced the often recurring main motive of this movement differently each time, so that it took on first a coaxing and caressing, and later a melancholy character. In this way the artist was capable of playing with her audience."[26] More evidence of Beethoven's appreciation of Ertmann is his

dedication to her of the A major Sonata op. 101, one of the most technically and psychologically challenging of all the sonatas.

Beethoven advanced beyond even this aesthetic framework in the
largest of all his sonatas, the "Hammerklavier" in B♭ major op. 106. He
described op. 106 as "a sonata that will keep pianists busy when it is played
50 years hence"[27] – a fairly accurate prediction, since apart from Franz
Liszt, Clara Schumann and Hans von Bülow, few pianists tackled the
immense challenges of this great sonata before the last decades of
the nineteenth century. Pieces like the "Hammerklavier" Sonata and the
"Diabelli" Variations tested the viability of the work-concept to an even
greater extent by pushing the conditions for adequate performance into
an unspecified future, according to Beethoven's favorite dictum, *ars longa,
vita brevis* ("art is long, life is short").

The "Hammerklavier" is the only one of the late sonatas to revisit the
four-movement plan characteristic of the early sonatas, such as op. 2,
op. 7, and op. 10 no. 3. An extraordinary role is assumed in each movement by B minor – a tonality Beethoven once described as a "black key." B
minor functions in the "Hammerklavier" like a focus of negative energy
pitted against the B♭ major tonic, creating a dramatic opposition with far-
reaching consequences. In op. 106, the conventional order of the inner
movements is reversed, with the scherzo placed before the great Adagio
sostenuto – the longest slow movement in Beethoven. Its tonality is F♯
minor, enharmonically a third lower than the tonic B♭, poised between the
overall tonic of the work and the focus of contrary forces in B minor. In
the ensuing slow introduction to the fugal finale, Beethoven distills the
intervallic basis of the whole sonata, reducing the music to a mysterious,
underlying level of content consisting solely of a chain of thirds in the
bass, accompanied by soft, hesitant chords in the treble.[28] This descending chain of thirds is interrupted three times by brief glimpses of other
music, the last of which is reminiscent of Johann Sebastian Bach. The
music thus suggests a search toward new compositional possibilities, with
the implication that Baroque counterpoint is transcended by the new
contrapuntal idiom embodied in the fugal finale, whose fiery defiance of
expression poses special challenges for listeners and performers alike.

Beethoven's final sonata trilogy, opp. 109–11, embodies other kinds of
narrative designs in which the finale becomes center of gravity of the
whole. In contrast to earlier works, such as the sonatas of op. 2, these final
sonatas project a directional process that is sustained across the individual movements, ultimately reaching fulfillment in culminations of lyric
euphoria. The finales of opp. 109 and 111 consist of variations on themes
in a slow tempo, whereas the fugal sections in the finale of op. 110 are metrically co-ordinated with the slow stanzas of the *Arioso dolente,* marked

Adagio, ma non troppo. The last movement of op. 109 begins and closes with a sublime, sarabande-like theme, whose motivic substance and melodic outline are foreshadowed in the opening movement. Here, as in the two companion sonatas, the coda of the first movement takes on an anticipatory role, tentatively foreshadowing the finale and assuming thereby a character of unfulfilled yearning.[29]

In the finale of op. 110, in A♭ major, Beethoven interweaves a lamenting *Arioso dolente* and spiritualized fugue, creating an unusual framework with parallels to the alternation of Agnus Dei and Dona nobis pacem in the last movement of his *Missa solemnis*. Both the depressive modality of the *Arioso* and the aspiring lyricism of the fugue are foreshadowed in parts of the first movement, but it is the comic scherzo-like second movement (Allegro molto) that seems to exert influence at the most crucial juncture: the double-diminution passage of the second fugue (Example 7.5a). This passage signals the imminent re-attainment of the tonic key of A♭ major and emergence of the triumphant closing lyric ascent. It also generates, in its radical structural compression of the fugue subject, deleting the second of the three rising fourths, a level of rhythmic energy that sustains the rapid figuration of the final passages, giving the effect that the theme is glorified by its own substance. The Meno allegro passage recalls a comic allusion in the Allegro molto to a folksong quotation, "Ich bin lüderlich, du bist lüderlich" ("I'm dissolute, you're dissolute") (Examples 7.5b, c). The import of Beethoven's inscription for the entire transitional passage, "nach u. nach sich neu belebend" ("gradually coming anew to life"), is embodied in this musical progression. The abstract contrapuntal matrix beginning with the inverted subject is gradually infused with a raw but vital energy, which arises not naturally through traditional fugal procedures but only through an exertion of will that strains those processes to their limits.

The two-movement design of the final Sonata in C minor op. 111 provoked Beethoven's publisher Moritz Schlesinger to inquire whether a third movement had been omitted from the manuscript. In the same vein, Thomas Mann, in the eighth chapter of his novel *Doktor Faustus*, has the fictional character Wendell Kretzschmar lecture on "why Beethoven wrote no third movement to the Piano Sonata Opus 111." A proper answer to this question would go to the heart of the aesthetic of Beethoven's third period. The turbulent strife of Beethoven's life-long preoccupation with the "C minor mood" seems to reach a climax in the opening movement of the sonata. Yet the fleeting appearance of the lyrical second theme in A♭ major, and its more sustained passages in C major and F minor in the recapitulation, represent a foreshadowing of the character of the *Arietta*, and they accordingly slow the music to Adagio. The plagal

Example 7.5
(a) Piano Sonata op. 110, mvt. 3, mm. 165–72

(b) Piano Sonata op. 110, mvt. 2, mm. 17–21

(c) Song, "Ich bin lüderlich"

cadences to C major in the coda build a bridge from the Allegro to the finale. Then the tension of the first movement is resolved, once and for all, as the unfolding variations on a lyric *Arietta* in C major achieve a synthesis of Being and Becoming. The progressive rhythmic subdivisions in the variations carry the music through the utmost agitation in variation 3 to the suspended, uncanny final passages. When the rhythmic intensification and registral ascent reach their climax, the original theme is recaptured, glorified by sustained trills and ethereal textures that music had never known before.

Variations

Already in his childhood, Beethoven had improvised variations on popular melodies by other composers. After his move to Vienna in 1792, he wrote out numerous sets of piano variations based on themes by such diverse composers as Dittersdorf, Grétry, Haibel, Mozart, Paisiello, Righini, Salieri, Süssmayr, and Winter.[30] The very closeness of these pieces to improvisation may help explain his reluctance to assign them opus numbers. Only in 1802 did he lift the variation genre into the mainstream of this artistic production with two sets of piano variations on original themes, op. 34 and op. 35. As Beethoven pointed out in a letter to his publisher, these works are "noticeably" different from his earlier variation sets; he therefore assigned them opus numbers, and, as he put it, "included them in the proper numbering of my great works, all the more, since the themes as well are by me."

Beethoven had used the theme of the Fifteen Variations and Fugue in E♭ major op. 35 twice previously: as the seventh of the Contredances for Orchestra WoO 16, and at the conclusion of the *Prometheus* Ballet op. 43, where Prometheus is celebrated by his two "creatures" – the original representatives of humanity. A sense of creative evolution is reflected here musically in the unusual compositional strategy of starting with the bass alone: only after several variations on the *basso del tema* does the composite theme emerge. The fragmentary, even bizarre effect of starting with only the bass is linked to the creation myth, whereby the awkward clay figures of Prometheus are gradually instilled with human life. The initial quality of unpredictability is sustained throughout this impressive work, which assumed even more importance by serving as the model for the *Eroica* finale, the seminal movement of the symphony, as Lewis Lockwood as shown.[31]

It may seem surprising that Beethoven's greatest variation set reverts to the use of a pre-existing theme, and a rather trivial one at that. The theme stems from the publisher Anton Diabelli, who in 1819 asked numerous composers to each contribute a variation; the collective project was designed to generate publicity for his firm. Beethoven initially refused. He disdained Diabelli's waltz as a "cobbler's patch" ("Schusterfleck") on account of its mechanical sequences, and did not overlook its trivial aspects, such as the prominent repeated chords that are played tenfold with a *crescendo* in each of the two opening phrases. Despite this initial reaction, Beethoven soon responded to Diabelli's invitation with a creative brainstorm: by the summer of 1819 he had composed not one, but a draft version including already twenty-three variations.[32] Only in 1823 did Beethoven complete this colossal work, which has been praised by Hans von Bülow as a "microcosm of Beethoven's genius"[33] and by Alfred Brendel as "the greatest of all piano works."[34]

In the end, even the banality of the theme assumed an important role. By subjecting Diabelli's waltz to parody and caricature, and poking fun at its shortcomings, Beethoven drew the waltz more deeply into the inner workings of the work as a whole. In variation 13, for instance, Beethoven

Example 7.6 (a) "Diabelli" Variations op. 120, theme

(b) Variation 13

(c) Variation 21

dissolves these repetitions into silence, whereas in variation 21 he merci-
lessly exaggerates the banality of the repeated chords (Examples 7.6a, b,
c). A comic obsessiveness characterizes variation 9, which is based
throughout on the turn figure from the head of the theme. One of
Beethoven's wittiest inspirations is the reference, in the unison octaves of
variation 22, to "Notte e giorno faticar" from the beginning of Mozart's
Don Giovanni. This allusion is brilliant not only through the musical
affinity of the themes – which share, for example, the same descending
fourth and fifth – but through the reference to Mozart's Leporello.
Beethoven's relationship to his theme, like Leporello's relationship to his
master, is critical but faithful, inasmuch as he exhaustively exploits its
motivic components. And like Leporello, the variations after this point
gain the capacity for disguise. Variation 23 is an etude-like parody of pianistic virtuosity alluding to the "Pianoforte-Method" by J. B. Cramer,
whereas variation 24, the Fughetta, shows an affinity in its intensely sublimated atmosphere to some organ pieces from the third part of the
Clavierübung by J. S. Bach.

The "Diabelli" Variations culminate in a Mozartian minuet whose
elaboration through rhythmic means leads, in the coda, to an ethereal

texture strongly reminiscent of the famous *Arietta* movement from Beethoven's own last sonata, op. 111, composed in 1822. Herein lies the final surprise: the *Arietta* movement, itself influenced by the "Diabelli" project, became in turn Beethoven's model for the last of the "Diabelli" Variations. The end of the series of allusions thus became a self-reference and final point of orientation within an artwork whose vast scope ranges from ironic caricature to sublime transformation of the commonplace waltz. In the last moments, Beethoven briefly alludes to the repeated chords from the waltz, and he concludes the cycle in the middle of Diabelli's thematic structure, poised on a weak beat. The unresolved tension of this surprising final chord reminds us that Beethoven's work is one of created, not congenital, harmony, and that in these closing bars we have reached "an end without any return" ("ein Ende auf Nimmerwiederkehr"), in the words of Thomas Mann's Kretzschmar in *Doktor Faustus*.

Small forms

Despite the importance of improvisation to Beethoven, he published only one fantasy for piano solo: op. 77 from 1809.[35] This piece is probably a revised version of the improvised solo fantasy Beethoven played at his famous *Akademie* concert of 22 December 1808, when the Fifth and Sixth Symphonies, the Fourth Piano Concerto, and the Choral Fantasy were first performed. The op. 77 Fantasy culminates in a set of variations in B major, following a free opening section abounding in thematic contrasts and sudden modulations, in a style reminiscent of C. P. E. Bach. The initial gesture of this work is a rapid descending scale, which seems torn, as it were, from the celestial ether; rather than support its key, G minor, Beethoven proceeds to the remote Db major, the key of the contrasting lyrical theme. The op. 77 Fantasy and the opening solo introduction to the Choral Fantasy both offer insight into Beethoven's considerable powers of invention outside the formal demands of the Classical sonata style.

Beethoven also made signal contributions in the category of the bagatelle: a short, intimate piano piece of lyrical or whimsical character. He had a long-standing interest in such pieces, some of which were connected to his larger compositions. The dance-like Allegro with Minore used as the penultimate movement of his Piano Sonata in Eb major op. 7 was originally sketched as a "bagatelle" independent from the sonata,[36] and the first movement of the Piano Sonata in E major op. 109 was also originally conceived as a bagatelle.[37] The most familiar of Beethoven's bagatelles is the popular *Für Elise*, which is known in a version dating from 1810. His first collection of such pieces, the Seven Bagatelles op. 33, dates from 1802. Several unpublished bagatelles from earlier years were revised and included in the Eleven Bagatelles of op. 119, brought out in 1823, together with freshly composed pieces, two of which are by-products of the "Diabelli" Variations.[38] When Beethoven began negotiating the publication of what became op. 119, in 1822, his portfolio of bagatelles contained about a dozen additional pieces, including the Scherzi in C minor WoO 52 and WoO 53, which were originally conceived for the Sonata in C minor op. 10 no. 1, as well as the Allemande in A major WoO 81, which was eventually incorporated into the String Quartet in A minor op. 132.[39]

Beethoven's last important composition for piano, the "Cycle of Bagatelles" op. 126, from 1824, binds a succession of six highly contrasted pieces with the integrative power that had long characterized his multi-movement works in other genres. Lyrical pieces in slow or moderate tempi alternate with more rapid, agitated ones until no. 6, in which a short and furious Presto frames a reflective Andante amabile e con moto. The play of contrasts and integration is lifted here into the realm of paradox, and Wilfrid Mellers has written that "coming from the greatest of all composers normally concerned with process and progression, this little bagatelle may count as Beethoven's most prophetic utterance."[40] Whereas the provocatively mechanistic Presto initially offers the raw material, as it were, out of which the Andante is shaped, the center of the bagatelle visits ethereal textures reminiscent of the *Arietta* movement of op. 111. Then the process is reversed: the adornments of art are stripped away to reveal the music from the beginning of the Andante followed by the frenetic Presto, whose fanfare of chords closes the piece. Beethoven's final bagatelle concludes by enacting its own deconstruction, and its circular design symbolizes that imaginative transformation of experience that lies at the foundation of art.

8 Beethoven's chamber music with piano: seeking unity in mixed sonorities

MARK KAPLAN

The essential problem in writing music for strings or winds with piano is immediately apparent: the sonorities do not readily mix. Stringed and wind instruments naturally produce sustained sounds, whereas a piano note decays from the moment it is struck – and decayed even more rapidly on eighteenth-century pianos than on today's. Hence, the expressive possibilities of the instruments are different and often contradictory; and as increases in virtuosity made their capabilities more specific, these differences become more pronounced. Despite this problem, chamber music with piano had a well-established and important role in eighteenth-century musical life, and the greatest composers were able to find ways for contrasting instruments to occupy the same musical space happily. Beethoven's role in this process was unique, because his years of creative genius coincided with a period of rapid development, both in instrumental design and instrumental technique. He was therefore a pivotal figure in the development of chamber music with piano – especially the still-young genres which will be the focus of this essay: duo sonatas with violin or cello, and trios with both instruments.

Much of this music was composed early in his career, from the mid 1790s until 1803, after which the seven remaining masterpieces (1808–15) integrated his earlier technical breakthroughs with later stylistic advances. Beethoven's choice of piano trios for his debut opus was a natural one: as a student he had experimented with both piano trios and piano quartets, and his teacher Haydn was the composer of several remarkable piano trios. The three op. 1 trios are not at all modeled on Haydn's trios in the way that they combine string and piano sonorities; Beethoven was already seeking his own answers to such textural problems. Before writing another piano trio, however, he concentrated on violin sonatas and cello sonatas, composing the op. 5 cello sonatas and the first nine violin sonatas between 1796 and 1803; so that the three later trios – opp. 70 nos. 1 and 2 (1808) and 97 (1811) – besides being formally and expressively more in accordance with Beethoven's middle period (as we would expect), are also markedly different from op. 1 in the way the three instruments contribute to the ensemble. Beethoven not only exploited every aspect of conventional instrumental sound, but helped to expand the range of sonority, in particular often requiring the strings to play in the manner of a piano, and occasionally the reverse as well. By the time he wrote the op. 102 cello sonatas, his mastery of the string–piano combination was so complete that he was free to concentrate on altogether different goals. It is interesting that after this, as Beethoven's expressive aims became ever more focused, he wrote no further chamber music with piano, instead channeling efforts into piano sonatas and string quartets.

The combining of keyboard and melodic instruments was, of course, well established before Beethoven. There was a long tradition of Baroque trio sonatas for various solo instruments with keyboard and basso continuo, and these developed along with changes in musical styles and increased levels of virtuosity, while retaining the basic instrumental roles of soloist and accompaniment.[1] At the other extreme was the Classical accompanied keyboard sonata, in which the (often expendable) role of the melodic instrument was mostly confined to providing filler for the quickly attenuating sounds of the keyboard.[2] Neither of these traditions addressed one of the primary ideals of chamber music, at least as we have come to think of it today: a fairly democratic treatment for all the instruments, which is usually (if simplistically) evaluated in terms of the distribution of thematic or motivic material. This concept was, however, quite alien to eighteenth-century thought. Examples of superb chamber music oblivious to democratic part-writing are found among Haydn's trios, as discussed by Charles Rosen.[3] However, the seeds for democracy among instruments were present in the technique of musical dialogue, which had long been established in diverse instrumental and vocal genres. As dialogue began to play a role in Classical chamber music with piano, it was often in a piano concerto-like context, especially in last movements.[4] The evolution from dialogue to a fuller form of conversation took place in the context of two major areas of development, one in instruments and the second in instrumental techniques. The late eighteenth century was a very active period for improvements in pianos, and Beethoven's interest in this process is well known.[5] Beethoven's pianos had substantially more sustaining power and tonal range than the instruments of only a generation earlier; and his piano writing features both far more legato than that of his predecessors and – in later works – the imitation of orchestral sonorities that became characteristic of later piano style. Stringed instruments and, especially, bows were changing as well: the Parisian bowmaker François Tourte (1747–1835) and his father Louis Tourte are generally credited with the design of the modern bow, which began replacing older types of bows in the 1780s. Not only did the new bows provide more power and sustaining capabilities, they also permitted a greater variety of articulation.

Modifications to the instruments themselves, adding to their power and tonal range, also began at this time.[6]

Significant technical advances in violin and cello playing also centered around Paris, especially after the arrival in 1782 of the Italian virtuoso Giovanni Battista Viotti (1755–1824), who remained for a decade, literally transplanting the vanguard of violinistic development from Italy to France. Viotti was not active as a teacher, but his influence was far-reaching: violinists who emulated his playing became the next generation of teachers, and they codified a method that evolved into the violin technique most prevalent today. Late eighteenth-century Paris also saw a corresponding development in cello playing, among the primary exponents of which was Jean Louis Duport, who wrote the first comprehensive treatise on cello technique (1806). From descriptions of Viotti and Duport it is apparent that both cello and violin schools emphasized tonal control, power, articulation, and expressivity, distinguishing them from other virtuosic styles that primarily emphasized left-hand dexterity in high positions (though Viotti continued to favor the use of high filigree writing as well).[7] For the cello, this had the effect of opening up a whole range of mid- and low-register possibilities, while for the violin the effects were most noticeable in the wide array of bowing patterns and strokes that entered common use. As a result of the French Revolution, the new styles of string playing spread more rapidly throughout Europe than otherwise might have been the case. In 1792, Viotti emigrated again to London, and later spent some years in Germany as well. Beethoven was familiar with his violin writing, and was personally acquainted with several prominent younger exponents of the French violin school.[8] Duport fled to Berlin in 1789, where he would later meet and play with Beethoven.

Such was the instrumental context in which Beethoven started to write chamber music with piano. As for the music itself, there was astonishingly little which could have provided direct models for Beethoven, though what did exist was of a very high standard: Haydn's piano trios and, from Mozart, a very fine quintet for piano and winds (a clear inspiration for Beethoven's early work for the same combination), two piano quartets, several trios, and well over a dozen violin sonatas. Neither Haydn nor Mozart wrote cello sonatas, although both composers took the cello seriously and wrote expressively and idiomatically for it. Mozart's great violin sonatas were available to the young Beethoven, and there is evidence that he used of some of them as formal models for his student piano trios and piano quartets.[9] Mozart's sonatas are remarkably inventive – often richer and more daring than the solo piano sonatas – and are built on a true dialogue between instruments, even if the keyboard is the first among equals.[10] His piano trios and piano quartets, most of them mature works composed from 1786 onwards, drew on his considerable experience with both violin sonatas and piano concertos; hence, they exhibit notably more instrumental interplay than Haydn's trios, especially where the violin is concerned. Even here, however, the cello is only rarely a protagonist; more often it supports either the piano or the violin.

These works by Mozart and Haydn comprised virtually the entire repertory of integrated chamber music with piano when Beethoven approached the genre. Knowing as we now do the ground that he was later to cover, it is easy to describe the op. 1 trios as "imitative," but I find the word inappropriate to Beethoven's temperament at any stage of his career. To draw upon the musical styles and works of the time is one thing, and this he did freely; to imitate them is quite another. From the first, Beethoven was clearly intent on asserting his own individuality and laying claim to new territory, even if his early means for doing so were neither so inherently revolutionary nor so confident and consistently successful as they later became. For example, there is a clear statement in the fact that the op. 1 trios, unlike any of Mozart's or Haydn's, are four-movement works, each with a scherzo or minuet. We can see a rather cocky intent to place the trio in the same serious category as a symphony or string quartet, an attempt which is at least mostly successful.

There is little resemblance to the piano-dominant style of Haydn's trio writing, and Mozart was certainly Beethoven's point of departure. The cello is very often independent of the piano's bass line, and there are thematic conversations among all three instruments, especially in development sections, as in the later trios of Mozart. Less typical of Mozart is the occasional division of a single theme among two or three instruments, which later become a favorite device of Beethoven's.[11] The manner in which material is passed between instruments often appears to be more self-conscious in Beethoven than in Mozart, as seen in a comparison of the conclusion of Mozart's Trio in E major K. 542 with that of the first movement of op. 1 no. 1 – endings which are in some ways quite similar. Mozart presents a very orderly passing of motivic material between two pairs of voices: piano right hand to piano left hand, then violin to cello, and the only asymmetry in the phrase comes from sustained chords added in m. 250 for a chromatic harmony. On the other hand, Beethoven changes the texture in each measure in less predictable ways that have clearly been carefully calculated to increase tension even before the *fortissimo*. Such unpredictability may explain the astonishment with which the trios were greeted, the novelty and originality that critics found in works which seem rather conventional to us today.[12]

Beethoven's concern with refining the instrumental relationships may be seen in his use at this time of what may be called compensatory dynamics: at times, one instrument has different dynamic markings from the others, and solely to prevent problems of balance. (See mm. 12 and 25–29 of the first trio, where the strings are marked *forte–piano* and *sfor-zando–piano* to the piano's *forte* and *sforzando*.) Such dynamic indications are particularly striking to the modern performer when motivated by the fear that the *piano* might not be sufficiently heard: with today's pianos the problems are usually the reverse. Beethoven soon abandoned this practice, and later works usually have more unified dynamics (except, of course, for reasons of musical content rather than for considerations of balance), or else indications in one part with nothing in the others.

One of Beethoven's most radical experiments in piano–strings relationships in the op. 1 trios occurs in the Presto of op. 1 no. 2, in which the movement is defined by a motif of fast repeated notes, not only idiomatic to the violin but essentially unplayable on the piano. Beethoven does modify the figure to trills or broken octaves to lighten the pianist's task, and later even finds virtue in necessity, having the violin imitate the piano's version (mm. 401–03); but clearly the material is originally conceived with the humorous lightness of the violin's figure.[13]

Although writing for the strings in the op. 1 trios is generally less adventurous than that for the piano, some peculiarly Beethovenian ideas are already present. Among these are a distinctive type of two-part texture for the violin in variation 5 of the Andante cantabile con variazioni from the third trio (later found in the G major Romance op. 40), as well as a staccato fanfare-like arpeggio figure in both strings in the Adagio of op. 1 no. 1 (also used in the F major Romance op. 50). Upon arrival in Vienna, Beethoven had taken violin lessons from Schuppanzigh and Krumpholz, and much of the violin writing can be differentiated into sections which he might have imagined playing himself and others beyond his reach. For example, the first movement of op. 1 no. 1 can be played almost entirely in the first position (though this is hardly recommended), whereas the awkward skips of a tenth in the last movement are difficult for the best professionals, suggesting that for material beyond his technical prowess, Beethoven relied on a more theoretical and, at this point, less thorough knowledge of the violin's possibilities.

From the first, Beethoven exploited the singing potential of the cello in its tenor and alto ranges, especially in slow movements. The Adagio of the first trio is notable for its extensive *cantabile* string material, with one such theme reserved exclusively to them. If such cello writing goes beyond anything in Mozart's chamber music with piano, there is still an inescapable Mozartian quality to the movement, largely because of the piano's improvisatory ornamental variations on the primary theme each time it returns.[14] A similarly Mozartian approach characterizes the Adagio of op. 1 no. 2, though this is less apparent because of a level of complexity that thickens the texture. However, some sections (e.g. beginning at m. 26) are deliberately thinned out to achieve a rarefied, ethereal effect (an intention already evident in the choice of the distant key, E major, for the movement), and these passages are similar enough to Mozart to justify, for once, the word imitative.

Still, the flavor of Mozart in this instance comes most strongly from the poignancy Beethoven achieved; and a clear argument against the concept of an imitative period is that Beethoven, though he could write so beautifully in this manner, chose so rarely to do so. In musical personality, the young Beethoven's humorous, boisterous and dramatic tendencies were much closer to Haydn; but here as well there are essential differences of temperament. Haydn's dramatic tendencies, and also much of his inventiveness and harmonic daring, have a somewhat gentlemanly aspect: he is like an inventor who creates for the sheer joy of it and, rather than consider the consequences of his inventions, simply casts them out into the world. Even in early works, Beethoven's drama and innovations have a greater earnestness that implies a more direct connection to personal experience. This quality is very evident in op. 1 no. 3, a dramatically charged C minor work, which played a pivotal, if not completely understood, role in the personal relationship between Haydn and Beethoven. This was the only one of the three trios about which Haydn expressed any reservations, which according to the surviving evidence seem to have concerned the trio's public reception more than the quality of the work itself. This distinction may have been lost on Beethoven, who took offense at Haydn's remarks, and continued to do so years later.[15]

The C minor was Beethoven's personal favorite among the op. 1 trios, and certainly it is the one which most fully explores dramatic possibilities as well as the use of harmonic change to increase and relieve tension. However, for complexity of relationships between instruments, it is more conservative than its siblings in its generally greater focus on the keyboard part: the coloristic possibilities of the strings are used excellently, but most often in support of a structure conceived in pianistic terms.[16] Perhaps, at this point in his development, he found it necessary to sacrifice politeness of instrumental interplay in order to achieve heightened drama. Such a trade-off between more ambitious emotional goals and textural inventiveness later became unnecessary as Beethoven's compositional technique matured. Indeed, one measure of his progress as a craftsman is an increasing ability to achieve diverse aims simultaneously, rather than individually.

This trade-off is still in evidence in the two op. 5 cello sonatas: while the first is remarkable for its instrumental and textural inventiveness – especially for the cello – the second is more musically and dramatically ambitious.[17] These sonatas, written during Beethoven's 1796 visit to Berlin, have the distinction of being the first cello sonatas with fully written out piano parts (as opposed to figured bass), and were thus of fundamental importance in defining the genre and its possibilities. Lewis Lockwood has described the connection between Beethoven and Jean Louis Duport, with whom Beethoven performed the works in Berlin, noting specific exercises in Duport's influential 1806 treatise on cello playing that are essentially identical to passages in Beethoven's sonatas, and clearly written in response to their new technical demands: Beethoven must have found it stimulating to work with a cellist of Duport's ability, for the cello parts are significantly more daring than those he had written only a few years before in the op. 1 trios.

To be sure, the piano part is still much more flamboyant than the cello writing, so much so that Joseph Kerman refers to these sonatas as "almost miniature concertos,"[18] and Tovey goes on a censorious tirade about the first one's virtuosity and cadenzas.[19] However, Tovey misses the obvious: virtuosity and cadenzas are appropriate because Beethoven was one of the supreme virtuosi of the time. The trip to Berlin was part of a concert tour, and it would have been unnatural for Beethoven not to have displayed his gifts as a performer – gifts not so easily separable at this stage of his career from his composing gifts.

If the piano writing in op. 5 no. 1 is what might be expected from Beethoven at this time, the variety in the cello writing is nothing less than astounding, as is the accomplishment of composing a work of such quality without prior models in the genre. The sonata starts with an introductory Adagio sostenuto (as does op. 5 no. 2), not a normal beginning for Beethoven at this time, and one he no doubt adopted in recognition of the cello's declamatory and rhetorical possibilities (e.g. opening or m. 22) as well as its singing potential (mm. 7–10). Mozart's Violin Sonata K. 379 has been mentioned as an inspiration for the introduction, and while this seems likely enough, it should be kept in mind that the op. 5 slow introductions, especially the second, are much denser than Mozart's, and the second has sufficient length and complexity of development to convey the emotional impact of a complete movement.[20] Lockwood outlines the variety of cello techniques appearing in op. 5, from double stops and occasional chords to pizzicati, arpeggio figures, and passages in broken octaves; and these – a world apart from the op. 1 cello parts – demonstrate Beethoven's newly found knowledge and interest in the instrument. Even more impressive is the care and originality with which he devised combined cello–piano textures. Some particularly striking ones include: the passage in op. 5 no. 1, mvt. 1, m. 194 (Example 8.1a), where the half-step at the very bottom of the cello is used even more evocatively than a similar figure in the Piano Sonata op. 57 (mvt. 1, mm. 10–14); a true blending of sonority in fast notes (2nd mvt., m. 241); the use of cello double stops for a drone effect (Example 8.1b, 2nd mvt., mm. 205ff.); instances of high piano filigree together with tenor-range cello melodies (Example 8.1c, op.

Example 8.1
(a) Cello Sonata op. 5 no. 1, mvt. 1, mm. 194–205

(b) op. 5 no. 1, mvt. 2, mm. 204–12

5 no. 2, mvt. 1, mm. 122–27); and, in the same movement, a powerful use of the low cello register in contrary motion to the piano's left hand, mm. 449–55 (Example 8.1d).

If, in the op. 5 cello sonatas, Beethoven was eager to explore and exploit the range of sounds most natural to a cello, his approach was quite

Example 8.1 (*cont.*)
(c) op. 5 no. 2, mvt. 1, mm. 122–27

(d) op. 5 no. 2, mvt. 1, mm. 449–55

different for violin sonatas, of which all but the last were composed in the years 1797–1803. Here we often find, rather, the reverse: Beethoven often took advantage of the new bows and techniques in order to push the violin's sonorities and articulations closer to those of the piano. This is clear near the beginning of the first sonata, op. 12 no. 1, m. 13: the violin takes over the piano's legato eighth-note figure (after a neat dovetail in m. 12), and the line has little strength or purpose when played with the natural violinistic fluidity appropriate to Mozart; Beethoven is depending on the violinist to articulate the notes in a more pianistic manner. The second theme presents a similar situation, again with legato eighth notes; then, in the recapitulation of the last movement, Beethoven confidently expects the violin's robust spiccato accompaniment to parallel a percussive piano bass part. Material that does not allow such unity of texture is rewritten: the legato violin line starting in m. 5 of the first movement is modified in m. 13 to emphasize the piano's ability to straddle a greater range and to downplay its weaker sustaining power. Mozart's very different approaches to the violin–piano texture nearly always featured the ingenious avoidance, rather than the solution, of problems. Where possible he chose material that could work equally well – though often differently – when played in the natural manner of both instruments, and our modern tendency to unify these sounds in a more Beethovenian way often goes counter to his music.

The most Mozartian of the Beethoven violin sonatas is op. 24, the so-called "Spring" Sonata, and even here it is only the first themes of the first and last movements that truly resemble Mozart. Nigel Fortune refers to the opening of the first movement as breaking with tradition in giving the theme first to the violin;[21] however, there is a strikingly similar precedent for this in Mozart's Sonata K. 301. Here, as in the Beethoven, the violin starts with first theme in the exposition and the piano in the recapitulation. Also parallel is the *crescendo* scale leading to a *subito piano* when the violin restates the theme at the recapitulation. Most striking, though, is the textural similarity itself, this being Beethoven's single use of Alberti bass figuration in a violin part.[22]

The quite dissimilar twin to op. 24 is the A minor Sonata op. 23, the two works having been intended to be published and perhaps also played together as a contrasting pair.[23] Where the fifth sonata (op. 24) is lyrical and benevolent, the fourth is brusque and menacing; where the fifth is expansive the fourth is, especially in the outer movements, terse and unrelenting with an agitation and brevity that foreshadow the String Quartet op. 95; where the fifth often allows a more Mozartian approach to performance, the fourth usually requires the more pianistic approach from the violin. It would, indeed, almost work as a piano sonata for three hands, except that Beethoven depends on tonal differentiation for his counterpoint, which would otherwise be too confined in range for the voices to be discernible (mvt. 1, m. 30) and also to create fleeting changes of perspective with voice switching (mvt. 1, m. 62). The fourth sonata is remarkable for its human relationship between the instruments. They converse like people – sometimes competitively (mvt. 1, m. 76), sometimes collaboratively (mvt. 2, m. 115), and sometimes simultaneously, as in the contrapuntal instance given above. They even manage to resolve differences of opinion and arrive at a consensus, whether in desperation (mvt. 1, m. 110, unifying at m. 118) or by gentle persuasion (mvt. 2, mm. 120–23, Example 8.2). If all sonatas are dialogues to some extent, op. 23 stands apart because its quickness of repartee – the overlapping of voices gives it a more naturally rhetorical cadence than the conventional politeness typical of dialogue in the Classical period.[24] Op. 23 relies on a two-note motif – two legato eighth notes either ascending or descending by a whole- or half-step – which is also used extensively in the sonatas op. 12 no. 2 and op. 47 (interestingly, all three are in A). Clearly, this motif provides limitless harmonic opportunity, but it was probably also attractive to Beethoven for violin sonatas because its very brevity and lack of

Example 8.2 Violin Sonata op. 23, mvt. 1, mm. 111–24

sustained notes makes timbral unity between the instruments more easily achieved when desired.

In the violin sonatas composed through op. 47 (the "Kreutzer" Sonata, 1802–03), there is a steady development both in sureness of violin writing and in textural diversity and richness. Among the three op. 12 sonatas, the third is in some ways the most ambitious, both for the expressive depth of the Adagio and for the level of violin virtuosity. The latter is introduced to match a very demanding piano part with a floridness occasionally reminiscent of the op. 5 sonatas; here, however, the violin sometimes joins in the spectacular effects. In the Adagio are the first signs (m. 66) of long legato indications in the violin part which exceed the limits of anything practically executable as a bowing. These, then, are non-instrumental phrasing notations, and Beethoven, who clearly loved his legatos, soon used them with abandon, letting them stretch over many measures, as in the last movement of op. 23.

The C minor Sonata op. 30 no. 2 and op. 47 contain violin writing as demanding and idiomatic as anything written to date, even by violinists. Indeed, the seventh, eighth and ninth sonatas display violin writing so virtuosic that we might expect to see identifiable violinistic influences from the French school violinists with whom Beethoven had contact – Kreutzer, Rode, and Baillot – as well as Viotti, whom Beethoven never met, but whose concertos he certainly knew.[25] However, Boris Schwarz has shown that these violinists concentrated their creative efforts on concertos, and that it is in Beethoven's Violin Concerto op. 61 and the Triple Concerto op. 56 that the most direct influence of the French school is to be found, rather than in these sonatas.[26] The instrumental writing in Beethoven's Violin Concerto provides a potentially rich field of inquiry, especially because of the wealth of changes to the violin figurations made by Beethoven in the manuscript. Unlike the manuscript emendations in the op. 69 cello sonata discussed later in this chapter (changes primarily having to do with subtle textural questions of interplay between the instruments), the Violin Concerto's manuscript emendations primarily affect the violin part itself, and provide detailed evidence not only of Beethoven's interest in French violin style, but also of his transformation of this style into something uniquely his own. There is, as well, a significant performance issue directly related to this: in traditions that date back to the nineteenth-century violinist Joseph Joachim, most violinists today adorn the extended sixteenth-note passages of the first movement with various complex bowing patterns – patterns derived from French school practices – despite the fact that there are no indications for these bowings in Beethoven's score. An examination of the autograph leads to the inescapable conclusion that Beethoven's modification of more typically French school figurations was always in the direction of simplification, and that the addition of bowing patterns to the concerto is inadvisable.

Most probably, the reason Joachim strayed in the direction of Viotti-like bowings was that he was trying to make traditional violinistic sense out of what is, in fact, much closer to piano writing. We have noted that Beethoven, in the chamber music, frequently crossed instrumental boundaries; and in the violin concerto the unusual relationship between soloist and orchestra is more typical of piano concertos of the time. The result is a concerto of a truly symphonic nature, with an orchestra part of unprecendented significance. This, and the magisterial length and character of the first movement, as well as the transcendent lyrical beauty of the second movement and the transition to the dance-like exuberant release of the Finale are, of course, the attributes primarily responsible for this work's place among the greatest violin concertos.

Still, to return to the violin sonatas, there is something of what Schwarz refers to as a French "military" characteristic in all three of them, especially in the last movements of op. 30 nos. 2 and 3; and there are specific figurations that may owe a debt to the French violinists, such as the broken octave and broken third figurations in the first movement of the so-called "Kreutzer" Sonata (mm. 59–60 and 246–47, Example 8.3), the articulations common in Viotti in the second variation of the second movement, and some highly demanding passages in the first movement of op. 30 no. 2, again with distinctive bowing indications. There was, however, no direct connection between Rodolphe Kreutzer and the sonata that has kept his name alive: Beethoven had written the work for the violinist George Bridgetower, but decided at the last moment to dedicate it instead to Kreutzer, who had made a very favorable first impression on him. Ironically, Kreutzer then refused to play the sonata, which he reportedly found "outrageously unintelligible."[27]

Example 8.3 Violin Sonata op. 47, "Kreutzer," mvt. 1, mm. 59–60 and 246–47

Two points about the "Kreutzer" Sonata deserve mention here. The two-note motif mentioned earlier, which would appear to generate the entire work, is in fact a by-product of a recycled three-note motif. The sonata was, from this point of view, composed backwards, for the third movement was written originally as the finale to op. 30 no. 1, in which the essential motif was the figure C♯–D♯–E. The development of this movement particularly emphasizes the last two notes with their semitone interval, opening the way for op. 47's first movement motif, E–F, which inverts to F–E for the second movement. Here we are compelled both to admire Beethoven's ability to construct a work of such power out of leftovers, and to wonder that he could have so fundamentally miscalculated the nature of his own work when he first wrote it, for the boisterous Presto with its tarantella characteristics would surely have been an unwelcome guest in the refined drawing room of op. 30 no. 1.

The second point has to do with the concept of democracy in chamber music referred to earlier, for the "Kreutzer" Sonata and the Cello Sonata op. 69 (chronologically the next chamber work with piano) may be said to usher in the age of fully democratic chamber music. They begin with such a self-conscious and declamatory instrumental symmetry that there can be no doubt Beethoven was making a deliberate statement of equality. We can even propose that op. 47 (especially the first movement) served a crucial role for chamber music similar to that of the *Eroica* Symphony for symphonic writing. There is a defiant staking out of new territory common to both works, and in both cases, Beethoven's subsequent works in each genre were markedly different from those before. In particular, we no longer find the trade-off between texture and drama mentioned in connection with opp. 1 and 5: Beethoven was able successfully to integrate the two.

Lockwood's insightful article on op. 69 discusses in considerable detail the relations between cello and piano, using as a point of departure Beethoven's autograph manuscript and the changes he made in this manuscript as he was composing.[28] This is one of Beethoven's messier autographs, and most of the emendations are for textural purposes, such as voice exchanges, registral shifts, changing of rhythms and articulations. It is interesting – and one of Lockwood's central points – that this painstaking work, involving considerable revision, was done at the very last stage of Beethoven's creation of the piece; that is, after completion of his sketchbook-work and after the sonata, in its essential form and sound, was already – in some sense of the word – "finished." Alan Tyson's article on the Trio op. 70 no. 2 also discusses a similar last-minute rewriting.[29] It would be interesting to see whether autographs of some of the works which seem to have involved some degree of choice between content and texture (e.g. op. 1 no. 3 or op. 5 no. 2) lack this type of revision; unfortunately, neither of these autographs is now extant. While referring the reader to Lockwood for a detailed discussion of op. 69, I will mention a few interesting points. The idea of opening the sonata with an unaccompanied stringed instrument is one Beethoven had already used in the "Kreutzer" Sonata, and he obviously found it compelling – it appears in three of the six remaining chamber works with piano: the Trio op. 70 no. 2, the Violin Sonata op. 96, and the Cello Sonata op. 102 no. 1. Aside from possibly reflecting Beethoven's growing interest in linearity, this also offered him the opportunity, through presenting a theme completely unadorned, of announcing its importance and imprinting it in the listener's ear, thus making it more recognizable when disguised through variation or buried in counterpoint. For example, in the first movement of op. 69, we have no trouble identifying mm. 38–41 with the first theme, despite the fact that the only similar gesture is the rhythm: the harmonies do not match, and while the melody superficially resembles an inversion it is really nothing of the kind. Beethoven's interest in such theme-imprinting may also account for one of the emendations that Tyson refers to in op. 70 no. 1: the opening of the last movement was changed from a violin and piano version to a final version with only piano. In op. 69, as in the violin sonatas, the cello is frequently called upon to articulate passages in a more pianistic than cellistic way, which was not typical of the op. 5 sonatas. But we also find the reverse situation: in some lyrical passages, such as in the development of the first movement (m. 107), it is clearly the pianist who is expected to use the instrument's resources to approximate the legato capabilities of the cello. As Beethoven once wrote to a piano manufacturer, "One can also sing with the pianoforte."[30] In general, the writing in op. 69 is thinner than in the early cello sonatas: another aspect of the greater textural sophistication of the later music is simply that greater compositional technique allowed Beethoven the possibility of using fewer notes with confidence. This enables increased cello clarity, and fast passages such as the many sixteenth-note runs in the last move-

ment of op. 69, or the "Kreutzer" Sonata-like figures in the first movement, m.115, are more successful than similar places in op. 5. The thinner
texture also allows some highly effective use of sustained notes in the
cello, notably the wonderful emerging G♯ at mm. 125–27 of the first
movement.

The same impressive mastery of resources distinguishes the op. 70
trios, which, like the pair of violin sonatas opp. 23 and 24, offer opposite
extremes of temperament. In these trios, when compared with those of
op. 1, the cello is more often paired with the violin than with the piano.
The generally benevolent character of the second trio is more typical of
Beethoven's music of this time, and like the op. 69 sonata, it is conspicuously democratic in its treatment of the three instruments: even the short
cadenzas in the last movement are dispensed with scrupulous fairness.[31]
In the rhythmically dynamic "Ghost" Trio op. 70 no. 1, the most daringly
experimental timbral effects are found in the Largo assai. Here the progressive diminution of note values in the piano – an example of a device
referred to by Alfred Brendel as a "foreshortening"[32] – work in conjunction with an exceedingly slow pulse[33] and some fine use of the murky
bottom sonorities of the cello (m. 17) to create an ever-building tension
that gives the work its not inappropriate nickname. The op. 70 trios are
typical of many middle-period works in their use of melodic material that
can be thought of as "constructed"; that is, clearly designed so as to
conform to specific symmetries and structures. In op. 70 no. 2, the
primary theme of the first movement provides an excellent example of
this: the decidedly non-vocal melody is carefully arranged in a series of
diminishing intervals which, once they are reduced to a semitone, resolve
into a scale that fills in an octave in a symmetrical pattern. Remarkable
here is the almost mathematical nature of the planning and also
Beethoven's complete disinterest in hiding it from us: unlike Mozart,
whose symmetries are generally hidden, Beethoven presents material that
tells the story of how it was constructed. This is, of course, completely
consistent with the personality of a man who preserved his sketchbooks
and left them for posterity.

The final four works that concern us – the last violin sonata, op. 96, the
last trio, op. 97, and the last two cello sonatas, op. 102, nos. 1 and 2 –
display different aspects of the boundary between Beethoven's middle
and late periods. The ideals of the middle period as taken to their limits
are exhibited in the expansiveness and grandeur of the op. 97 "Archduke"
Trio, qualities which extend beyond sheer length and character to include
sonority as well. This is the only trio in which Beethoven reaches for
orchestral sound in ways that clearly anticipate Brahms. In order to do so,
he relies heavily on the depth of the lowest cello register, on the wide range

of the piano, and on thick chordal sonorities shared by all three instruments. In this context, democracy among voices again becomes irrelevant; and in an instance such as mvt. 1, m. 33, the symphonic gesture of the entire ensemble is more important even than the cello's primary motivic material, which is, indeed, very likely to escape the conscious attention of the listener. Sections in which the texture radically thins out, such as m. 181, are evocative of wind solos in the fifth or sixth symphonies. Another orchestral device is the thematic use of pizzicato in the first movement development.

The op. 96 violin sonata is quite different – an intimate and thinly textured piece in which the melodic ranges of violin and piano are often kept close and intertwined. Even the two hands of the piano are sometimes unusually close together, as in the Trio of the third movement, where there is even some technical danger of the hands becoming entangled. This sonata contains passages in which the violin is called upon for cello-like sonorities, as in the recapitulation of the chorale melody in the Adagio espressivo, or in the long F♯ pedal tone in the Adagio variation of the last movement. Beethoven wrote the piece with the French violinist Rode in mind, and while Rode was less than successful with the work,[34] there was probably no contemporary violinist who could have fared much better with its often elusive musical language and deceptively innocent-looking technical problems. Beethoven was now beyond learning instrumental possibilities from the virtuosi of the day; instead, he was posing challenges for the future.

After opp. 96 and 97, a few fallow years with relatively little output were followed by the two op. 102 cello sonatas, works which stand out for their innovations in formal and aesthetic areas as well as the textural and instrumental ones that are the focus here; by this time, Beethoven's mastery of the instruments and their relations was merely a tool in the service of his more general *avant-garde* artistic goals. Astonishing here are the compression and economy of material and the abrupt emotional changes – sometimes rather like stream-of-consciousness – with which Beethoven experimented, confident that his structures were strong enough to maintain unity. This pair of sonatas, together with the Piano Sonata op. 101, announced the advent of Beethoven's late period. As Brendel notes in his essay on the late style, even the extensive and adventurous experimentation in earlier works could not prepare Beethoven's contemporaries (or, indeed, us) for the new and unprecedented worlds that were to follow. For example, the Adagio of op. 102 no. 1 is similar in many respects, including texture, to the Adagio variation in the last movement of op. 96; yet as improvisatory and moving as the earlier movement might be, it seems tame next to the repressed wildness of the cello sonata, with its chromaticisms that keep leading farther than one expects.

The speech-like quality is also carried farther than ever before. We have mentioned the rhetorical aspect of op. 23, and there are certain similarities between its first movement and the Vivace of op. 102 no. 1 (not only the rhetorical nature, but also the terseness, the use of triplets to create restlessness, the turbulent character strewn with *sforzandi*, and the key of A minor); however, it is, again, the later work that paradoxically sounds even more humanly natural because of such unexpected elements as the unprepared Bb in m. 89, held as a pedal-tone by the cello through a fleeting far-away chorale-like interlude that dissolves into the recapitulation.

In this late period the music parallels the seeming unpredictability not only of speech but also of thought. Just as we experience very few thoughts that are complete in themselves, the music has few points of conclusive cadence; instead, Beethoven creates extended areas where we are left suspended, with often incomplete themes swirling around us. For example, at the recapitulation mentioned above, Beethoven withholds the expected D minor chord at the down beat of m. 94; and on the second beat, when he does move to D minor, he keeps it in the unstable second inversion. Adding to the instability is the texture: the *tremolo* chords in the piano are typical of this period, as are extended trills which also contribute to a state of suspension. Another example of Beethoven's new way of dealing with material is found in the opening Andante of this sonata. As in op. 69, the cello opens with a solo statement of a straightforward diatonic theme; but instead of the piano repeating the cello's statement – which would have fulfilled both Classical and post-Classical "democratic" expectations – the piano presents a response much more in keeping with a natural thought process (Example 8.4). It is clearly based on what the cello stated, but not in a simply definable way; rather, it shows the involvement of a second personality. In this introductory movement, the complete theme is repeated three more times – in thirds between cello and piano, in thirds for piano alone, and with both instruments in parallel first-inversion triads – and each time it is harmonically diverted towards the subdominant, though it never arrives there. Beethoven continually frustrates our expectation of a cadence by resolving to tonic chords in either first or second inversion; for example in the middle of mm. 20, 22, and 23. Then, in the middle of m. 24, when we are sure there must be a cadence, a brief dominant cadenza occurs, which finally does resolve. Yet, even here the texture of the broken chords in the bass forestalls any definite stability. The result, at the end of this short C major movement that is never really in C major, is that even three solid measures of C major

Example 8.4 Cello Sonata op. 102 no. 1, Introduction

do not make us feel completely at home, and the change to A minor (of which there has been not the least suggestion), while unexpected, also feels completely organic.

If it is beyond the scope of this survey to do justice to the op. 102 sonatas, yet a few more points should be made. Op. 102 no. 2 contains the only full-scale slow movement among the cello sonatas, and it is worth waiting for: the use of a chorale-type melody is similar to the Adagio

Example 8.4 *(cont.)*

espressivo of the op. 96 sonata, but where that one exuded benevolence, this explores darkness and pain with an understated intensity that is more direct and effective than many of Beethoven's earlier and more openly dramatic attempts in this direction. Like the op. 96 Adagio, that of op. 102 no. 2 proceeds directly into the next movement, in this case a sort of miniature "Hammerklavier"-Sonata fugue that starts, surprisingly, with a childlike questioning naïveté, before building to a concentrated serious-ness. This fugue is only the most obvious example of a pervasive, sure-footed and rather "uncompromising" (Brendel)[35] use of counterpoint – one of the defining aspects of the late period. The independence of voices inherent to this counterpoint is, of course, vital to our discussion of texture, as is the previously mentioned destabilizing and atmospheric use of trills and tremolos. Also notable is a propensity for thinner writing, especially in the second sonata, which often distills to one line in each hand of the piano – or sometimes even one hand alone – together with the cello. However, the most striking general aspect of texture in these sonatas is simply the degree of inventiveness: in op. 5 and op. 69, Beethoven confronted textural issues in order to ensure that a vital voice or rhythmic gesture would not be obscured – in other words, to prevent or alleviate problems. Here, however, to an unprecedented extent, texture is used proactively to create deliberate effects that are at times extraordinarily evocative (e.g. mm. 59–66 in the Adagio of op. 102 no. 2).

The op. 102 sonatas were written in 1815, and in his remaining twelve years of life Beethoven wrote no further chamber music with piano. Nigel Fortune suggests that this may have been due to the deterioration, with deafness, of Beethoven's powers as a pianist, and a consequent disinterest in social music making.[36] I find this less than convincing, for it presupposes that even in this last period Beethoven's own physical use of the piano was the primary motivating force for his works with piano. The abstractness and technical challenges of his late piano sonatas indicate the contrary; and in any case he was already quite deaf when he composed the op. 102 sonatas.

Another possibility is that, for reasons of temperament, perhaps related to his increasing personal isolation, Beethoven's explorations were leading him to extremes of either grandness or intimacy. If we view op. 97 as going in the former direction and op. 96 in the latter, it may well be that Beethoven felt that he had taken chamber music with piano – a genre naturally somewhat in the middle – as far as he could toward those extremes. The solo piano could approach both, with opp. 106 and 110 as representative examples; and intimate quartets or, on the other hand, monumental symphonic works offered Beethoven more scope than he could find in chamber music with piano.

The absence of a body of late period chamber music with piano beyond the op. 102 sonatas may well account for the rather slight attention this repertory has received from scholars, at least by comparison to the quartets, piano sonatas, or symphonies. This is regrettable, if understandable: there is a natural fascination with the very latest works of Beethoven, together with a less justifiable tendency to see so many of the earlier works as merely "leading up to" the final crowning ones. Hopefully it is clear from this chapter that the innovation and musical genius in the chamber music with piano make it a repertory in every way the equal of Beethoven's other great instrumental genres.

9 Manner, tone, and tendency in Beethoven's chamber music for strings

JOHN DAVERIO

I

In his chamber music for strings, Beethoven made incredibly rich contributions to an entire family of genres: trio, quartet, and quintet. This music comprises the sort of metagenre that Walter Benjamin had in mind when, writing about Proust's *A la recherche du temps perdu*, he maintained that all great works of art either "found a genre or dissolve one."[1] One could make that claim for Beethoven's string chamber music in general and of his quartets in particular, even if it is not easy to pinpoint the precise means through which the composer either founded or dissolved a genre.

On at least one point there can be no doubt: Beethoven viewed his chamber music for strings as a privileged repertory. Consider his attitude toward the common practice of arranging chamber works for other media. One special case aside, Beethoven did not recast his string chamber music for other instruments, though there are several examples of the reverse procedure in arrangements either made by Beethoven himself or completed under his supervision, for instance, the reincarnation of the Wind Octet op. 103 as a string quintet (op. 4), or the arrangement of the Piano Trio op. 1 no. 3 for string quintet (op. 104). Furthermore, his recasting of the E major Piano Sonata op. 14 no. 1 for string quartet – a task that Beethoven felt only he could have accomplished satisfactorily – amounts to a wholesale transformation of the original.[2] Hardly a measure of the piano sonata is left untouched in matters of register, texture, dynamics, accompanimental figuration, or rhythm, and a rationale for every modification can be found in the composer's desire to "translate" the source work into the language of the new medium.[3]

Yet Beethoven was never tempted to make such translations of his chamber works for strings. (His arrangement of the *Grosse Fuge* op. 133 for piano four-hands [op. 134] hardly counts, for it is merely a note-for-note rendering undertaken to facilitate study of the quartet movement, and devoid, apart from the opening flourish, of any pianistic touches.) When other composers attempted something of the kind, the results were often found wanting by contemporary critics, such as the reviewer of an arrangement of op. 18 no. 4 for piano four-hands who commented that Beethoven's quartets, "even if skillfully arranged, will lose more than those of other masters."[4] One is left with the impression that Beethoven's string quartets, owing to their ultra-refinement of style, suffered more than other instrumental genres when arranged for different media.[5]

To be sure, the quartet shares this ultra-refinement with the string trio and string quintet. According to the entry for *Quartett* in Gustav Schilling's *Encyclopädie*, which not surprisingly cites Haydn, Mozart, and Beethoven as the preeminent contributors to the genre, the string duo, trio, quintet, and sextet all draw on the technical and aesthetic categories associated with the quartet.[6] The discussion of string chamber music in Carl Czerny's *School of Practical Composition* is based largely on early- and middle-period Beethoven (who receives twice as many examples as either Haydn or Mozart), and here too the trio and quintet are said to partake of the same ideals as the quartet.[7] We will not do justice to Beethoven's string trios by viewing them as preparatory exercises for bigger and better things; on the contrary, he approached these works just as seriously as he would the later quartets. This is not only true of the C minor Trio op. 9 no. 3, which foreshadows the storm and stress of op. 18 no. 4, but also of the unabashedly sunny G major Trio op. 9 no. 1. The *concertante* textures in the latter work hark back to the idiom perfected by Mozart in his E♭ major Divertimento K. 563 (the model for the early String Trio op. 3), but the prefacing of the first movement with a slow introduction and the appearance of elaborate sonata forms in all movements except the Scherzo betray Beethoven's desire to lend the genre a new weight and substance. Likewise, the Quintet op. 29 exhibits the formal expansiveness often associated with the middle-period quartets, while the D major Fugue op. 137 and the unfinished Prelude and Fugue in D minor (Hess 40), both for string quintet, look forward to the fascination with contrapuntal textures that informs the late quartets.[8]

None of this, however, provides evidence of the founding or dissolution of a genre. Indeed one could easily argue that Beethoven's chamber music for strings remains well within traditional bounds. The level of technical proficiency needed to play his first violin parts seldom exceeds that already required to negotiate the Trio in the Menuet of Mozart's K. 589 (which includes passages with marked similarities to the first-movement coda of Beethoven's op. 74) or the finale of Haydn's op. 76 no. 2, to cite a few obvious examples. Precedents for Beethoven's attempt to achieve continuity on the large scale by linking movements with transitional passages – an often-cited feature of his middle- and late-period style – can be found in Haydn's op. 20 no. 2 and op. 54 no. 2. The expansive forms of Beethoven's middle-period quartets are no larger than those in the opening movements of Haydn's op. 77 quartets or of Mozart's Quintet K. 515.⁹ Still, listeners, players, and critics alike are left with the impression that Beethoven accomplished something fundamentally new, especially in his string quartets, that he pressed the genre to a point of no return. Where, then, does the novelty reside?

To begin with, we might say that in his quartets Beethoven decisively altered a basic feature of the mode in which such compositions were offered for consumption: the very notion of an opus or "work." Up through op. 59, he adhered to the eighteenth-century custom of publishing either three or six more or less independent quartets as a single opus, while thereafter only single works were allotted an opus number. (Already in 1797 Beethoven issued a single piano sonata under an opus number: the Sonata in E♭ op. 7.) A vestige of the older practice appears to survive in the later chamber music: after all, precisely *three* quartets resulted from Prince Nikolas Galitzin's commission of November 1822 (opp. 127, 132, and 130). At the same time, Beethoven's conscious effort to forge palpable relationships among discrete works departs significantly from tradition. As many writers have observed, opp. 130, 131, 132, and the *Grosse Fuge* all make prominent use of a four-note configuration consisting, in its most common form, of a rising half-step, a leap upward of a diminished seventh or minor sixth, and a descending half-step.¹⁰ In fact, certain aspects of the genesis of all the late quartets suggest that these works comprise a unified corpus. The sketches for op. 127 show that, like opp. 132, 130, and 131, this quartet was originally intended to have more than the traditional four movements (the "extra" movements would have been a character piece entitled *La gaieté* and a brief Adagio before the finale). In all likelihood, the *Alla danza tedesca* from op. 130 was first envisioned as the fourth movement of op. 132, where it would have appeared in A major instead of G major. What began as part of the last section of the op. 131 finale ultimately provided the basis for the theme of the third movement (Lento assai) of op. 135.¹¹ Thus, significant elements of the finished works and of the process leading to their completion indicate that Beethoven has replaced the traditional opus – a series of complementary but independent works – with a system of interrelated compositions, each of which was weighty enough to receive its own opus number.

We can gain further insights into Beethoven's transformation of genre by examining what Ludwig Finscher calls the theory of the string quartet.¹² According to Finscher, this theory drew on two principal ideas: first, on the notion that the four-voice texture was the ideal medium for the presentation of lofty musical ideas, and second, on the analogy between few-voiced chamber music and a conversation among intelligent speakers. Both ideas had a long history, but they were first applied to the string quartet in the 1770s. Thereafter, in critical and theoretical accounts of the late eighteenth and early nineteenth centuries, each idea gave rise to a number of corollaries. The privileged status of the four-voice texture, for instance, became closely bound up with notions of the quartet both as a vehicle for the contrapuntal or learned style and as an object of study. At the same time, comparisons between the quartet and the art of conversation often imposed a hierarchy on the interlocutors and treated the genre as a vehicle for the comic style and as an object of elevated diversion. In other words, implicit in the theory of the quartet is a series of dialectical pairings: between equality and hierarchical disposition, between strict and free styles, and between reflection and diversion. It could be argued that Beethoven exploited the tensions between these pairings more thoroughly than any composer before or after him.

In the slow movement of op. 18 no. 2, for instance, two statements of an ornamented aria (Adagio) frame a central Allegro. While the opening statement is dominated by the first violin, thus evoking the *quatuor brillant* popular in France during the early nineteenth century, the cello comes into its own in the second statement, so that an elaborate *concertante* texture reminiscent of Mozart's late quartets and quintets results. But the two soloists are not treated in quite the same way. Reluctant to grant the cello equal rights, the violin reminds the rest of the group of its traditional role as *primus inter pares* in the ninth bar of the second Adagio, where the thirty-second notes of the corresponding bar in the first Adagio are replaced by an extravagant roulade in sixty-fourths.

Although the conflation of sonata-form rhetoric and fugal techniques often provided Haydn and Mozart with a venue for high comedy, Beethoven intensified the dialectic between learned and comic styles in the finale of op. 59 no. 3. The breathless, almost frantic quality of the movement is a direct consequence of its opening theme, a chatty fugue subject whose incredible length issues from a series of varied repetitions and sequences. This high-spirited spoof on the learned style reaches a highpoint in the development section, where a comic derivative of the subject – hurled from the top to the bottom of the texture – knows no better than to march up an octave and back down again.

A reflective attitude on the part of listeners and players is a condition for the appreciation of all of Beethoven's quartets, but the tension between reflection and diversion is particularly marked in his late contributions to the genre. Writing in 1827 and echoing the claim of many nineteenth-century critics that the late quartets do not divulge their secrets easily, the reviewer of op. 127 for the *Berliner allgemeine musikalische Zeitung* maintained that the work required repeated hearings in order to be understood. Only after careful study of the score will "the unfamiliar harmonies [of the quartet] seem like the white streaks of the Milky Way."[13] Indeed, it was probably not by chance that the scores and parts of the late quartets were published more or less simultaneously (in contrast, the scores of op. 18, op. 59, op. 74, and op. 95 were not issued until between nineteen and twenty-eight years after the appearance of the parts). An organization such as the Beethoven Quartet Society, founded in London during the 1840s, even took as one of its express aims the study of the late quartets from score.[14] The dialectic between initial befuddlement and subsequent illumination born of study – a theme closely associated with the reception of much twentieth-century music – is intimately related to the first reactions to Beethoven's late quartets. And even if Beethoven's chamber music for strings was not the first repertory to embody the tensions we have considered, it certainly brought them to the surface.

In analyzing Beethoven's transformation of generic norms, we should also keep in mind that the composer came of age during a period when the concept of genre itself was undergoing intense critical scrutiny. In the influential *Vorlesungen über dramatische Kunst und Literatur* (1808–09) of August Wilhelm Schlegel, a normative outlook on genre gives way to an historical point of view in which the homogeneity of the classical genres was contrasted with the heterogeneity of their modern counterparts, without thereby implying a negative value judgment of the latter. On the contrary, the generic hybridity of Shakespearean drama, a result of the mixture of tragic and comic elements, was just as aesthetically viable for Schlegel as the supposed purity of classical drama.[15]

August Wilhelm's writings represent a distillation of the thinking of his brother Friedrich, who imparted further dimensions to the new view of genre in a notebook entry of 1797 regarding the novel, the *ne plus ultra* of romantic literary forms: "The various types of novel [*Romanarten*] are determined by manner, tone, and tendency [*Manier, Ton, Tendenz*]. But for the classical genres, style, content, and form [*Styl, Stoff, Form*] are the determining factors."[16] Implicit in these statements is a series of binary oppositions wherein the first member of the pair describes the classical artwork, and the second its modern analogue: style/manner, content/tone, and form/tendency. In pairing style and manner Schlegel probably drew on a celebrated essay by Goethe entitled "Einfache Nachahmung der Natur, Manier, Stil" (1789). But while Goethe makes a value judgment (he views "manner" as the artist's ability to create "his own language to express in his own way what he has grasped with his own soul," whereas "style" designates the highest level of art since here the artist detects "some order in the multiplicity of appearances"), Schlegel views style and manner as value-free characteristics of different phases in the history of art.[17] In his second pair, Schlegel sets the clearly delineated images of classical poetry (content) against the finely nuanced – and sometimes obscure – moods of modern art (tone). And finally, the ascription of "tendency" to Romantic prose addresses the replacement of the self-sufficient, rounded forms of Classicism with the intentionally fragmented structures of modernity.[18]

These observations can provide us with a useful framework for an analysis of Beethoven's rethinking of generic norms. In the first half of the nineteenth century his works were both praised and blamed for embodying precisely those traits that the Schlegel brothers defined as touchstones of modern art. In a diary entry of 16 June 1816, the young Franz Schubert traced the "bizzarrerie" of current musical trends to the influence of "one of our greatest living artists" – certainly he meant Beethoven – who "unites and confuses the tragic and the comic, the pleasant and the repulsive" without compunction.[19] Yet Hermann Hirschbach, an early apologist for Beethoven's late music, expressed his admiration for the "novelistic" character of the late quartets.[20] Moreover, Beethoven and his circle were well aware of the literary accomplishments of the Schlegel brothers. An enthusiastic reader of Shakespeare in A. W. Schlegel's translation, Beethoven was introduced to the *Vorlesungen über dramatische Kunst und Literatur* by his friends and aristocratic patrons.[21] During his last years, Beethoven kept abreast of Friedrich Schlegel's career as journalist, critic, and diplomat, and was even encouraged by Count Moritz Lichnowsky to set Schlegel's translation of a story from the *Mahabharatà* of India.[22] In short, the ideas of the principal spokesmen for a romantic worldview were very much in the air in Beethoven's household.

Given this context, I would like to suggest that in the string chamber music of his earlier period Beethoven strove to establish an individual *manner*, in his middle phase he effected a transformation of the *tone* of the string quartet and quintet, and in his late quartets he challenged the aesthetic unity at the heart of Classicism by resorting increasingly to *tendency*.[23] (To be sure, all of these categories coexist throughout Beethoven's creative life, but in my view one element dominates in each of the various phases of his career.) Furthermore, some of the late works barely remain within the proprietary bounds of the quartet genre; in fact, they threaten to dissolve it.

II

Music historians often use the term "style" in two quite different senses. On the one hand, it may refer to a family of prescriptions and strategies shared by all composers of a period. When we speak of a "Classical style," for instance, we implicitly allude to the existence of just such a *lingua franca*. On the other hand, "style" may designate an individual mode of expression, a repository of personalized gestures that account for an artist's distinctive voice. In the latter case, we are in fact dealing with the artist's "manner."[24] Beethoven implied that he had attained an individual manner as a composer of string chamber music when, in a letter of 1 July 1801, he asked his friend Karl Amenda not to circulate the earlier version of what would become op. 18 no. 1, adding: "For only now have I learnt how to write quartets."[25]

Nonetheless, manner is unthinkable without style, that is, without the background provided by the works of those figures whose no less individual manners come together to create the dominant style of the day. In his chamber music for strings, Beethoven no doubt found this background in Haydn and Mozart. As has been frequently pointed out, both earlier composers left their imprint on Beethoven's first genuine contributions to the genre.[26] At the same time, his distinctive manner is just as pronounced in those works that at first appear to owe most to his predecessors.

During the decade before the publication of op. 18, Haydn completed his quartets opp. 71, 74, 76, and 77. Among the traits of these works that must have impressed Beethoven most deeply is the motivic economy of their sonata-form movements. But none of these pieces is quite so densely saturated with a fundamental motive and its derivatives as the first movement of Beethoven's op. 18 no. 1, in which the opening two-bar figure pervades every aspect of the design.[27] And here lies an essential ingredient of the Beethovenian manner, for the motive serves not only as an agent of unity, but also as an emblem of obstinacy and disruption within the ensemble. Only during the initial stage of the second group (mm. 57–71) is it absent, but immediately thereafter it reappears in dialogue between the cello and first violin. The fact that it is introduced in the upper reaches of the cello register – and is repeated twice more in the same range – lends it the character of an individual who can't bear to be left out of a conversation for long. Rather than supporting a discourse among four intelligent interlocutors, the motive seems to disturb it.

Beethoven's reliance on Mozart frequently extends to matters of large-scale design. At least two of the movements from op. 18 – the Scherzos of op. 18 nos. 4 and 5 – bear prominent traces of quartet movements by Mozart that Beethoven is known to have put into score: the finales of K. 387 and K. 464.[28] Here too, however, the surface similarities to the models are overwhelmed by Beethoven's individual manner. The finale of K. 387 and the Scherzo of op. 18 no. 4 conflate fugal techniques and sonata-form procedures,[29] and both movements likewise delineate a trajectory from imitative to homophonic textures. But Beethoven's movement embodies a contradiction between the nature of the thematic material and its subsequent development – a contradiction not present in Mozart's work. The main subject of the K. 387 finale is a deliberately archaic figure in long notes, ready-made for fugal treatment, while Beethoven's opening theme, despite its elaboration in a fugal exposition, is an easy-going German dance. Beethoven makes the point gracefully but emphatically at the end of the movement, where the tune is fitted out with a lilting, waltz-like accompaniment.

Although Beethoven continued to invoke earlier models in his middle-period chamber works[30] – and in the works of his later years as well – we sense strongly that he was interested in more than merely emulating his predecessors. Specifically, a fresh approach to the content of the musical text and a concomitant modification in its "tone" are both constitutive for the "new way," which, according to Czerny, Beethoven adopted around 1800.[31] It is common knowledge that Beethoven's middle-period chamber music is notable for its absorption of symphonic elements, but this feature alone cannot account for the new tone of this music. Writing in 1799, and acknowledging what was by then a widespread practice, August Kollmann related that chamber music for one-on-a-part ensembles can be "set in the style or character of a Symphony as well as a Sonata."[32] The new tone of Beethoven's quartets (and quintet) of the years 1801–09 seems rather to emanate from a confluence of several factors: an emphasis on musical topics derived from "public" genres such as the symphony and concerto, the placement of these topics in unusual contexts or their combination in unexpected ways, and the unfolding of lyrical ideas over larger spans than previously encountered in Beethoven's music.

None of the favored musical topics of the middle-period chamber music lacks precedents in the earlier literature. To take a few examples from the "Razumovsky" Quartets op. 59: the hymnic Molto Adagio of op. 59 no. 2 has a counterpart in the slow movement of Haydn's op. 76 no. 5; the use of popular tunes in op. 59 nos. 1 and 2 concords with the spirit if not the letter of any number of Haydn's quartet movements; the first violin's extravagant passage work leading into the finale of op. 59 no. 1 is firmly rooted in the virtuoso tradition of the *quatuor brillant*. What is striking in op. 59, however, is Beethoven's constant allusion to genres associated with a sizable community of listeners or performers, that is, his reliance on gestures drawn from the world of the theatre, the public concert, and the church. In addition to the hymn, the folk-song, and the concerto, these works abound in references to the march, and, of course, to the symphony. Nor is this feature surprising, for the Razumovsky quartets were stimulated in part by the violinist Ignaz Schuppanzigh's establishment in 1804 of a quartet whose *raison d'être* was public performance. But the public for which this group performed was a decidedly select one: probably no more than a hundred people could comfortably fit into the space where the players held their concerts, a hall attached to the restaurant Zum römischen Kaiser.[33]

The paradoxical situation of the quartet in early nineteenth-century Vienna – suspended midway between public and private venues in its mode of performance – is aptly reflected in the Razumovsky quartets, whose new tone can be said to derive from the accommodation of gestures drawn from the public genres to the chamber idiom. Beethoven's handling of march topics offers a case in point. Often Beethoven subjects these gestures to some form of rhythmic or metric differentiation, as in the middle segment of the first group in the first movement of op. 59 no. 1 (mm. 19–28), where the accentuation of the march-like theme suggests a metric displacement by half a bar. In the finale of the same quartet, the second group includes another march tune, this one driven by persistent dotted rhythms. Initially presented by the lower voices (mm. 206–09), the theme is combined with a figure in the violins in which the same dotted pattern is displaced by an eighth note, producing a propulsive rhythmic counterpoint. In both cases, an exoteric (or public) topic is transformed by an esoteric compositional technique.[34]

A comparable duality informs Beethoven's approach to symphonic topics, many of which stem directly from his own works. The principal theme of op. 59 no. 2, for instance, clearly alludes to the celebrated opening of the *Eroica*, where Beethoven contrasts a pair of hammer-strokes with a *cantabile* response. But the two openings are actually worlds apart, the quartet theme a more highly differentiated – and more tortured – relative of its symphonic cousin: the affirmative tonic hammerstrokes and triadic melody of the major-mode *Eroica* give way in the minor-mode quartet to an interrogative gesture (moving $I-V^6$), a cryptic, meandering answer, and a further heightening of tension through the transposition of the passage from tonic to Neapolitan.

In his middle-period quartets, Beethoven not only metamorphoses the topics of the public genres to accommodate them to a new context, he also combines them (and less genre-specific topics) in unexpected ways. The Allegro vivace of the first movement of op. 59 no. 3, for instance, is particularly rich in topical allusiveness. The opening first violin line represents an unusual cross between march and cadenza, though neither topic provides the actual content of the passage. On one hand, the topics neutralize one another; on the other hand, both appear in attenuated forms: the music is neither metrically square enough for a march nor brilliant enough for a cadenza. What remains, in other words, is an almost ineffable tone distilled from two of the most familiar topics of the period.

The special tone of op. 59 no. 1 also derives from a singular combination of topics. Here Beethoven makes telling use of the strategies for formal expansion and continuity he had developed earlier in the *Eroica* Symphony, and not only in the quartet's first movement, where we might expect them, but also in its second. The Allegretto vivace e sempre scherzando substitutes for the customary minuet or scherzo, but it hardly keeps to the modest dimensions of these traditional movement types; instead it unfolds as a broadly conceived sonata form replete with intensely developmental passages and a protracted coda (mm. 394–476). At the same time, the movement proceeds well beyond the conventional boundaries of the form; its twists and turns include a curiously bifurcated exposition (mm. 68–154 can be viewed as a reinterpretation of the exposition, mm. 1–67), a false recapitulation in Gb, the flat submediant (from m. 239), and an almost whimsical handling of tonal relations once the recapitulation actually gets under way (an entire segment appears a fifth *higher* than originally presented; cf. mm. 68–99 and 304–35). These features result not only from the blending of two formal paradigms – sonata and scherzo – but, in a deeper sense, from the incursion of the scherzo's playful essence, its characteristic tone, into a sonata-like design. The element of play is even apparent in matters of texture and ensemble: witness the manner in which the melodic substance of the movement assembles itself from motivic scraps – a teasing ostinato and a cryptic rejoinder – scattered among the voices at the opening. Hence the tone of the movement is a function of precisely those qualities that make it so difficult to classify.[35]

Concurrent with Beethoven's proclivity for goal-directed, developmental forms in the middle-period chamber music is a complementary penchant for lyricism. The first movement of the C major Quintet op. 29 represents something of a breakthrough in this respect. Here the decisive aspect is not merely Beethoven's employment of a number of lyrical themes, but rather his adoption of a pacing that tends toward leisurely, expansive unfolding.[36] The opening idea seems to inscribe circles around itself: both the first violin and cello simultaneously trace a neighbor-note pattern around the pitch C, with the lower instrument providing an exact mirror image of the melody in the violin; an undulating accompaniment in the viola adds to the general air of calm; finally, the varied repetition of the entire eight-bar phrase offers textural amplification in lieu of dynamic change. The expansiveness of the second and closing groups (mm. 41–93) hinges on Beethoven's enrichment of the tonal palette through modal mixture (A major vs. A minor) and a "purple patch" in the submediant (F) – techniques that were certainly not lost on Schubert.

Lyricism takes a somewhat different turn in op. 74. One of the first reviewers of the quartet was puzzled by Beethoven's decision to conclude the work with a set of variations, but as demonstrated by Elaine Sisman, the form of the finale is in many respects a logical consequence of what has transpired in the preceding movements. The varied treatment of the "harp" music in the first movement, the alternation of refrain and episodes in the second movement, and of Scherzo and Trio in the third, the rich embellishments of the hymnic main theme of the second movement – all of these traits foreshadow the design of the finale.[37] Most important for our purposes is their contribution to the quartet's lyric tone, which is not only a function of the thematic content, but even more a product of its treatment. The family of strategies employed in op. 74 (figural variation, alternation, embellishment) stand in opposition to the dynamic, goal-directed processes that regulate the musical flow over long stretches of the op. 59 quartets. Together they create a new and deeply expressive tone that will continue to inform Beethoven's musical language in the late quartets.

The *Quartetto serioso* op. 95, completed on the heels of op. 74 in 1811, likewise embodies traits that resonate with the late quartets. Specifically, its design is characterized by the gnomic quality that the early Romantics associated with "modern" as opposed to "classical" genres. As we have seen, Friedrich Schlegel expressed this difference by means of a simple binary opposition between finished "forms" and incomplete or fragmentary "tendencies." The latter category looms large in the reception history of Beethoven's late quartets, and indeed was often adduced to account for the difficulties of this music. According to Friedrich Rochlitz, the C♯ minor Quartet op. 131 posed a formidable – though not insurmountable – impediment to ready comprehension through its recourse to "whimsical fragmentation [*Zerstücken*] and hide-and-seek."[38] But what earlier reviewers often cast in a negative light can be turned to positive account if we concede that the fragment as a form in its own right may act as an ideal medium for conveying esoteric thought, and that the appearance of incompletion in "modern" art may serve as a powerful statement of the impossibility of attaining absolute aesthetic perfection.[39] In Beethoven's later string quartets, "tendency" assumes a number of guises, including radical compression of utterance and obliquely mediated contrasts at the local and global levels, and Beethoven further complements these features with an increasingly ironic attitude to musical form, a rhetorical strategy that questions a fundamental premise of the theory of the quartet.

Joseph Kerman has lucidly described the extreme abbreviation that characterizes the F minor Quartet op. 95: "one senses Beethoven's impatience (or fury) with conventional bridge and cadential passages of every kind – the more or less neutral padding material of the classic style."[40] The third movement (Allegro assai vivace ma serioso), for example, outwardly follows the plan of Beethoven's big, middle-period scherzos – A B A B' A' – but, as Kerman notes, the closing A' (Più Allegro) brings only the last twenty-four bars of the initial forty-bar A section in a reduction bordering on the grotesque.[41] In fact, the initial A itself is already a fragment. Consisting of a single, repeated strain (not the customary two), it begins in the minor dominant, C minor – the harmonic instability of which is intensified by the fact that the notated downbeat is perceived as an upbeat – but rapidly moves toward the tonic and remains there for the rest of the section. What we have, then, are the final segments of an implied three-part form: a retransition and a restatement of an "absent" A section.

A much larger piece, such as the opening movement of the second "Galitzin" quartet, op. 132, deals with its apparently fragmentary materials quite differently. The first group juxtaposes two ideas: (a) an Assai sostenuto featuring an imitative elaboration of the four-note cell that in varied forms appears in opp. 130, 131, and the *Grosse Fuge*; and (b) an Allegro dominated by a languid march tune distributed between cello and first violin. Both ideas are open-ended, incomplete, and – at first blush – incompatible. Much of the remainder of the movement, however, is devoted to showing that these seemingly disparate gestures are or can be related. In the first group, Beethoven establishes such a relationship in a highly oblique way (see Example 9.1). The return of the march in mm. 23–26 is coupled with an inversion (or permutation) of the four-note cell (F–E–G#–A), and in retrospect, the same combination is seen to have informed the first statement of the march, where segments of the inverted cell are rhythmically altered or hidden in the texture: its first two notes (F–E) come at the end of the first-violin cadenza in mm. 10–11, while the second pair of pitches (G#–A) are tucked away in the second violin line in mm. 12–13.

This relationship is initially difficult to grasp not only on account of the fragmentary quality of the elements combined but also because of Beethoven's uncanny treatment of the ensemble. Just as the march is split between first violin and cello (mm. 11–14), and then among the three upper voices (mm. 15–18), so too are segments of the four-note cell dispersed throughout the texture (first and second violins, mm. 10–13; viola and cello, mm. 13–16; first and second violins, mm. 23–26). Yet on reflection, we realize that here too Beethoven effects a rapprochement. The first violin appears to extend the march tune beginning at the last beat of m. 16, but the pitches of the extension (F–D#–F–E) are none other

Example 9.1 String Quartet op. 132, mvt. 1, mm. 1–27

than a variant of the second half of the four-note cell, and thus a logical outgrowth of the preceding appearance of the first half in the cello (mm. 15–16). With this simple gesture, Beethoven reveals the complementarity of march and motivic cell, and also of the curiously dispersed lines that wend their way through the ensemble.

When Beethoven wrote on the engraver's copy of the C♯ minor Quartet op. 131, upon sending it to his publisher Schott, that the work was "patched together from stolen bits of this and that," he surely meant his comment to be taken facetiously.[42] The C♯ minor quartet is one of his most tightly integrated compositions; indeed, for many critics it represents the apogee of Beethoven's achievement in the genre. But oddly enough, his statement comes very close to describing the remarkable compositional background for the second movement (Allegro ma non tanto) of op. 132. The middle section of the movement is built out of three dance-like episodes, all of them drawn from the many such pieces in a popular idiom that Beethoven composed between 1795 and 1800. The first episode, a musette, evolves from the four-bar vamp to an A major *Deutscher Tanz* for orchestra (WoO 8 no. 8); the second, shared by viola and first violin, derives from the second strain of a *Ländler* in the same key, and also for orchestra (WoO 13 no. 11); and the third, which flows directly from the second, recalls the melody of an A major *Allemande* for keyboard (WoO 81).[43] Beethoven arranges these fragments of earlier dances in a fragmentary manner: one tune hardly plays itself out before another begins. The technique seems more redolent of Stravinsky than of the early nineteenth century. Moreover, the dances are metrically altered, their easy-going triple time shifted one beat "to the left." The spirit of this procedure – aptly dubbed a "medley" principle by Kerman[44] – also informs the fifth movement (Presto) of op. 131, a droll piece in duple time which Beethoven patterned after his middle-period scherzos: A B A B A + coda. Here the contrasting B section evokes a dance medley whose fragmentary quality is underscored by the lack of a transition between the first dance, in E major, and the last two, in A major.

The discrepancy between the accessible content (or tone) of both movements and a formal pattern, the medley of fragments, which seems strangely out of place in a string quartet, offers a partial explanation for the sharp divergence of opinion among early critics of Beethoven's late music. While the majority of writers, whether proponents or not, found it to be enigmatic at best and inscrutable at worst, Robert Schumann counted himself among those "for whom Beethoven's late works [are] popular in the highest sense and clear as the sky."[45] Hermann Hirschbach, whose essay "Ueber Beethoven's letzte Streichquartette" appeared in four installments of the *Neue Zeitschrift für Musik* during the summer of 1839, shared Schumann's sentiments. For him, this supposedly arcane music was in fact teeming with jollity, good humor, and wit.[46] But as he also understood, the distance between Beethoven's playfulness and his pointed critique of the forms and materials of his time was a short one. And this brings us to an important complement to the "tendencies" or fragmentary utterances in which the late quartets abound. Specifically, the discrepancies among content, form, and context that we have noted in the scherzo-like movements of opp. 132 and 131 speak to the presence of an ironic dimension in this music.

As the rhetorical device whereby the speaker says one thing but means another, irony represents an affront to the discursive mode of the string quartet: it can be extraordinarily difficult to carry on a conversation with an ironist. More significantly, irony allowed Beethoven to expose as illusory the aesthetic wholeness of the musical language that he inherited from his predecessors but applied toward his own ends. Hirschbach heard in the finale of op. 127 "the most original, maddest humor imaginable," and supported his claim by calling attention to the "satirical" alternation of A♭ and A in the main theme and the "mocking" quality of the theme's final appearance, where it is transformed from duple meter to 6/8. The entire movement, he concluded, was conceived against an "ironic background," yet "in order to make fun of the world and its inhabitants, one must have long reflected on them."[47] Beethoven not only "reflected" on the ironic potential of melodic and rhythmic details in this movement, but also on one of the most sensitive moments in the sonata form: the point of reprise. The immense "false" recapitulation of the opening theme – which appears first in the subdominant, A♭ (mm. 145–76), and then in the tonic (mm. 187ff.) – has none of the good-natured wit usually associated with this formal ploy; it goes on far too long for that. Rather, it creates a curious bulge that deliberately sets the proportions of the movement askew. An even more radical employment of the same strategy occurs in the "trio" section of the second movement (Vivace) of op. 135. Here a frantic dance tune inches up from F to G and finally to A, where it gives way to an ostinato figure repeated nearly fifty times in the lower voices, over which the first violin leaps erratically.[48] Thus in both the finale of op. 127 and the second movement of op. 135, the continuity of the musical flow is intentionally cast in an ironic light. Organic wholeness gives way to "tendency."

The fragmentary quality that we have observed at the local level in Beethoven's late quartets operates at higher levels of structure as well. The overall design of op. 130 provides an excellent example. The slow movement of the Classical string quartet often brings together lyrical ideas and their embellished projections or variants, but in op. 130 these traits become the topics of separate movements: highly ornate melodic lines characterize the third movement (Andante con moto ma non troppo), while ultra-expressive lyricism is localized in the celebrated Cavatina. Similarly, the minuet or scherzo of the Classical quartet frequently unites the graceful gestures of the dance with witty rhythmic play. In op. 130, however, each characteristic is embodied in an independent movement, the witty side of the typical scherzo in a gnomic Presto, and the elegance of the typical minuet in the *Alla danza tedesca*. Therefore the sprawling six-movement design of op. 130 is the outcome of subjecting the affective unity of the Classical quartet to a process of fragmentation. Still, fragmentation or "tendency" alone will not account for all the difficulties posed by what remains to this day the most problematic of Beethoven's late quartets. The chief difficulty, of course, involves Beethoven's decision to replace the original finale, the *Grosse Fuge*, with a new finale at once lighter in tone and more modest in size. There is a strong likelihood that questions of genre – its limits and its possibilities – directly impinged on this decision.

Some writers consider the *Grosse Fuge*, which appeared with the rest of the quartet when it was first published, to be the "true" finale of op. 130.[49] In their opinion the new finale represents Beethoven's half-hearted capitulation to the wishes of his publisher Artaria, who exerted pressure on the composer through his friend Karl Holz. For Stefan Kunze, however, the fairly common practice among modern-day performers of restoring the *Grosse Fuge* to the quartet amounts to an "arrogant disregard for Beethoven's intentions," while the new finale should be viewed as a result of the composer's having taken to heart the public's rejection of the fugal finale.[50] The most controversial interpretation maintains that the late Bb major quartet is potentially *two* quartets, one ending with the *Grosse Fuge*, the other with the new finale, and each characterized by its own narrative trajectory.[51] But it seems plausible that if Beethoven had wished to retain the *Grosse Fuge* as an integral part of op. 130 (or had he wished to issue two separate quartets), nothing would have prevented him from doing so. In the summer and autumn of 1826, when the new finale was conceived, he was neither so physically nor psychologically debilitated that he couldn't have insisted on his preference. Hence I am inclined to agree with Kerman, who sees in the replacement of the *Grosse Fuge* "an acknowledgment (however reluctant, bad-tempered, greedy, etc.) that [Beethoven] saw something wrong with the way it sat in the quartet."[52] What, then, was wrong?

Before addressing the question directly, it will be worth recalling that there is nothing in the quartet repertory quite like the *Grosse Fuge*. Its design can be roughly summarized as follows:

1. *Overtura* — various meters (proleptic introduction)
2. *Fuga* — C (double fugue in Bb)
3. Meno mosso e moderato — 2/4 (fugato in Gb)
4. Allegro molto e con brio — 6/8 (episode in Bb)
5. Allegro molto e con brio — 6/8 (developmental fugue, beginning in Ab)
6. Meno mosso e moderato — 2/4 (fugato in Ab)
7. Allegro molto e con brio — 6/8 (reprise of episode; + coda)

In terms of their meter, tempo, and tonal scheme, these sections can be grouped into an introduction (section 1) and three "movements," as in a sonata or symphony, with section 2 functioning as an initial Allegro, section 3 as a slow movement, and sections 4–7 as a conflation of scherzo and finale. At the same time, the *Grosse Fuge* draws heavily on the tonal scheme and rhetorical disposition of the sonata form, with sections 2 and 3 acting as exposition, section 5 as development, and sections 6 and 7 as recapitulation. Obviously, the work also draws on a whole array of contrapuntal genres, including fugue, double fugue, fugato, and cantus-firmus variations.[53] (In Beethoven's hands, these genres take on an extreme character: while imitative textures normally represent the quintessence of the quartet's conversational idiom, here they often create the impression of fierce arguments among the members of the ensemble, especially in sections 2 and 5.) Allusions to dramatic or operatic genres emerge in the opening *Overtura*,[54] in the use of thematic reminiscences that help to unify the whole sprawling structure, and in the sublime *cantabile* of section 3. The notion of linking together a series of distinct sections or quasi-movements in turn recalls the keyboard fantasia tradition, and, for at least one writer, the symphonic poem.[55]

It would be misguided to pinpoint any one of these genres as the decisive one. What Beethoven created in the *Grosse Fuge* is rather a metagenre in which the canonical types – symphony, sonata, fugue, and so forth – are represented by some, but not all, of their constitutive features. If a "Classical" genre emanates from the confluence of style, content, and form, it could be said that what remains of the genres combined in the *Grosse Fuge* are some but not all of their qualities: the "manner" of the Classical sonata, the "tone" of a fugue, the "tendency" of a symphonic work.[56]

There is compelling logic in Beethoven's initial plan to conclude the late B♭ major quartet with the *Grosse Fuge*. Indeed, the earlier quartet repertory provides ample precedent for closing with a fugal movement: witness Haydn's op. 20 nos. 2, 5, and 6, and op. 50 no. 4, Mozart's K. 387, and Beethoven's own op. 59 no. 3. Moreover, on at least two previous occasions Beethoven had deemed a long, complex design comparable to that of the *Grosse Fuge* to be peculiarly fitting for the conclusion of a multi-movement work. But when a design such as this appears in the finales of the Third and Ninth symphonies, the earlier movements prepare for it not only in terms of their length and breadth, but also by way of their motivic density and seriousness of tone. In the late B♭ major quartet, however, only the opening movement remotely approaches the *Grosse Fuge* in breadth. As we have seen, the middle movements are *intermezzi* in which the unified affects of the Classical slow movement and scherzo are split into disparate "tendencies." In short, Beethoven must have realized that the *Grosse Fuge* threatened to upset the balance of power in the B♭ major quartet, dwarfing what had gone before – even the profoundly moving Cavatina that precedes it – through its sheer size and intensity.[57] His replacement of the *Grosse Fuge* with a new finale demonstrates a genuine concern for proportion – and also for generic propriety.

The new finale, though less challenging for listeners and players than the *Grosse Fuge*, represents more than a concession to popular taste. Beethoven's last completed movement includes many echoes of its earlier counterpart: the opening Gs in the viola ironically recall the emphatic initial gesture of the *Grosse Fuge*; its finely wrought *obbligato* textures answer to the gritty counterpoint of the original finale; the A♭ major episode prefacing its development corresponds to the first stages of section 5 of the *Grosse Fuge*; and finally, the closing phrases of this episode (mm. 132–40) bring a motivic relative of the four-note cell that runs through the *Grosse Fuge* and many of the other late quartets. The sonata form of the new finale may be no match for the imposing design of the *Grosse Fuge*, but its episodic asides and extended coda lend the movement considerable dimensions. Even with its new finale, the late B♭ major quartet nearly dissolves the genre that Beethoven played no small part in founding.

10 Sound and structure in Beethoven's orchestral music

LEON BOTSTEIN

In 1918, Paul Bekker argued that the symphonies of Beethoven had been revolutionary and still captured the imagination of listeners in a unique way. It was not the color and variety of Beethoven's instrumental sound or his ingenuity as an orchestrator that set his symphonic works apart, but rather his exploitation of the sheer volume and presence of sound; Beethoven opened up the sonic power implicit in the orchestral forces of Mozart and Haydn, and the symphony now became more than a sonata for orchestra.[1] Bekker suggested that Beethoven composed with a new "idealized picture of the space and listening public" in mind; his goal was to reach a "mass" public with the symphony, and to create a "community" through the act of shared listening. That community was far reaching, representing humankind, a spectrum of listeners that extended beyond the aristocracy and embraced those liberated from the shackles of the past by the ideas and events surrounding the French Revolution. Beethoven's orchestral music, through its implied extra-musical narratives and its impact on listeners, became associated not only with Romanticism but also pre-1848 political liberalism.[2]

Bekker construed Beethoven's political and social ambition as a causal element in the act of symphonic composition. Beethoven sought a clear break with an older tradition of symphonic writing that had been directed at a circumscribed public consisting of the elite connoisseur and patron in favor of a strategy that could reach beyond and forge solidarity within a wider audience. He did not strive to emulate "beauty" in music in a manner readily appreciated by a public convinced of its refined sensibilities. Hence, in Bekker's view, he departed from a reliance on Mozartian melodies as thematic subjects in the symphony and showed a marked preference for "easily grasped" and "riveting" motivic gestures. For Bekker, Beethoven was the quintessential "sentimental" composer, in Schiller's vocabulary of praise, who was succeeded, at best, by the "naive" music of Schubert and Bruckner. Bekker's characterization of Beethoven's symphonic agenda, despite its formulation in early twentieth-century political categories, was an extension of the ideology of symphonic composition articulated by Johann Georg Sulzer in the mid 1770s. The purpose of larger-scale instrumental composition was to "maintain a listener in the same emotional state for a period of time."

Main themes must have "sufficient clarity and comprehensibility of expression such that anyone hearing it will immediately understand this language of the heart." Repetition and development were essential in order to sustain extra-musical meaning. Within instrumental music, the symphony was particularly suited to "grandeur, passion and the sublime"; it was a genre of "dignity."[3]

Beethoven's unique contribution, as Bekker surmised, was the transformation of the tradition of the sublime and the dignified towards monumentality, dramatic intensity, and universality, conceived in a political and social as well as aesthetic sense. This was already recognized by some contemporary critics: E. T. A. Hoffmann noted, comparing Ludwig Spohr's First Symphony with Beethoven, that Beethoven did not keep within the "bounds of calm dignity," particularly in his choice of motivic materials. That contemporary listeners recognized this change was crucial to the construction of a nineteenth-century musical culture in which Beethoven emerged as the pivotal historical protagonist.[4] Bekker's emphasis on monumentality and spiritual universality in Beethoven's orchestral music reflected his intent to connect its sustained aura in the *fin-de-siècle* concert repertoire with Mahler's symphonies (e.g. Mahler's Eighth Symphony as the successor to Beethoven's Ninth). Bekker's method drew on an appeal to criteria beyond the boundaries of textual analysis. However polemical his prose was in terms of the cultural politics of 1918, his approach is reminiscent of strategies taken by Beethoven's contemporaries. The most influential views were those of Hoffmann, for whom Beethoven's instrumental work "unveils before us the realm of the mighty and the immeasurable . . . it sets in motion the machinery of awe, of fear, of terror." Hoffmann took care to link his allusions to the overpowering sound of the music, the "shaft of blinding sunlight" to Beethoven's "rational awareness" and his command of form: "all is directed towards a single point." The objective was to "sustain one feeling in the listener." There was no lack of "real unity and inner coherence," since in Beethoven, as in Shakespeare, the focus on communicating a particular sensibility and meaning – even of infinitude – was complete.[5]

The striking presence of the orchestral sound and the extremes of Beethoven's orchestral style were sometimes rejected: H. G. Nägeli criticized in 1826, with some disdain, the "exaggerated piling up of sonority" and the "false consequences of the emphasis on colossal character [*materiellen Colossalität*]" of the music.[6] But the overpowering effect of the orchestral sound led critics in the 1830s to stress in Beethoven a novel sense of integration and unity. Gottfried Wilhelm Fink found in Beethoven's orchestral music an organic approach to compositional development which successfully reconciled individuality and subjectivity with an overarching sense of a totality; Beethoven developed in his "giant works," his symphonies, the proper scale and materials for communicating an all embracing universality utilizing a striking array of disparate elements and contrasts. The focus on monumentality did not necessarily preclude an appreciation for the music's dynamism and drama. In 1837 Ferdinand Hand highlighted the dramatic dimension in Beethoven's symphonic music, particularly the conception of the orchestra representing a chorus, as in Greek tragedy. Beethoven's orchestra suggested gravity and profundity that "moved the concerns of humankind"; his formal procedures reached a sense of universality by using the orchestra to generalize the particular. Yet within this noble agenda, as Robert Schumann observed, Beethoven attacked the public at the very moment it seemed most comfortable and relaxed, ready to return to a more limited and purely aesthetic experience; using the orchestra, he hit listeners over the head with a stone – or at least threw one at them – a characteristic later identified with Mahler's modernist tendencies and his subversion of audience complacency and aestheticism.

Even though Bekker conceded that Beethoven's orchestral music was widely known in its piano versions, he argued that its real magic could only be encountered properly in an orchestral performance in a public space; the piano reductions were to the music as reproductions in art books were to large-scale canvases. Bekker took a somewhat different view from Hoffmann, even though both considered the material sound of the instruments in a grand space properly crucial to an appreciation of a work's true character. As Hoffmann observed, a Beethoven symphony achieved the massing of sound, the contrasts, the broad strokes and sharp outlines characteristic of an altarpiece or large painting designed to be viewed by large masses of people within an imposing public arena; it was resistant to adaptation for the intimacy of the sitting room.[7]

Carl Dahlhaus offers a synthesis of Bekker's early twentieth-century line of argument and the claims of early nineteenth-century criticism by linking the special prestige accorded to instrumental music in the early nineteenth century as an aesthetic and philosophical vehicle, as "sublime" (following the evolution of such claims from Sulzer to Hoffmann), with the monumental dimensions of sound, purpose, audience, and space that interested Bekker. Monumentality and the dramatic, which was a category derived in part from the late eighteenth-century notion of the noble and the sublime (and from literary parallels to music), were reconciled in Beethoven's orchestral music, which represented a fusion of late eighteenth-century ideals of taste, connoisseurship, and learning (*Bildung*) and a novel public function, suggestive of Jürgen Habermas's notion of the emergence of a public realm (*Öffentlichkeit*) before 1848. The highest form of aesthetic appreciation, the capacity to grasp the autonomous ideas and qualities of instrumental music required "pure" musical thinking; with Beethoven it acquired a second and equally integral meaning, as the medium through which humanistic ideals that transcended the individual, the subjective, and the purely musical could be communicated. Beethoven's orchestral music acquired special significance as the carrier of new political and social ideas; it reflected back on the listener an image of the self consistent with a new age. The dimension of his orchestral music, particularly the symphonies, that revealed this possibility was its sonic scale; it reflected psychological sensibilities and political aspirations encouraged by the music's texture, dynamic extremes, and aggressive presence.[8]

The impact of Beethoven's symphonies has been twofold. On the one hand, after his death, the symphony as genre achieved a unique prestige as an experience of solidarity (i.e. the objective and universal) and personal engagement (i.e. the subjective and the individual) at the same time that it remained tied to highly prized aristocratic traditions of taste and connoisseurship. On the other hand, Beethoven's example was paralyzing through its evident novelty and boldness, making imitation by successors nearly impossible and deviation from the Beethovenian model daunting at best. Symphonic thinking, as Dahlhaus argued, therefore was forced out of the confines of the symphony and invaded other musical genres, even as later composers also grappled with the Beethovenian challenge in their own symphonic works.[9] Beethoven's orchestral music, as Bekker knew, was the anchor of the repertory of the late nineteenth-century orchestral concert; it served as the proper measure of any venture into orchestral composition (including the tone poems of Richard Strauss) in which intimacy, formal complexity (and the use of procedures linked to sonata form), and subtlety were attempted on a grand dramatic and sonic scale with either overt or covert extra-musical meanings. Bekker even argued that the clarity with which Beethoven commanded the texture and power of the orchestra had been sacrificed by the greatest exponents from the two generations after Beethoven. Mendelssohn, Schumann, and Brahms avoided the all-embracing idealism and ambition of Beethoven and intentionally darkened – if not muddied – the orchestral sound.[10] Through the writings of A. B. Marx, a normative theory of instrumentation and orchestral sound took hold (even for those who explicitly sought to circumvent it such as Liszt), tied to an idealized conception of symphonic structure based on thematic development. The dominant ideal of orchestral sound and compositional procedure was based on a mid nineteenth-century view of Beethoven's decisive historical example.[11]

By the early twentieth century, the Beethoven symphonies had achieved unique status as emblems of modernity's finest aesthetic achievement as well as its worst dilemma: such heights would never again be reached. They were the yardstick against which all subsequent orchestral music had to be measured.[12] The symphonies represented at once the culmination of Classicism and the model of Romanticism. Precisely for this reason, so-called improvements to Beethoven's orchestration (such as those by Mahler), although always controversial, were accepted as necessary, to ensure the inherent and unquestioned contemporaneity of the music.[13]

Since the texts of the orchestral music of Beethoven have become inseparable from the traditions of their performance and reception, it makes sense to approach the symphonies and overtures not in terms of the chronology of composition, but rather in terms of the ways they have been differentiated, in the popular imagination, by subsequent generations.[14] One symphony stands out as the most talked about, most played, and most influential: no. 5 in C minor op. 67, which was begun in 1803 and finished in the years 1807–08. Symphony no. 6 in F major op. 68, the *Pastoral*, which Beethoven composed during the same period as no. 5 and premiered at the same concert in 1808, has been performed less often than nos. 3 and 7, but it immediately took on a special role as a harbinger of Romanticism through its experimentation with tone painting and programmatic expressiveness. Because of its program the Sixth Symphony has remained the most controversial symphony after the Ninth, and yet it was the program that made it very influential in the later nineteenth century.[15] Following the Fifth Symphony in popularity and familiarity are Symphony no. 3 in E♭ major op. 55, which was finished in 1803 and premiered in 1804, and Symphony no. 7 in A major op. 92, written in 1811 and 1812 and first performed in 1813. The Third Symphony, the *Eroica*, has held the second place of honor right after no. 5, owing to its significance in the Beethoven canon as representing a dramatic advance in the evolution of the composer's mature style. The many well-known accounts regarding its initial dedication to Napoleon have lent it a particular aura.[16] Although Symphonies 3 and 7 have been almost as popular as 5 on the concert platform they have exerted somewhat less of a hold on the popular imagination, even though the theme of the *Marcia funebre* of the Third Symphony became almost as popular as the opening bars of Symphonies 5 and 6.

Symphony no. 1 in C major op. 21, completed and first performed in 1800, has suffered by comparison, owing to its reputation as being Haydnesque and less truly Beethovenian in the sense established by Symphonies 3 and 5. Symphony no. 8 in F major op. 93, composed in 1812 and first performed in public in 1814, has maintained an affectionate and stable but subordinate place among the symphonies. Symphony no. 2 in D major op. 36, composed in 1801 and 1802 and premiered in 1803, and no. 4 in B♭ major op. 60, written in 1806 and performed in the spring of

1807 and the winter of 1808, have remained the least familiar of the nine, although no. 4 has benefited from its placement between 3 and 5. And then of course there is Symphony no. 9 in D minor op. 125, completed in 1824, which for future generations of composers and listeners has been in a class by itself, reserved for special adulation and emulation as well as consternation and skepticism.[17]

Posterity has shown good instincts. In terms of chronology, the popular placement of the Ninth Symphony in a special category is justified, since it was completed more than ten years after the Eighth. Historically speaking, Symphonies 5 and 6 form a pair. Both performer and listener can benefit from a close comparison of these two seemingly contrasting yet interrelated works. Symphonies 3 and 7 possess similarities in terms of structure and scale, particularly in their second and third movements. Likewise, Symphonies 1 and 8 contain affinities with one another, as do 2 and 4. The "Battle Symphony," *Wellington's Victory, or The Battle of Vittoria* op. 91, from 1813, although termed a symphony by Beethoven, has been conveniently but understandably excluded from the canon of Beethoven's symphonies and orchestral works. It is, however, a significant source for the understanding of Beethoven's approach to orchestral sound and his notions of the narrative possibilities of instrumental music.[18]

The centrality of the nine symphonies has helped to sustain the popularity of the overtures. But – in their own right – these works have held a secure place in the concert repertory, in part owing to their more overt correspondence between drama and music. The overtures encouraged theorists such as Marx to examine the interrelationships between sonata form and dramatic narrative, particularly the ways in which formal procedures corresponded with idealized projections of human reflection, psychological development, and aspirations regarding self-realization. The most famous and popular overtures have been *Egmont* op. 84 (1810), *Leonore* no. 3 op. 72a (1806), and *Coriolan* op. 62 (1807). The next tier of performance frequency includes *Fidelio* op. 72b (1814) and *The Creatures of Prometheus* op. 43 (1801). *The Ruins of Athens* op. 113 (1811), *The Consecration of the House* op. 124 (1822), and *Leonore* no. 2 op. 72a (1805) – unfortunately too often overshadowed by no. 3, although it may be a more compelling work – still appear less frequently. *Leonore* no. 1 op. 138 (1807) and *King Stephen* op. 117 (1811) remain the least familiar.

II

The analysis of the nine symphonies of Beethoven in terms of form and structure is nearly inexhaustible as a subject and it has been well covered.[19] It can be misleading to separate matters of orchestration – issues of how Beethoven uses the orchestra – from structural questions, but isolating these aspects is revealing, because Beethoven's ear for instrumental color, texture, and timbre was, as Bekker suggests, integral to his compositional process. Despite the conceits of twentieth-century modernists, particularly Alban Berg, neither a piano reduction of a Beethoven symphony nor an analysis that does not take into account the character of the instrumental voices in the context of issues of structural, harmonic, or thematic development can do justice to the music or reveal its formal properties. The ideological apparatus favored by Schoenberg (taken in part from Adolf Loos's 1908 essay, "Ornament and Crime," which inspired a convenient separation of the decorative and ornamental from musical ideas and structure) is not germane.[20] In Beethoven these variables are intertwined. The use of piano reductions may be strategically necessary as an intermediate step in analysis, but the extraction of elements of instrumental specificity and color only temporarily simplifies the task. Even the effect of the massing of orchestral forces is lost. In the end, as Peter Gülke argues (not only for Beethoven but also for Mahler and Bruckner), the physicality of the orchestral sound in Beethoven's symphonies and overtures is more than an elaborate facade or the mere sensual realization of abstract musical ideas.[21]

The creation of sounds coming from the entire orchestra, the roles given to solo wind instruments, the varied demands made on the different constituents of the orchestra, and the mode of integration and combination of the elements of the orchestra were part and parcel of Beethoven's originality and novelty – particularly his role for the Romantic movement as the champion of inner subjectivity.[22] Too often we assume that Beethoven's ideas somehow "forced" an extension of traditional instrumental practices and possibilities, as in the case of the use of the violins in the *Leonore* Overtures nos. 2 and 3 (the virtuosic solo bridge section to the codas) and in the *Egmont* Overture (the extensive writing for the upper registers). The reverse seems more plausible: that Beethoven heard in his imagination what violins could sound like in high registers or in rapid unison asymmetrical solo figurations. Thus innovative aural projection of instrumental sound in its material realization could lead to motivic and thematic ideas and their elaborations. Ideas and their materiality are inseparable in Beethoven, and this helps explain why, when "extreme" uses of instruments occur, listeners are struck with notions such as rebellion, radicalism, individuality, and subjectivity. The notion of orchestration as an act subsequent and subordinate to compositional invention does not fit the Beethoven symphonies. The orchestral substance of musical events is indivisible from the form, the core structure, and the ideas that are – in and of themselves – adequately represented in piano reductions or described in terms of pitch, rhythm, and harmonic structure in analytic prose and diagrams.

The sound of the symphonies, from the moment of their first appearance, captured the imagination of contemporary listeners. The sequence of B♭s, followed by E♭ and F and B♭ an octave lower, hammered out by the two horns in the transition to the second group (mm. 59–62) in the first movement of the Fifth Symphony, serves its function in large measure because of the bold instrumentation. Likewise, the choice of two bassoons in mm. 303–06 in the parallel passage in the recapitulation does more than underscore the expected harmonic contrast. The famous opening of the movement, which calls initially for clarinet doubling and then bassoon doubling of the strings followed by the use of the whole orchestra in m. 18 and subsequently a *fortissimo* statement in m. 22 without trumpets and timpani, is a calculation in the service of a particular sound on which the structural logic of the movement depends. The same observation holds for the dramatic use of the timpani in the second movement of the *Eroica* and in the Scherzo of the Ninth Symphony. Instrumentation was a basic element of the genesis, allure, and greatness of these works.

A remarkable aspect of Beethoven's use of the orchestra is the sheer variety and extreme range of color, texture, and sound that he achieved without adding substantially to the forces used by Haydn and Mozart. Only Symphonies 3, 5, 6, and 9 use more instruments than can be found in Haydn and Mozart: doubled winds (flute, oboe, clarinet, bassoon), doubled brass (two horns, two trumpets), timpani, and strings. The *Eroica* Symphony, which marks the first time Beethoven used more than the traditional complement of two horns in an orchestra, employs only one additional French horn. In the Fifth Symphony, three trombones, piccolo, and a contrabassoon appear, but only in the last movement. The use of trombones had numerous precedents, particularly in late Mozart (e.g. *The Magic Flute,* the C minor Mass K. 427/417a, and the Requiem). But Beethoven's use of trombones and the contrabassoon owes most to Haydn's instrumentation in *The Seasons.* In Symphony no. 6 the parallel to *The Seasons* is apparent, since the trombones appear for the first time in the remarkable "Storm" of the fourth movement, which was directly inspired by the uncannily similar storm in the "Summer" section of Haydn's oratorio. Beethoven's use of the contrabassoon and piccolo in Symphonies 5, 6, and 9 also can be compared to passages in Haydn's oratorio and, in the case of the former, to *The Creation* as well. In the first three movements of the *Pastoral* Symphony, Beethoven is once again content with the conventional forces of his predecessors.

The Ninth Symphony tells a somewhat different story. Four horns are part of the basic sound. Trombones appear in the Scherzo and again, with contrabassoon, piccolo, and percussion (triangle, bass drum, and cymbal), in the last movement. Here an operatic precedent can be adduced, yet once more the practice of Haydn is evident (e.g. in the case of the percussion, consider the closing chorus of "Autumn" in *The Seasons*), since the use of this expanded sound palette in the orchestra coincides with the presence of chorus and solo voices. In the last movement of the Ninth, Beethoven of course departs entirely from the orchestral symphonic complement and appropriates conventions from opera and secular and sacred oratorio. Nevertheless, in the purely orchestral moments of the last movement he explores the extremes of sound and register, using contrabassoon and piccolo to powerful effect.

In Beethoven's orchestral music, perhaps only the use of four horns marks a sustained departure from Haydn and Mozart. Four horns are required for *King Stephen*, all three *Leonore* overtures, *Egmont*, *Fidelio*, and *The Consecration of the House*. Apart from the last of this group (which is chronologically close to the Ninth Symphony), each of these has an explicitly dramatic narrative. The influence of such a clear programmatic and dramatic function also explains the enlarged orchestra Beethoven employed for *Wellington's Victory*, which, in addition to percussion, requires six trumpets as well as piccolo and trombones.

Given Beethoven's essentially conservative instrumentation, why does his orchestral music sound so distinctive and radically different from that of his predecessors and contemporaries? Here are a few basic suggestive but not exhaustive answers:

Dynamics and punctuation

The distinctive feature of Beethoven's sound world that remains most evident to the lay listener is his manipulation of stable instrumental groupings – including the frequent use of the entire orchestral tutti – to create an exceptionally wide and rapidly shifting range of dynamics. The placement and use of dynamic shifts are integral compositional elements in Beethoven, particularly when a reduction or increase in the forces used is not the mechanism by which dynamic punctuations and shifts in the dynamics are achieved. Beethoven separates dynamic level from color and timbre and renders it a discrete element through orchestration. A classic example is the introduction to the first movement of Symphony no. 4 (Example 10.1). A sustained *piano* is punctuated periodically by *sforzandi* (with slight increases in the ensemble) and then erupts into a *fortissimo*. In the *fortissimo*, Beethoven adds timpani and trumpets, but in the previous thirty-five bars all other instruments are at work communicating a delicate balance of timbres, colors, and dynamic contrast.

Perhaps the most revealing markings in Beethoven are levels of *forte* (most often *più f*, *f*, and *ff*) and the *sforzando* (*sfz*), *sforzando–piano* (*sfp*),

Example 10.1 Symphony no. 4 op. 60, mvt. 1, Introduction

and to a lesser extent the *forte–piano* (*fp*). Beethoven layered sound, carefully reserving double *forte*. Yet even within a sustained *ff* sound, as in the closing bars of the first movement of Symphony no. 9, he called for *sf*, with the whole orchestra playing. Likewise, Beethoven combined punctuation and differing levels of sound with crescendo and diminuendo. But he rarely failed to employ surprise and sudden dynamic shifts. The other side of the coin to Beethoven's nearly bizarre habit of shocking the listener with abrupt interjections and sustained increases in volume is, obviously, his use of extreme levels of softness. Here again, Beethoven used stable sound groupings and often the whole orchestra. The third movements of Symphonies 3 and 7 offer fine examples of subtle uses of *piano* and *pianissimo* with quite large forces. But it is the use of the *sforzando* that is most characteristic of Beethoven.

Example 10.1 (*cont.*)

The other technique that Beethoven employed to achieve radical dynamic contrasts and powerful interruptive and sudden punctuations was to disaggregate the elements of the orchestra. Here again Symphony no. 4 makes the point. In the first movement, Beethoven achieved a variety of color and shadings by breaking down the orchestra, using solo instruments and single voices in the strings, and alternating winds with each other and strings. He even resorted to single lines, as if to heighten the sense of impending contrasts and the echo of those already heard. The same observation holds for the first and third movements of the *Pastoral* Symphony. In the last movement, Beethoven shifted from massive full sound to solo sounds abruptly, as in the closing bars. In this movement he also found ways, using the whole orchestra, to have accentuated moments speak through effective uses of *sforzandi* within a full orchestral sound.

The orchestral unison

Classic treatises in orchestration have pointed correctly to Beethoven's skillful use of solo woodwinds and horns, as well as novel combinations of winds and brass. But equally striking are his full orchestral unisons and different registrations of the same pitches or pitch sequences when the entire orchestra is playing. This is perhaps the aspect that inspired Bekker to stress the sheer force of Beethoven's orchestra, which clearly set the stage for a technique we more readily associate with Bruckner. Beethoven exploited a wide range of registration as well as density in doublings that give weight to the sound. Two unison passages are exemplary, one from the first movement of the Ninth Symphony (mm. 17–20) and the other from the *Coriolan* Overture (mm. 84–91). At the same time, under the rubric of unisons, Beethoven's skill in layering rhythmic patterns and the use of the entire orchestra in moments of frenzied activity to assert an overriding rhythmic grid without loss of clarity is stunning. The last movements of Symphonies no. 7 and no. 8, in quite different ways, show how he marshaled the entire orchestra to assert and underscore a single rhythmic pattern. This technique accounts for the effectiveness of the dramatic outbursts of energy which we associate with Beethoven. The reinforcing of repeated patterns using the whole orchestra over a sustained period of time gives the music a driving insistence. Repetition does not become static. Symphony no. 9, particularly in the first movement, represents this aspect of Beethoven's use of the orchestra most powerfully.

An early example of Beethoven's use of orchestral massing on behalf of a motivic cell and harmonic change can be found in the introduction to the first movement of the Fourth Symphony. The *ff* passage, three measures before the Allegro vivace, on an F major chord that extends the harmonic journey from the opening B♭ minor to B♭ major – including the prior allusion to D minor – emphasizes the surprise. The harmonic effect is heightened significantly by orchestration, particularly the As in three octaves in the violins that immediately precede the *ff* (marked *pp crescendo*). This is the first *ff* outburst in the work and the first use of trumpets in the ensemble. Similar brief interjections of an *ff* massing of the orchestra, in fact, become a distinguishing feature of the Allegro vivace. The transition to the recapitulation is a brilliant example of how Beethoven reassembled his orchestral forces and varied not only thematic and harmonic ideas from the exposition, but orchestral devices as well.

The roles of the oboe, clarinet, bassoon, and horn

The oboe solo in the recapitulation of the first group in the first movement of the Fifth Symphony became a normative example of oboe solo writing in nineteenth- and twentieth-century treatises on instrumentation. Also exemplary are the roles of the oboes in the *Marcia Funebre* of the *Eroica,* and in the third movement of the *Pastoral.*[23] Equally distinct are the opening bars of Symphony no. 7 and the use of the oboe in the development section of the first movement and later at m. 300 of that movement.[24] Beethoven's reliance on the oboe per se was not unusual. Two oboes, together with a pair of horns, were basic to the eighteenth-century Classical orchestra. Therefore it is primarily through the use of clarinet and bassoon that Beethoven transformed the role of the woodwinds in the orchestra. The passage for solo clarinet and bassoon in m. 101 in the A major section of the second movement of the Seventh Symphony provides a fine example. The use of the clarinet throughout Symphony no. 4 (particularly in the second movement) and in the finale of Symphony no. 3 also deserves mention. Most famous of all is the role the clarinet plays in the final movement of Symphony no. 6. The flexible and prominent use of the clarinets by Beethoven changed the possibilities for color and timbre in the disposition of the whole wind section in contrasting groupings, particularly in the combination of oboe and bassoon; flute, oboe, and bassoon; and clarinet, bassoon, and oboe. The second movement of the Fifth Symphony and the third movement of the Ninth (Example 10. 2) make this point brilliantly.[25]

Beethoven also extended the possibilities of the bassoon – as he did with the viola and cello – beyond its traditional role as a bass-line support instrument in the Classical orchestra. His approach to the bassoon reflects the influence of Mozart, who used this instrument to great effect, particularly in his piano concertos. Beethoven gave a solo role to the bassoon in the second movements of the Fifth and Sixth Symphonies, and with the horns, oboes, and clarinets established the unusual and riveting sonority of the opening bars of the second movement of the Seventh. The wind choir at m. 23 of its first movement shows Beethoven's particular affinity for the oboe–clarinet–bassoon combination. A fine example of

Example 10.2   Symphony no. 9 op. 125, mvt. 3, mm. 83–90

his use of the bassoon as a solo instrument can also be found in the last movement of Symphony no. 2 at m. 98, in the first movement of Symphony no. 4, the Allegro vivace at m. 65, and in the last movement, particularly at m. 184. It is important to note that Beethoven was keenly aware of how exposed and unusual this passage was. He let the bassoon play solo (followed by the cellos), but when the comparable passage returns at m. 297 he gave it to the clarinet, doubled by the violin, until he created a reminiscence of the earlier event by letting the bassoon finish the solo passage – *pp* – followed by a wild *ff* extended elaboration of the figuration by the strings. Widor in particular praised the use of the bassoon in this symphony.[26] Beethoven explored the upper reaches of the bassoon sound, thereby permitting it to combine with the oboes and clarinets more than with the horns – a role the bassoons often play in late Haydn symphonies (e.g. in Symphony no. 99). A remarkable and virtuosic use of the bassoons can be found in the opening section of *The Consecration of the House* (Example 10.3).

The shift in the use of the bassoon towards the upper winds helped

Example 10.2 (*cont.*)

create the space in the orchestra for Beethoven to experiment with an
expanded, prominent, and varied role for the French horn. The subtle and
extended use of the French horn is one of the salient features of
Beethoven's orchestration technique. These instruments not only provide
harmonic background, or combine with trumpets and timpani in tuttis,
but they also state and vary themes. And they play a lyrical role. In
Symphonies no. 3 and no. 5, and the trio of the third movement of no. 7,
not to mention the *Fidelio* Overture or the rest of the Seventh Symphony
and all of Symphony no. 9, the French horn claims a unique melodic, harmonic, and rhythmic role – a central one – in Beethoven's orchestra. The
horns work with the woodwinds as well as with the brass, as in the case of
the second movement of Symphony no. 8. The prominence of the horns
helps to distinguish Beethoven's orchestral sound.

Experimentation with the string choir
Beethoven's use of an expanded range on the violin in the upper register
and his daring experimentation with extended solo figuration by the

Example 10.3 Overture *The Consecration of the House* op. 124, mm. 44–48

entire violin section has been noted earlier. Equally striking is his varied conception of pizzicato, martelé strokes, and staccato. Although Beethoven picked up where Haydn left off (Haydn's role as the orchestral experimenter par excellence can never be overstated; neither can Beethoven's debt to him in matters of orchestration), he went much further. In the voicing of the five-part string section of the orchestra, Beethoven increased the independent melodic and solo alto role played by the viola section. He utilized the contrabass section independent of the cellos as no previous composer had. As Widor noted, judging from his symphonies, Beethoven would have been the ideal composer to write a double bass concerto.[27] By strengthening the role of the basses he created the opportunity for the cello section to function apart from providing the bass line, permitting it to take on a greater lyric and thematic role in the orchestra. Consider, for example, the use of the violas and cellos within the opening of the Allegro con brio of Symphony no. 2 and in the second movement of the Fifth Symphony. The cellos play a notable leading role at the end of *Coriolan*. In terms of the bass section, the second movement of Symphony no. 3 and the last movement of no. 9 are the most obvious examples of Beethoven's exploration of the possibilities of the lowest string register. These three changes – expanded independent roles for the viola, cello, and bass – greatly expanded the possibilities offered in terms of color and texture by the string section. This is most apparent when Beethoven employed the string section as the main engine, so to speak, in variation form, as in movements 2 and 4 in the Third Symphony, movement 2 in Symphony no. 7, and movement 3 in Symphony no. 9. The widening of the range of string color enabled him to use the strings to achieve a kind of transparent yet harmonically interesting sound in a *piano* dynamic unlike anything heard in Mozart or Haydn. In addition, Beethoven exploited the possibility that a string section can realize both angularity and rhythmic contrast if used as an obbligato-like background. This is perhaps most evident in the last movement of Symphony no. 7, particularly in its closing moments.

Beethoven's string writing capitalized on more than the homogeneity of the sound offered by the mass of strings that dominates the orchestra. He understood the possibilities inherent in string instruments to achieve contrasts in timbre and conflicting colors. The use of double stops and broken chords – the repeated statement of chords in the strings and the punctuation of lyric textures by a nearly percussive use of string instruments with single notes – are hallmarks of Beethoven's string orchestral sound. The scherzi of his symphonies offer the best examples. Last but not least, the strings in Beethoven are brilliantly used as the orchestra *in nuce*, as in the openings of Symphonies nos. 5, 6, and 9, to announce the basic elements of the movement. But it is in his use of the strings – discontinuously – in short interventions alternating with winds or with winds and brass as a percussive and rhythmic entity that much of the novelty in string use resides. The strings lose their exclusive dominant role in providing the continuity of the line. Symphony no. 7 reveals this aspect of Beethoven's technique most consistently.

The timpani

It has already been noted that Beethoven relished punctuation and discontinuity in his orchestral textures as a necessary component of the statement and elaboration of his motivic and thematic material. No instrument was better suited to assist in this task than the timpani. The last movement of the First Symphony contains an early example, from mm. 219–37, where the timpani, not as a solo instrument but as part of the texture, assume a leading role. The timpani become emancipated from their traditional coupling with trumpets, as becomes clear in Symphony no. 3, not only in the second movement, but in the last movement as well. The transition from movement 3 to 4 in the Fifth Symphony is justly famous for the role the timpani play. Most famous of all may be the solo role given the timpani in the second movement of

Symphony no. 9. (A close second comes from the "Emperor" Concerto in E♭ op. 73 (1809), in the final movement.)

One of the most lasting contributions made by period-instrument orchestras to our understanding of Beethoven's orchestration is the restoration of the forceful, piercing, and unintegrated sound the timpani certainly made in Beethoven's day, given the size of the orchestra and the character of early nineteenth-century instruments. During the late nineteenth century and early twentieth, a quite different, anti-Beethovenian orchestral sound ideal took hold. An effort was made to have the sound of the timpani blend in with the rest of the ensemble. The use of thicker heads and the turn away from wood- and leather-topped sticks became fashionable. A seemingly less strident, warm sound replaced a harsh, nearly military drum sound. This practice, combined with the larger and more lush string sound of later orchestras, particularly in the sonorities produced by basses and cellos, robbed Beethoven's use of the timpani of the stark, arresting, and prominent role he clearly assigned it in his symphonic and orchestral music. Given that contemporaries of Beethoven and conservative musicians from succeeding generations found Beethoven eccentric and even mad, the elaborate and leading role he gave the timpani could easily have been a source of such critical skepticism. Yet it is precisely the support the timpani give Beethoven's habits of punctuation and the textures of his tuttis – not to mention the solo independent structural role solo timpani often play – that remains a hallmark of Beethoven's orchestral sound.

Orchestration as a counterbalance to perceived structural repetition or sameness

Taken as a whole, Beethoven's innovations in the use of the orchestra can be understood as undermining the routine and regularity of Classical symphonic structure and, therefore, the standard expectations of listeners. Beethoven followed Haydn's path in expanding the elements of surprise, wit, and ingenuity in symphonic form. In each of the nine symphonies – in recapitulations, in first-movement sonata structures, in returns in rondo form, in restatements in scherzi, and in the composition of codas – alterations in instrumentation and explicit changes in timbre, color, and texture achieved by instrumental shifts and substitutions are crucial.

As we have observed, the early Romantics found in Beethoven a new orchestral sound and a new palette. They welcomed an increased spectrum of possible sonorities.[28] At the same time, nineteenth-century observers believed that Beethoven had transformed the multimovement Classical symphony of Haydn and Mozart into an organic compositional whole. The interrelationships between motivic elements between first and last movements, as in Symphony no. 5, or the progressive narrative experience of no. 6, were cited in defense of this view. So too was the return of material from previous movements in the last movement of the Ninth Symphony and the fusing of the third and fourth movements of Symphony no. 5. This perception of a tendency to organic unity in the symphony was underscored by Beethoven's use of the orchestra, e.g. in movements 1 and 4 in Symphony no. 3. His orchestration undermined the symmetries of symphonic form and his symphonies sounded as if they eschewed repetition and developed organically – but in an evolving linear, albeit revolutionary, manner. The symphonies rebelled against the expectation of sameness and surface coherence. Listening to Beethoven became an evolutionary and transforming journey. The architecture of his symphonies seems dynamic and not static. Insofar as this perception is accurate, it is rooted in the variegated use of the elements of the orchestra in the face of related, if not repetitive, material. Beethoven's employment of contrasting instrumental choirs, his novel combinations of instruments, and his shifts in assigning solo roles in the middle and end of movements support this Romantic view of his symphonic work.

Ideas and statements given to one instrumental group in an exposition are often taken over by another one in a development and recapitulation. Instrumentation in Beethoven works against stasis, highlights harmonic shifts, and works against the pitfalls of facile recognition of the structural and formal necessities of return, restatement, and closure. At the same time, given the increased transparency, power, and variation in the sound Beethoven achieved, in each of the symphonies he used the orchestra's combinatory power to underline and demarcate conclusions. No discussion of his genius as an orchestrator can omit reference to the weight he gave to endings, not only of movements, but of entire works. Symphonies 3, 5, 7, and 9 are obvious examples, but so too are the closing moments of nos. 2 and 4.

Having sacrificed conventions of continuity, Beethoven invented orchestral timbres that could ensure sufficient weight for closure, as in the last movement of Symphony no. 5. Only in the *Pastoral* Symphony is the ending inward and brief. The beginning of the use of extended endings in symphonic music, particularly in last movements, can be traced to the consequences not only of Beethoven's compositional ideas considered independently of instrumentation, but also of his highly differentiated use of the orchestra prior to closing a work. He was the master of orchestrating dramatic moments and powerful arrival points within the symphonic form, as Symphonies 3, 5, 7, and 9 demonstrate. Therefore he had to solve the problem, in terms of orchestration, of ensuring that his endings would carry the proper sense of gravity and finality. And this he did with uncanny success.

III

The orchestral works of Beethoven, owing to their enormous prestige and their singular place in the symphonic repertory, are by far the hardest orchestral music to conduct. The daunting challenges inherent in the scores themselves are only made more difficult by the unique weight of competing performance traditions handed down to performers. The presence of an enormous library of recordings on compact disc spanning practically the entire twentieth century has made the issue of tradition and expectation in performance nearly unbearable. Conductors, once content to grapple with competing live performances, oral traditions, and memory, now face extraordinary documentary evidence. Not only are orchestral musicians also aware of this, but contemporary listeners have gained their familiarity with Beethoven from recordings as well.

At one end of this legacy of Beethoven performance is the Wagnerian and Mahlerian approach, which suggests that each subsequent generation re-interpret Beethoven in order to realize his universal and essential power. The most-often cited twentieth-century equivalent of this tradition of profound re-interpretation has been Furtwängler, despite his avowed admiration for Schenker's ideas. Freedom in the choice of tempi, shifts in the pacing, and orchestration techniques are applauded. At the other end of the spectrum of inherited performance traditions are the achievements of those conductors who derived much of their insights from an engagement with the modern ideology of reconstructed period performance practices and the use of period instruments. One thinks particularly of the performances and recordings of Roger Norrington and Nikolaus Harnoncourt. Somewhere in the middle lies the mid-century anti-romantic tradition of Beethoven performance established by Toscanini, Erich Kleiber, George Szell, and Fritz Reiner, which sought to rid the performance of Beethoven from *fin-de-siècle* expressive excesses.

Although it is hard to do, a conductor – especially one leading a big orchestra of modern instruments – must set these examples aside and avoid imitating past generations. Nonetheless, in terms of orchestral sound, the challenge faced by conductors and orchestras in the performance of Beethoven is how to reconcile the natural weight and power of the sound with the need to achieve transparency and an essential degree of anti-Wagnerian lightness. We still struggle with the legacy of Beethoven as seen and heard through Wagner's eyes and ears. It is all too easy to overbalance the winds with the modern complement of strings. If one resorts to doubling or re-scoring (as Mahler did), one still risks losing the clarity of articulation and the subtle contrasts in timbre and color. Reducing the string ensemble runs the risk of producing an overly thin

sound. Beethoven's orchestration underscores the angularity and abruptness of his symphonic style. Yet it is also all too easy with a modern orchestra to reduce the shocking punctuations and flatten out the lyricism and
the details of structure and form by evening out the differences between
intense energy and delicacy, and collapsing the distance between drama
and contemplation.

In the sound of the symphonies, the balance between coherence and
continuity on the one hand, and differentiation and discontinuity on the
other, is hard to find. A useful principle is to honor the unique sounds
Beethoven assigned to instruments and groupings and to resist achieving
a blended and often blandly uniform full orchestral sonority. Beethoven's
inner ear can always be trusted. The unity and logic of his compositional
working-out of his ideas through instrumentation need no assistance
from the conductor through an effort to generate some sort of integrated
sonority. Beethoven's orchestrations, regardless of the size of the orchestra, the tempi, the hall, or the instruments used (e.g. twentieth-century
timpani, valve horns, and modern steel strings), can speak clearly
throughout his dynamic range. Above all, the parity between wind and
string sound, the extremes of treble and bass, the clarity of inner voices,
and the prominence of brass and timpani – all written into the score –
await realization in the context of a wide range of interpretations based
on choices that depend on factors broader and less tangible than
Beethoven's own retrospective metronome markings, instrumentation,
and use of the orchestra.

11 Beethoven's songs and vocal style

AMANDA GLAUERT

When the poet Ludwig Tieck sought to distinguish the styles and methods of instrumental music from vocal music in 1798, he set a precedent for championing the freedom and independence of instrumental music to express the inexpressible and sounded one of the principal themes of German early Romanticism. E. T. A. Hoffmann's review of Beethoven's Fifth Symphony is perhaps the most famous example of the enthusiasm for this newly heightened appreciation of the power of instrumental music.[1] The consequences of this new perspective for vocal music were, however, less immediately exciting. Music for the voice was confirmed as being in subordination to language and related to everyday experience, for, according to Tieck, "it is, and always will be, elevated declamation and speech."[2] Romantic poets might still strive for the expression of the ineffable in their language, but their aspiring to the potential of instrumental music was essentially a yearning for what they could never claim in their own sphere. In his novella *Musical Joys and Sorrows*, Tieck's characters discussed whether an ideal singing voice might not bring poetic expression nearer to the ineffable. In the words of the fictional singing teacher Hortensio:

> A tone if it is correctly produced must rise up like the sun, clear, majestic, becoming brighter and brighter, the listener must feel in it the infinitude of music. The singer must not give the impression that he cannot sustain the tone to the end.[3]

Yet the results of Hortensio's teaching, as described by Tieck, were not encouraging; his pupil sang like "a calf being led to the slaughter, with not a trace of style or method."[4]

The kind of vocal production Tieck apparently preferred was inspired by J. A. Schulz's *Lieder im Volkston* of 1782: a simple, unadorned vocal style, following closely the contours and rhythms of the text, and sung from the heart.[5] The possibility of song speaking directly from the heart was viewed as the source of its authentic and distinctive power. For the poet Achim von Arnim, even if instrumental music approached the ineffable, "the power of simple song allows everyone to call mightily into the heart of the world."[6] This kind of straightforward conceptual distinction – instrumental music reaching outwards, vocal music inwards – was clearly attractive to writers of the time. The songs of Schulz and Reichardt were praised for avoiding the complexity of symphonic music and for the intimacy of their melodies that anyone might sing and identify with. Beethoven's symphonies earned praise for astonishing audiences with their boundlessness, yet Tieck was not afraid to criticize Beethoven's songs and other vocal works for failing to honor generic distinctions with their inappropriate complexity and restlessness. In fact it was probably inconceivable to him that one artist should encompass both musical viewpoints. And if a choice had to be made between considering Beethoven as an instrumental or vocal artist his choice fell, not surprisingly, on the former.[7]

How Beethoven himself might have viewed the matter is less easy to determine. There is certainly much evidence that he found it hard to gain a natural vocal style. Through his teacher Neefe in Bonn, Beethoven would undoubtedly have been aware of the aesthetics of a simple vocal style. Like Schulz and Reichardt, Neefe was taught by Johann Adam Hiller, once described as the vocal composer closest to the heart of the German people in the late eighteenth century.[8] Composed under Neefe's influence, Beethoven's first surviving song is a setting of a poem by Bürger, a poet dedicated to writing truly popular poetry, whose texts were often set by Neefe and Schulz. Yet the simple melody of Beethoven's "Schilderung eines Mädchens" WoO 107 of around 1783 fits awkwardly with the words and blurs the rhyming pattern of the poem's first two lines. Such awkwardness might be expected from a young composer. However, when he came to set Matthisson's "An Laura" WoO 112 about a decade later, Beethoven was still struggling to find an appropriate vocal idiom. Reichardt once said it was very difficult to create a song in the true style of folksong;[9] according to Schulz, one had to capture the essence of folksong's language of the heart and not merely imitate external character.[10] The young Beethoven was quite capable of the latter, as suggested by his "Trinklied" WoO 109 and "Punschlied" WoO 111 of around 1790, but in such occasional drinking songs he was not concerned about individuality or originality. "An Laura" was a quite different case. The stretching of the vocal line in the first bar shows the composer grasping at the poetic image of Laura in paradise, but the melody's high-points strain against the flow of the text and undermine the song's simplicity (Example 11.1).

Beethoven's discomfiture with vocal writing was compounded by his well-known reluctance to present images in his music and to aim for the immediately graspable, even in song.[11] Schiller spoke of folk-like songs as a natural vehicle for what he called the "naive" artist, one who limits himself to speaking directly out of his experience and showing the sublime within the everyday.[12] This contrasts with the "sentimental" artist

Example 11.1 "An Laura" WoO 112, mm. 5–11

who struggles with his material, seeking to convey through it and beyond it his idea of a greater reality.[13] It is much easier to identify Beethoven with the second of Schiller's artistic categories, and if he still persisted with song and other vocal idioms, it may be that he saw them as a means to a greater compositional end. As a young man, his wish to impress musical circles in Vienna and conquer all areas of composing activity undoubtedly formed part of his motivation.[14] But in the composer's late period, when his drive to introspection appeared most strongly, his sense of the wider significance of vocal idioms emerged in a highly distinctive fashion. The most famous example of this is undoubtedly the Ninth Symphony. In the finale, as Robert Winter has observed, Beethoven placed two kinds of vocal style side by side, "the step-wise, even-rhythmed flow" of the popular style and the "angular dance-like bursts" borrowed from the instruments.[15] These are both dissolved later in the finale in the emphatic music for the "Seid umschlungen," which seems to belong to no recognizable vocal style, except that its modal character has encouraged some writers to identify it with a chorus in ancient Greek drama.[16] At the decisive moment of resolution and climax the popular "Ode to Joy" theme is bound with the "Seid umschlungen," the two having probably been conceived together,[17] to suggest that contrasting styles can be synthesized to form a unity. The musical categories of the vocal and instrumental, the simple and the complex, the angular and the smooth are transcended in honor of Beethoven's conception of an all-embracing symphonic style.

Yet the fact that the moment of stylistic dissolution in the Ninth Symphony is still associated with vocal textures makes it a provocative gesture on Beethoven's part. In his late works the composer is usually assumed to have absorbed vocal styles into the instrumental: witness the eloquent quasi-vocal styles which Joseph Kerman has identified in the late quartets.[18] But, the Ninth Symphony's "Seid umschlungen," which Wagner said showed Beethoven drawing a new power from the prosodic rhythm of the words themselves,[19] suggests the direction might be reversed and the vocal seen to encompass the instrumental. A similar conclusion might be drawn from Beethoven's *Missa solemnis*. Writers have observed how the instruments often appear to take the initiative from the voices, by preempting an expressive statement of the text or continuing and completing the vocal lines.[20] Yet in a letter to Zelter of 1823, as part of his attempt to interest the composer in his work, Beethoven discussed the possibility of adapting the *Missa solemnis* for *a cappella* performance, a principle which he praised with reference to the works of Palestrina, the composer who Beethoven believed established the model for true church music.[21]

From our experience of the late works, it seems Beethoven relished confounding expected aesthetic notions. Thus one should not be surprised at his directly challenging Tieck's categories and seeking to find the sublime and immeasurable within vocal music, even within vocal styles more traditionally conceived than those in the Ninth Symphony and *Missa solemnis*. The song-cycle *An die ferne Geliebte* op. 98 of 1815, the "quiet herald of the late style,"[22] has long been accepted as Beethoven's successful transformation of a familiar folksong idiom. The linking of simple strophic songs into a continuously unfolding network of tonal and thematic relationships is recognized as one of the most poignant examples of Beethoven drawing out immediate musical details to encompass the immeasurable.[23] His setting of the first phrase of the text, "Auf dem Hügel sitz' ich spähend" (On the hill I sit gazing), captures the sense of distance that the poet feels between himself and his beloved, and also establishes a measure of the musical distance to be covered by the cycle as a whole. For at the moment of vocal emphasis upon the tonic, the melodic fulfillment of the high E♭ on the first beat of m. 3, the piano withdraws its rhythmic and harmonic support, seeming to provoke the expressive falling away in the voice's following descending sixth, E♭ to G. And when the piano does enter on the second beat of m. 3, it substitutes the submediant for the more expected tonic chord (Example 11.2).

The melodic and harmonic emphasis upon G and C in this example, mediant relationships that both link closely to the tonic triad and suggest a potential for open-ended harmonic departure, anticipates the subsequent course of the cycle. G becomes the tonality of the second song, and C that of the fifth. Even the flatward pull of the subdominant A♭, as represented by the tonality of the third and fourth songs, might be said to relate to the "falling away" from the tonic seen in Example 11.2 in helping avoid any large-scale assertion of the dominant. The subdominant is taken up at the beginning of the sixth song, as part of the drawing together of the threads of the cycle in a close reworking of Example 11.2. The melodic resolution onto the high E♭ is now supported by tonic harmonization in the piano, as though some of the emotional distance between the lovers

Example 11.2 *An die ferne Geliebte* op. 98, first song, mm. 1–3

were resolved. In the words of the poet, his songs have helped to create a link between them. Yet as the echo of the first song comes back at the beginning of the sixth verse to reinforce this poetic notion, the C minor triad of Example 11.2 returns too, reintroducing the sense of harmonic space. Even in the motivic reminiscence over the tonic E♭ at the end of the piano postlude, the sound of the falling sixth leaves an impression of melodic openness. At the end of the cycle one knows that the poet and his beloved will always remain apart and the musical image of Example 11.2 retains some of its immediate impact, even when having been composed out as the basis for a large-scale tonal and thematic process.

In *An die ferne Geliebte* Beethoven is acknowledged to have reconciled the simplicity of a traditional folksong aesthetic with his characteristic concern for the immeasurable. However, writers are more reluctant to allow any such creative transformation of folksong ideals to have taken place within the collections of folksong melodies which he arranged for George Thomson between 1809 and 1816.[24] It is true that the compositional circumstances seemed less propitious. In the song-cycle there is evidence that Beethoven worked directly with the poet Alois Jeitteles; but in the folksong collections Thomson provided him with the melodies ready-made and gave precise instructions for their arrangement. Despite Beethoven's repeated requests, Thomson did not send him the texts along with the melodies.[25] There were thus an unusual number of constraints upon him. However, if one accepts that Beethoven was particularly concerned to explore the idea of musical boundaries in the late style, then it is possible that he might have found such extreme limitations challenging. As he noted in his diary, "[t]he Scottish songs show how unconstrainedly the most unstructured melody can be treated by harmonic means."[26]

The Welsh folksong "When Mortals all to rest retire" WoO 155 no. 15 certainly supports such a positive interpretation. Beethoven pointed out enthusiastically to Thomson how he had extracted a repeated-note motif from the melody given to him and made a feature of it in his introduction.[27] From the beginning the attention of the listener is thus drawn to

Example 11.3 "When Mortals all to rest retire" WoO 155, no. 15, mm. 1–7

this punctuating cadential figure which underlies the rhyming sequences in the first four bars of the vocal melody. However, such cadences remain marked only on the melodic surface, for underneath Beethoven inserts a C pedal which blurs the voice's patterns (Example 11.3). Such procedures become more extreme as the song progresses, since almost every vocal cadence is undermined by some overlapping of the expected tonic and dominant chords. The effect is greatly to extend the line of the song; the repeated notes of the motif pass into the bass-line's pedals to create a most unexpected flattening out of harmonic perspective. In his letter to Thomson, Beethoven wrote that he hoped the rhythm of the verses, when added, would help to stress the motif which he had highlighted; but in a sense the poetic impact of his music was assured. For the relationship here between the vocal line and its harmonization focused attention on the detail of the words and their immediate meaning, whatever they might be, while simultaneously suggesting the more elusive resonance which is the secret of all poetic utterance. Thus by working with the detail of the vocal melody, Beethoven again succeeded in bringing his characteristic concern with harmonic extension into the confines of a simple song and linking it to a poetic text.

As Barry Cooper has pointed out, the folksong collections are full of such imaginative touches,[28] and one wonders whether having a pre-existing melody was not a significant release for the composer, relieving him from the burden of having first to find a natural-seeming vocal line. Looking over the whole of Beethoven's song output, it was certainly some time before he reached the subtle manipulation of vocal details seen in these examples from his late period. As the composer himself said in a letter to the librettist Friedrich Kind:

> When sounds stir within me I always hear the full orchestra; I know what to expect of instrumentalists, who are capable of almost everything, but with vocal compositions I must always be asking myself: can this be sung?[29]

Thus the greatest of Beethoven's early songs are not surprisingly those where an instrumentally conceived texture or idea forms the point of departure and the voice is pushed beyond its natural confines, seeking to maintain its balance amongst a flow of rhythmically generated figures.

A famous example of such instrumental inspiration is Beethoven's song *Adelaide* op. 46 of 1794, which has been seen to outstrip his instrumental works of the same early Viennese period in its daringly expansive formal outline. The piano's triplet accompanying texture provokes a stream of melodic variation in the voice as well as an increasingly wide circle of tonal modulation. An overriding balance of melodic contour and tonal shape is retained throughout the song, but there are few obvious signposts of thematic return such as one might expect from a more tightly constructed instrumental movement. Instead the voice maintains certain recognizable cadential patterns and preserves a general impression of matching phrase-shapes, even though the actual motivic details of the melodic line are constantly changing. There is thus a sense of mutual responsiveness between the voice and piano throughout the song's expansive dimensions. The voice varies its settings of the name "Adelaide" in response to the instrumental momentum, but also offers an important thread of continuity for the whole, the concentration on the beloved's name representing a vestige of song-like containment.

Some commentators have felt that Beethoven's *Adelaide* actually transcends the boundaries of song and should be defined as an aria or cavatina.[30] The distinction between genres is difficult to make.[31] Certainly in Vienna, lyrical poems of the kind connected with the emergence of the *Lied* were often set in elaborately Italianate fashion, as well as in *Volkston* styles.[32] And even the song-composers of North Germany, like Reichardt, regularly drew on the operatic traditions of German *Singspiel*. If one looks at Beethoven's first operatic arias, "Prüfung des Küssens" WoO 89 and "Mit Mädeln sich vertragen" WoO 90 of around 1790 to

1792, and compares them with his first song in quasi-operatic style, "Selbstgespräch" WoO 114, written at the same time, the vocal style of the arias seems more contained, even though they blend aspects of Italian style into their *Singspiel* idiom.[33] Both of the arias begin with short balanced phrases, and these remain the basis of the continuing dialogue between voice and instruments, serving as a point of departure and return. The word-setting is effective and unpretentious, if rather neutral when compared with the heightened treatment of similar melodic patterns in "Selbstgespräch." In the song the two-bar piano introduction initiates a rising flow of sixteenth notes which is taken up directly by the voice, and helps extend its simple step-wise phrases into a sweeping seven-bar phrase ending in the dominant.

Thus the intensity of the vocal writing in this quasi-operatic song is markedly greater than in the examples in *Singspiel* style, reflecting a different kind of involvement with the text. Indeed in song the text has always the potential to be claimed by the composer as an intimate confession in a way impossible within opera, and the choice to adopt an operatic style is often perceived to come from the composer's own feeling for the text, not merely from a desire to impress his audience or a particular singer. When Beethoven came to set Bürger's two poems "Seufzer eines Ungeliebten" and "Gegenliebe" WoO 118 in 1794 he probably knew the simple settings by Schulz. Yet he chose to adopt an exaggeratedly operatic idiom for his setting of the first poem, complete with *opera seria*-style recitative. The first impression this gives is one of formality; the style of the song is actually very close to the concert aria *Ah! Perfido* op. 65, which Beethoven composed in 1795 under Salieri's instruction, in order to improve his command of Italian declamation. The gracious triple-meter melodies in E♭ into which both song and aria resolve are so similar in contour that one can sense how Beethoven must have borrowed the style from his teacher or other Italianate models.

The sense of formality remains throughout *Ah! Perfido*, even when an Allegro in C minor follows the calm of the Adagio. For here Beethoven turns back to the *tutti* style of the first recitative passages and encapsulates it in a grand declamatory gesture for the voice. He then alternates this style with a slower, more melodic figure in E♭ reminiscent of the Adagio, thus bringing together the material of the work in an ordered sequence. In "Seufzer," the calm of the E♭ aria style is brushed away with far greater spontaneity than in *Ah! Perfido*, as the first song is linked with the second. The continuously flowing instrumental semiquavers of "Gegenliebe" suggest a passionate immediacy as the poet stops looking at the rest of creation, whose happiness he cannot share, and demands a response from the beloved herself. The style of this second setting is still as expansive as

Example 11.4 "Gegenliebe" WoO 118, mm. 1–8

an aria in the scale of its rhythmic repetitions, but if the instrumental flow
were removed the voice might be singing one of Schulz's appealingly
direct folksong-style melodies (Example 11.4). The awkward text setting
is not in keeping with Schulz's style, but when heard in context it becomes
the natural consequence of the voice being pushed forwards by the
piano's rhythmic intensity.

The particular effect Beethoven achieves in "Gegenliebe" is of a simple
vocal style being emotionally transported by the accompaniment into a
tumbling flow. A critic attaching importance to idiomatic vocal styles
might complain that an instrumental texture was in danger of swallowing
up the vocal line, but in this song Beethoven had certainly succeeded in
one primary objective of a vocal composer, that of conveying emotion
through the voice. The style of melody in Example 11.4 is immediately
familiar as the basis for the Choral Fantasia and the "Ode to Joy" theme of
the Ninth Symphony, as well as for the more exultant vocal styles of
Fidelio. It also contributed much to Beethoven's successful song-settings
of Goethe's poems in the later 1790s, "Maigesang" op. 52 no. 4 and "Neue
Liebe, neues Leben" op. 75 no. 2. With such a style Beethoven was able to
capture the concentrated energy and excitement of Goethe's verse in a
way that eluded the simpler settings of Zelter and Reichardt.

It is well known that Goethe himself did not approve of Beethoven's
expansive instincts in setting verse, believing that all song-composers
should keep within the formal boundary of the poem, avoiding textual
repetition and all kinds of open-ended musical development. Beethoven
was quite prepared to challenge poetic authority if necessary; he once said

to Czerny that the composer needed to rise above the poet in his set-tings.[34] However, his respect for Goethe was such that he was prepared to try keeping to his strictures, if only as an experiment. When in 1808 he composed four settings of Goethe's famous lyric for Mignon "Nur wer die Sehnsucht kennt" WoO 134, he attempted to honor the extreme compression of the single-stanza poem and its relentless rhymes. In the first three songs the sense of a tightly enclosed form is reinforced by the second half of the poem being set as a strophic repetition of the first. In each case the entire song is dominated by the first line's simple descent to the tonic, with little resistance from the piano textures and only a slight rise of vocal contour at the third line of the poem before the first half of the song closes with a repetition of the first vocal phrase. This pattern of enclosure is rendered more poignant in Beethoven's fourth version of the poem by a greater textural expansiveness and a delay in the moment of return until the last two lines of the poem. Yet even here the sense of musical restriction is so strong that Mignon seems to be speaking in a numbed voice, without the intensity characteristic of Goethe's poem. Beethoven himself seems to have had a disparaging view of these songs and noted on the autographs that he did not have time to finish a good setting.[35] Yet he still published them in 1810, as though wishing to point out all the problems caused by conforming to Goethe's commands.

There is little doubt, however, that the struggle to create a self-contained song form – without inhibiting instincts for musical growth and contrast – engaged Beethoven's interest even if he required greater flexibility in the realization than ever Goethe envisaged. Even in his early song output one can find isolated examples, such as his setting of Hölty's "Klage" WoO 113 (c. 1790), where the composer seems to be testing the boundaries of simple sectional forms and turning the formal limitations to his advantage. From the opening of "Klage" he engages in a careful balancing act with the vocal line, making it hover between closure and openness while the piano underlines the melodic details rather than immediately urging the voice into expansiveness (Example 11.5). The melodic pause upon the mediant at the end of the first two-bar vocal phrase both hints at a further descent to closure on the tonic, and a holding off from E to allow the vocal line to expand. After the impact of the E♯ in the third bar, pushing the vocal line away from the tonic, the rhythmic pattern and melodic contour of the phrases does become freer. So the piano's breaking open of the cadence to the first section of the song, ready for a much more expansive second section, still comes as a response to the vocal detail as it unfolds. The quasi-operatic style of the second section brings an unexpectedly vivid contrast, a fully dramatic presentation of the poetic change of tense as the poet moves from considering his

Example 11.5 "Klage" WoO 113, mm. 5–15

contented past to facing a desolate present. Yet musically Beethoven prevents this section settling too much into its own style. It is drawn into a final third section and tolling cadences which announce musical closure and the poet's imminent death. The first section's hovering between openness and closure is thus acted out, if in rather rougher strokes, in the contrasting vocal styles of the following two sections. Detail and form develop together, even if without the immediate harmonic and motivic logic that one comes to expect from the later Beethoven.

"Opferlied" WoO 126 of 1794 presents perhaps a better example of a song in which the details of the vocal line continue to be stretched out in an unbroken chain, so that the whole song is heard as one all-inclusive musical phrase. With a restraint reminiscent of Gluck, Beethoven strips away the voice and piano parts to the barest melodic and rhythmic outlines. But he draws the vocal line beyond a simple step-wise profile with judicious use of melodic leaps, making each step in the steady syllabic sequence reach beyond the immediate phrase to the larger melodic sweep. "Opferlied" was a favorite song of Beethoven's, representing a vocal style of calm exultation such as balanced the overspilling joy characteristic of "Gegenliebe." He used a similarly taut but restrained style for five of his six Gellert songs op. 48 of 1802, achieving particularly in the third song, "Im Tode," a remarkable intensity in the subtle but relentless extension of a single vocal phrase. Such unity of mood was most appropriate for these hymn-like poems, though in ruling out any elements of contrast or expansion, such an idiom remained limited and failed to provide a real answer to the ambitious aspirations for song revealed in "Klage." In a sense Beethoven created the greatest realization of this hymn-like style

Example 11.6 "Kennst du das Land?" op. 75 no. 1, mm. 1–7

outside song, in his sonatas, quartets, and symphonies where he could weave it into contrasts on a much larger scale.

The promise of "Klage" remained largely unfulfilled until Beethoven's engagement with the poems of Goethe finally bore fruit in two undisputed masterpieces, "Kennst du das Land?" op. 75 no. 1 of 1809 and "Wonne der Wehmut" op. 83 no. 1 of 1810. In setting the first poem, another lyric for Mignon, Beethoven employed a clear strophic form as with his setting of "Nur wer die Sehnsucht kennt," but now he charged the form with much greater emotional complexity in a way that Goethe found both provocative and disturbing.[36] At first Beethoven makes Mignon ask her question – "Do you know the land?" – as though the answer were quite straightforward and near-at-hand. The rise and fall of the syllabic phrases, the balancing of tonic and dominant harmonies, create an immediate image of simplicity (Example 11.6). Yet a basic reversal has taken place in the usual succession of "question and answer" phrase-shapes. The "answer" or closing melodic statement comes first in mm. 1 and 2, followed by a question which ends up on the dominant. When this pattern is repeated with further emphasis on the dominant in m. 7, Beethoven uses it as the opening for a sudden contrast of key and pianistic texture. The motif of the first two bars returns seven bars later at the close of the section, but it has lost its aura of simplicity and it too now hovers on the dominant. And although the next section brings a balancing emphasis upon the tonic A major, the lurch into a faster 6/8 tempo suggests that without this greater urgency the "answer" would be in danger of slipping away. Taking his interpretation of Goethe's poem as a whole Beethoven makes it clear that there is no doubt in Mignon's mind of the land she is yearning for. With the three strophic repetitions there is an overall balance between phrases, between tonal "question" and "answer," even with the textural intensifications of the third verse. Yet given the strange shifts from section to section within each verse Beethoven also manages to suggest the greater restlessness which underlies Mignon's desire for her homeland, the longing for spiritual peace which in some sense evades all resolution.

Example 11.7 "Wonne der Wehmut" op. 83, mm. 1–4

"Wonne der Wehmut" is perhaps an even more remarkable example of Beethoven's new ability at this period to plumb the tensions of musical contrast and return within a basically simple vocal style and tight formal framework. The paradoxical message in Goethe's poem that only by keeping the tears of grief flowing can the unrequited lover experience a full life, is fully met by the ingenuity with which Beethoven spins out the precisely paired rhythms of his first two bars into longer and longer vocal phrases (Example 11.7). The piano's thirty-second notes create the immediate image of flowing tears, which is soon matched by all manner of rhythmic and harmonic extensions to the vocal line. Yet the voice continues to be directed toward matching cadence-points based on the two-eighth-note patterns underlying Example 11.7, patterns which constantly renew expectations of a return to the tonic. Thus the poet's flow of tears is interpreted quite appropriately by Beethoven as part of a conscious directing of the emotional instincts and a controlled response to the workings of passion. At no point are the flowing textures allowed to mask the song's underlying patterns of formal containment.

Such a meeting of emotional expression and rational control in song should warn commentators against dismissing Beethoven's *Lieder* as peripheral to his true oeuvre (as Carl Dahlhaus has implied).[37] The persistence with which the composer pursued effective and satisfying song styles speaks much for his commitment to the genre and for its links with his main compositional concerns, particularly with his urge to unite the sensuous and rational, as reported by Bettina Brentano.[38] The final and perhaps unexpected stage in his struggle with song idioms came with a series of ten songs extending from "Der Gesang der Nachtigall" WoO 141 of 1813 to "So oder so" WoO 148 of 1817. For these songs join with the folksong settings commissioned by Thomson and *An die ferne Geliebte* in revealing Beethoven's return in his late period to the issues of Schulz's folksong aesthetic. Having failed to find a natural *Volkston* manner in his first songs, the composer now found his way back to nature "by the paths of reason and freedom," to quote Schiller.[39] Certainly his setting of "Der

Example 11.8 "Der Gesang der Nachtigall" WoO 141, mm. 7–12

Gesang der Nachtigall" by Herder, one of the main early Romantic folk-song collectors, shows great ease in its appropriation of a tuneful pastoral idiom. The song combines a naive imitation of the nightingale's song in the piano prelude with the subtleties of a teasingly repetitive line for the voice. Although on the surface the voice's infectious dactylic rhythms seem to fall entirely into straight one-bar phrases, subtle elisions also pull them into a longer six-bar shape. Only the two-bar refrain is allowed to remain simple and self-contained, so keeping the pastoral image intact (Example 11.8).

With this song Beethoven could lay claim to having completed his distinctive appropriation of the vocal styles of his time, from the expansively operatic to the most simple folksong style. He could also claim to be capable of adjusting the formal context for his appropriation from the large scale of symphony and opera to the smallest scale of the *Lied*, and to be able to reverse expectations of a particular style from within its smallest details. Thus the subtle play of openness and closure, of instrumental and vocal perspectives, which is so valued in *An die ferne Geliebte* and seen as the beginning of a rich history for the nineteenth-century *Lied* grew out of a whole range of songs which betray the same vital expressive potential. Beethoven's struggle to find a distinctive vocal style can in no way be allowed to have inhibited his success in vocal music. Indeed, perhaps it should be recognized that the struggle itself became an important means of his realizing some of his deepest compositional concerns, and of showing precisely how the simple and immediate might lead toward the immeasurable.

12 Beethoven's essay in opera: historical, text-critical, and interpretative issues in *Fidelio*

MICHAEL C. TUSA

Despite its familiarity, its secure place in the operatic canon, and the large body of literature that surrounds it, Beethoven's *Fidelio* continues to pose challenges to interpretation and understanding. Its complicated genesis, performance history, and transmission present troublesome philological questions that in certain cases may never be fully resolved. And its position as the sole opera of a composer known primarily for his instrumental music makes it a difficult work to place within the context of his artistic development. But if *Fidelio* is nearly as much a problem for critics and scholars as it was for the composer himself, it is also a central work, an understanding of which is crucial for any attempt to comprehend Beethoven's ambitions and accomplishments, his self-critical spirit, and his world-view.

Whose *Fidelio*? the historical background and the textual problem

The complex text-critical issues that surround *Fidelio* are perhaps best approached through a review of the biographical circumstances that led to its creation and revisions. In 1803 Beethoven accepted a commission for a new opera from Emmanuel Schikaneder, the impresario of the Theater an der Wien, who himself provided the composer with a libretto entitled *Vestas Feuer*. Beethoven began to compose Schikaneder's text in the autumn of that year, but he quickly abandoned it; by early January 1804 he had decided to have an extant French libretto, Jean-Nicolas Bouilly's *Léonore, ou L'amour conjugal*, adapted into German by Joseph Sonnleithner.[1] Nearly two years later, on 20 November 1805, the opera premiered at the Theater an der Wien as *Fidelio, oder Die eheliche Liebe*.[2] It was withdrawn after only three performances, a consequence in part of bad timing – Vienna had recently been occupied by Napoleon's forces – and in part of audience indifference to the work.[3]

Having experienced his opera in the theater, Beethoven and a second poet, Stephan von Breuning, revised it during the winter of 1805–06. This second version of *Fidelio*, reduced from three acts to two, returned to the stage on 29 March 1806, but the opera enjoyed only one additional performance before it was again withdrawn. It received no further public performances in Vienna until 1814,[4] when three members of the Court Opera approached him for permission to revive it for a performance for their benefit. Beethoven took the opportunity to enlist a third librettist, Georg Friedrich Treitschke, to refashion the text while he himself significantly revised the music. With its premiere on 23 May 1814 *Fidelio* at last established itself as one of the core works in the German operatic repertory.

A number of fundamental issues arise from the foregoing. The question of how the different versions relate to each other is exceedingly difficult to answer, primarily because the very first version of 1805 has not survived intact. Many of the autograph and copyists' sources written for it were discarded and lost as their texts were superseded by the replacements of 1806 and 1814. Extant editions of the so-called "Ur-*Leonore*" offer at best only compromises that fill out the surviving torso of the 1805 version with elements from 1806 and 1814.[5] The 1806 version is much less of a problem, thanks to the discovery in the 1970s of a manuscript score with autograph annotations in Prague, which Beethoven sent to the Bohemian capital in 1807 for an anticipated production at the Estates Theater.[6] For this production – which did not take place – Beethoven also composed the so-called *Leonore* Overture no. 1, in actuality the third in chronological order.[7]

Even the familiar 1814 version poses a number of textual questions, in particular, the degree to which the received version of *Fidelio* corresponds to Beethoven's final wishes. Treitschke's correspondence with theaters suggests that the composer and librettist both felt strongly that the opera worked better without Rocco's Act 1 "gold aria," a piece omitted from the first six performances and re-instated at the seventh, given for Beethoven's own benefit on 18 July 1814. More startling, in view of the dramatic and musical significance of the piece, is Treitschke's recommendation that theaters might also omit Leonore's great first-act aria, which was similarly withheld until the seventh performance of 1814.[8] Beethoven ultimately did include both arias in the authorized piano–vocal score published by Artaria in 1814, but the fact that the composer never published the opera in full score perhaps gives the 1814 *Fidelio* a less finished quality than works that he did see through the press, during which process he often made substantive last-minute revisions.[9]

The potentially "open-ended" status of the 1814 *Fidelio* raises another fundamental question. Is *Fidelio* best regarded as (1) a single work that after much trial and error achieved a final version that supersedes all prior versions (a view that Beethoven himself seems to have endorsed in a number of comments in 1814[10]), as (2) three different but equally authentic "works" corresponding to the three productions supervised by the composer, or as (3) a fluid entity embodied not only by a number of discrete stages marked by landmarks like composer-sanctioned performances and publication but also by preliminary and intermediate manuscript versions?[11] The question obviously cannot be answered categorically, as one's response will depend on one's interest and purpose. I will adopt the point of view that *each* stage of the opera's history reveals something different and important about Beethoven and his evolving relationship to opera. Though we shall probably never have the complete "Ur-*Leonore*" of 1805, it is nevertheless important to understand as fully as possible, on the basis of the surviving sources, the ambitions of a composer at the peak of his creative powers entering the operatic arena for the first time. But it is equally important to understand how his experience of the work in the theater and direct contact with the exigencies of singers and audiences alike prompted the revisions of 1806. And with the *Fidelio* of 1814 we confront a composer at a significantly different stage of his life and career and a fundamentally different moment in the history of Austro-German society.

Aspects of the libretto

With regard to plot, characterization, and music-dramatic structure, *Fidelio* largely follows Bouilly's *Léonore, ou L'amour conjugal*, a two-act *opéra-comique* that premiered at the Théâtre Feydeau on 19 February 1798 with the music of the composer-tenor Pierre Gaveaux.[12] Years later the librettist claimed that his so-called *fait historique*, the story of a woman who disguises herself as a young male to rescue her husband from unjust imprisonment, was based on "a sublime act of heroism and devotion of one of the ladies of Touraine" during the Reign of Terror.[13] Recent research suggests, however, that Bouilly more likely drew upon various acts of spousal fidelity and courage during the darkest days of the Revolution, some of which he no doubt personally witnessed as a government official in Tours.[14]

Characteristic of the "mixed" dramaturgy of the late eighteenth century, Bouilly's libretto combines characters from the lower end of the social spectrum (in this case the working-class Rocco, Marzelline, and Jaquino) and their usually sentimental or mundane concerns with aristocratic characters (Leonore, Florestan, Pizarro) who are placed in potentially tragic situations. Bouilly emphasizes this division linguistically, by giving the lower-class characters a less elegant dialect than the elevated speech of the aristocrats. Though potentially disconcerting to modern audiences and critics more accustomed to the uniformly tragic dramaturgy of post-Wagnerian serious opera, the heterogeneity of Bouilly's libretto has a compelling logic of its own. For the sake of verisimilitude, Leonore's disguise as an orphaned youth and her acceptance as such by Rocco and Marzelline plausibly grant her entrance to the prison and, ultimately, access to the cell where her husband is hidden. Further, the dramatic mixture allows certain themes to be developed from both "high" and "low" perspectives. The topic highlighted in the alternative title of the opera, marital love, runs through both dramatic spheres, gaining increasing weight as the action shifts from Rocco's household into the dungeon. If in the early scenes it is seen from the *petit-bourgeois* viewpoint of Marzelline's idyllic daydreams of domestic bliss with "Fidelio" and Rocco's financial pragmatism, the meaning of marriage deepens considerably when we finally learn Leonore's real identity and appreciate the risks that she has taken and will take for the sake of her husband.

Exactly how Beethoven came to select this libretto is unknown, but a number of factors must have made it particularly attractive to him. From a practical point of view, Beethoven probably sought to capitalize on the Viennese vogue since 1802 for French *opéra-comique* and the pronounced popularity of operas with similar plots of liberation, which expressed the tumult and anxieties of the Revolutionary era. The heterogeneity of the libretto was also advantageous, as it offered Beethoven a framework that would allow for a wide variety of expression and compositional types, as we shall see below. Beyond such pragmatic considerations, however, elements in *Léonore* doubtless resonated strongly with his own moral, ethical, and political views. Its tale of successful struggle against repression struck a sympathetic chord with a love of freedom and an essentially optimistic worldview shaped by the Enlightenment.[15] Florestan's stoic perseverance in the face of overwhelming suffering must have appealed to a man who, in his own life, had only recently overcome the devastating realization of his incurable deafness.[16] In the character Leonore Beethoven, who allegedly regarded the libretti of Mozart's comic operas as "lewd" (presumably because of their sometimes irreverent treatment of topics like love and marriage),[17] found an ideal effigy of womanhood, of marital commitment, and of the redemptive power of love, as well as a symbol of the potentiality of the human spirit to aspire to and attain nearly unthinkable goals. And her selfless decision in the grave-digging scene to liberate the as-yet-unrecognized prisoner regardless of his identity exemplifies the Kantian categorical imperative that appears to have resonated strongly with Beethoven's own moral code.[18]

Sonnleithner's libretto (1805) follows Bouilly very closely, in many instances translating the French word for word into German.[19] The most conspicuous dramatic initiatives in Sonnleithner's version are: (1) the linguistic elevation of the working-class characters, who now express themselves in High German rather than dialect; (2) a tendency to place the virtuous characters in a better light, so that Marzelline is less coy with Jaquino, Rocco less venal, and Leonore more remorseful about her deception; (3) the more frequent invocations of God for assistance and consolation;[20] and (4) the identification of a just king as the ultimate arbiter of Pizarro's punishment. The last two changes may well have been helpful in getting the libretto approved by the censor,[21] and may also reflect Beethoven's own religious and political views at this stage in his career, although these are notoriously difficult to pin down.[22]

Of greater consequence in the 1805 libretto is the expansion of the role of music in the presentation of the drama, a clear barometer of Beethoven's operatic ambitions (see Table 12.1). To the pieces present in the French libretto Sonnleithner added a new aria (1805/8), a new duet (1805/9), two new trios (1805/3, 1805/6), and two new quartets (1805/4, 1805/16). He also extended Bouilly's two act-ending choruses into multi-sectional finales (1805/12, 1805/18), inventing for the first of these a new dramatic situation for Pizarro and his guards in order to effect a more emphatic conclusion than the subdued ending of Bouilly's first act. Because most of the new pieces were inserted into the first act of Bouilly's libretto, Sonnleithner and Beethoven decided at a relatively late stage to divide it into two acts, a decision that prompted the addition of yet another piece, an instrumental introduction, to the start of the new Act 2 (1805/7).[23] Sonnleithner's new pieces also have a decided impact on characterization, especially that of Pizarro, whose transformation from a speaking role in Bouilly's libretto into a singing one through his new aria (1805/8) and participation in ensembles makes him an altogether more imposing and credible villain.

Sonnleithner's expansion of the musical dimensions of the libretto had, however, brought with it various undesirable consequences that Beethoven and Stephan von Breuning sought to address in the 1806 revision (refer again to Table 12.1).[24] Sensing that the beginning of Act 1 dwelled too long on the Marzelline–Fidelio side-plot, Breuning reverted to Bouilly's two-act organization, deleted Rocco's aria (1805/5),[25] and redistributed other pieces related to the side-plot (1805/3, 1805/10) to later points in the first act so as to allow important strands in the principal serious plot, Pizarro's scenes and Leonore's monologue, to emerge more quickly. As Martin Ruhnke points out, the fact that Leonore's *scena* now follows immediately upon the sinister Pizarro–Rocco duet highlights her role as an opponent to Pizarro's repressive regime.[26] New stage instructions

Table 12.1 *Léonore, Leonore,* and *Fidelio*

Bouilly/Gaveaux. Léonore (1798)	Sonnleithner/Beethoven. Leonore (1805)	Breuning/Beethoven. Leonore (1806)	Treitschke/Beethoven. Fidelio (1814)
Ouverture, f–F	Ouverture ["*Leonore* no. 2"], C	Overture ("*Leonore* no. 3"), C	Overture ("*Fidelio*"), E
Act I	*Act I*	*Act I*	*Act I*
1. Couplets (Marcelline), g/G	1. Arie (Marcelline), c/C	1. = 1805/1	1. = 1805/2
2. Duo (Marcelline, Jaquino), C	2. Duetto (Marcelline, Jaquino), A	2. = 1805/2	2. = 1805/1
	3. Terzett (Marzelline, Jaquino, Rocco), E♭	3. = 1805/4	3. = 1805/4
3. Chanson (Roc), B♭	4. Canon [Quartet] (Marzelline, Leonore, Rocco, Jaquino), G	4. = 1805/6	4. = 1805/5
	5. [Arie] (Rocco), B♭		5. = 1805/6
	6. Terzett (Rocco, Marzelline, Leonore), F		
	Act II		
4. Duo (Marcelline, Léonore), A	7. "Introduzione del Atto 2do," D[a]	5. Marcia, B♭	6. = 1806/5
	8. [Arie] (Pizarro), d–D	6. = 1805/8	7. = 1805/8
5. Romance (Léonore), f/F	9. Duetto (Pizarro, Rocco), A	7. = 1805/9	8. = 1805/9
	10. Duetto (Marzelline, Leonore), C		
6. Air (Léonore)[b]	11. Arie (Leonore), E	8. = 1805/11	9. = 1805/11
		9. = 1805/10	
		10. = 1805/3	
7. Chœur (Prisonniers), D	12. Finale, B♭/G/E♭/–/B♭[c]	11. = 1805/12	10. = 1805/12, with new conclusion
Act II	*Act III*	*Act II*	*Act II*
8. Recitatif./Romance (Florestan), c	13. Recitatif./Arie (Florestan), f/A♭/F?/f[d]	12. = 1805/13, shortened	11. = 1805/13, with new conclusion, f/A♭/F
9. Duo (Roc, Léonore), E♭	14. [Melodram?]/Duett (Rocco, Leonore), a[e]	13. = 1805/14, without Melodram	12. = 1805/14, with Melodram
10. Trio (Florestan, Roc, Léonore), G	15. Terzett (Florestan, Rocco, Leonore), A	14. = 1805/15	13. = 1805/15
	16. Quartett (Pizarro, Florestan, Leonore, Rocco), D	15. = 1805/16	14. = 1805/16
11. Duo (Florestan, Léonore), f–F	17. [Recit. &] Duetto (Florestan, Leonore), G	16. = 1805/17	15. = 1805/17, without recitative
12. Chœur (+ Florestan, Léonore), B♭	18. Finale, c/A/F/–/C	17. = 1805/18	16. = 1805/18, with new opening movement and revised conclusion
13. Finale (Chœur general), C			

[a] This piece is not specified in the 1805 libretto and is not published in Hess's edition of the 1805 *Leonore*. Hess assumes that the B♭ major March was performed at this point in 1805, but the March is clearly a piece from 1806. See Brenneis (1990) for details.

[b] This Air is not set to music in the published score of Gaveaux's opera, possibly because of its religious sentiments.

[c] In the 1805 libretto the term "Finale" is placed not at the start of the prisoners' chorus, but instead at Leonore's outburst in line 24, "Noch heute . . ."

[d] The original version of Florestan's aria does not survive. See Tusa (1993) and Lühning (1997) for details.

[e] A Melodrama is not specified in the 1805 libretto and an 1805 version of the Melodrama does not survive. However, sketches in Mendelssohn 15 show that Beethoven planned a melodrama at this point in the 1805 libretto implies that there had been a melodrama at this point, and the Prague score of the 1806 version implies that there had been a Melodrama in 1805.

clarify the gestures and emotions of the characters,[27] and a new change of scenery in the middle of Act 1 promotes visual variety lacking in the first version.[28] And in a few cases – the Marzelline–Leonore duet, the Act 2 Trio, and the Act 2 Finale – Breuning altered texts of pieces that Beethoven had already composed, doubtless at the composer's request.[29]

G. F. Treitschke's revision of 1814 continues some of the lines of development begun by Breuning (see again Table 12.1).[30] The dramatic action in Act 1 is streamlined by the removal of the two "comic" pieces that Breuning had shifted toward the end of the act, the Marzelline–Leonore duet and the Rocco–Marzelline–Jaquino trio.[31] To set the opera in motion more energetically, Treitschke exchanges the positions of the first two numbers, an inversion that allows the opera to begin *in medias res* with the Marzelline–Jaquino duet.[32] More theatrical, too, than the segment that it replaces is the new conclusion of Florestan's aria ("Und spür' ich nicht linde sanft säuselnde Luft?"), a quasi-delirious (and prophetic) vision of Leonore as a liberating angel; yet various commentators have felt that this change diminishes somewhat the heroic stature of a character who in the discarded, original conclusion had accepted his miserable fate with supreme stoicism.[33] Treitschke also intensifies the symbolism inherent in Breuning's juxtaposition of Leonore's soliloquy with the Pizarro–Rocco duet by giving her a new recitative that expressly contrasts his lack of humanity with her own trust in hope ("Abscheulicher! Wo eilst du hin?", a text inspired by the comparable *scena* in Paer's *Leonora*).[34]

To a much greater extent than either of his predecessors, Treitschke departs from Bouilly's original plot. The release of the prisoners at the end of the first act is no longer a regular part of their daily regimen but a special event that Rocco permits at Leonore's urging.[35] This seemingly minor change gives rise to a new conclusion for the Act 1 Finale, whereby an angry Pizarro orders the prisoners back to their cells, to which they regretfully return as the soloists look on and comment. Treitschke's solution affords a more persuasive and emotionally complex conclusion than the bombastic exchange between Pizarro and his guards that Sonnleithner had concocted as the final segment for the act. Even more consequential are the changes that Treitschke made to the denouement, purportedly to move the conclusion of Act 2 out of the dungeon and into the open light.[36] In the 1805 and 1806 versions, as in Bouilly's libretto, the trumpet calls that interrupt the standoff between Leonore and Pizarro by no means resolve all dangers for the protagonists. Indeed, at the end of the quartet Rocco disarms Leonore, leaving her and Florestan alone in the dungeon unsure of their fate; only in the course of the Act 2 Finale, with the Minister's appearance in the dungeon and his recognition of the long-lost Florestan, is the happy ending assured. In contrast, Treitschke takes pains to let Florestan and Leonore understand as soon as possible that the trumpet signals mark the end of their suffering: Jaquino announces to all the arrival of the Minister immediately after the second fanfare; Rocco allows Leonore to keep her pistol and makes a comforting gesture before he accompanies Pizarro out of the dungeon to greet the Minister; and he soon returns to explain (in spoken dialogue that is normally cut following the Florestan–Leonore duet) that Florestan's release is likely. With the suspense lifted, Treitschke's Act 2 Finale functions principally as a cantata-like celebration of justice, freedom, and Leonore's great accomplishment, fittingly set in the full daylight of the prison courtyard.

But as several writers have noted, this new denouement is not without its own problems.[37] Quite apart from the fact that it effectively removes any dramatic suspense approximately one half-hour before the opera concludes and that it compelled Beethoven to discard one of the most striking sections in the 1805 and 1806 versions of the opera, the poignant accompanied recitative preceding the Florestan–Leonore duet, Treitschke's ending poses an unanswerable question: why does the King (through the Minister) grant amnesty to the other prisoners?[38] To be sure, the Minister's words suggest that they have been victims of unjust imprisonment, of some "night of crime" that has weighed heavily upon all. But since Florestan is expressly the only prisoner *not* on Don Fernando's roster of state prisoners (and thus the only known victim of Pizarro's abusive power), the other prisoners must have been legally incarcerated as enemies of the state, that is, of the King. This paradox leads to the suspicion that the scene is primarily intended symbolically, as a euphoric metaphor for the Austrian people's own sense of liberation from the anxieties and hardships of the Napoleonic wars. Little did they suspect in early 1814, however, that benighted times would soon descend again, now at the hands of their own leaders in the age of Metternich.

Beethoven as a composer of opera

In approaching Beethoven's compositional achievement in *Fidelio*, let us again consider the three versions in chronological order; in this way we can properly situate the work in the context of his career.[39] Following closely on Beethoven's breakthrough to a "new path" in instrumental works like the *Eroica* Symphony and the "Waldstein" Sonata, the 1805 version of the opera represents nothing less than his attempt to conquer the operatic world with a work that would demonstrate an encyclopedic competency in the genre, a "summa," as Heinrich W. Schwab has recently described it, of known operatic styles (comic and serious, lyrical and declamatory, Italian, French, and German), forms (strophic, through-composed one-section forms, multi-sectional forms), and genres (songs, arias, recitative, melodrama, contemplative and active ensembles, finales, and even a canon).[40]

At the same time, however, the *Fidelio* of 1805 is the work of a novice opera composer whose prior experience in vocal and theater music can only have partially prepared him for the great challenge of a full-length opera; it is therefore hardly surprising that much of the work is dependent on models. That *Fidelio*'s mixture of types is reminiscent of the heterogeneity of Mozart's German operas, particularly *Die Zauberflöte*, is significant and hardly a coincidence.[41] Beethoven looked to his great Viennese predecessor for guidance in his first opera; extant copies in his own hand of pieces from *Don Giovanni* and *Die Zauberflöte* attest his study of Mozart's ensemble technique in preparation for his own work.[42] Several pieces in *Leonore* betray melodic and/or structural resemblances to Mozartian prototypes, and certain of the pieces in the 1805 *Leonore*, like the E♭ major trio (1805/3), Leonore's aria (1805/11), and the Act 3 Trio (1805/15), seem to take as their starting point specific Mozartian models, respectively the Pamina–Papageno duet from *Die Zauberflöte*, Fiordiligi's Act 2 aria from *Così fan tutte*, and the Act 2 Trio from *Don Giovanni*. The overture of 1805 (*Leonore* no. 2), may be seen as a typically Beethovenian intensification of programmatic impulses inherent in Mozart's mature opera overtures. Essentially Mozartian too is a large-scale tonal structure that reconciles key selections made on the basis of conventional character and situation associations (e.g. C major for topics of love or heroism, G major for pastoral themes, A major for duets, D minor for revenge arias, and so forth) with concerns for symbolism and coherence *within* the opera. Thus the 1805 Overture and the Act 3 Finale frame the opera in C major, a key that occurs at several points in the drama that express love and/or hope. The progression from C minor to C major in the first vocal piece, Marzelline's aria (1805/1), to signify a move from present uncertainty to future marital bliss, anticipates the more drastic symbolism of the Act 3 Finale, in which the ambiguous and mis-understood threats of the opening offstage C minor chorus resolve eventually into the C major celebration of spousal love.[43]

Yet the Mozartian background is only one part of the equation. By his own admission Beethoven was captivated by the French operas that had conquered the Viennese theaters,[44] and *opéra-comique* elements abound in the music of *Leonore*, like the minor/major alternation in Marzelline's strophic aria (a common feature of the *romance*), the use of *mélodrame* (spoken dialogue with orchestral accompaniment) at a particularly sinister point in the drama, the jagged melodic profile of much of Pizarro's music, and novel, atmospheric effects in the orchestration, like the unusual tuning of the timpani to a diminished fifth in the *Introduzione* to Florestan's aria. It is possible that Beethoven knew and took hints from Gaveaux's setting of *Léonore*, which was published in full score and there-fore easily available,[45] but his main source for the French style was Cherubini, a composer whom Beethoven held in the highest regard and whose *Les deux journées* he studied in preparation for *Leonore*.[46]

The music of the 1805 version of the opera establishes a number of basic premises that remain constant through all three versions. For one thing, it serves to delineate three principal dramatic planes. Rocco's household is mostly characterized by stylistic features inherited from comic opera traditions of the eighteenth century: relatively rapid, syllabic declamation; detached articulation in the orchestra and voice; pitch repe-tition (especially in Rocco's music); a largely consonant harmonic-tonal language; and strophic forms. The occasional coloratura that creeps into Marzelline's music reminds us, too, of her ancestry in stock soubrette characters like Despina. Beethoven's music for Marzelline, Jaquino, and Rocco has often been found a bit ponderous, lacking the light touch that flowed so easily from Mozart's pen. Perhaps this is true, but in my view, the somewhat serious tone of this supposedly "lighter" music seems appropriate: just as Sonnleithner's text avoids the trivializing *patois* of Bouilly's "comical" characters, so too Beethoven's music asks us to see the dignity of these modest people.

Florestan and Leonore occupy a different plane stylistically. In accor-dance with Mozartian precedent for the depiction of aristocratic, heroic characters, their music draws upon Italianate *opera seria* traditions. They express themselves in a more sustained, *cantabile* manner than do the members of Rocco's household, and although the fact of Leonore's pre-carious disguise as "Fidelio" means that she must in public accommodate her style to that of Rocco's family, at moments when she is alone (1805/11) or lost in her thoughts (in the ensembles 1805/6 and 1805/14) she blossoms into elaborate coloratura. Formally their great soliloquies are also indebted to the Italian tradition of multi-sectional *rondò*-arias with obbligato instrumental accompaniments; Beethoven obviously found the strophic *romances* specified at the corresponding points in Bouilly's libretto too insignificant for his heroes.[47] We have already noted the indebtedness of Leonore's great aria (1805/11) to Fiordiligi's "Deh, per pietà" from *Così fan tutte*, with which it shares the key of E major, the topic of marital fidelity, and use of obbligato horns,[48] but Beethoven characteristically goes beyond the model in the use of *three* horns instead of two, in the greater length and complexity of the coloratura, in the greater fervency of the prayerful slow section, and in the heroic dynamism of the fast concluding section. And with the original version of Florestan's solo scene (1805/13) Beethoven seems to have envisaged an unusually expansive piece in five sections of which the fourth, a section in F major with obbligato flute, is lost.[49]

With the *Introduzione* to Florestan's aria, an unsurpassed musical evocation of the horrors of the dungeon, we come to the third principal realm in the opera, Pizarro's sadistic world, which Beethoven characterizes through means – derived in part from Revolutionary-era *opéra-comique* – that would have been judged abnormal or disruptive by the stylistic norms for early nineteenth-century music: disjunct (i.e. non-lyrical) melodic profiles, dissonance (particularly that of the diminished seventh chord), chromaticism, tonal instability, unusual tonal goals, syncopation, "dark" scoring (with prominent brass instruments that remind us of his political power), aberrant formal structures, and the like. So omnipresent is this sinister background that some of its stylistic codes take on quasi-leitmotivic functions, although Beethoven eschewed the more obvious manifestations of thematic recall developed in the *opéras-comiques* of Méhul and Cherubini.[50] Thus even before we meet Pizarro, Rocco's first mention of 'der Gouverneur' in the Act 1 Trio (1805/6) elicits unison chromatic motion that casts a sudden pall over the music. Similar effects occur in the prisoners' chorus in the Act 2 (or 1) Finale (1805/12), where they are reminded of their constant surveillance ("Sprecht leise, wir sind belauscht"),[51] and in the opening section of the Act 3 (2) Quartet (1805/16), where, in unison with a slowly rising chromatic bass, Pizarro identifies himself as Florestan's tormentor and would-be assassin.

Along with a recognition of opera's need for musical characterization, Beethoven of course brought to the composition of *Fidelio* an unexcelled understanding of musical form and process honed by years of experience in instrumental music. This background plays no small role in giving the opera its unique musical strengths. Throughout the work the motivic-contrapuntal treatment of the orchestra contributes immeasurably to dramatic expression, whether through reliance on a primary motive to create a unity of mood (as in the grave-digging duet), or through juxtaposition of contrasting motives and textures that underline gestures and changes of mood (as in the Rocco–Pizarro duet). Beethoven's powers of thematic development also make themselves felt at various points in the opera in both the orchestral and vocal parts. The Act 1 Trio for Rocco, Leonore, and Marzelline (1805/6), for example, relies largely on three motives (Example 12.1).[52] The first two of these (a and b), presented during Rocco's opening quatrain (m. 1, m. 3), are evidently associated with the idea of courage, an association that becomes explicit when

Example 12.1 *Leonore* (1805) Trio, no. 6, basic motives (a) mm. 1–5

(b) mm. 21–23

Leonore's text clarifies the meaning of the second motive (b) in an imitative dialogue with the winds at mm. 13–15 ("Ich habe Mut . . ."); the third motive (c), introduced by the violins during Leonore's solo (m. 21) and reiterated during Marzelline's first solo, is clearly related to concepts of love and marriage. What is more, the first of the motives (a) is treated not only as a recurring accompanimental figure in its own right (e.g. mm. 14, 32, 163–65), but also as a source of elements that are developed through the course of the piece. Its rhythm, an anacrusis of three eighth notes leading to a downbeat, is soon transferred to vocal figures (e.g., m. 4) and returns at the start of both the second (mm. 84–85) and third (mm. 135ff) principal sections of the ensemble; a diminuted form of the motive – triplet sixteenths leading to the beat – punctuates the end of the first principal section (mm. 79–80). The chromatic motion of the first four notes is also abstracted from the original motive for use elsewhere in the piece: in retrograde in Rocco's part at mm. 7–9; at mm. 31–35 in the first bassoon as a linear scaffold (f^1–$f\sharp^1$–g^1–$a\flat^1$) for a rising sequential treatment of the second motive (b); and in augmentation $(c^1-c\#^1-d^1-d\#^1-e^1)$ at mm. 81–84 at the first invocation of Pizarro.[53]

Equally characteristic is the way that Beethoven shapes musical forms to help articulate dramatic actions and meanings, doubtless one of the principal lessons that he absorbed from his study of Mozart's operas. Elements of sonata style in several "action" ensembles (1805/2; 1805/6; 1805/9; 1805/15) underscore dramatic elements: the use of differentiated melodies and motives to characterize the various participants and moods in the piece; modulation from tonic to a related key to punctuate the completion of the first major stage of poetic-dramatic structure; tonally unstable middle sections that mark some increase in tension or new dramatic development; and thematic reprises that underscore recurring dramatic ideas or draw an analogy to some prior condition. Just as significantly, the frequent divergences between these operatic forms and the conventional formal procedures of instrumental music serve to articulate dramatic meanings. When in his duet with Marzelline Jaquino returns and resumes his awkward proposal, the music effects a thematic recapitulation, but the fact that it is in the wrong key, the flattened supertonic B♭ major, suggests that his efforts will be to little avail.[54] And the many departures from sonata-style norms in the Pizarro–Rocco duet (1805/9) – the delayed definition of the tonic key at the start of the piece, the unorthodox modulation to the mediant key C♯ minor (rather than to the dominant key) for the close of the "exposition," and the unusual double statement of the reprise section – provide music-structural correlatives to the sinister situation and Pizarro's devious and desperate character.

Even pieces with little dependence on sonata-form archetypes provide ample evidence for Beethoven's close co-ordination of dramatic meaning with musical structure. To suggest changes in character and situation, the grave-digging duet modifies the rondo structure implied by the poetic form of the text and dramatic action through increasingly drastic variations of the second and third statements of the refrain ("Nur hurtig fort, nur frisch gegraben . . ."): the second statement of the refrain breaks off prematurely as Leonore turns her attention to the prisoner, whom she vows to save regardless of identity, and the third statement of the refrain is severely compressed to signal the increased urgency of the situation.[55] Completely *sui generis* is the structure of the celebrated quartet (1805/16), the dramatic climax of the opera that owes much of its tremendous effect to the way that musical processes track and magnify its eventful and emotionally charged action: (1) the orchestral accompaniment associates a principal orchestral motive with Pizarro (Example 12.2); (2) long-range bass ascent – an approach to progression and mod-

Example 12.2 *Leonore* (1805) Quartet, no. 16, principal motive

Example 12.3 *Leonore* (1805) Quartet, no. 16, bass progression, mm. 1–130

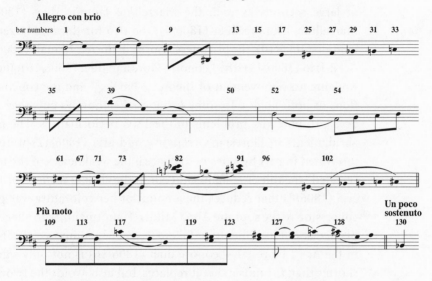

ulation common to instrumental fantasias and the development sections of sonata forms – is here correlated with the constant increase in dramatic tension up to the call of the off-stage trumpet (Example 12.3); (3) disruptions of diatonic harmonic progression through deceptive cadences and chromatic detours underscore the successive interruptions of Pizarro's murderous plan, beginning with his own digression ("Doch erst, er soll es wissen") and continuing through the series of Leonore's ever more dramatic interventions ("Zurück," "Töt' erst sein Weib," and "Noch einen Laut und Du bist todt!"); and (4) an unresolved diminished-seventh chord (vii°⁷/V) at the end provides an apt musical symbol for the unresolved dramatic tension at the conclusion of the original version of the quartet.[56]

Inasmuch as the compositional revisions of 1806 and 1814 represent, with a few exceptions, adjustments and refinements to rather than rejections of the basic premises of the 1805 version, we shall conclude this overview with a brief consideration of the principal musical changes of each subsequent stage.[57] The significant shortening of musical pieces in the 1806 version suggests that Beethoven saw a major flaw in the length of the first version, an inference that is perhaps corroborated by the presence of slightly faster tempo indications in certain movements of the 1806 score and by the conversion of the Melodrama back into spoken dialogue.

Beethoven scoured the work for passages that could be abbreviated or eliminated without damage to the drama. Many of his cuts entail minor incursions on the structure, like the removal of phrase repetitions, the curtailing of instrumental ritornellos, or the contraction of two measures into one. However, a substantial number of pieces witness the excision of large sections as well: the Marzelline–Jaquino duet (1806/2); the Marzelline–Leonore duet (1806/9); the trio for Rocco, Marzelline, and Jaquino (1806/10); the prisoners' chorus in the Act 1 Finale (1806/11); the Act 2 Trio (1806/14); the Leonore–Florestan duet (1806/16); the F major Andante assai movement of the Act 2 Finale;[58] and the concluding sections of both finales. In some instances Beethoven's cuts may also have been prompted by problems in the 1805 performances. The presumed abridgments in Florestan's recitative and aria (1806/12) were perhaps motivated in part by a desire to conceal the weaknesses of the tenor who "created" the role.[59] A significant cut in the closing sections of Leonore's aria (1806/8) that reduces the amount of her coloratura was possibly a concession to the soprano Anna Milder-Hauptmann, who allegedly complained about its difficulty.[60] Likewise, a newly composed closing section in the Act 2 Florestan–Leonore duet (1806/16) is not only significantly shorter than the music that it replaces, but also avoids the two sustained high Cs that Beethoven had required of Leonore in 1805.

Whatever opinion one may hold about the cuts – whether they represent unfortunate mutilation of an organic whole or salutary pruning of undramatic padding – the version of 1806 also comprises revisions the merits of which are beyond debate. The B♭ *Marcia* composed in 1806 as a replacement for the D major "Introduzione del IIdo Atto" is a fascinating miniature whose quirky rhythms seem a caricature of a march, perhaps again suggesting the perverse and skewed world of Pizarro's prison. With the addition of a contrabassoon to its instrumentation the grave-digging duet takes on an even more sepulchral aura.[61] The new concluding ritornello for the Florestan–Leonore duet effects a rapid transition from the exultation of their reunion to a more subdued mood, consistent with the quiet endings that prevail in the dungeon scene and also with the continuing doubt about their fate. And of course, in taming some of the bolder formal aspects of the 1805 overture – most obviously by providing a recapitulation to the structure – Beethoven produced the so-called *Leonore* Overture no. 3, a piece that easily ranks among his greatest creations.

Beethoven's attitudes about the 1814 revision of *Fidelio* are quite well documented by his correspondence with Treitschke. Naturally, the revisions of the libretto led to the most important musical changes. Owing to the reversal of the first two pieces of Act 1 Beethoven wrote yet another overture, the E major *Fidelio* Overture, forgoing the programmatic character of its predecessors (as well as the C major tonal frame for the opera as a whole) for the sake of a more compact "curtain raiser."[62] For the new conclusion of the first-act Finale he replaced the martial exhortations in Pizarro's *Aria con coro* ("Auf euch will ich nur bauen") with the chiaroscuro of the ensemble "Leb wohl du warmes Sonnenlicht." With Florestan's aria the revision tended in the opposite direction, as the new F major Poco allegro with obbligato solo oboe for Florestan's ecstatic vision is more brilliant and emphatic than the original, stoic F minor ending. The new denouement occasioned a number of important musical changes: a full cadence to tonic D major at the end of the Act 2 Quartet to signal that the threat to the heroes has effectively ended;[63] the deletion of the remarkable recitative preceding the Leonore–Florestan duet; and the composition of new music for the start of the Act 2 Finale, the celebratory C major chorus "Heil sei dem Tag" and Don Fernando's announcement of the King's general amnesty.

But the distance that separated the composer of 1814 from his earlier work seems to have prompted him to reconsider much of the music not affected by the textual changes; as he complained to Treitschke: 'Let me add that this whole opera business is the most tiresome affair in the world, for I am dissatisfied with most of it – and – there is hardly a number in it which *my present dissatisfaction would not have to patch up here and there with some satisfaction . . .'* (original emphasis).[64] To a certain extent Beethoven proceeded as he had in 1806, eliminating a number of brief passages that had entailed extraneous repetitions or prolongations.[65] Several of these new cuts clarify musical and/or dramatic points in striking ways; for instance, a simple truncation in Marzelline's aria produces a vast improvement in the long-range approach to the upper registral boundary (cf. 1805/1, mm. 27–29, and 1814/2, mm. 23–24),[66] and rhythmic compressions in the Rocco–Pizarro duet (1814/8, mm. 135–36) and in the Act 2 Trio (1814/13, m. 81) clearly lend a sense of greater urgency that is appropriate for the moment. As opposed to the 1806 version, however, large-scale cuts are quite rare; apart from the deletions effected by the changes in the libretto, major cuts are for the most part confined to significant abbreviations in Leonore's aria – in particular the deletion of the first section of the Allegro ("O du für den ich alles trug') – again perhaps a concession to the soprano Milder-Hauptmann.[67] By 1814 Beethoven also realized that shorter is not always better, for he restored the Melodrama (1814/12) and several phrases that he had deleted in 1806 (e.g., mm. 91–94 in the Act 1 Trio [1814/5], mm. 27–28 in the Act 2 *Introduzione* [1814/11], and mm. 239–42 in the Act 2 Finale [1814/16]), expanded the recitative (and probably also the Adagio) of Florestan's aria (1814/11) to approximately the original dimensions of 1805, and

partially reinstated the reprise of the Act 2 Trio (1814/13). A new passage
for chorus in the coda of Pizarro's aria (1814/7, mm. 89–104) allows us to
hear more clearly that even his own guards live in fear of him.

Beyond his concern for cuts and expansions, the Beethoven of 1814
found much else to change in the opera. A number of adjustments in the
declamation result in closer matches of musical expression and verbal
meaning. To cite just one characteristic example: in the Allegro of
Leonore's aria the phrase "ich wanke nicht" (1814/9, m. 75) is rhythmically reshaped so as to shift the downbeat from the word "wanke" (waver)
to "ich," thereby giving the line a stronger sense of *her* personal resolve.[68]
Similarly, numerous revisions of declamation, melodic contour, texture,
orchestration, harmony, and dynamics in the great Act 2 Quartet
(1814/14) allow for a more vivid projection of words and feelings than do
the earlier versions; these include the more jagged contour of Pizarro's
opening solo, the unaccompanied revelation of Leonore's identity ("Töt'
erst sein Weib"), the more differentiated treatment of dynamics, orchestration, and harmony in mm. 88–93 and 94–99 for Leonore's dual pledges
of consolation for Florestan and ruin for Pizarro ("Ich bin sein Weib,
geschworen / Hab' ich ihm Trost, Verderben dir"), and the new treatment
of dynamics at the start of the final section.[69] At a broader level of expression, the reconception of vocal texture and orchestral sonority in the
Sostenuto assai section of the Act 2 Finale (as well as the deceptive
cadence from V/A to F with which it now begins) adds immeasurably to
the aura of incredulous relief and pious gratitude expressed in this
"Augenblick." A new stretta for the Act 2 Finale rounds off the opera with
music that is not only more thematically cogent than the music that it
replaces – unlike the 1805/06 versions, the new conclusion is based on the
principal melodies of the *Schlußchor* itself – but also more emphatically
jubilant. Lastly, a number of revisions, like the imitations incorporated
into the Adagio of Leonore's aria (1814/9, m. 49, mm. 51–52), the Act 2
Introduzione (1814/11, mm. 18–19), and the A major Meno Allegro of the
Act 2 Finale (1814/16, mm. 110–20, 155–60), simply result in more interesting, richer music *per se*, surely something for which no opera composer
ever need apologize.

Throughout his career Beethoven repeatedly toyed with the idea of composing a second opera, but he never again seriously pursued any such projects, allegedly because of his dissatisfaction with the libretti offered
him.[70] Doubtless his increasing deafness worked against a return to the
theater. His experiences with *Fidelio* must also have disinclined him to re-
enter the operatic arena. For a composer accustomed in instrumental
composition to the freedom to follow his musical imagination wherever it

might lead, the many demands of opera – to match musical expression to specified emotional states, to accommodate the very real limitations of opera singers, and to achieve immediate success with paying audiences – must have seemed unusually confining, a sentiment that may well be summed up in a single diary entry from 1816: "Leave aside operas and everything else; write only in your manner . . ."[71] But precisely because opera was not his true metier, the one extraordinary essay in the genre that he did complete will always occupy an especially cherished place in the pantheon of his great works. Peripheral though it may be, his only opera reveals, as do few of Beethoven's other works, the full measure of the man: his idealism, his ambition to absorb and transcend the best of the Classical heritage, his dogged determination to attain perfection, and his faith in the power of his art to elevate and ennoble those who experience it.

13 Probing the sacred genres: Beethoven's religious songs, oratorio, and masses

BIRGIT LODES

Beethoven lived at a time when Christianity and its institutions were losing much of their power, yet the influence of religion is felt not only in his explicitly sacred and liturgical works but also in works such as the Ninth Symphony, *Fidelio*, and the "Heiliger Dankgesang" from the A minor String Quartet. Since Beethoven, who was baptized as a Catholic, never really subscribed to any one of the many distinct theological currents of his time, it is difficult to obtain a coherent picture of his religious views from the multiplicity of ideas that, as documentary evidence proves, occupied Beethoven's interest.[1] Still, a pattern emerges in his independent pursuit of religious questions that is reflected in his choice of texts to set: for him, religion was something not just dogmatically given and represented through the Catholic Church, but rather to be understood from a human perspective and experienced in its relevance to one's own life – a position that differs as essentially from the Baroque orientation toward the hereafter as from the mysticism and otherworldliness of Romanticism.

The "Gellert" *Lieder* op. 48 and other songs with sacred texts

With the first unmistakable signs of hearing loss and the deep personal, musical, and ideological crisis that followed, Beethoven began to grapple increasingly with religious ideas. At this time he came to know the *Geistliche Oden und Lieder* of Christian Fürchtegott Gellert (1st edn., Leipzig, 1757). From these fifty-four texts he chose six with revealing content: "Die Ehre Gottes aus der Natur," for example, recalls ideas in poems by Christoph Christian Sturm from *Betrachtungen über die Werke Gottes im Reiche der Natur . . .*, a book which he may have encountered while still in Bonn and later definitely read,[2] and "Vom Tode," to which the ideas of the last section of the Heiligenstadt Testament (October 1802) closely correspond,[3] seems to reflect his preoccupation with thoughts of death.

Gellert's poems were among the most frequently set texts in the second half of the eighteenth century.[4] C. P. E. Bach composed some of the most remarkable and musically most demanding settings (1758 and 1764), which Beethoven may have known. Bach's strophic settings are distinguished by an unpretentious tone, a simple and often chorale-like melodic line that is doubled in the treble part of the keyboard, and an almost complete absence of music for keyboard alone. Beethoven broke with this precedent in his own *Lieder*, which date from between 1798 and 1802. "Bußlied," the last of Beethoven's settings, has special significance within his entire song repertory because of its great length and its through-composed bipartite construction. Moreover, in the fast second part, for the first time in the history of the German *Lied*, a varied, virtuosic piano accompaniment is placed against an unvaried vocal part (compare with the later *An die ferne Geliebte* op. 98, 1815). Even the first five, despite their simplicity, include more keyboard figuration than the Bach pieces. There are preludes, interludes, and postludes in the piano, and the melody, which is not always identical in the vocal and piano treble parts, contains surprises, such as the large leap in no. 2, m. 10. Despite the regularity of the line lengths and rhythms in the poems, Beethoven varies phrase-lengths (no. 3) or, for expressive purposes, the vocal declamatory rhythms (no. 2). In no. 4 he composed two musical strains for the first two poetic strophes, thus achieving a larger overall form (ABA'). In preparing the songs for publication he shifted "Bußlied," the most substantial setting, to the end,[5] thus achieving an effective conclusion of the entire group.

At the same time the songs have conspicuously "religious" traits, especially the first five: contrapuntal textures, the avoidance of melismas and word-repetitions, the preference for unvaried chorale-like rhythms, half notes as the preferred rate of declamation (frequently with an alla breve marking), and even, in no. 2, a postlude for the piano that is reminiscent of a chorale prelude for organ in which the vocal melody is distributed among the parts of the strict contrapuntal texture (Example 13.1). In these *Lieder*, it seems, Beethoven for once consciously wanted to approximate church idioms.

Using religious texts in solo songs with piano was not a common practice among Viennese composers, but Beethoven set a number of other such texts in this manner, including "An einen Säugling" WoO 108, 1784?, "Der Wachtelschlag" WoO 129, 1803, "An die Hoffnung" op. 32, 1805, and op. 94, 1815, "Abendlied unterm gestirnten Himmel" WoO 150, 1820. These *Lieder*, some of which represent his earliest engagement with spiritual themes in music, are relevant in several important ways for his later religious works. In these works, he found musical solutions for certain types of textual ideas that he would later fall back on and develop further: among these are flickering chord repetitions as an image of the stars,[6] a IV–I cadence to end an open statement pointing toward the future (first in the "Bußlied" op. 48 no. 6, then in the *Missa solemnis*, from the Gloria

Example 13.1 "Die Liebe des Nächsten" op. 48 no. 2, mm. 15–29

up to the Agnus), the idea of developing a movement from a single note to which a line is added (op. 48 no. 1, WoO 129, Kyrie of the C major and, modified, the D major Mass; see below) or the vivid musical juxtaposition of the noise of war and trust in God (WoO 129, mm. 51ff.; *Missa solemnis*, Agnus Dei, mm. 338ff.).

Christus am Ölberge op. 85

Beethoven may have begun work on his only oratorio, *Christus am Ölberge*, at the end of 1802, thus only a few months after completing the "Gellert" *Lieder*.[7] Having recently been employed at Schikaneder's Theater an der Wien, he glimpsed the possibility of using the theater during the coming Lenten season for an academy in which he would present himself in public for the first time as a vocal composer. The recent introduction of three important oratorios to the Viennese repertory, Haydn's *Seven Words*, *Creation*, and *Seasons*, which were first performed during Lent in 1796, 1798, and 1801 respectively, posed a challenge to Beethoven's ambition to establish himself as a composer in all the important genres.

As the subject for his oratorio Beethoven selected an excerpt from the Passion story of Jesus (the prayer on the Mount of Olives in nos. 1–3 and the arrest in 4–6).[8] The fact that virtually no oratorio setting of the Passion story had been performed in Vienna during the preceding years in itself suggests that the choice of text was not a matter of convention, but rather had personal meaning for him. The plot deviates from the traditional story in a significant way: the events are more powerfully centered on Jesus the person, who is presented as an individual in all his changing feelings. Certain phrases in the Heiligenstadt Testament and Beethoven's letters from the time closely resemble the language and the ideas from passages in the oratorio, providing strong evidence that in his own time of crisis Beethoven identified with the figure of Jesus.[9]

In Jesus he saw an exemplary person whose moral precepts he wished to follow. The "godliness" of Jesus was not the central idea for him, and there is even evidence that he doubted this aspect of Catholic theology.[10] Instead, he stressed the Christian concept of love. This emerges clearly in the recitative and trio from no. 6, in which Beethoven's music sensitively expresses Peter's angry rejection of Jesus's message of love (see mm. 74ff.) – a very human reaction – but after Jesus has instructed him again to love his enemies (now in recitative-like direct speech rather than an aria) Peter finally agrees to preach this holy law.

Many unusual features of the work, some of which are still controversial, follow from the oratorio's emphasis on the human side of Jesus:

> Rather than the usual oratorio bass, Jesus is set as an operatic tenor/suffering hero; in his first appearance he sings a recitative with a dramatic aria and solo cadenza and later (no. 3), a duet with a seraph that resembles a love duet.
>
> An earlier version of the libretto includes stage directions,[11] some of which Beethoven vividly rendered into music: for example, the last measures of no. 3 realize the indication "Christ falls down on his knees." The publishers removed these indications and wanted the libretto to have a more abstract, less human disposition, but Beethoven vehemently opposed this suggestion.
>
> After the oratorio had been performed in Vienna at least three times, Beethoven revised it early in 1804, creating the version known to us today. The few preserved excerpts from the original version,[12] above all from the first aria, suggest that he was eager to dynamize and individualize formal processes, to achieve intensely vivid text setting (e.g. the unaccompanied vocal part in mm. 176ff.), and to strengthen theatrical and dramatic elements (e.g. the powerful vocal cadenza at the end of the aria).
>
> Church-music elements are only coloring in *Christus*: they appear only in conjunction with specific textual contexts, such as in the seraph's recitative in no. 3: "So spricht Jehova," mm. 7–13 (Grave, simple declamation in the vocal part, wind accompaniment stile-antico whole and half notes, an embellished Renaissance-style cadence in mm. 12–13); there are, to be sure, also longer imitative passages, as

well as a fugal final chorus on a grand scale ("Preiset ihn") reminiscent of an oratorio chorus by Handel or Haydn.

It is the dramatic conception that makes *Christus am Ölberge* a central work in Beethoven's gradual progress toward composing an opera. Alan Tyson and Sieghard Brandenburg, among others, have pointed out affinities with specific operas and have criticized the oratorio for its derivative stylistic diversity. Nevertheless, Beethoven also found individual solutions, as I want to illustrate by the scene-complex in nos. 4 and 5.

Immediately after Jesus has welcomed death (recitative, no. 4), for he will die to save humankind, the mercenaries who seek him are heard in the distance ("Alla Marcia").[13] Jesus reacts in a recitative ("Those who have come to catch me are approaching," "Die mich zu fangen ausgezogen sind, sie nahen nun"). Here Beethoven expresses what Jesus thinks and says, while the soldiers look for him, without departing from the standard sequence recitative–aria (see the use of the dotted search-motive for the soldiers, and the motivic connection of Jesus's words to the recitative in no. 4). By musically tying together two simultaneous but spatially separated events (the soldiers' search and Jesus talking), Beethoven creates the illusion of a three-dimensional stage-setting.

This effect becomes even stronger when, immediately after Jesus's important words "Doch nicht mein Wille, nein! Dein Wille nur geschehe," the marchlike search-motive returns and tension increases, culminating in the excitement (the A major chord, the dominant) at the beginning of the Allegro molto. With the soldiers' sudden intrusion ("Hier *ist* er"), the music resolves into a unison, fortissimo D under a fermata – a harmonic and rhythmic analogy to the libretto's dramatic action and rhythm of declamation. Jesus's disciples awaken at the noise but, confused from drowsiness, ask themselves what will happen to them. That this dramatic conception had a powerful impact on contemporary audiences becomes clear in reviews of the performance: "The choruses of the soldiers, 'Wir haben ihn gesehen,' etc. had the greatest effect. It was all the talk as the audience exited and for several days afterward. At the words 'Hier ist er! Ergreift ihn! Bindet ihn!' many felt so deeply affected that, according to their own statements, for a moment they feared for their own lives."[14] Beethoven would go still further in this dramatic direction in *Leonore*.

Beethoven became caught in a critical crossfire because of these very qualities of scenic and dramatic immediacy in an oratorio. In one review of the score (published in 1811), a critic explained that in general an oratorio – as opposed to a drama, which portrays a "present-tense," unexpected occurrence – represents an event "already known to us, but whose inner motivation, the accompanying feelings, are brought to life."[15]

Numbers 4 to 6, above all the trio, thus seemed too theatrical to this critic, while the role of Jesus's disciples was "extremely common and trivial" in text and music. Also lacking was a "solid fugue," according to this review, which seems to have a North German-Protestant aesthetic basis. In 1828, however, a critic for the *Berliner allgemeine musikalische Zeitung* distinguished between Beethoven's "Catholic" oratorio and a "Protestant" oratorio by Louis Spohr: Catholicism tries to translate secrets and prophecies of the holy script into temporal terms, "to transplant them from the realm of inner reflection into that of sensual perception,"[16] making it inevitable that Beethoven's music, too, should appear as "dramatically sensual perception" and show "Christ and the Angel . . . as humans," reminding us of "nothing higher." However one chooses to evaluate the difficult questions of genre aesthetics raised by *Christus am Ölberge*, within Beethoven's personal development as a dramatic composer it remains a crucial work in which the theme (which preoccupied Beethoven at this time) of the hero who overcomes fear and suffering emerges with particular distinctness.

Mass in C op. 86, and *Missa solemnis* in D op. 123

Genesis, first performances, and publication

In the spring of 1807 Beethoven received a commission from Prince Nikolaus II Esterházy to compose a Mass for the name-day celebration of his wife, Princess Josepha Maria Hermengild. Since the Mass in C op. 86 is Beethoven's first completed work for the divine service, it is understandable that he looked for orientation in other Masses, including the six late Masses by Joseph Haydn, also composed for Esterházy. Special emphasis should be placed on his reliance on Haydn's *Schöpfungsmesse* Hob. HXII:13 because it is documented in the sketches for the first part of the Gloria.[17]

Beethoven conducted the first performance of his Mass on 13 September 1807 with a large orchestra. Although there is evidence that the Mass was inadequately rehearsed, its unconventional music – in comparison with the familiar Masses by Haydn and Hummel – seems above all to have caused displeasure. To a countess friend Prince Nikolaus wrote: "Beethoven's Mass is unbearably ridiculous and vile. I am not convinced that it could in honesty even be published. I am angry and ashamed about it."[18]

The *Missa solemnis*, too, had its origin in a specific occasion, the celebration of Archduke Rudolph's enthronement as Archbishop of Olmütz on 9 March 1820, although this time Beethoven began composition without a commission. It was an act of personal feeling and esteem: it was to Rudolph, his patron, student, and friend, that he directed the words in the autograph above the Kyrie: "From the heart – may it go – to the heart!"[19] But he took so long on the work that the Mass could not be performed for the ceremony – only the Kyrie and parts of the Gloria were ready by then – and, interrupted by work on the Piano Sonatas opp. 109, 110, and 111, was not completed until the end of 1822.[20]

Both masses occupy a position between liturgical music and religious music for the concert hall. Beethoven performed excerpts from the C major Mass in his famous concert of 22 December 1808 and permitted Breitkopf & Härtel to publish it with a German translation of the text (for use in concert performance) under the Latin. The *Missa solemnis* went far beyond the liturgically justifiable range of expression (Beethoven characterized it to various publishers as his "greatest" work and wanted to sell it for a higher price than the Ninth Symphony[21]), and, in the event, the premiere did take place in a concert hall (7 April 1824, St. Petersburg), as did the first Viennese (partial) performance on 7 May 1824.

Music and text in the Mass in C and the *Missa solemnis*
The Kyries: humankind and transcendence

"The general character of the *Kyrie* . . . is heartfelt devotion, from which [comes] the warmth of *religious* feeling, 'Gott erbarme dich unser,' without therefore being sad. Gentleness is the fundamental characteristic. . . . despite '*eleison* erbarme dich unser' – cheerfulness pervades the whole. The Catholic enters church on Sunday in his best clothes and in a joyful and festive mood. The Kyrie eleison in the same way introduces the entire work."[22] Beethoven thus described the Kyrie of his C major Mass on 16 January 1811 and in so doing defended himself against the underlaying of a German text, in which concepts like "the Almighty," among others, are found. While many earlier mass-settings present powerful praise of both God and aristocratic authority, Beethoven proceeds from "the warmth of religious feeling," "gentleness," and "joyfulness." For him the focus lies neither on God nor on princes, but rather on the human being entering the church, in whom emotions should be stirred and devotion awakened.[23]

For this reason, probably, the bass section alone begins the Kyrie, intoning a single pitch (Example 13.2). Unaccompanied by the brilliance of instruments, the voice of the pleading people opens the Mass and, after the entrance of the other choral voices and strings in m. 2, will continue to lead the instrumental voices in the entire movement. Trumpets and timpani, typically ceremonial instruments, are silent throughout the Kyrie.

Example 13.2 Mass in C, Kyrie, mm. 1–11

From this rhythmicized single tone, the tonal space (a stepwise rising line in parallel thirds against the pedal point on c), harmony, and dynamics slowly unfold up to m. 9, which touches on a surprising E major chord but immediately afterwards cadences in C major (mm. 10f. and 14f.). The first Kyrie (mm. 1–36) is permeated by the opening Kyrie intonation and the stepwise rising line, often in thirds; the C major to E major chord progression becomes the tonal scaffolding for the entire movement (Kyrie in C major, Christe in E major, Kyrie in C major).

Example 13.3
(a) Sonata op. 53, "Waldstein" first mvt., mm. 1–4 (beginning of first theme); mm. 34–38
(beginning of second theme in m. 35)

(b) Mass in C, Kyrie, mm. 36–40 (Christe theme)

C major and E major are also the keys of the two themes in the opening movement of the "Waldstein" Sonata op. 53 (Example 13.3a and b): the first, like the Kyrie theme, beginning with a single tone, rising from the depths, animated – departure; the second, like the Christe theme, static, high-pitched, chordal, cadencing – goal (mm. 35ff.). The modulation from E major back to C major proceeds in precisely the same quick and surprising manner[24] in both the sonata and the mass movement (Example 13.3c: compare mm. 82f. and 84f. in op. 53 with mm. 76f. and 78f. in op. 85). However, parallels between the first Kyrie and Christe and

Example 13.3 (*cont.*)
(c) op. 53, first mvt., mm. 82–85 and op. 86, Kyrie, mm. 76–79

the exposition of a sonata-form movement break down at the latest in mm. 84ff.: instead of the unchanged repetition of the exposition or the beginning of the development the slightly varied Kyrie returns. Since in a mass – as opposed to a sonata – a recapitulation of the second thematic area (Christe) is hardly possible and harmonic closure cannot be achieved in this way (the modulation to E major is omitted and replaced by a brief cadence in C major, mm. 109–12), Beethoven integrates the unusual E major region by frequently juxtaposing C major and E major during the course of the movement.

The ABA′ form arising from the tripartite structure of the text presents the challenge of organically connecting the individual sections. In addition to the web of motivic and harmonic connections stemming from the very beginning of the movement, there are other significant integrating features: (1) continuous motion (uninterrupted eighth notes) pervades the Kyrie and Christe in a similar manner (one exception: the *a cappella* Christe statement in mm. 37–40) and only gradually subsides in the final measures; (2) the Christe eleison melody can be understood as inverting the rising line of the Kyrie; (3) the boundaries between the second (Christe) and third (Kyrie) formal sections are strikingly blurred: at the end of the Christe eleison text (m. 68) the Kyrie motive enters – at first set instrumentally, then also vocally, in each case only the antecedent phrase followed by fragmentation – but still in the E major of the middle section; the tonal return does not take place until m. 84.

In the literature on the C major Mass it has not been recognized that Beethoven drew on several aspects of the first movement of the "Pastorale" Sonata op. 28. Its form also develops organically from the opening phrase and avoids conspicuous contrasts; closely related to the beginning of the Kyrie is the opposition of a low pedal point that first appears all by itself and the melodic line (in this case, descending). As in the transition to the third formal section of the Kyrie, Beethoven divides the thematic and harmonic articulation of the form in the sonata movement in order to blur the boundary of the second theme and support the sense of organic flow. Contributing to this quality in the sonata – as in the Kyrie – is the continuous pulse (quarter notes), which is interrupted only in a few formally significant places. The sonata and the Kyrie both depart from the usual texture of melody-with-accompaniment in their almost continuous four-part writing (the apparent accompanimental eighth notes in the Kyrie also have their basis in the chordally conceived melodic style),[25] and in both movements fragments from the first theme dominate the thematic-motivic work (compare the development and coda of the sonata with the end of the second formal section, mm. 68–78, and coda, mm. 113ff., in the Kyrie: in each case fragmentation leads to inactivity without dramatic confrontation).

The parallels between the opening movements of earlier piano sonatas and the Mass demonstrate the latter's close connections to Beethoven's instrumental music. Nevertheless, he avoided simply transferring the formal schemata of instrumental music to Mass movements, as Mozart and Haydn often did; instead he applied instrumental techniques – linkage; contrasts; harmonic, thematic, and motivic processes – to tie together the distinct parts of the text-generated form. It is not surprising that there should be similarities to precisely that piano sonata (op. 28) in which Beethoven sought to minimize drama and contrast in the first movement of a sonata. With these qualities he succeeded in "irresistibly" awakening in the listener an "edifying" feeling, "through which the heart is led to devotion in the *Kyrie*."[26]

In 1824, Beethoven voiced similar sentiments about the *Missa solemnis*:

my primary goal in composing this grand Mass was to awaken and permanently instill religious feelings in both the singers and listeners.[27]

Indeed the character of the Kyrie in the *Missa solemnis*, marked "Assai sostenuto. Mit Andacht," is similar to that in the C major Mass. The relationship is manifest in the thematic material (gradual unfolding in parallel thirds between the bass parts and first violins in mm. 6–12, between clarinets and bassoons against the tonic pedal in mm. 23ff., 27ff., 31ff. – the feeling of devotion slowly mounts; see Example 13.4), in the formal structure (motivic connections within and between the three text-generated parts, no dramatization of the return to the A section, even more changes in the second Kyrie – to round off the form – than in that of the C major Mass), and in the foreshadowing in the opening phrase of the tonal plan of the movement (B minor, the key of the Christe, is introduced as a chord in mm. 3 and 18). In the C major Mass considerable harmonic tension between sections offsets motivic and expressive evenness; in the *Missa solemnis* a less tense harmonic scaffolding opposes a large diversity of motives: in each case Beethoven was concerned to balance one parameter with the contrary tendency in the other.

The two settings differ decisively, despite the various connections. Although the Kyrie is the shortest movement of the *Missa solemnis*, it is in many respects more grandly conceived than the Kyrie of the C major Mass.[28] The thematic material does not develop from one scarcely audible low pitch; rather, the tonic supports a powerful, dotted tutti chord undoubtedly meant to be heard as a musical sign for God.[29] The emphasis is not on illustrating the immaterial, but rather on creating a musical analogy to the realization that for a human being the greatness of God remains intangible and unimaginable by desensualizing sound (see the unusual entrance "before the beat").[30] Therefore the divine is consistently set against the human (see above all the varied repetition of the introduction with the vocal parts from m. 21 [see Example 13.4]: after the grand Kyrie statements [mm. 21ff., 25ff., 29ff.] comes the individual human reaction in the solo voice [mm. 23ff., 27ff., 31ff.] with calm linear progressions in the winds). This is a programmatic exposition of that which will remain the underlying idea of the *Missa solemnis*: the impact of the almighty divinity on individuals who can only vaguely perceive his unattainable greatness. Such unmediated juxtaposition of the irreconcilable domains of God and humankind plays a central role in the organization of the Gloria and Credo.[31] In both movements, Beethoven's concern for the meaning of the text (he sought an adequate musical expression for every sentence or even single words)[32] results in block-like musical sections that butt up against each other abruptly.

Example 13.4 *Missa solemnis*, Kyrie, mm. 21–33

Example 13.4 (cont.)

Example 13.5 Declamation of "Et incarnatus est" in the Credo of both Masses

Mass in C, mm. 134–37

Et in- car- na- tus est   de spi-ri-tu sanc-to

Missa solemnis, mm. 126–29

Archaisms: "Et incarnatus est"

Well-established topoi – such as the beginning of the Kyrie – and archaic
sonorities help shape the aural impression of the *Missa solemnis*. Yet
Beethoven, who before and during the composition of the Mass had been
studying early music (e.g. Palestrina), did not simply adopt these traditions: he chose them consciously, from a distance, as an alternative to the
language of the Classical style. Among these idioms – a dimension
scarcely discernible in the C major Mass – are such harmonic characteristics as the frequent use of the fourth scale degree (associated with plagal
cadences and the ambivalent relationship between the chords on the
fourth and first scale degrees, which in the *Missa solemnis* can be heard
sometimes not only as subdominant and tonic but rather also as tonic and
dominant), and the avoidance of the leading tone, especially audible in
the "Et resurrexit" (Credo, mm. 188–93), along with prose-like declamation and rhythmic irregularities that work against the sense of well-
defined meter.

Beethoven used historical styles not only as "a leaven of modernity,"[33]
but also semantically, as in the "Et incarnatus est." The setting in the C
major Mass resembles the section in the *Missa solemnis* in its identical
speech-determined rhythm (Example 13.5) and in the distinct designs of
the sections "Et incarnatus est" (homogeneous, in the *Missa solemnis* with
gradually expanding orchestration) and "et homo factus est" (dialogue
between an individual voice and a group, distribution of melodic material
among various parts). Yet Beethoven sets the sections in the *Missa solemnis* more clearly in relief against each other and, above all, interprets their
textual meaning more powerfully through musical analogies. He trans-
fers the inconceivable secret of "Et incarnatus est" into mysterious,
foreign music-historical worlds:[34] that of accompanied plainsong (single
voice, Dorian mode, but, nevertheless, accompanied and with text-setting
based on modern principles of metrical accentuation), that of vocal
polyphony (mm. 132ff., but with a nimbus-like pulsation in some of the
woodwinds and a flute symbolic of the Holy Ghost in its "disembodied"
detachment from the beat), that of liturgical recitation (mm. 141ff., *falso-
bordone*), which in its remoteness from meaningful articulated speech

conveys that the true sense of "Et incarnatus" remains inconceivable for human beings.[35] The "historical" is thus used semantically: to express what cannot be understood rationally, the sacredly distant, placed in opposition to the familiar style of the "Et homo factus" (return of functional harmony; the melody is suggestive of a consequent phrase thus forming a musical analogy for arrival).

Agnus Dei

From a musical – not a liturgical – point of view, the Agnus Dei, the last part of the Ordinary, presents the problem of bringing the entire work to a persuasive conclusion. To round off the C major Mass cyclically, Beethoven refers in the final seventeen measures to the music from the beginning of the Kyrie (an independent recasting of the "Dona ut Kyrie" convention of using the music from the Kyrie for the "Dona nobis pacem" section of the Agnus); the close of the Agnus in the *Missa solemnis* is connected motivically with the "germinal motive" that permeates the entire Mass (e.g. Kyrie, mm. 4–7).[36] Harmonic tension from the Kyrie is reintroduced and resolved in the Agnus of both masses. In the "Dona nobis pacem" of the Mass in C, C major and E major are brought together several times in cadential progressions; the Agnus Dei of the *Missa solemnis* begins in B minor, the "black" key of the Christe, and "opens" to D major only in the "Dona nobis pacem".

The "Dona nobis pacem" is traditionally set to different, usually more serene music than the repeated "Agnus Dei, qui tollis peccata mundi, miserere nobis." Beethoven follows this custom, although in neither Agnus is he satisfied with a simple sequence of two parts: in the C major Mass – apparently for the first time in the history of Mass-settings – the somber C minor sphere of the Agnus reappears in the "Dona nobis pacem" (mm. 65–82). This is not done only to make the form more coherent; it also has a psychological interpretative function: peace cannot be established immediately and unconditionally; there must be another fearful appeal to the Lamb of God. The unexpected recall of the Agnus Dei music within the "Dona" section resembles an important aspect of the latter movements of the Fifth Symphony: the C minor sphere of the open-ended scherzo returns (mm. 152–205) within the radiant C major of the finale;[37] there are also parallels to *Christus am Ölberge* in the idea of "overcoming" and the key-scheme C minor–C major.

In the Agnus of the *Missa solemnis*, the text "Agnus Dei . . . miserere nobis" also returns in the "Dona nobis pacem," but now it appears within several, in part purely instrumental, contrasting sections, in which Beethoven expresses musically the kind of "peace" he had in mind: the unusual "war episodes" (mm. 164–89, 326–53; war music as in a *battaglia*,

Example 13.6 *Missa solemnis*, Agnus Dei, mm. 266–72

operatic accompanied recitative to illustrate fear) represent the threat to "outward peace."[38] In the war episodes foreign material in an alien key enters – so to speak, "from outside." In the representation of the threat to "inner peace" (mm. 266–326), which is a completely new idea in the history of the Mass, well-known material from earlier in the movement reappears in such a form that the music seems to come apart as an analogy for disturbed inner peace (cf. Example 13.6):[39] The lower theme is derived from the "pacem" motive (cf. choral soprano, mm. 107ff.), but several pitches are deleted, it includes ties across the bar, and stands in opposition to the meter. The upper theme is related to the counterpoint to the "pacem" motive (cf. choral bass, mm. 107ff.), but it is now disjunct, inter-rupted by many rests – it is no longer peaceful. After the first entry the two fugato themes both shift in different directions by a fourth (interval between entries now a seventh); they thus clash and the entire passage is harmonically unstable. The question of what exactly Beethoven wanted to depict here has until now remained unclear, though "inner peace" was extraordinarily common in his time as a theological image, which sug-gests that it was not Beethoven's own subjective invention. In his work *Ueber den innern Frieden*,[40] widely read around 1800 and possibly also known to Beethoven (at least in its content), Ambrosius von Lombez described inner peace as the (positive) impact of God upon the individ-ual.[41] When absent, "impatient ardor," "conflicting impulses," and "turmoil" prevail in the human heart (cf. Beethoven's music in mm. 266ff.).[42] Each individual possesses the potential for inner peace in himself, but it can be activated only by God – a non-abstract God whose acts directly and personally affect mankind.[43] Beethoven's vivid setting of the prayer for inner (religious) and outer (secular) peace in the Agnus, which far transcends the usual limits of liturgical settings, reveals how convincingly Beethoven was able to interpret the content of the Mass text in his music.[44] By May 1819 at the latest, he had become acquainted with various writings by the theologian Johann Michael Sailer, to whom he wanted to send his nephew for instruction. In conceiving and completing the *Missa solemnis*, especially the "Et incarnatus" and "Dona nobis pacem," Beethoven had expressed in music in exemplary fashion Sailer's appeal that believers should not simply parrot the prayers from the liturgy, but rather try to penetrate intellectually their spiritual meaning.[45] The profound interpretative dimension is, as required by Sailer, balanced by the stirring of warm human feeling (Sailer's "religion of the heart").

Conclusion

Theodor Adorno once posed the question: "Is the aesthetic problem of the Missa [solemnis] its reduction to the universal-human?"[46] In my view this is the aesthetic problem in all of Beethoven's religious works *before* the *Missa solemnis*. After Beethoven had concerned himself with the human dimension of faith in *Christus am Ölberg* and the C major Mass, he succeeded in the *Missa solemnis* in finding the appropriate expression of the incomprehensibility of the divine and its effect on humankind. The human being still stands in the center – even in the *Missa solemnis* – but apprehends transcendence and its effects.

For Adorno the *Missa solemnis* was a problematic work, and this kept him from finishing a planned monograph on Beethoven. Although this "alienated masterpiece" is not infrequently performed, in his view it is usually received with paralyzed admiration rather than analytical acuteness. As Adorno correctly recognized, one can scarcely penetrate the aesthetic essence of the *Missa solemnis* through the perspective of middle-period procedures (e.g. thematic work): the *Missa solemnis* breaks the musical and expressive boundaries of everything that came before it. To describe how it differs from the works of the middle period requires emphasizing its similarities to other late works (among them the "Hammerklavier" Sonata, the Ninth Symphony, the late piano sonatas and string quartets) with respect to formal design, harmonic configuration, instrumentation, symphonic dimensions, effects of contrast, thematic organization, contrapuntal techniques, fugues, connections between individual movements, and much more. In recent years several far-reaching studies on these aspects, above all those by William Drabkin and William Kinderman, have appeared in English.[47] Here I have tried to suggest another possible approach, namely to present Beethoven's ideas about religion and expression, and their compositional realization in the *Missa solemnis* in the context of his earlier sacred and liturgical works.

The entire repertory of Beethoven's religious music had a very mixed reception because of the shift in evaluative criteria, especially for religious music, at the beginning of the nineteenth century, which made

Beethoven, his listeners, and his critics walk a "tightrope" with no certain outcome. "Functional" music and genre traditions increasingly lost their aesthetic value; they could not survive the requirement that compositions be "original," "individual," "products of." In each of his sacred and liturgical works (songs, oratorio, and Masses) Beethoven expanded existing norms, just as he did (and is recognized for having done) in the instrumental genres. In so doing he created in the masses true and great "works of art."

Translated by Margaret Notley

PART IV

Reception

14 "With a Beethoven-like sublimity":
Beethoven in the works of other composers

MARGARET NOTLEY

Beethoven made instrumental music seem to matter as it had not before. Charles Ives interpreted the "oracle" at the beginning of the Fifth Symphony as "the soul of humanity at the door of the divine mysteries, radiant in the faith that it will be opened – and the human become the divine,"[1] because the music apparently struck him, as it has many of the rest of us, with the vividness of revelation. Like the opening of the Fifth Symphony, the fusion of introduction and first theme in the Ninth, the point of recapitulation in the *Eroica*, and the interconnectedness of the C♯ minor quartet all have an aura of compelling significance. Ives chose to claim a portion of Beethovenian grandeur for American culture and himself by placing the Fifth Symphony's motto at the center of a theme in the *Concord* Sonata. And, indeed, much of music history after Beethoven reads as a series of engagements – aggressive, inspired, ironic, elegiac – with his greatness and the potential that he had revealed.

A new world of sound and a new subjectivity

Richard Wagner's reactions to Beethoven, voluminously documented in his own writings and in the recollections of his associates, exposed a number of key themes in the reception of Beethoven and his music; his observations will therefore serve as an occasional guide in this survey. Wagner attributed his very awakening as a musician to the Ninth Symphony: "I was struck at once, as if by force of destiny, with the long-sustained perfect fifths with which the first movement begins: these sounds, which played such a spectral role in my earliest impressions of music, came to me as the ghostly fundamental of my own life."[2] Here as elsewhere, he isolated a crucial moment in the music: the sixteen-bar opening is remarkable for its thematic void and tonal ambiguity, its emphasis on sheer sound, and its suggestiveness: repetitions of the notes of the hollow fifth slowly expand the registral space and timbral resources to bring into existence the universe of the symphony. Like more typical sonata-form first themes, the introduction/theme comes back repeatedly to function as a beginning, each time renewing the sense of "a background of infinite spread."[3] All subsequent orchestral works in D minor that open with sparse thematic material against a harmonic plateau (the Overture to *Der fliegende Holländer*, Brahms's First Piano Concerto, Bruckner's Third and Ninth Symphonies, Mahler's Third Symphony, etc.) appear fated to be linked with Beethoven's Ninth.[4] In many instances the reference seems obvious and even trivial, but in others (not necessarily in D minor), composers have given the opening a semantic twist by modifying its formal function and taking the emphasis on sound to a new extreme. Wagner himself did this when he concretized its implications in the celebrated Prelude to *Das Rheingold*, filling 136 measures with an E♭ triad to evoke an absolute, nonrecurring beginning, the creation of the world of *Der Ring des Nibelungen*: the notes of the "chord of nature" enter as if through spontaneous generation – the overtones of the basses' lowest string (retuned to E♭), for example, already audibly sounding the second partial soon to be played by the bassoons – the increasing animation that ensues likewise seeming to generate the first *Leitmotif* of the tetralogy.

Gustav Mahler and Alban Berg reworked Beethoven's essay in sublimity from their more skeptical, turn-of-the-century perspectives. Berg reinterpreted its initial tonal obscurity in the nontonal context of his *Three Orchestral Pieces* op. 6 (completed in 1915). As the point of departure for the first piece, a "Präludium," Berg used only unpitched percussion instruments: their indeterminate sounds lead to the tuned pitches of other instruments before themes take shape and then develop. Toward the end the opening events occur in reverse order, the instruments gradually dropping out in a return to amorphousness that signals impending closure. This characteristic Bergian form places the Beethovenian opening in a different light. If the form is construed as circular, returning to its point of origin to start the same process again, it implies, as Theodor W. Adorno wrote, "hopeless confinement"; if understood as a construction that comes together and then apart, the form might conversely suggest ephemerality.[5] In either case, Berg had come up with a distinctly modernist slant on a moment from Beethoven.

Though the premises of Berg's opening parallel those in the Ninth Symphony, he may not have consciously modeled the movement on that distant prototype; critics have tended to associate the "Präludium" with Mahler rather than with Beethoven.[6] Mahler himself appears to have drawn directly on Beethoven's Ninth in his own First Symphony, completed in 1888. The symphony opens on the solitary pitch A – eventually revealed as the dominant – in nine string parts, which from the beginning cover the entire musical space in an attempt to suggest, as his friend Natalie Bauer-Lechner recalled from conversations with him, that "with the first note . . . we are in Nature."[7] Unlike both Beethoven and Wagner,

Mahler has made "Nature" seem strange: all except the lowest of the parts play harmonics. Against this defamiliarized background noise, melodic fragments that include hunting motifs and stylized nature sounds drift in and out as the setting gradually comes into focus. Here the opening dominant, swollen to sixty-two measures, serves as a discrete slow introduction to a monothematic exposition; introduction and theme only later become more integrated. Mahler composed the symphony with a program in mind: he intended the folk-like sonata theme, for example, to represent a young hero and alter ego of himself.[8] Like many other composers, Mahler wished to amplify, distort, and also give more specific meaning to elements and procedures associated with Beethoven. But the mystique of absolute music proved too strong, and he suppressed his program.

Positioned center-stage in aesthetic controversies of the time, the tension between programmatic and absolute music, along with the related inclination of composers like Mahler to inject more of themselves into their works, played dominant roles in nineteenth-century compositional reception of Beethoven's music. Both trends were grounded in his own practices; indeed, most of the apparently novel features in his music did not originate with him. To cite only one well-known precedent, Justin Heinrich Knecht wrote a pastoral symphony, "Le portrait musical de la nature," with programmatic titles that anticipate those in Beethoven's Sixth.[9] Beethoven immediately distinguished his symphony from that particular model through the heading for his first movement, "The awakening of happy feelings upon arrival in the country," by insisting on the presence of a sentient human subject in the landscape painting.[10] To an unheard-of degree he communicated a personal voice in his instrumental compositions, and subsequent composers adopted techniques, such as thematic recall and *attacca* connections between movements, through which he conveyed a heightened sense not just of formal unity but of lived experience. In 1854 Wagner went so far as to read the C♯ minor String Quartet op. 131, Beethoven's most extreme experiment in through-composition, as a day in the composer's inner life, an interpretation he liked well enough to incorporate in the long centennial tribute of 1870.[11] The paradox of including a quasi-programmatic exegesis in that essay in which Wagner most exhaustively displayed his late turn toward a Schopenhauerian aesthetic of absolute music is symptomatic of the ambivalence of many musicians toward the absolute/programmatic dichotomy: for example, while Beethoven inspired both Felix Mendelssohn and Hector Berlioz, in many respects almost musical antipodes, to write programmatic orchestral works, they both later expressed reservations about such music.[12]

Berlioz had concentrated his compositional efforts on vocal genres until he heard the Third and Fifth Symphonies in 1828 performances under François-Antoine Habeneck at the Paris Conservatoire; as he later wrote, "Beethoven opened before me a new world of music,"[13] the possibilities of purely instrumental composition. In his famous commentaries on the nine symphonies, Berlioz understood the Fifth as musical self-expression: "It is his intimate thoughts that he means to develop, his secret sorrows, his pent-up anger, his dreams full of dejection, his nocturnal visions, and his outbursts of enthusiasm."[14] In his initial and most influential compositional response to Beethoven, the *Symphonie fantastique* (completed in 1830), Berlioz adopted the programmatic slant, five-movement format, and, in the third movement, the pastoral imagery of the Sixth Symphony; he also exaggerated the subjectivity that Beethoven had made explicit in the heading for the first movement of his symphony. The *Symphonie fantastique*, as is well known, dramatizes Berlioz's obsession with the actress Harriet Smithson. An early draft highlights the theatricality of the program and the paradoxical distance between Berlioz and his work:[15] "The composer imagines that a young musician . . . sees for the first time a woman who possesses all the charms of the ideal being he has dreamed of, and falls desperately in love with her."[16] This is followed by the description, carried over into the final draft, of how "through an odd whim, whenever the beloved image appears before the mind's eye of the artist it is linked with a musical thought," the *idée fixe* that pervades the opening Allegro agitato e appassionato assai and reappears in each succeeding movement. Witnessing the events from several removes, "the composer" imagines the "young musician" recalling the beloved one/theme. The dramatic situation has become more concrete in Berlioz than in Beethoven, and he has objectified a version of himself as the protagonist.

Mendelssohn did not approve of the *Symphonie fantastique* or its program.[17] Though committed through Beethoven's example to referential or even narrative music, Mendelssohn chose to allude to its subject matter in a title – *A Midsummer Night's Dream*, the *Reformation Symphony* – rather than produce a fully developed program. And Berlioz's theatrical rendering of events relating to his own life was foreign to him. Yet in the central monument to his early, deep engagement with Beethoven's late style, the A minor String Quartet op. 13, Mendelssohn did respond to the seeming self-referentiality in such movements as the Molto adagio of Beethoven's A minor Quartet op. 132 with its headings "Heiliger Dankgesang eines Genesenen an die Gottheit" and "Neue Kraft fühlend."

Mendelssohn may well have begun composing his own A minor

quartet around the time of Beethoven's death (26 March 1827), for he indicated that he had completed the first movement on 28 July 1827 and the finale on 26 October of the same year,[18] and certain passages in the quartet so clearly echo string quartets by Beethoven that they must be understood as homage. The first theme of the opening movement resembles that in Beethoven's A minor quartet, and recitative introduces Mendelssohn's finale, as it does Beethoven's. Mendelssohn, moreover, has clearly borrowed a formal idea from the slow movement of another quartet, that in F minor op. 95, an Allegretto ma non troppo with chromatic fugal interludes, for his own Adagio non lento.[19]

Mendelssohn sent the autograph of the A minor quartet to his friend Adolf Fredrik Lindblad and, in a remarkable letter, articulated his ardent appreciation for the way that one movement leads into the next in Beethoven's C# minor quartet:

> [The opening fugue] closes in a very somber manner in C# major, all [the instruments] play C#; and then it (the next movement, that is) enters with so sweet a D major and such little embellishment! Do you see, that is one of my points! The relationship between all 4 or 3 or 2 or 1 movements in a sonata and the others and the parts thereof.[20]

Although Mendelssohn admired the implicit *attacca* connections between movements in Beethoven's quartet (there are no solid double bar lines between them), he did not apply the technique in his own quartet. In the finale, however, he did use thematic recall – much more lavishly than Beethoven himself ever did – to synthesize the movements; themes also change their stylistic orientation at crucial points, a restrained version of the fantastical transformations that take place in the imagination of Berlioz's "young musician." The recitative that opens the movement is succeeded by more idiomatically instrumental sonata-form themes, establishing the characteristic dialectic of styles in this finale. At the beginning of the development, the treble line of the recitative becomes a fugue subject, presented in one four-part exposition; toward the end of the development, portions of the fugal interlude from the second movement reappear; at the very end, the recitative comes back to introduce the recapitulation. The coda begins with a chain of themes previously in instrumental, but now in recitative style: two statements of the slow movement's fugue subject surround one of the finale's main theme, vocal-style transformations that culminate naturally in the return of the song-derived slow introduction from the first movement.

Mendelssohn designated a song that he had composed shortly before ("Frage" op. 9 no. 1) as the quartet's so-called "Thema": he told Lindblad to expect to "hear it speak with its notes in the first and last movements, in all four movements with its feeling."[21] Motives that had set the words "Ist es wahr?" appear in the slow introduction to the first movement and at the end of the finale, which concludes with a more substantial passage from the song. The quotations provide a formal frame for the quartet, and the lyrical *ich* of "Frage," an aesthetic persona whose "feeling" as expressed in the song suffuses all four movements. Taking a more understated but also less mediated approach, Mendelssohn, like Berlioz, wants us to understand his work as portraying the inner life of a poetic subject. To Beethoven's younger contemporaries, who could adopt a Beethovenian stance with Mendelssohnian subtlety or the flamboyance of Berlioz, instrumental music seemed capable as never before of conveying individual emotional experience. Composers could also rework Beethovenian techniques and passages against the grain: a later generation, as we have seen, suggested its changed world view by distorting the awe-inspiring opening of the Ninth Symphony. Music had acquired a new eloquence with Beethoven.

"Through Beethoven music learned to think"

> Do we not, in truth, ask the impossible of music when we expect it to express feelings, to translate dramatic situations, even to imitate nature?
>
> (Igor Stravinsky[22])

Seizing on the aspect of Beethoven's style that would arguably prove the most influential in the twentieth century, its thematic/motivic work, Wagner found in the symphonic first movements a continuously meaningful musical texture, "always enthralling through so vivid a movement that the listener cannot escape its impression, but rather, strained to extreme attention, must grant melodic significance to every harmonic note, indeed every rhythmic pause."[23] Wagner's narrowly focused view of Beethoven's symphonic style seems to have allowed him to envision a technical basis for "endless melody" in the music dramas that he would soon compose. Characteristically, he stressed the coerciveness of the unprecedented motivic saturation: "the listener cannot escape its impression." Other musicians would choose to understand the same facet of Beethoven's style as an advance not in musical rhetoric, but rather compositional logic.

Carl Dahlhaus has observed that such logic had always been a particular hallmark of chamber music.[24] Beethoven set inhibitingly high standards in the string quartet, as in the symphony and also the piano sonata, the genres on which he had the most profound impact. A case in point:

Johannes Brahms finished a string quartet that satisfied him only after many abortive attempts, and its completion occasioned a drastic change in his style. The opulent, expansive lyricism of the string sextets and first chamber works with piano gave way to the tense – and undeniably exciting – compression of the C minor String Quartet op. 51 no. 1, a stylistic disjunction that cannot be explained simply by the six-year gap between the early chamber music and the first two string quartets.[25] Brahms may have been emulating Beethoven's laconic F minor String Quartet op. 95 in his own C minor quartet, in which every moment contributes to the unfolding of the themes' potential, every note is thus motivic, and every formal connection logical. Arnold Schoenberg considered Brahms a progressive composer in part because of his further distillation of this Beethovenian feature.[26]

In 1927, the centennial of Beethoven's death, at a time when many composers were denying that he had meaning for their work, Schoenberg's student Erwin Stein argued that the total thematicism in Beethoven's music guaranteed its continuing relevance.[27] In preliminary remarks, Stein asked tendentiously, "What does the most personal of artists have in common with the 'new objectivity?'" His ultimate answer was that "through Beethoven music learned to think," and that this "thinking" actualized itself in his compositions through the development of themes and motives. Stein considered Schoenberg to be Beethoven's true heir because he insisted that "everything must be thematic, nothing decoration."[28]

For his vast, yet motivically dense one-movement String Quartet in D minor op. 7 (completed in 1905), Schoenberg himself cited Beethovenian models: the C♯ minor quartet and the first movement of the *Eroica*. Schoenberg wrote that the quartet had inaugurated "the period of greatly expanded forms," which allowed no breaks between movements yet still encompassed "all the four characters" of tradition.[29] And, because the "great expansion" of form in his D minor quartet "required careful organization," he had kept the *Eroica* movement at hand to help him deal with fundamental problems in composition: "how to avoid monotony and emptiness; how to create variety out of unity; how to create new forms out of basic material; how much can be achieved by slight modifications if not by developing variation out of often rather insignificant little formulations."[30]

Schoenberg thought of his quartet as a sonata form – like Beethoven's symphonic movement – reconfigured along these lines:[31]

Exposition–Development–Scherzo–Dev. 2–Recapitulation–
Slow movement–Recap. 2–Rondo–Coda

But what does "sonata form" mean here? Beyond the inclusion of all four types of movement in one and the constant motivic development, the music is distinguished by extreme chromaticism, often by a temporary suspension of tonal orientation. As a result of these features, the significance of, for example, "development" or even "thematic group" has changed. Thus, although the beginning of the quartet displays the rhythmic incisiveness of many opening themes, this first group is as volatile as the transition, which in Classical style is a site for increased activity and, usually, a form-defining modulation; moreover, Schoenberg considered the intensely elaborated first group to last *ninety-six* measures and likewise developed the transition at length (seventy measures) through imitation. Perhaps the huge scale and compendious form required the sections standing for functional parts of a sonata-allegro exposition to have as much substance and self-sufficiency as those representing entire movement-types.

What did Schoenberg have to learn from the *Eroica* a full century after the fact? As his words suggest, he drew special inspiration from Beethoven's thematic work, the wealth of ideas and relationships among them. And the constant thematic "becoming" in the quartet was driven by idioms of Beethoven's dynamic rhetoric – the repeated intensifications and arrivals, the brevity of most stable passages – which allowed the various themes, transitions, developments, and movement-types to come together into a convincing quasi-sonata whole. For its overall trajectory does broadly resemble that of the *Eroica* and other sonata-form first movements: developmental activity increases before the recapitulation of the first group, and the movement becomes progressively more stable in the recapitulation, which includes the slow movement and rondo sections.

As in Beethoven's first movement, where the initial chords present the full registral range and act as a frame for the cellos' theme,[32] the very scoring of Schoenberg's opening – the cello's chord, the register of the violin in which the theme appears – is an important point of reference, which in the quartet serves to help make the moment of recapitulation clear despite the less than tonal context. From the *Eroica* movement – his stated model for the quartet, after all – Schoenberg may also have learned the unifying effect of related, strongly profiled cadential passages placed in various parts of the form.[33] For example, the descending chromatic figure in mm. 9–13, supported there and, at times, elsewhere by whole-tone chords (Example 14.1a), resurfaces throughout the D minor quartet, functioning in particular to articulate the sonata-form framework, as before the recapitulation of the first group (mm. 21–37 after I) and before the coda (mm. 81–85 after N). Unadorned whole-tone scales appear in

Example 14.1
(a) Schoenberg, String Quartet no. 1 op. 7, mm. 11–13

(b) Schoenberg, String Quartet no. 1 op. 7, mm. 28–33 after G

other transitional sections: for instance, before the return of the opening in the ternary first group (mm. 62–64) and in the connection between the trio and varied restatement of the scherzo (Example 14.1b).[34]

Long-distant, nearly literal, repetition helps hold together the huge movement, but it is through subtly modulated motivic change that the music might be understood to "think": slight variations of just two motives, for example, produce the pliant treble line at the beginning of the quartet (the motives evolve more radically after m. 4). In his formal overview of the quartet Schoenberg showed some of the most obvious large-scale interrelationships, those between the various themes of the sonata-allegro and other movement-types – the opening of the scherzo (at E), for example, is a transformation of the transition idea (second violin, mm. 3–9 after A) – but the thematic work throughout the D minor Quartet invites close consideration.

Stein found the closest Beethovenian parallel to the "strictly thematic unity," the "malleability of the motives and their rich relationships" in the D minor quartet not in the *Eroica*, but rather the *Grosse Fuge* op. 133, a work of special interest to a number of twentieth-century composers:[35]

> The rhythmic and melodic variations that the shape of the primary theme (in the fugue, countersubject) undergoes manifest a principle similar to, and, above all, have the same significance as, Schoenberg's variation technique. It is, so to speak, the pondering of a musical idea.[36]

Stein's initial ploy had been to present all the ways in which Beethoven might seem to have no meaning for contemporary composition and had included an assertion that the new classicism rarely referred to Beethoven as a model. This generalization, of course, did not always hold true. In his younger years, Igor Stravinsky had felt an aversion to Beethoven – or, more precisely, to attitudes toward the music – but by the mid-1920s he was actively studying the music for his own purposes,[37] and late in life wrote that he had "found new joy in Beethoven," singling out the *Grosse Fuge* as "pure interval music," "a perfect miracle," "an absolutely contemporary piece of music that will be contemporary for ever."[38]

The Concerto for Two Pianos, finished in 1935, may be Stravinsky's most significant compositional response to Beethoven: according to his own account, he had "steeped" himself in Beethoven's variations and fugues while composing the third and fourth movements, and he pronounced himself "very fond" of the fugal finale.[39] At certain moments Stravinsky also simulated Beethoven's emphatic approach to the climaxes made possible through the conventions of Classical syntax. As formulated by Leonard Meyer, a "syntactic climax" involves the "primary parameters" of melody, harmony, and/or rhythm in "an action in which the tensions of instability are resolved to the relaxation of regularity," such as typically occurs in Classical sonata forms at the point of recapitulation.[40] In the Concerto for Two Pianos, Stravinsky underscored the entrance of the first movement's opening theme (m. 11) with a sweeping (unstable) introduction, and though the movement as a whole is not easily reconciled with sonata form, he managed to incorporate sonata-form processes of retransition and recapitulation: after a section with fast surface rhythms and many syncopations, a wrenching metric modulation (mm. 167–69) leads into a repetition of part of the introduction (mm. 169–74 = mm. 5–10) and then of the opening theme itself (mm. 176ff.), set magnificently in relief.

Such qualities in the music apparently led Virgil Thomson to hear Beethoven immediately as the inspiration for the concerto.[41] In a review of a 1944 performance, Thomson wrote that "as in most of Stravinsky's music from the last twenty-five years, its style is its subject," and argued that the subject of the concerto appeared to be the style of Beethoven's final piano sonatas filtered through Stravinsky's sensibility. Focusing on a number of disruptive features – e.g., "angular and strong" melodic material, "violent" emotional content, transitions achieved "brusquely and without grace" – Thomson concluded that "the whole picture of the later Beethoven music . . . is complete, with all its mannerisms and all its perfectly real seriousness." Without going into detail, he also noted "a certain grandeur of expression," suggesting that this was "the conscious manner of the piece," even more so than in Beethoven, "because the concerto is a study of another man's stylistic achievement."[42]

Stravinsky seems to have modeled his last movement directly on that of Beethoven's A♭ Piano Sonata op. 110: both finales include two fugues, the second based on the inverted subject of the first, and each is preceded by a slower nonfugal section. Stravinsky must have paid close attention as well to the types of thematic manipulation evident in the second fugue of op. 110. After presenting the inverted subject in a three-voice exposition, Beethoven treats the uninverted subject to inexact diminution (mm. 152ff.), augmentation (mm. 161–68), and then double diminution (mm. 168ff.), which, with additional distortion of the original rhythm and intervals, ultimately dissolves it (m. 175): the subject, in short, becomes a motive and then an unmarked figure, as the finale modulates from G major back to A♭. Against the new figuration, the fugue subject enters in the bass and is again transformed; this final elaboration (mm. 185–209) is indistinguishable from the apotheosis of a theme at the end of a sonata form.

The fluid interplay between fugue subject, motive, figure, and theme in the finale of Beethoven's sonata surely influenced Stravinsky's own approach in the Concerto for Two Pianos. The concerto's finale cannot be considered apart from the third movement variations, for the two share thematic material and Stravinsky himself made it clear that he thought of them as one entity.[43] The "Quattro variazioni" display his idiosyncratic conception of "theme" as neutral succession of pitch-classes; this movement has two such themes, each the length of a short phrase. No rhythmic configuration of the notes is presented as primary, nor does either theme have an invariable contour: pitches can be displaced by one or more octaves. (Example 14.2a shows the first appearance of the more important of the two themes.) Arranged in its most compact form in the fourth variation, the first theme becomes a quasi-ostinato figure (Example 14.2b); the second theme likewise rotates through in the manner of an ostinato. When the first theme reappears as the opening phrase of the fugue subject, it necessarily gains a fixed profile, which also allows it to be systematically inverted (Example 14.2d and e). Like Beethoven, Stravinsky freely augments and diminishes his thematic material to underscore crucial formal junctures – e.g. the end of the variations, the opening of the Preludio (Example 14.2c), the conclusion of the first fugue and transition to the second – and, furthermore, ties these modifications to shifts in the central pitch roughly analogous to modulations in traditional tonal music. Thus, though the fugue subject and its inversion center on D, each ending a half-step away from that pitch, Stravinsky centers the final, augmented statement on E, introducing chromatic alterations to make it come to a grand close on the E "tonic" of the concerto's first movement (Example 14.2f).

Example 14.2a–f Stravinsky, Concerto for Two Pianos

a. Quattro variazioni, Var. 1 ♪ = 76

p, ma poco marcato

b. Var. 4 ♩ = 96

c. Preludio e Fuga, opening; Lento ♩ = 50

d. Fuga à 4 voci ♩ = 66

f ben marcato

e. Le stesso tempo della Fuga nell'inversione

f. Largo ♩ = 44

ff marcatissimo

Stravinsky, Schoenberg, and Brahms, as well, might prefer to speak soberly of organization, motives, intervals.[44] Yet in those works in which they took Beethoven as a model, each of them responded not just to the complexity of the thematicism, but also the vitality of the motivic evolution and the monumentalization of formal process in his music. In their concern with Beethovenian techniques, they also absorbed the rhetorical purposes that the techniques served. While abstract logic may have seemed more appropriate than intense eloquence to these three composers for their theorizing, Wagner clearly grasped something of continuing significance – even to them – by stressing the latter aspect of Beethoven's style.

Citation and style as symbol

Composers have quoted works by Beethoven to a number of expressive ends, though recently voiced skepticism about Schumann's apparent allusion to Beethoven's *An die ferne Geliebte* in his C major Fantasy op. 17 highlights the problem in assuming that one composer has referred to another: the resemblance may be incidental. Schumann himself never explicitly commented on a connection between the end of the Fantasy's first movement and Beethoven's song-cycle; furthermore, the tradition that links the two works seems to date only from the early twentieth century.[45] Yet the excerpt makes wonderful sense as a quotation from *An die ferne Geliebte* in the work itself and in relation to more than one stage of its complicated genesis. The movement's evolving themes culminate in this stable fragment; as Charles Rosen has observed, it "appears not as a reminiscence of another composer, but as at once the source and the solution of everything in the music . . . the entire movement of Schumann is a preparation for, and development of, the concluding phrase."[46] And Schumann had for a while intended to bring the passage back to close the finale, much as Beethoven connected the first and last songs in his cycle.[47] Schumann composed the opening movement, originally meant to stand on its own as a fantasy, during the period when Friedrich Wieck would not allow him to see his daughter, Schumann's future wife Clara, thus at that time his "distant beloved."[48] An intentional reference would also have been appropriate when Schumann later added two movements to produce a "Sonata for Beethoven," a publication scheme that came to nothing:[49] what had begun as a personal message would have become a public tribute to the composer.

Dmitri Shostakovich wrote the finale of his last work, the Sonata for Viola and Piano (1975), as such homage, "an adagio in memory of Beethoven," but told its dedicatee, the violist Fyodor Druzhinin, not to let that "inhibit" him, adding the not incontrovertible statement that "the music is bright, bright and clear."[50] After an extended solo passage for viola; the piano enters with arpeggios, initiating references to the Adagio sostenuto of Beethoven's "Moonlight" Sonata op. 27 no. 2 that will run throughout the rest of the movement. With the arpeggiated accompaniment, based on the functional chords of common-practice tonality, come shards of Beethoven's melody: repeated notes set to a dotted rhythm, the characteristic move up a half-step and back, the octave leap between the end of one phrase and the beginning of the next. Throughout this swan song, Shostakovich interweaves twentieth-century idioms introduced in the viola solo with the fractured traditional syntax of the paraphrased material. The sonata manages to close on a "clear, bright" C major triad, each of its notes achieved successively through protracted voice-leading. The many allusions to the "Moonlight" Sonata, however, never culminate in a "whole" fragment, the impossibility of such fulfillment deepening the elegiac poignancy that, notwithstanding Shostakovich's comments, marks the composition: we hear the adagio against the complete sonata movement.

In certain compositions, references to Beethoven serve to call up a wide range of associations. In the closing phrase of his late work for twenty-three solo stringed instruments, *Metamorphosen*, Richard Strauss quoted the opening of the "Marcia funebre" from the Third Symphony and inserted the cryptic words "IN MEMORIAM" below it. Strauss composed the piece, on commission from the conductor Paul Sacher, between the late summer of 1944 and the following spring. For years German commentators have suggested that the quotation had to do with Strauss's sorrow over the destruction of Munich by the Allied forces;[51] it also appears to encode his reaction to the debasement of German culture – Beethoven representing its past glory – under the Nazi regime. Timothy L. Jackson has proposed that the work, with its Goethean title, probes an inversion of the classical conception of metamorphosis, according to which, "by discovering the divine within, man could metamorphose into the godly . . . In Strauss's essentially tragic view, self-knowledge reveals the bestial, not the divine, in man."[52]

Ives, as we have seen, alluded to Beethoven for more positive and transparent purposes, prominently incorporating the opening notes of the Fifth Symphony in all four movements of his Piano Sonata no. 2 ("Concord, Mass., 1840–1860") the first version of which he composed between about 1907 and 1919:[53] most extensively in the first, "Emerson," and third, "The Alcotts." In the *Essays Before a Sonata* that Ives wrote to accompany the composition, he claimed disingenuously that he had termed the four pieces a sonata "for want of a more exact name."[54] To call his work a piano sonata was obviously to invoke European tradition, more specifically one of the genres most closely connected with Beethoven, and to imply serious ambition and high-mindedness. In the *Essays* Ives made it clear that he wished to align Thoreau and, especially, Emerson with Beethoven, that he found Beethovenian greatness in nineteenth-century Concord. Ives linked the composer even with the household headed by the impecunious, impractical Bronson Alcott: "And there sits the little old spinet piano Sophia Thoreau gave to the Alcott children, on which Beth played the old Scotch airs, and played at the Fifth Symphony."[55] The opening theme of "The Alcotts," at the center of which lie the first few notes of Beethoven's Fifth, has been identified as the "human-faith melody" that Ives mentions in the part of the *Essays* devoted to that movement: "All around you, under the Concord sky, there still floats the influence of that human-faith-melody . . . reflecting an innate hope, a common interest in common things and common men – a tune the Concord bards are ever playing while they pound away at the immensities with a Beethoven-like sublimity."

"Beethoven-like" or, more commonly, "Beethovenian" does indeed evoke the sublime; the adjective has, for example, become permanently attached to a peremptory style of musical discourse, especially if set in the C minor of the Fifth Symphony. Even if Franz Schubert had not used the first six measures of Beethoven's C minor Variations WoO 80 for his late piano sonata in that key (D. 958), its stormy 21-bar opening would be heard as Beethovenian.[56] Schubert's borrowing was most likely overdetermined, at once an act of self-assertion and a tribute by a dying composer to a recently deceased one. He must also have realized that he could expand Beethoven's oddly truncated theme into a powerful beginning for a large-scale sonata theme. After the transformed counterstatement with which the transition begins (mm. 21–26), Schubert thoroughly assimilated the borrowed theme to his own style, thereby both fulfilling the requirement of originality, accentuated after Beethoven, and effectively preparing the poised inwardness of the theme in E♭ that follows.

Even when unanchored to a key, *maestoso* defiance calls forth the inevitable association, as in the following description of Pierre Boulez's Second Piano Sonata (1947–48): "After more than twenty years, the Beethovenian vehemence of this sonata still astounds the ear."[57] A number of critics have connected his Second Sonata to the most gnarled and explosive of all piano sonatas, the "Hammerklavier" op. 106. Boulez did place his own sonata in the traditional four movements, with nods toward sonata form and fugue in the first and fourth, and possible fleeting references to Beethoven's sonata.[58] But it is above all the sense of titanic rage, of pushing the instrument to its limits, that inspires comparisons with the "Hammerklavier." Boulez would later assert that after composing the Second Sonata, he never again referred to past forms, that the work records his effort to obliterate them: "It was probably the attempt of the Viennese School to revive older forms that made me try to destroy them completely."[59] And the particular, unspoken figure whom he chose to confront in this act of aggression was, of course, Beethoven.

Yet the grand serenity of certain slow movements also sounds "Beethovenian": virtually all of Bruckner's adagios, for example, as well as many by Béla Bartók seem to strive to recapture the spirituality of such slow movements as the "Heiliger Dankgesang" from the late A minor String Quartet op. 132.[60] Critics have frequently understood the Adagio religioso of Bartók's Third Piano Concerto (1947) to refer directly to that

movement, just as they have heard the beginning of his First String
Quartet (1908) as a response to the opening fugue of the C♯ minor
quartet.[61] Although intervallic correspondences to some extent justify
these interpretations, Bartók more basically drew on certain characteristic textures – chorale style, slowly unfolding imitation – adaptable to his
own twentieth-century voice.

In the 1970s George Rochberg recreated the Beethovenian adagio
more precisely in such movements as the variations (Adagio sereno) of
his Third String Quartet and the fugue (Adagio religioso) of his Fourth
String Quartet. Like Bartók and Ives, if perhaps not Strauss and
Shostakovich toward the end of their lives, Rochberg could believe in the
attainability and appropriateness of, in Ives's words, "Beethoven-like sublimity," and without feeling compelled to acknowledge the pastness of
Beethoven's musical language. Critics who found his wholesale imitation
of the style of the Beethoven adagio disturbing[62] expressed the view of
many listeners: that Beethoven could be emulated, his works assimilated
or broken, but that his style could not simply be "forged" and remain
effective. While the possibility of Beethovenian grandeur in the twentieth
century might be affirmed or denied without stirring up controversy,
post-Beethovenian originality continued to press its claims; composers
could still be expected to come up with new terms on which to face the
great man.

15 Beethoven's music in performance: historical perspectives

ALAIN FROGLEY

The history of performing Beethoven is in essence the history of our entire Western culture of musical performance as it has evolved since the end of the eighteenth century. One is even tempted to write "Western culture" *tout court*. The ways in which we have kept alive the creations of one of the most potent icons of our civilization, the written instructions of the printed scores mediated by individual performers and by changing performance conventions, speak eloquently of deeper issues – of cultural value, tradition, authority, the individual and society, written versus oral communication, intuition versus reason. At a more concrete level, Beethoven's music underpinned the formation both of the fundamental performance institutions of modern musical life, including the character and makeup of our public concerts and recitals, and of the very idea of a mass culture of "serious" music that elevates edification over mere enter-tainment. And from Franz Liszt's use of selected sonatas in the nascent modern piano recital, through to the adoption of Beethoven by the "authentic" performance movement in the 1980s, Beethoven's music has assumed a variety of contrasting symbolic meanings – Romantic rebel, disciplined Classicist, proto-Modernist – all of them heavy with prestige and authority, whether covertly or openly invoked. The attempt to project these meanings has shaped specific decisions about performance practice – the size of performing forces, details of tempo and articulation, the structure of concert programs – and these in turn have influenced the changing images of Beethoven's art.

This history has been paradoxical as well as complex. Beethoven's music has played the dominant role in the careers of some of the most celebrated performers and conductors of the last century-and-a-half, many of them composers in their own right: Liszt, Wagner, Bülow, Mahler, Toscanini, Furtwängler, Schnabel, to name just a few. While his music has been held in awe as the visionary outpouring of an individualistic genius, its fortunes have nevertheless depended on charismatic performers whose personalities have often come close to eclipsing – or at least sub-suming – that of the composer in the eyes of the public; and while all have sought to be faithful conveyors of Beethoven's intentions, differing views as to how these intentions can be divined have led to interpretations so divergent as to throw into grave doubt the whole notion of the musical work as a stable entity. If the slow movement of the Ninth Symphony takes just over eleven minutes in Roger Norrington's version, and close to twenty in Wilhelm Furtwängler's, in what sense are we still dealing with the same piece? In this context, formulations such as "Furtwängler's Beethoven" become more than verbal conveniences. While such questions are hardly restricted to this composer, they strike one here with unusual force: can the music of Beethoven, undisputed master of form, timing, and compositional control at every level, really be this malleable if responsibly performed?

Such issues have been given fresh relevance in the past decade or so in the heated debate surrounding the adoption of Beethoven's music by the so-called historical performance movement.[1] In addition, this has coincided with a surge of interest in studying performance as an historical topic in its own right, with important implications for analysis and criticism, rather than merely as a source of "authentic" performance practices, for which anything after the composer's lifetime is normally disregarded.[2] In the light of such concerns, I intend here to sketch the rich history of performing Beethoven in terms of a few pivotal issues that focus shifting images of the composer, and the place of his music in broader performance culture. There will be no attempt to offer a "how-to" primer in performance practice, although topics relevant to such questions will inevitably be touched upon. And I shall start with Beethoven himself, who in his struggles to realize in practical terms the sounds of his imagination was frequently the first "interpreter" of his music.[3]

From the horse's mouth?

Essays of this kind typically begin with a commitment to seek out the composer's own intentions for performances of his or her music, and at one level the desirability of such a goal seems obvious. Yet it is fraught with problems, and even if we set aside the broader controversy surrounding "intention" in works of art, and its role in performing music, Beethoven presents an unusually difficult case.

This is not for a lack of potential evidence. In addition to the indications found in the scores themselves, there is a wealth of material to be culled from the composer's letters, conversation books, and the accounts of contemporaries. All Beethoven's major works were performed during his lifetime, and in most cases with his direct involvement, either as pianist or conductor (and sometimes both), or as a consultant at rehearsals.[4] Furthermore, since his death the bulk of his output has continued to be performed: there has never been a Beethoven "revival" or any need for one. This has ensured an unbroken lineage of performers descended from Beethoven, as it were, initially through those who knew and worked with him or, in a handful of cases, were actually taught by him. Of the latter, Carl Czerny was the most influential; he published detailed instructions on the performance of Beethoven's piano works,[5] and also taught the young Liszt, among others: the succession that runs Czerny–Leschetizky[6]–Schnabel – and beyond – is a particularly impressive one.

In a living tradition, however, such pedigrees can be deceptive. In Beethoven's case one cannot be confident that they preserved with any detailed fidelity the master's own practices: even those closest to the composer and writing as early as the 1830s and 1840s frequently contradicted one another, and Czerny's testimony is not always internally consistent; and, as with most historical witnesses, the memories of Beethoven's associates were clearly colored by their own biases, particularly in relation to changing performance styles after the composer's death.[7] But they are hardly to be blamed: even when we try to go directly to the horse's mouth, as it were, many factors confuse the historical record. Not least among these, as we shall see presently, are the problematic example set by Beethoven's own performances, inconsistencies within his documented remarks on performance issues (his attitude towards the metronome, for example), and the complicating issue of his deafness.[8] Much may be inferred, of course, from our broader knowledge of performance practice in Beethoven's Vienna, but here several broader factors urge caution. While Beethoven went further than any previous composer in trying to fix every detail of his works in notation, he clearly assumed that this notation would be realized in terms of the prevailing performance practice of his day – at least he left no general instructions to the contrary. Yet he lived at a time when much of this was in flux, and in some areas, such as the execution of trills and the introduction of the metronome, moving closer to present-day practice; his music made technical and interpretative demands on performers that went well beyond contemporary conventions; he was dissatisfied with most performances of his music; and, as with so many aspects of his art, his attitudes to performance reflect a strong tension between the ideal and the actual.[9]

Nevertheless, there are several areas in which we can be certain that Beethoven conceived his music in terms of sounds and practices strikingly different from those encountered in modern performances.[10] First and foremost, the instruments of his day produced a more sharply differentiated range of timbres than their modern equivalents, and, when in combination, more transparent textures; this holds true equally for the strong identities of instruments within the orchestra, and the vivid contrasts between different registers on the piano (there were moreover several distinctive varieties of piano in use, of which Beethoven was most fond of the especially touch-sensitive and clear-toned Viennese designs). In orchestral music clarity was further enhanced – at least judging from recent performances on period instruments – by an absence of continuous vibrato and extended legato phrasing, a more even balance in the numbers of strings and wind than is found in a modern orchestra,[11] and the use of a smaller number of players overall. That said, Viennese orchestras varied wildly in both size and competency, reflecting a heterogeneous assortment of social, financial, and acoustic conditions; Beethoven's symphonies were performed during his lifetime by as few as thirty-five players and as many as ninety (although a figure somewhere in the middle was more typical), and amateur performers often played alongside professionals.[12]

On a different front, when performing piano concertos and chamber music with piano Beethoven would have added ornamentation to the written-out keyboard part. He did not trust other pianists to embellish his music, however, even if they were pupils: in 1816 Czerny was sharply rebuked for adding notes in a performance of the Quintet for Piano and Winds op. 16.[13] Yet to the special case of concerto cadenzas he took a different attitude: even though he wrote out compositionally sophisticated cadenzas in manuscript, he made no attempt to publish these, leaving other pianists to improvise or compose their own.[14] This underlines the fact that for much of Beethoven's career it is difficult to separate sharply performance and composition. Although during his first decade in Vienna he was known as much for piano playing as for composition, even as a virtuoso he was admired above all for his improvisations, where composer and performer came together;[15] likewise, improvisation played an important role in Beethoven's compositional process, some works clearly existing as fluid scenarios for improvisation before they were fixed in notation. And even when performing notated music, by himself or others, Beethoven impressed listeners with the spontaneously passionate character of his playing. Yet it is precisely this emphasis on improvisation and unpredictability which limits the usefulness of Beethoven's own playing as a specific guide to performing his music – except in implying an overall freedom that he never willingly licensed to others.[16] As a conductor, Beethoven was also famously volatile and unpredictable, whether directing from the keyboard or using a baton (he was one of the first to experiment with the latter method).[17] Some problems stemmed from the ad hoc character of many of the ensembles involved, and from a lack of adequate rehearsal time; nevertheless, the results were chaotic on occasion.[18] We might at this juncture be tempted to adapt on Beethoven's

behalf an old adage: "do as I write, not as I do." But for all the unprecedented effort Beethoven put in to preparing his scores for publication,
with sometimes multiple sets of proofs and lengthy letters to publishers
(though he was not a good or enthusiastic proofreader), even his printed
scores contain numerous ambiguities and inconsistencies in their performance indications. One senses here an inevitable clash between
Beethoven the composer for posterity, trying to fix a work once and for
all, and Beethoven the spontaneous performer, ever sensitive to the multiple possibilities inherent in his material.

Nowhere is this tension felt more strongly than in the domain of
tempo, a subject which has generated more debate than any other issue of
Beethovenian performance practice. Beethoven himself never doubted its
critical importance for his music – Schindler reports that the composer's
first question about any performance at which he was not present was
"How were the tempi?"[19] – and it runs like a cantus firmus throughout the
history of performing his music: so many issues of character, expression,
and structural articulation depend upon it. It may seem ironic that the
music of a composer celebrated as a rhythmic innovator should be so
bedeviled by ambiguity and controversy in this fundamental aspect of
musical time. The psychology of tempo is always a complex matter,
however; and, more specifically, Beethoven's music once again participated in a process of transition, in this case from an eighteenth-century
approach predicated on a small number of basic tempo indications –
allegro, adagio, etc. – which by custom implied certain broadly standard-
ized speeds, towards the much more finely differentiated and wider
overall range of tempi typical of the nineteenth century. As time went
on, Beethoven's indications became increasingly complex in their
qualification of basic terms: "unfettered genius," as he once put it, could
not be bound by a system in which "Allegro" meant much the same for
every piece over which it appeared.[20]

In the light of such concerns, it is perhaps no surprise that Beethoven
welcomed the invention of the metronome in 1813, since this enabled
composers for the first time to indicate tempo in precise and objective
terms. Indeed, he became the first major composer to use metronome
markings, which he supplied for all nine symphonies, the string quartets
up to op. 95, the "Hammerklavier" Sonata, and a handful of minor
works.[21] Yet far from settling tempo issues in the works concerned, these
markings have generated much heated and complicated debate. Above all,
the tempi indicated have seemed too fast to many musicians.[22] The controversy is sure to continue, but the consensus of modern scholarship, and
the fruits of the historical performance movement, all suggest that
Beethoven's markings must be taken very seriously indeed, even if they

are not always followed absolutely literally (the $\downarrow = 138$ marking for the first movement of the "Hammerklavier" still seems astonishing). It is clear that Beethoven viewed the metronome as his best chance of ensuring that performers would be able to understand and project in their playing the unique and often delicately poised physiognomies of his creations.

Nevertheless, Beethoven had profound reservations about the metronome, and still believed that finding exactly the right speed depended on more intuitive considerations: "feeling also has its tempo," as he wrote alongside the metronome mark in the autograph of the song "Nord oder Süd."[23] The insight of the performer is even more critical to a second, related issue, namely the modifying of an initial tempo with ritardandos, accelerandos, and passages of contrasting stable tempi not explicitly indicated by the composer. Once again, balancing the often conflicting evidence is a delicate process, but this much seems clear: while Beethoven felt that an appropriate initial tempo should remain throughout as a background benchmark, he also believed that tempo must be modified as a piece progresses, in order to highlight formal junctures, characterize different themes, and articulate expressive contrasts and structure in general.[24] How far should the tempo be modified? Even with the advent of the metronome Beethoven made no attempt to mark such fluctuations. No doubt they would have been prohibitively numerous, and the composer probably also felt that, having been guided towards the right initial tempo, sensitive performers should instinctively understand what was required by way of subsequent modifications; yet the implication is also that these modifications were to be subtle enough that assigning meaningfully contrasting metronome marks would run the risk of exaggeration and rigidity. In his later music he specified numerous localized ritardandi, but these do not answer questions about larger-scale modifications, and, in the end, we are still left very much in the dark. Such questions are particularly important in the late works, whose subtle subversions of conventional characterisitics and structures often depend on hair-trigger distinctions of timing; ironically, as Beethoven legislated more and more detail in his music, notation proved limited in conveying its true spirit, and it depended more than ever on a perceptive performer.

This reminds us that tempo cannot easily be divorced from other considerations: a tempo that makes sense on a piano of Beethoven's own time, for instance, may seem quite inappropriate on a modern Steinway. Most important of all is the relationship of tempo to articulation and rhythmic style, to the whole area of musical punctuation. Many questions remain unresolved here, not least how far Beethoven's copious articulation markings – much more detailed than those of his predecessors – relate to the actual mechanics of beginning and ending notes, or to more conceptual questions of structural definition; certainly some of his longer slurs are not practicable as truly continuous streams of sound. As a pianist, Beethoven was famous for his legato playing, his ability to generate a singing tone and sustain this across long phrases; yet contemporary descriptions inevitably reflect expectations of the relatively detached articulation typical of the late eighteenth century. What does seem clear is that despite the increased importance of legato effects, much of Beethoven's music was still conceived in terms of keyboard fingerings, string bowings, and other practices that created on the whole a more sharply etched rhythmic profile than their modern equivalents, and a substantially wider repertoire of articulation types. And some modern scholars and performers have also argued that contemporary concepts of rhetoric and poetic declamation are essential to understanding Beethoven's approach to rhythm, including tempo: here once again, controlled flexibility appears to be the guiding principle.[25]

A disputed inheritance: the mid-nineteenth century

> The genuine artist lives only for the work, which he understands as the composer understood it and which he now performs. He does not make his personality count in any way. All his thoughts and actions are directed towards bringing into being all the wonderful, enchanting pictures and impressions the composer sealed in his work with magical power.[26]

After his death, Beethoven's music went on to become the core of the canonic performance culture that emerged in the mid-nineteenth century: the "imaginary museum of musical works" which is still with us today.[27] This edifice was founded on the public concert; the symphony orchestra and its repertory formed the central structure, but even the traditionally more intimate media of chamber and solo piano music were now often transplanted to the larger forum: the museum thus had three wings, dominated respectively by Beethoven's symphonies, string quartets, and piano sonatas.[28] Vital to the new institution were two closely related ideas: first, the concept of the musical work as a stable and unique art-object that transcended ephemeral performance events, and whose every detail was fixed by its composer;[29] second, the image of the composer as heroic genius, whose works could inspire and even edify a new bourgeois audience bent on self-improvement. But could the vision of genius be communicated by just any competent performer playing the score "as written"? At first glance, E. T. A. Hoffmann's words quoted above, which effectively define the position that came to be known as "Werktreue," or "fidelity to the work," might appear to support this view:

if the performing artist is to be completely self-effacing, then transmitting strictly what the composer has written is surely the best (the only?) course. On closer examination, however, matters are not so simple: the performer must understand the work "as the composer understood it"; and if its essential qualities have been sealed up with "magical power," presumably nothing less is required to unlock them again – simply reading the notation is obviously quite inadequate. Clearly, the performer must be almost as remarkable an individual as the composer. And since Hoffmann's remarks come in the context of an essay on Beethoven, the stakes are high indeed.

Hoffmann was one of the first writers to interpret Beethoven's music in terms of Romanticism (his famous account of the Fifth Symphony appeared in 1810), stressing its daemonic, mysterious qualities, and its evocation of the infinite and the spiritual. This view was commonplace by the 1830s, and it inevitably tempted the more daring performers, now also being cast as Romantic heroes, to break up Hoffmann's delicate alloy of inspired humility, and to go well beyond the composer's text in order to "bring into being" the wonders sealed therein. Around 1830, for instance, Berlioz was present at a performance where Liszt added trills, tremolos, and "impassioned chords" to the first movement of the "Moonlight" Sonata; more radically, in 1835 Liszt performed the same sonata with the first movement arranged for orchestra alone.[31] He treated op. 26 with similar freedom, once playing the first movement on an organ, and another time combining it with the last movement of the "Moonlight."[31] Yet Berlioz, whose own Romantic credentials are not to be dismissed lightly and who admired Liszt enormously, was horrified by such licenses; and this highlights the fact that even during the heyday of musical Romanticism, sharply divergent views existed as to the proper limits of "interpretation" in Beethoven's music, and on the performance of his music in general. Ignaz Moscheles and Clara Wieck, the two other virtuosi who pioneered public performance of Beethoven sonatas in the 1830s, took a more sober and "faithful" approach than Liszt (although they sometimes played only selected movements from a sonata, a common practice at the time).[32] Indeed, Liszt himself later repented of his *péchés de jeunesse*, and even in his younger days he had on occasion adhered strictly to the score. In the latter part of his career he treated the text of Beethoven's works with great respect on the whole, even down to the controversial metronome marks in the "Hammerklavier" Sonata. It was in this very work, however, that he also took the most significant liberties of his later Beethoven performances, improvising an introduction that gradually yielded up the first movement, adding octaves to some of the trills in the fugue, and possibly reversing the order of the middle movements.[33] Like the composer-performer Beethoven before him, Liszt was impetuously unpredictable, and if a piece inspired him enough, he could not always resist responding to it as co-creator as well as executor (as is evident from his transcriptions and concert paraphrases of music by many different composers, of course). What Beethoven would have thought of this treatment of his music is another matter. It is important, nevertheless, that liberties taken in the spirit of sincere Romanticism be distinguished from the more cynical or haphazard disfigurations – movements played out of order, partially cut, or omitted altogether, and changes in instrumentation and scoring for instance – that Beethoven's music routinely suffered in concession to public taste or inadequate performing resources up to the middle of the nineteenth century.[34]

That composers loomed large in debates about Beethoven performance should not surprise us (and not only because many of them earned a living as performers and critics). As well as underpinning an emerging "museum" culture, Beethoven was also central to live issues in the composition of new music, in particular what might be dubbed crudely the struggle between Classicism and Romanticism, objective form and subjective expression, or, to invoke a wider framework, Apollonian and Dionysian aesthetics. Janus-faced, his music embodied the polarities at issue both within individual pieces, and between different genres and periods within the oeuvre as a whole, particularly between the first and last style-periods.

Such tensions were articulated most clearly in the area of conducting, whose relative novelty encouraged many practitioners to put their methods and opinions into print. In the quarter-century after Beethoven's death, his music accelerated the ongoing transition from orchestral direction by a keyboard player (the last vestige of Baroque continuo practice), alone or in tandem with the principal violinist, to the modern practice of a conductor with a baton (though there remained pockets of resistance beyond mid-century). The conductor now became the equal of a pianist or other solo performer, except that his "instrument" was the orchestra; indeed, he provided an individualistic and potentially heroic focus for the otherwise dispersed identity of a large – and ever larger – ensemble.[35] The period 1830–60 saw the emergence of two primary viewpoints concerning the proper role of the conductor; these have shaped the history of conducting, and of performance in general, right up to the present day, and, again, Beethoven's music loomed large in their formation.

On one wing were Berlioz and Mendelssohn; they defined the approach we find perhaps most familiar today, which, in theory at least, treats the composer's score as the ultimate authority in performance decisions. As Berlioz vividly put it:

> the sun, in lighting up a picture, reveals its exact design and colour. It does not cause either trees or weeds to grow; or birds or serpents to appear, where the painter has not placed them.[36]

Inevitably, this discouraged the use of tempo modifications that were not specifically marked in the score, as well as changes in orchestration, or any other additions to the text; less inevitably, it also came to be associated with rhythmic precision, tight ensemble, and clarity of execution in general, and favored tempi that, as well as being steady, were on the fast side.[37] On the other wing was Wagner. Whereas Mendelssohn and Berlioz saw their role in terms of reproducing or recreating the composer's vision, Wagner viewed conducting as a creative act. Although he also preached fidelity to the composer's intentions, and did not tamper lightly with the text, for him the score was nevertheless a contingent representation of a conception that lay some way behind or beyond it. Only from an intuitive, empathetic understanding of the idea, in particular its projection in the structural melodic backbone that Wagner called the *melos*, could a correct interpretation of the notation emerge.[38] The most important job of the conductor is to articulate the changing character of the *melos*, and for this, Wagner argued, tempo modifications are essential; composers do not generally mark these, because they must emerge naturally from a deep understanding of the music, and so tempo is the arena in which the conductor becomes a true co-creator. Wagner's own conducting, not surprisingly, emphasized flexible tempi, including speeding up as well as slowing down, even though this exacerbated the already poor ensemble typical of many nineteenth-century orchestras. For Wagner, Beethoven marks a watershed in the history of music and the role of the performer: whereas tempo flexibility is occasionally required in earlier music, in Beethoven it underpins his whole style, and, given his seminal influence on the next generation of composers, it thus becomes the norm for modern music.[39]

The mystical aura of Wagner's approach, and his emphasis on the flexible unfolding of a long melodic line, accord well with his own music, of course, and invite us to connect it with Beethoven's – an association Wagner was always keen to encourage. Mendelssohn and Berlioz, especially the former, likewise highlight issues that reflect their own compositional concerns. Both schools claimed to bring out the composer's intentions, but one adopted a more metaphysical view of this concept, and by implication a more important role for themselves as "interpreters" of works rather than mere performers. Mendelssohn's performances were perhaps stiffer than Beethoven would have wished; Wagner, on the other hand, probably went further in tempo modification than Beethoven envisaged – but then one remembers reports of the composer's own impulsive performances, and is left to wonder.

Another area of widely diverging practices was that of "retouching" Beethoven's orchestration to accommodate changes in instrument construction and playing techniques, some of which, such as the more powerful sound of the strings, profoundly changed dynamic balance within the ensemble; also significant were the acoustical demands of new, larger performance spaces. Most musicians believed that some kind of modification was essential, especially in the elaborately scored and texturally complex Ninth Symphony, and such retouchings can be heard even on quite recent recordings.[40] Wagner's alterations in the Ninth range from relatively straightforward adjustments of balance, to more interventive changes which highlight his analytical understanding of the voice-leading, and thus constitute an element of "interpretation." An example of the latter category is his re-writing of the flute and first oboe parts in mm. 138–43 of the first movement, designed to clarify what he believed to be the structural melodic line: this involves reshaping the oboe part at one point, transposing the flute down an octave at another, and adding new dynamic and tempo indications (see Example 15.1; Wagner's additions are shown in square brackets or on the middle stave).[41] Yet such tinkering appears timid beside Mahler's audacious novelties, which included the use of timpani to hammer out the famous "Fate" motif in the Fifth Symphony, and the introduction of effects typical of Mahler's own music, such as the shrill E♭ clarinet added to the score of the *Eroica*, or the placing of wind-players offstage in the "Alla marcia" section from the finale of the Ninth[42] – surely a composer-performer trying to recast Beethoven in his own image. Nevertheless, even the specialist conductors that were emerging during this era – figures such as Willem Mengelberg and Bruno Walter – also took significant licences, although not generally as extreme as Mahler's.

The period between c. 1870 and 1914 marked the height of a highly romanticized, Wagnerian school of Beethoven performance that touched all areas of his output,[43] and which although always controversial, gradually came to predominate; it was reinforced by, and helped reinforce, parallel trends in the critical and theoretical reception of the composer, and rising German nationalism was a powerful background presence. The era is epitomized by the influential figure of Hans von Bülow, who also draws together a number of threads pursued here. As pupil and son-in-law of Liszt, close (though later estranged[44]) associate of Wagner, and in his multiple roles as pianist, conductor, and teacher, Bülow was heir to and

Example 15.1   Symphony no. 9 op. 125, mvt. 1, mm. 138–43 with Wagner's retouchings

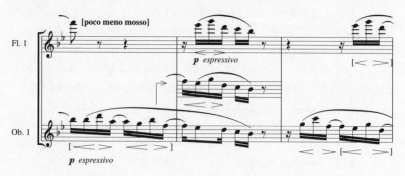

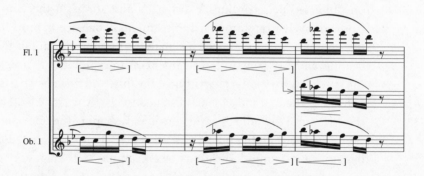

transmitter of a powerful tradition. Something of the uncompromising loftiness of his view of Beethoven can be gleaned from the fact that he once played all five late piano sonatas on a single program, and on another occasion conducted the Ninth Symphony twice in one evening.[45] And he could make performance a medium for explicit historical-critical commentary: in playing any of the last five sonatas, he customarily improvised a prelude evoking an earlier sonata which in his view thematically adumbrated the later work. His edition of the piano sonatas, made in conjunction with Sigmund Lebert and Emmanuel Faisst, was widely used from its appearance in 1871 until well into the twentieth century. In recognition of Beethoven's increasingly important role in piano pedagogy, a plethora of editions of the sonatas appeared during the nineteenth century; reflecting the priorities of the day, these recorded the interpretations of particular teachers and virtuosi rather than offering anything by way of textual criticism of existing scores. Bülow's edition clearly embodies Liszt's approach, to the extent that the master himself used it in his teaching late in life.[46] Not surprisingly, it is boldly interpretative, suggesting programmatic associations in many cases, and, more concretely, offering detailed

Example 15.2 Piano Sonata op. 57, mvt. 1, mm. 30–47 in edition by Hans von Bülow and Sigmund Lebert

a) Without keen insight into the Master's thematic work, without a clear understanding of the process of the arising and passing-away of the several motives, an intelligent and intelligible interpretation of his works is impossible. As detailed analysis would swell this instructive edition to an "unpractical" bulk, and oral instruction by the teacher being, moreover, far more fruitful of good than written treatises, the Editor must content himself with occasional hints, leaving their exploitation to practical teaching. Take note, just here, of the melodic "passing-away," more particularly from the rhythmic point of view:

A. Rhythmical diminution. **B.** Melodic disappearance of the descending second.

b) While observing the exact rhythmic precision demanded by the correct interpretation of this melody, which arises from the inversion of the first motive, be very careful to play the intermediate 16th-notes without over-sharp emphasis, an avoidance of which ought never, on the other hand, to lead to indistinctness.

suggestions for tempo modification. In the first movement of the "Appassionata" Sonata, for instance, a change from ♩. = 126 to ♩. = 112 is indicated at the second theme, with a resumption of the initial tempo at the closing theme (see Example 15.2; all the tempo markings and accents, the articulation of the left-hand part in the first five bars, and the slurring of the accompaniment to the theme are Bülow's).

After Wagner: modernism and authenticity

By the end of the century a reaction began to set in against what some saw as the arbitrariness and undisciplined subjectivity of the Wagnerian approach, as a fetish for unconnected moments of cheap sensation, manufactured by exaggerated fluctuations of dynamic and tempo. Felix Weingartner, the most eloquent spokesman of the backlash, coined the dismissive term "tempo-rubato conductor," and blamed Bülow for the phenomenon – perhaps unfairly.[47] But it was not until the emergence of Toscanini as a major Beethoven conductor in the mid-1920s, as conductor first of the New York Philharmonic and then of an orchestra created for him specially at NBC radio, that a decisive challenge was mounted to Wagnerian principles of interpretation. Toscanini's hard-headed view that Beethoven's scores must be followed to the letter if the composer's true intentions were to be revealed – although he broke this rule more often than is sometimes suggested, particularly in the earlier part of his career[48] – is something that nowadays we may be inclined uncritically to take as a truism, but it cut right against the grain of the dominant performance practice of the time. A large number of "traditional" modifications to Beethoven's scores in performance had become typical by the late nineteenth century, which, in addition to orchestrational retouchings of the kind discussed earlier, included certain customary rhetorical pauses and changes of tempo (the latter operating over and above the general flexibility of tempo that seems to have been the norm even up until World War II[49]): all this Toscanini largely spurned.

His approach echoed in more extreme form Berlioz's and Mendelssohn's views of more than fifty years earlier; for a variety of reasons, however, the artistic and cultural climate now became unusually friendly to such ideas and their propagation. As Richard Taruskin has pointed out,[50] the widespread anti-Romanticism of the 1920s, typified by Stravinskian neo-Classicism and other modernist movements touting a new 'objectivity' in art, formed a harmonious backdrop for the brilliant clarity and at times remorseless rhythmic vigor of Toscanini's conducting; the second wave of modernism that followed World War II finally elevated his approach into a new orthodoxy. And although he was a European, Toscanini's willingness to challenge old orthodoxies – he was scathing on the subject of tradition – and his preference for American over European orchestras could not help winning him accolades in the New World. Other powerful factors were also at play, not least the populist impact of the new recording and broadcasting industries, and the related development of high-powered publicity for classical artists; in both these areas, Beethoven's prestige was a valuable commodity.

The advent of recording had a powerful impact on many different aspects of musical life; for historians, it makes possible the study of actual performances, rather than merely writings about performance (early limitations on sound quality or modern editing techniques notwithstanding).[51] Recording and broadcasting came to play an important role in the media-fueled polarization and rivalry that developed between Toscanini and the other most celebrated Beethoven conductor of mid-century, a rivalry that brought to an unusually sharp point opposing philosophies born in the previous century. Wilhelm Furtwängler was the last great representative of the Wagnerian school of conducting, shaping his performances through almost continuous and often substantial tempo modification (tempi within the exposition of the *Eroica* symphony's first movement, for instance, could fluctuate by almost twenty points on the metronome),[52] and emphasizing singing structural lines and darkly rich orchestral mass, often at the expense of unity and clarity of ensemble; indeed, he made his priorities clear when he commented that the great musical works were about "spiritual problems" that could not be brought out by literal adherence to the score.[53] Yet in Furtwängler's case at least, such performances were not founded on passing whims of the moment: Nicholas Cook has argued convincingly that Furtwängler's interpretations of Beethoven project sophisticated structural analyses, based on principles close to those of the theorist Heinrich Schenker, with whom the conductor had close contact. And Furtwängler, like Schenker, believed that in performing great works, there was essentially only one correct interpretation (allowing of course for some flexibility in detail).[54] But in any case, musical issues became fatally enmeshed with politics: Furtwängler's decision to remain in Germany when the Nazis came to power, albeit as a sometime dissenting voice, was compared unfavorably to Toscanini's staunch anti-Fascism and his abandonment of Italy for the United States. When war broke out, and as the radio "V for Victory" morse-code signal explicitly invoked Beethoven as a supra-national symbol of democratic freedom, any connection with what modern Germany had become was disastrous; Furtwängler's reputation never completely recovered, even after the war, and with him a whole school of interpretation, already compromised obliquely by its Wagnerian ancestry, was tainted directly by its association with Nazism. Yet his recordings live on, as revelatory documents of a long and profound tradition that died with him.

In addition to preserving complete cycles of the symphonies under Toscanini and Furtwängler, the legacy of mid-century Beethoven recordings includes Artur Schnabel's magisterial account of the complete piano sonatas, made in the early 1930s, and celebrated recordings by the Busch string quartet. Schnabel, while considerably less literal than Toscanini, advocated close adherence to Beethoven's text; most controversially, this included following pedal markings that blur together harmonic progressions, and trying to honor the composer's metronome marks in the "Hammerklavier," which in the case of the notorious first-movement marking of ♩=138 leads to near-disaster in his 1935 recording.[55]

Despite such literal touches, however, there is a range of rhythmic nuance and compelling temporal flux in Schnabel's playing – he indicated modest tempo modifications in his edition of the sonatas – that makes much post-1945 Beethoven performance seem either rigid or flaccid in comparison. Ironically, as the LP age recorded more and more Beethoven performances for posterity – in a survey compiled in the bicentenary year of 1970, *High Fidelity* listed no fewer than sixteen complete sets of the symphonies, twelve of the sonatas, and five of the quartets[56] – the range of different performance styles was becoming narrower and narrower, with artists taking few risks, and the majority following Toscanini rather than Furtwängler in their attitude to the text. Perhaps it was inevitable in this climate that notable exceptions to this rule, such as Leonard Bernstein and Glenn Gould, should veer towards the histrionic or the downright bizarre in an effort to escape the mold.[57]

By far the most important development of recent years, however, and one which has shaken up hard the creeping homogeneity of Beethoven performance, has been the surge of "historically informed" performances using period instruments and techniques. This began as a trickle in the 1960s and 1970s, with pioneers such as Austrian pianist Paul Badura-Skoda and the German ensemble Collegium Aureum, but became a veritable flood in the 1980s, to the extent that at the time of writing half-a-dozen cycles of the symphonies played by period groups are now available on CD (there have been fewer recordings of the solo piano music and chamber works). Whatever the controversy surrounding the actual historical basis of such approaches, they have been wonderfully refreshing and thought-provoking. Beyond shedding light on general features of timbre and texture of the kind touched on above, period-instrument groups have gone further than ever before in trying to realize Beethoven's metronome marks – even the most extreme – and thoroughly reconsidered many areas of rhythm and articulation. The results have often been startling. For instance, in the recording of the Seventh Symphony by the Orchestre Revolutionnaire et Romantique under John Eliot Gardiner, the dominant rhythmic figure of the first movement, notated ♪♩♩ ♪♩♩, is articulated in a way that is almost impossible to notate but can be rendered approximately as ♪♩♩ ♪♩♩ ; combined with a fractional anticipation of the initial dotted eighth note as the figure is repeated, this creates an agogic effect which imparts unprecedented energy to an already electrifying movement.[59] Whether or not there is anything "authentic" about this reading beyond its overdotting – it may in part have been suggested by early nineteenth-century bowings – to this listener at least it seems to offer something both genuinely new and which helps bring out more fully the intrinsic character of the movement. Such imaginative conceits have become more and more common in historically informed performances of Beethoven, countering their earlier tendency to fetishize context as well as text.

A familiar subtext of the historical performance movement has been the battle over whether Beethoven is a Classical or a Romantic composer: if Furtwängler makes him the direct progenitor of Wagner, Gardiner forcefully reminds us that Beethoven studied with Haydn. And such radically new – and perhaps also old – approaches to Beethoven can once again be linked to broader developments in our society: analyzing the historical performance movement as a whole, Richard Taruskin has drawn attention to parallels with recent legal theory (a connection noted first by lawyers themselves), which has turned its attention increasingly to the unstable and political relationship between written texts and interpretative acts.[59] But whatever their origin, such developments – responsibly pursued – guarantee that Beethoven's music will not be exhausted for us: they make us hear these well-worn pieces as if they were new again. Furthermore, plurality of performance styles ensures the life of our musical culture; a greater awareness of these styles and of their origins will surely encourage its continuing health. Whether we could ever revive, or should wish to revive, the interpretative world of Furtwängler is doubtful. On the other hand, it would be regrettable if the historical performance movement established a new orthodoxy that sharply limited the range of accepted approaches to performing Beethoven. Whether or not his music is really "better than it can ever be performed," to use a striking phrase of Schnabel's, the possibilities within it certainly cannot be exhausted by any one school or approach. And in any case, even if we do our best to follow his intentions, the ambiguous historical record leaves open a wide range of interpretative paths to follow. Which is surely a good thing – both for us and for Beethoven's music.

16 The four ages of Beethoven: critical reception and the canonic composer

SCOTT BURNHAM

Of the reception of Beethoven's music these last two hundred years, one thing is clear: there has been little trace of the tidal cycles of popular and critical approbation suffered by almost every other important composer. More specifically, no significant ebb tide has yet been charted in the reception of his music. Or it may be that his fortunes are subject to a tide table of an exceedingly grander temporal scale: perhaps Beethoven will go out of fashion for the next two hundred years, only to return with force in some unthinkable new world. And yet, his image – however abiding – has not simply stood in place over the last two centuries, like some historically inert monolith. One may mark discernible stations in the critical reception of his life and music, points in the historical flow that seem to gather into a larger narrative.

I would like to construct four such stations, each anchored to a symbolic milestone in the history of Beethoven reception: 1827, death of Beethoven and birth of the artist as Romantic revolutionary and hero; 1870, centenary of Beethoven's birth and symbolic rebirth of the composer as a spiritual and political Redeemer; 1927, centenary of the composer's death and symbolic death of the figure of the Romantic artist in favor of that of the law-giver and natural force; and 1970, bicentennial of the composer's birth and symbolic birth of the culturally constructed hero. Beyond tracing the vibrant afterlife Beethoven has enjoyed in mainstream Western musical thought, the resulting trajectory illuminates a perhaps typical process of canon formation, whereby a canonic subject is gradually transformed into a canonic object.

1827 Beethoven as Romantic hero

> Just as the behemoth storms through the sea, so [Beethoven] swept through the frontier limits of his art. From the gurgling of the dove to the roaring of thunder, from the most ingenious weaving together of idiosyncratic artistic materials to that fearful extreme, when cultivation passes over into the unruly caprice of nature's struggling forces, he has taken the measure of everything, comprehended it all.
> (Franz Grillparzer)

Speaking on the occasion of Beethoven's funeral, the poet Franz Grillparzer describes the famous composer's music as something akin to a force of nature, equally at home with a bird's gentle song and with the senseless fury of a storm, knowing no externally imposed boundaries in the service of a comprehensive musical art. Grillparzer goes on to claim that Beethoven will perforce have no successors: anyone who comes after him will have to begin all over again, "for [Beethoven] only stopped where Art itself stops."[1] Grillparzer's oration thus sets the tone for much of the subsequent reception of Beethoven, a reception initially founded on the Romantic figure of the artist as hero. In a sustained effort of superhuman will, Beethoven creates his own world, a world coterminous with the world of musical art. His all-embracing musical activity notably includes that distinctly Romantic transit between the cultivated and the chaotic, the civilized and the primitive.

Some years later, Grillparzer privately condemned the crossing of this line, the relinquishing of cultivation. Here is a diary entry from 1834, in which Grillparzer felt compelled to list distinct reservations toward Beethoven's music:[2]

> Beethoven's harmful effects on the world of art, despite his inestimably high worth:
>
> 1. The first and foremost necessity of a musician – the refinement and rectitude of the ear – suffers under his audacious combinations and their all too often indulged admixture of musical howling and yowling [*Tongeheuel und Gebrüll*].
> 2. By leaving lyricism well behind him [*Durch seine überlyrische Sprünge*], he stretches the concept of order and coherence in a piece of music to the breaking point.
> 3. His frequent overstepping of the rules makes them appear to be dispensable, whereas such rules are the inestimable expression of a healthy and unaffected sensibility.
> 4. He replaces the preference for a sense of beauty with a taste for the engaging, the robust, the overpowering, the intoxicating [*das Interessante, Starke, Erschütternde, Trunkenmachende*] – and it is precisely music, of all the arts, which fares the worst with such an exchange.

Disregard for the rules, harsh, wild sounds, loose construction, and over-powering outpourings (note how the intensification of the nominatives in item 4 is itself Beethovenian – from something which engages one's interest to something which overwhelms and intoxicates): these things seem to injure Grillparzer's sense of musical propriety, even while he recognizes the overriding importance of Beethoven's music.

If Grillparzer's concern over such loss of cultivation marks his fundamentally Biedermeier sensibility – the classic Biedermeier novel, Adalbert Stifter's *Der Nachsommer* (1857), devotes hundreds of unruffled pages to the cultivation of gardens and the arts – his split judgment resonates with many characterizations of the composer and his music that were already in circulation. The combination of reverence for Beethoven's music and lack of understanding of, or even lack of sympathy for, certain less than decorous aspects of that music is fundamental to the view of Beethoven circa 1827. There was a growing sense that a full appreciation of Beethoven's music would be relegated to a more educated and experienced posterity. In his obituary for the composer, the critic Friedrich Rochlitz wrote: "If his boldest, most powerfully gripping works are not yet honored, enjoyed, and loved, it is only because there are still not enough people who comprehend them and can form an audience for them. This number will grow, and so too will his fame."[3]

Robin Wallace, in documenting the reactions of critics contemporaneous with Beethoven, has used the phrase "awed but skeptical" to characterize the general attitude toward Beethoven's music of critics writing for the *Allgemeine musikalische Zeitung*.[4] Somewhat belying Rochlitz's hopes for posterity, this combination of awe and skepticism is still in evidence decades later in the writings of the critics Wilhelm von Lenz and Aléxandre Oulibicheff.[5] Lenz, in particular, made frequent reference to Beethoven's "chimera," meaning those passages where the composer goes beyond the dictates of musical taste into something monstrous and willfully transgressive. Thus the difficulties in Beethoven's music are fabled difficulties, and they add to his stature as an uncompromising artist: the struggles of the embattled, heroic artist are more sublime than euphonious.[6]

In his fear of the loss of musical cultivation in the face of Beethoven's imposing greatness, Grillparzer adumbrates the terms of a dichotomy which was to galvanize nineteenth-century thought on music: that of beauty and the sublime.[7] We shall see this dichotomy raise its head again, now adorned with a Prussian *Pickelhaube* (spiked helmet), when we consider Wagner's 1870 monograph on Beethoven.

Grillparzer was not the first, or even the most influential, literary personage to take a stand on the phenomenon that was Beethoven. A much more lasting contribution to the myth of Beethoven as an artistic hero was made by E. T. A. Hoffmann, the Berlin lawyer, musician, music critic, and fantastical man of letters. In a series of seminal essays and reviews he established a critical tradition that worked to substantiate the myth of Beethoven as an artistic hero.

As the representative of a more purely Romantic sensibility than was Grillparzer's, Hoffmann had no problems with the difficulties of Beethoven's music but rather heard in them the unmistakable signs of the presence of the inexpressible, the signature of the truly Romantic. Writing about Beethoven's Fifth Symphony in 1810, he suggested that "[Music] is the most romantic of all arts ... Music reveals to man an unknown realm, a world quite separate from the outer sensual world surrounding him, a world in which he leaves behind all feelings circumscribed by the intellect in order to embrace the inexpressible."[8] Hoffmann went on to pronounce his now famous distinctions between Haydn, Mozart, and Beethoven:[9]

> Haydn and Mozart, the creators of modern instrumental music, first showed us the art in its full glory; but the one who regarded it with total devotion and penetrated to its innermost nature is Beethoven ...
>
> Haydn's compositions are dominated by a feeling of childlike optimism. His symphonies lead us through endless, green forest-glades, through a motley throng of happy people ...
>
> Mozart leads us deep into the realm of spirits. Dread lies all about us yet withholds its torments and becomes more an intimation of infinity ...
>
> In a similar way Beethoven's instrumental music unveils before us the realm of the mighty and the immeasurable ...
>
> Haydn romantically apprehends the humanity in human life; he is more congenial to the majority. Mozart takes as his province the superhuman, magical quality residing in the inner self. Beethoven's music sets in motion the machinery of awe, of fear, of terror, of pain, and awakens that infinite yearning which is the essence of romanticism.

The triumvirate Haydn, Mozart, and Beethoven, the three pillars of the Viennese Classical Style, here find their classic characterizations: Haydn is but touched by the spirit of Hoffmann's distant realm – the result is a prelapsarian and pastoral music; Mozart crosses the threshold of that realm, and brings back intimations of infinity; Beethoven actually lives in the spirit-realm, takes on the full terrors of interiority, and sweeps the listener along with him into that infinite space.[10] By positioning Beethoven as the most powerfully possessed of the three, Hoffmann initiates the common view of the hierarchy and historical evolution implied in the succession of Haydn, Mozart, and Beethoven. Beethoven completes this dialectical triad and becomes the ideal Romantic artist, the only one truly at home in Hoffmann's spirit-realm of the infinite.

And how does Beethoven's music express infinity for Hoffmann? Through the music's teeming abundance and the way that its exuberant, almost chaotic, variety seems grounded by an underlying unity.[11] Perceiving that unity is an act of critical intuition akin to sensing the unity of creation amidst its overwhelming variety: the same mystical faculty of mind is put into play, and it brings with it the intimation of eternity.[12] Hoffmann helped create a situation rare in music history: the little understood works of a still living composer were accepted on faith as masterpieces of organic conception and sublime revelation, each held together by a deep and mysterious continuity which, in Hoffmann's words, "speaks only from spirit to spirit." In other words, Beethoven's music was heard to register less with the visible world of intellect than with the invisible domain of the spirit.

On the other hand, Hoffmann offers concrete evidence for his sense of coherence in Beethoven's music. In the Fifth Symphony review, he discusses the long-range development of thematic material, and he emphasizes the intense psychological engagement the music engenders. This combination of thematic process and psychological intensity clears the way for the anthropomorphic subject that is still frequently associated with Beethoven's themes and motives in criticism and analysis.

It is important to note that Hoffmann lived and worked in Berlin. In the early nineteenth century, Berlin was a city of growing cultural and political stature, home of a new university (founded in 1805 by Wilhelm von Humboldt) which professed a bold agenda for the merger of the concerns of the state and the arts. After Hoffmann's death (in 1822), the phenomenon of Beethoven's music would increasingly come to strike the perfect note with the cultural charter of this city of new beginnings. This was achieved largely through the proselytizing efforts of the Berlin critic and theorist Adolph Bernhard Marx, who was significantly influenced by Hoffmann's musical writings. Marx promoted the music of Beethoven not primarily from a literary perspective but from the cutting edge of contemporary musical thought.[13]

As one of the nineteenth century's most influential musical thinkers, Marx ultimately managed to institutionalize a view of Beethoven not far from Hoffmann's own. Although Marx spoke to Hoffmann only once (Hoffmann died shortly after Marx's arrival in Berlin), his first substantial publication was in fact an appreciation of Hoffmann's role as a musical thinker, which he wrote in 1823 as an appendix to Julius Hitzig's biography of Hoffmann and which adumbrates many of the great themes of his own critical agenda. In the following year, the Berlin music publisher Adolph Schlesinger appointed the thirty-year-old Marx as head editor of a new music periodical, the *Berliner allgemeine musikalische Zeitung*, a weekly newspaper which Schlesinger hoped would compete with the ever popular *Allgemeine musikalische Zeitung* of Leipzig. Given Marx's lack of journalistic experience, Schlesinger's choice was something of a gamble. And yet Marx's inexperience had a signal advantage that far outweighed any drawbacks: by not coming from an established journalistic tradition, Marx could more easily create a new ideal for the musical journal. Rather than concentrating on the detailed reporting of musical events, Marx's paper would provide a forum for higher-minded issues – it would treat music as a vital part of cultural and intellectual *Bildung*. Most importantly, the *Berliner allgemeine musikalische Zeitung* would prepare the public for a new age in musical art.

The founding composer of Marx's new age, the age of ideal music, was Beethoven. Marx viewed the whole of music history as a grand three-stage process of music's spiritual development. The first stage is simply one of "blessed play" – music learns the nature of its own parameters through childlike play and experiment; the second stage involves the expression of feelings; and the third rises to the expression of transcendent, spiritual content. While the music of Mozart culminates the second stage, Beethoven is the composer of the crowning ideal stage. The spiritual content Marx sought and found in Beethoven's instrumental music was not some timeless ideational essence, Romantic, Platonic, or otherwise, but rather the concretion of idealized and – given Marx's and Beethoven's historical provenance – politically charged human values, such as freedom and overcoming. Marx's leap into the compulsions of the moral domain adds a crucial note to Hoffmann's view of music's spiritual nature as the Romantic intimation of the infinite. For now the spirit of music is anchored in the moral bedrock of the age; and perhaps here we have again passed from the ethos of Romanticism to that of the Biedermeier-Vormärz.

Like Hoffmann before him, Marx argued that it was up to the critic to attempt to understand Beethoven's works, a task that would take more than one hearing, as well as a certain gift for divination. Marx's brief for musical hermeneutics consolidated the first stages of a continuing tradition of interpreting Beethoven's music as a kind of secular scripture. And this was not all. Marx went on to write one of the nineteenth century's most influential treatises on musical composition. Best known as the theorist who codified sonata form, he did so almost exclusively on the model of Beethoven's piano sonatas. Thus the pertinacity of the theoretical model of sonata form is mutually symbiotic with the work-oriented Beethoven paradigm in music criticism and analysis.[14]

The journalistic, pedagogical, and theoretical writings of A. B. Marx went a long way toward the canonization of Beethoven's music, which served both as the model for Marx's influential theory of musical form (and sonata form in particular) and as the foundation for what he deemed a new age of music history, based on the high spiritual claims of Beethoven's instrumental music.[15] For Marx and his generation, Beethoven was both a revolutionary herald of the future of Western music and the culminating figure of that music's history; we shall next encounter Beethoven elevated beyond the flesh and blood artist-hero to a more supratemporal mythological hero. It is Richard Wagner who rolls away the stone from Beethoven's tomb and finds that he is no longer there, that he has been resurrected.

1870 Beethoven as Redeemer

> [T]oday it behooves us to show that, through this musician Beethoven, who speaks in the purest language of all peoples, the German spirit redeemed the spirit of man from profound disgrace. (Richard Wagner, *Beethoven* [1870])

What can Wagner mean by this? His words fashion Beethoven as a Christ figure, who brings the word of a holy power (the German spirit) to concrete, redemptive expression: as a universally understood language, Beethoven's music is the purest speech of all.[16] But in what sense can Beethoven and the German spirit be said to have redeemed humankind from spiritual disgrace? What in fact is the German spirit? And how is Beethoven's music a pure language?

We need first to be reminded of a remarkable and momentous coincidence: the year 1870 marks both the composer's hundredth birthday and Bismarck's triumph over Napoleon III in the Franco-Prussian War. Wagner's commemorative monograph on Beethoven makes the connection quite explicit, and he is not alone in this. There were a number of birthday celebrations for the composer in which he was unabashedly proclaimed as a political hero of the first stripe.[17] Thus Beethoven's symbolic rebirth as a redeemer is made to coincide with the symbolic birth of German unity that was attended by the Prussian victory over that old adversary, the French.

In addition to providing an appreciation of the German spirit, Wagner wished his Beethoven monograph to be perceived as a contribution to the philosophy of music.[18] Like Schopenhauer, Wagner associates music with the immediacy of the Will. This allows him to make a case for music's unique ability to commune with our most inward beings. Throughout the monograph, Wagner exploits a facile dichotomy between the inner world and the outer world, in order to privilege music and the ear over and against the plastic arts and the eye. The outer world is governed and perceived by the eye, which is satisfied with beauty and semblance; the inner world is the realm of the ear, which listens for the sublime. The outer world is a waking state that offers only appearances; the inner world is associated with the dream and with things spiritual, with prophecy and transcendence.

But music can in fact be the means of reconciling the two worlds, for with music, the outer world speaks to us in a way that resonates with our deepest being. Here Wagner defines music as the art that emerges from "this immediate consciousness of the unity of our inner essence with that of the external world."[19] Thus music itself is now a form of revelation, a philosophy of deeply inward experience. And it was Beethoven who brought music from the status of a debased artform to this sublime calling.[20]

In an interpretative move that, according to K. M. Knittel, irrevocably altered the subsequent reception history of Beethoven's late style, Wagner treats the composer's deafness not as a rationalization for some of the perceived difficulties of his later music but as an enabling condition for his preternatural inwardness.[21] Not unlike the blindness of the seer Teiresias, Beethoven's deafness becomes a martyrdom that guarantees his immortality.[22]

Beethoven's enhanced inwardness accounts for the power and magic of his music. Unhampered by any superficial and outward reliance on appearances, his music is galvanic; its every aspect "is raised to the supreme importance of a direct outpouring of his spirit."[23] Hence Wagner's famous formulation that everything in this music becomes melody, even the silences: he hears Beethoven's music as an all-encompassing effusion that coheres like one great melody. In this way, Beethoven emancipates melody from the detrimental and inconstant influence of fashion, elevating it to a universal human *Typus*.[24] This is why Wagner feels able to describe Beethoven's music as "the purest language of all peoples." Its inwardness, as from a pure source unsullied by the circumstances of mundane reality, creates a universality that "seems to set our deepest being into motion."[25] Such inward depth is natural, universal, and pure. And its presence is sublime.

Wagner's association of the inward with the sublime is absolutely crucial to his view of the role played by Beethoven in the triumph of the German spirit. For the German, "that which is pleasing is denied; as compensation, his truest thoughts and actions are inward and sublime."[26] The German spirit dismisses all that is merely pleasing; it, in fact, cannot be pleased. And thus a deaf composer's difficult music becomes the warrant of Germany's sublime destiny.

At the end of his monograph, Wagner reaches the point of great moment for his contemporary readers: if the inner world is the realm of the Germans, the outer world is inhabited by – the French. And now is the time to throw off the French yoke: "While German arms are victoriously driving toward the center of French civilization, we are suddenly seized with shame over our dependence on this civilization, shame that openly demands a rejection of Parisian fashionmongering."[27] When Beethoven freed music from the fetters of fashion he already began the process of this "most noble conquest"; the Beethovenian symphony brought "the new religion, the world-redeeming annunciation of sublime innocence" to a desecrated paradise.[28]

We may now refine Wagner's earlier definition of music as that which emerges from the consciousness of the unity of inner and outer worlds. What seems clear from the entire thrust of his monograph is that it is Beethoven's music which emerges from a consciousness of the unity of inner German essence and the outer world. This is how Beethoven's music redeems the spirit of humankind; it recreates the world in its own profound image, rescuing the world from the beautiful snares of the merely fashionable.

In his oft-cited interpretation of the Quartet in C♯ minor op. 131 – the centerpiece of his Beethoven monograph – Wagner actually portrays the composer engaged in this formidable task of remaking the world.[29] For Wagner, this arguably cyclic quartet (transformed material from the opening movement features heavily in the finale) becomes a mythopoetic symbol – it is figured as a day in the life of "our saint," one which takes him from waking back to sleeping. Wagner's image of a passing day is not only a cogent way to portray the unity of the whole work (all its movements are heard as part of the same trajectory); it also enjoys a venerable symbolic patrimony, invoking the great myths of cyclic return.

Wagner construes Beethoven's fugal first movement as a prayer of penance, uttered upon waking, in melancholy apprehension of the day ahead. The composer's prayer is answered: the D major second movement is the lovely consoling memory of a submerged dream image. And now Beethoven is ready to work. During the transitional third movement, he turns to his magic world. In the ensuing variation movement, he fully exercises his restored magical powers, transforming a graceful and profoundly innocent figure with unheard of variety, to his unremitting delight. He then turns his gaze outward in the fifth movement (Presto), illuminating the outer world with his inner happiness. Next he regards life itself, sinking into contemplation (in the Adagio sixth movement) about how he might make life dance (in the seventh and final movement). He wakes once again, and creates the "dance of the world itself," standing above this wild storm of heaven and hell in the smiling security that it is but a playful fantasy after all. And then night beckons, and his day is done.

From daybreak to nightfall – for Wagner, the whole piece replicates and reflects this larger cycle by means of an alternating series of dream states and waking states, of inward contemplation and outward propagation. The melancholy of the first movement is a condition of waking; it echoes the great fall of humankind. The second movement, like some Platonic memory, harks back to an earlier dream (remembering the last time the cycle was enacted?). Next, the creator submerges himself again in his interior world, emerging to illuminate the world in his own image and then, after yet another submersion, actually recreating the world. Finally he rests, presumably to begin it all again at another dawn.

The result is a typically Wagnerian mythic stew, a conflation of the Judaeo-Christian creation myth with cyclical/mythical history and "the works and days" of human life (waking, remembering, finding oneself, emerging, creating, resting, and so on . . .). Beethoven himself is portrayed as a creator, whose mythic day consists of so many border crossings between visible and invisible worlds, inner and outer states. As such, his quartet – in Wagner's reading – may also be said to embrace the rhythm of Western epic, replete with outward journeys and inward, chthonic episodes; in its urge to contain everything within the space of a single day it is not unlike the Bloomsday of Joyce's *Ulysses*. Wagner needs all of this in his attempt to describe the creative process of the redeemer of Western music and the German spirit.[30]

Ultimately, Wagner's conjunction of inward spirituality, self-aggrandizing metaphysics, and a fervent nationalism both political and militant stands as a modern instantiation of that age-old formula for empire building: the symbiotic combination of a powerful idea and material power. His easy equation of music and philosophical depth, of art and the spiritually sublime, and his claim for the natural superiority of the invisible and inward over the visible and outward, together spell the particular attractions of the nineteenth-century Germanic empire of the spirit. In this vision, Beethoven's music becomes a powerful transhistorical force, engaged in a much larger struggle than simply pointing the way to future developments in musical style.

Yet, as always, Wagner's mirror distorts, tending to reflect and concentrate extreme elements. Other contemporary authors were decidedly less mythical in their treatment of Beethoven. In fact, this may well count as the great age of empirical musical biography. Surely Thayer's fact-centered approach to the biography of Beethoven seems the very antidote to Wagner's grandiose mythologizing. And Thayer's *Life of Beethoven* shared the reliable company of Jahn's biography of Mozart and Pohl's of Haydn. In line with literary Realism, the biographer was wont to stick to what were perceived as the facts; at the same time, music theorists began to invoke the natural sciences, with psychology and cognition replacing more Romantic views of the human spirit, while Gustav Nottebohm's groundbreaking work on Beethoven's sketchbooks provided evidence of all-too-human creative struggles on the part of the composer. Indeed these more empirical efforts form the level ground against which Wagner's enormous success may be gauged, for like his theater at Bayreuth, Wagner's oeuvre created a great resonant space extending above and below the German landscape, promising an ennobling escape into the billowing heights and boundless depths of the German spirit.

But the overarching theme of German musical thought toward the end of the nineteenth century – that to which all these different enterprises tended – was the emergent ascendancy of the Viennese Classical Style into something like an essentialist norm, the alpha and omega of Western musical history. And the ruling spirit of this imposing musical plateau was Beethoven, increasingly understood as a Classical composer in the broadest sense. In the section that follows, we will observe that Beethoven becomes not only Classical, but universal and natural as well, as the vision of what music could be shifted to a determination of what music should be.

1927 Beethoven as lawgiver and bearer of Classical values

> He did not revolutionize [musical] art; he did not invent new artistic means, laws, or forms; he released neither himself nor others from the traditional rules of his art ... And just as he respected the laws of art, he respected those of reality. He never separated art and reality, never understood music as unconditionally absolute or used music as a surrogate for religion. His greatest works in fact serve the expression of moral concepts: the idea of Christianity and of the moral upbringing of man.
>
> (Arnold Schmitz, *Das romantische Beethovenbild* [1927])

Here, on the occasion of the centenary of Beethoven's death, the German musicologist Arnold Schmitz presides over the symbolic death of the Romantic image of Beethoven. In this manifesto-like peroration, Schmitz systematically deflates, point by point, the prevailing nineteenth-century view of the composer.[31] Schmitz's litany practically stands Grillparzer's nervous list on its head: we now discover that Beethoven did not overthrow authority; he did not dispense with rules; his music did not create its own religion but rather served Christian morality. In one century, Beethoven has gone from a symbol of exhilarating progress and enticingly dangerous revolution to one of upstanding normalcy and healthy morality.

If Wagner's vision of Beethoven and unconscious creation invoked a twilight state of dreams and wakings, we are now fully awake. For Schmitz purports to rub the sleep from our eyes, to dispel and banish all such fogs and vapors, to see Beethoven in the light of day, successfully delivered from the night sickness that is Romanticism. Where nineteenth-century critics portrayed the composer as genial child of nature, revolutionary, magician, and high priest, Schmitz seeks to recover the "genuine Beethoven" and his historical greatness – a greatness now seen to lie in Beethoven's service to the ideals of Classicism and moral well-being.[32]

Schmitz's assumption that there is an identifiably genuine Beethoven, no longer in need of the distorting shadows that both unnerved and thrilled the likes of E. T. A. Hoffmann, grounded a more general agenda of sober reclamation undertaken by many prominent voices of German musical scholarship. This effort formed the common denominator of many of the German-language essays and books written to commemorate the 1927 centenary. In his own 1927 book on Beethoven, August Halm declared that "it behooves us to re-educate ourselves concerning Beethoven; to this end, a certain cool consideration may be more helpful than a purely emotive enthusiasm, such as has been far too often encouraged by custom."[33]

The call of writers like Schmitz and Halm to reject a tradition now perceived to be perniciously subjective found a receptive audience in postwar Germany. For they were addressing a wounded culture having every reason to distance itself from the ecstatic extremes of Romanticism and, more immediately, Expressionism, a culture more than ready for a *neue Sachlichkeit*. And there was a powerful political motivation for this view of Beethoven: downplaying the idea of Beethoven as a revolutionary worked to dissociate the composer from French revolutionary ideals. This proved crucial in many of the right-wing, ultra-nationalist readings of Beethoven which appeared around 1927 in Germany.[34]

In line with this new agenda, musical thought in 1920s Germany takes a decidedly objective turn, namely, the turn to form. Halm himself conceptualized music as an objective, spiritual power, made visible through its form.[35] And he celebrated Beethoven's music above all as a triumph of formative power, of *Gestaltung*.[36] Thus Beethoven's music registers on a supra-individual level – Halm discourages interpretative conflations of the music with the personality of the composer, claiming instead that even the most individually idiosyncratic passages in Beethoven's music serve a coherent whole. As an example of this, he cites the famously premature horn call in the first movement of the *Eroica* as an expression not of some personal whim but of Beethoven's overmastering sense for form.[37] Here we observe Beethoven's music becoming more and more objective, the personal idiosyncrasies of his musical style heard more and more as supra-individual, natural forces.

Beethoven enjoyed pride of place in Halm's grand view of the forces of music history. Halm understood instrumental music to be the highest testimony to the viability and power of music. And within instrumental music, he distinguished two great "cultures": the fugal and concerto forms of Bach, and the sonata forms of Beethoven and Bruckner. He described sonata form as the "conclusive form of great music."[38] It is an altogether higher *Gestaltung*, for in its dramatic temporality and a priori finitude it comes closest to life itself. As Halm exclaims: "This is a truly living music; this is earthly life!"[39]

As a life force, Beethoven's music counts as a natural phenomenon, but it is emphatically not to be heard as nature allowed to run riot. In the sentence that concludes Halm's book we hear that Beethoven's great achievement is to have formed a great unity out of the metamorphosing temporality of life: "Where Beethoven succeeded – and succeeded so perfectly that we can practically grasp the idea with our hands – was in [creating] a music of phases, of transformations, of ages and lifetimes, that nonetheless forms an inseparable, grandiose unity: this was an achievement [*Errungenschaft*] in the history of the musical spirit whose worth will never be exceeded."[40]

Halm's apotheosis contains all the reigning elements of what has been called the Beethoven paradigm: the music's message is utterly palpable (the idea that can be grasped with the hands); the music achieves a unique integration of compelling temporal process and oneness on a grand scale; and this achievement is understood to be an *Errungenschaft*, an achievement that had to be struggled for (as opposed to a *Leistung*, for instance). Beethoven is still a hero, his music is unmistakable in its message and force, and it attains and expresses the highest synthesis of the temporal and the spatial, the dramatic and the epic, the circumstantial and the monumental.

Other signal trends in the growing analytical literature around Beethoven rallied to the same call of synthesis and unity. The rise of motivic analysis, for example, culminating in the Schoenbergian ideal of the developing variation, can be understood as a way of charting both the music's temporal process and its synchronic integrity. The motive had already been characterized in the theoretical work of several nineteenth-century theorists (such as A. B. Marx and Hugo Riemann) as a kind of seed, an elemental, germinal utterance. But whereas this idea remained for them largely a suggestive metaphor, analysts now transformed it into unswerving law and sought to demonstrate it in case after case.

In one of the more proselytic treatments of this burgeoning agenda, published in 1925 and entitled "Die Sonatenform Beethovens: Das Gesetz," Walter Engelsmann describes Beethovenian thematic/motivic process with a metaphor that promises even more inevitability than the usual metaphor of organic growth: "We thus understand the Beethovenian motive as the germinal seed [*Keim*] of the sonata, from which the course of the work explodes outward – without addition – only through variation of its proper content."[41] The motivic seed now harbors an explosive force [*Explosivkraft*], and the unfolding of the form becomes an inevitable, supercharged trajectory. After thus bringing the organic metaphor into line with the age of modern warfare, Engelsmann closes his article with the following formulation, laying down the law of his title with stentorian capitals:

> He who is capable of understanding all [Beethoven's] remaining works as having grown in the same sense, will be able – with me – to form this law: EVERY SONATA OF BEETHOVEN IS DEVELOPED, IN ALL ITS PHRASES, SECTIONS, AND THEMES, FROM A SINGLE MAIN THEME OR MAIN MOTIVE.[42]

If Engelsmann's words articulate a directive that was to keep motive hunters happily motivated for decades to come, the inception and rise of Schenkerian depth analysis was to enjoy a more widespread credibility and respect, at least among Anglo-American scholars. For with its deeply submerged *Ursatz* and the various middleground stages lying between the *Ursatz* and the sounding foreground of the composition, Schenker's theory appeared capable of exploring and charting those trackless interior spaces that Wagner and others could only shadow forth. In the 1920s, Schenker promoted and developed his new analytical methodology in a series of analyses published in a journal entirely devoted to his own work and tellingly titled *Der Tonwille*. The metaphorical implication is clear: music has a will of its own, is a natural world unto itself. Schenker's elaborate subtitle includes the phrase "in witness of unchanging laws of musical art." Again the concept of natural law is invoked – music is a natural force, subject to its own laws. And Beethoven's music would, for Schenker, be a primary witness of these laws. For Beethoven's Fifth Symphony was the subject of Schenker's flagship analysis in *Der Tonwille*, and, indeed, each important stage of Schenker's thought is marked with an imposing analysis of a work by Beethoven.[43]

Both motivic analysis and Schenkerian depth analysis purport to objectify the intuitively perceived suasions of temporality, process, and unity in the music of Beethoven. This was the nascent age of structuralism, after all, an age of enhanced confidence in the ability of the human mind to plumb its own depths, to descry the very forms and structures of its thought. The emphasis on musical form – especially so-called inner form – in the writings of critics and analysts such as Halm and Schenker may well serve as the transitional link in completing the shift from nineteenth- to twentieth-century views. With the rise of psychology and notions of latency, a science of the unconscious continued to develop, wherein the inward is joined with the profound, and the two are shown to be subject to laws as immutable as those which govern the transactions of the natural world. This agenda reveals the kinship between these two ages, for all their cries to the contrary. Analysts of the twentieth century sought to objectify the still prevailing assumption about the profundity and interiority of Beethoven's music; continuing a trend begun so earnestly by Hugo Riemann, they sought to enunciate the invisible laws underlying the musical surface. The compelling quality of Beethoven's music is thus associated with the compulsions of natural law – anything so compelling must be law – as the process of objectification continues.

Related to the idea that Beethoven's music is best understood as an expression of natural musical law is the emergent view, in the discourse surrounding Beethoven in 1927, that his music expresses healthy normality and moral wellbeing. Here too, the values of form and balance are generally invoked – Classical values, to be sure. For example, even while railing against the "a priori fancies" of German music theorists, the great English critic Donald Francis Tovey advocated a similar emphasis on form.[44] The difference was in his approach: whereas Riemann went to great systematic lengths to develop his notion of the prototypical eight-bar period, Tovey concentrated on the proportions and details of individual musical forms as they moved through time; he insisted that such close study of foreground detail was a sine qua non for an understanding of form.[45]

Tovey was interested above all in demonstrating the temporal logic of Beethoven's forms. In a well-known essay written in 1927, Tovey undertakes to show the "fundamental normality" of the same piece celebrated so portentously in Wagner's 1870 monograph: the late Quartet in C♯ minor op. 131, a work that was generally considered to be Beethoven's most original and idiosyncratic. The burden of Tovey's analysis is a demonstration of how the various movements draw on the sonata-form ethos, by now the prevailing mark of musical normality. By the end of his analysis, Tovey's watchword is unity: motivic and harmonic links between the finale and the first movement prompt him to declare that "[t]he wheel has come full circle. The whole quartet is a perfect unity, governed by the results of the initial event of the first movement . . ."[46] With the detection of this unity, Tovey seems to consider his case clinched: op. 131 is, after all, a strict and reasonable conception.

In a compelling and sympathetic account of Tovey's achievement as a critic, Joseph Kerman emphasizes his Victorian sensibility.[47] It is this sensibility that prompts Tovey to characterize the values of form, balance, and unity (and even drama, the mainspring of the Classical style in his view) as healthy, normal values, values that evince a strongly positive moral force. And Tovey is not alone in understanding Beethoven primarily as a model of ethical wellbeing. In two other essays stemming from 1927, the renowned German musicologists Guido Adler and Hermann Abert independently arrived at the same conclusion: the combination of urgency, form and balance in Beethoven's music lends that music a moral force that is thoroughly Classical.

Both Abert and Adler talk about the music as holding great opposing forces in balance. According to Adler, in Beethoven's music "the demonic [*Dämonie*] . . . binds itself with crystalline reason and clear understanding. Each holds the balance over and against the other."[48] Above all, form is to be ranked over *Idee* as the determining factor in his music.[49] For Abert, Beethoven balances the heroic with the contemplative. He notes, for instance, that works with a fully developed scherzo always contain a big Adagio (which represents the urge to sink into the All, as opposed to the scherzo, which strives to maintain one's own self in the face of the All). This dichotomy of Self and All is initially presented in the first movement as a primal conflict (*Urkonflikt*), a powerful play of opposites, which are then separated in the middle movements and ultimately synthesized in the finale.[50] Again the values of balance and synthesis, Classical values, come to the fore.

Finally, both men find ethical force at the foundation of Beethoven's art. Implicit here is an admission that there is dangerous energy at large in this music – remember Adler's *Dämonie* – energy that is somehow contained and/or balanced by an act of will. Indeed, Abert talks about Beethoven's "powerful ethical will,"[51] Adler about his "urge for truth."[52] Beethoven confronts the entire range of human experience with unflinching honesty. Adler defines Beethoven's fundamental essence as straightforwardness (*Gradlinigkeit*) and true ethos (*wahres Ethos*).[53] And Abert, who studied Classics in Berlin and wrote a dissertation on the ethos of Greek music, culminates his essay by associating Beethoven with a beloved Classical ideal, that of beautiful nobility and goodness (*kalokagathía*).[54]

Beethoven's music became for this generation the unsurpassable model of a redeeming, Classical art. For Tovey, his music sounds as the epitome of Victorian normality and health; for Abert and Adler it is a viable moral force, a force for truth and goodness. Such things seemed in short supply in the wake of the Great War: the Beethoven of 1927 stands as a fitting representative for all that this battered age feared had been lost in the madness. Now his music no longer fights for a fabled future, as it was heard to do one hundred years earlier, but for a stable and reassuring past, increasingly capable of being objectified; there is now less of "the starry skies above" and more of "the moral law within."

1970 Beethoven as cultural force and cultural product

> Between Beethoven then and Beethoven now stands the history of Beethoven reception.
> (Hans Heinrich Eggebrecht)

Thus begins Hans Heinrich Eggebrecht's 1970 monograph entitled *Zur Geschichte der Beethoven-Rezeption*.[55] It would be hard to situate the subject of his study, the history of Beethoven reception, more immediately and dramatically; beyond this, Eggebrecht's words broach an arresting predicament: there is now no longer any such thing as direct, unmediated access to Beethoven. Schmitz's landmark book of 1927 already served to make one aware of Beethoven reception. But Eggebrecht goes further. If Schmitz's prevailing agenda was to get at the real Beethoven by cleansing his image of the intervening reception tradition, Eggebrecht argues that there is no "real Beethoven" waiting beneath the accretions of history; rather, Beethoven is fully and irrevocably a construction of that history. Eggebrecht's monograph articulates a broad shift from the study of an essential Beethoven to the study of the ways we construct him. As such, his work underwrites the last stage in our own trajectory: for the rise of reception studies signals the birth of our awareness of the constructed hero, now more fully an object, a product of cultural and ideological forces.

Eggebrecht's words, above all, emphasize our sense of distance from Beethoven. They signal a loss of faith in an immediate connection to Beethoven, a recognition that what we have been clinging to all these years is a myth, a construction. What happens when this connection is lost? We might be tempted to answer that it is no longer Beethoven himself who is the subject of our collective scholarly archeology but the Beethoven myth. If we can no longer hope to reach the master himself with our efforts, we can at least console ourselves with the fascinations of two hundred rich years of reception history. Following Eggebrecht, authors as diversely motivated and trained as Ulrich Schmitt, Martin Geck, David B. Dennis, Tia DeNora, and myself have traced this history, with its often nefarious appropriations and constructions of Beethoven.[56]

And yet there is much work that continues to flourish in the study of Beethoven's sketches, the clarification and interpretation of biographical issues, as well as interpretative studies that purport to get closer to Beethoven's actual compositional intentions. Thus it is not simply the case that we have collectively forgone the study of Beethoven himself; instead, what now characterizes all these studies is the urge to get behind and beyond the myth, to understand the phenomenon Beethoven not as something messianic and by definition larger than life but as the human object of various forces – be they cultural, ideological, economic, political, or psychological.

One manifestation of this effort is the work being done to assign Beethoven a meaningful place in a broader cultural history (or ideological history), to reinsert him into the flow of human time, above which his music has always been heard to rise, as a timelessly valid aesthetic force, whether Romantic, Classical, or natural. Beethoven is now often studied as a cogent element of history-bound cultural practice: William Kinderman, Thomas Sipe, and Maynard Solomon, for example, have argued that Beethoven's music projects certain Schillerian aesthetic values;[57] the work of Adorno – who came to light for Anglo-American musicology in the late 1970s, thanks to the brave efforts of Rose Rosengard Subotnik – linked Beethoven with Hegel;[58] and some of my own work has situated Beethoven within the value system of the *Goethezeit* as a whole. All of these authors attempt to find Beethoven within the image of his culture, to bring his music back into the arena of cultural practice after years of formalist exemption from the perceived contamination of history.

Another symptom of our age is the way in which we attempt to reconstruct an image of Beethoven in the fashion of a mosaic, as we collectively fill in the picture of Beethoven's personal and compositional paraphernalia, the contents of his pockets, the types of paper he wrote on, the specifics of the concert and patronage scene, the hard data of his popularity and his presence, what he was worth, etc. Our once highly touted spiritual bond with the composer is bracketed off as the insidious sign of ideological prepossession, or, at the least, as something irrelevant, personal, and anecdotal. Taking its place is a perhaps sublimating mania for knowing everything external that we can about him. In this sense, we have traded invisible bond for visible surfeit. Thus we are busy reconstructing something like a Beethoven for the digital age, a Beethoven of ever finer resolution, each square of the mosaic requiring its own team of specialists, each square becoming itself a mosaic, in a kind of fractal proliferation. No longer can any one person control a vision of the whole.

Related to this tendency is a process that may well be analogous to the ritual dismemberment of the hero, namely, the translation of the mythic composer into the objects of kitsch. Here is perhaps the ultimate objectifying of Beethoven, his imposing figure pulverized into a steady tide of commercial flotsam, representing a new kind of universality: the Beethoven doorbell, busts of all sizes and materials, refrigerator magnets, T-shirts, a popular disco version of the Fifth Symphony, and the movie *Beethoven*, not actually about the composer but about a slobbering St. Bernard of the same name who galvanizes a nineties family in suburban America. Kitsch objects that involve musical sound invariably rely on the amputated opening motive of the Fifth Symphony as both sound-bite and talisman; there could hardly be a more cogent symbol of the dismemberment of Beethoven.

If the proliferation of kitsch objects is a way of undermining the myth by turning inside out the exalted attractions of the reliquary and bringing Beethoven's alleged universality up to speed in the age of global communication and commercialism, there are other, more studied attempts to debunk the myth and destroy its hold on us. Within the realm of reception studies, these include the work of Ulrich Schmitt, who associates the nineteenth-century taste for Beethoven with the taste for power and speed that was propagated by such technological advances as the railway system. This kind of linkage is demythologizing in itself, for the bond of the spirit is explained away as a fascination with technology. Another striking move toward the demythologization of Beethoven is Tia DeNora's analysis of the politics of musical patronage in Vienna; she argues that the perceived greatness of Beethoven's music might be largely a politically motivated construction of the Viennese aristocracy, who were fostering an emergent ideology of "serious music." Or consider those studies whose authors explore the sinister side of Beethoven reception, charting the many insidious political appropriations of the composer: Martin Geck on the *Eroica*, Andreas Eichhorn on the Ninth, David B. Dennis on Beethoven and German politics. Nothing curdles one's awe of this music faster than the realization of the extent to which it was useful to fascism. Another contemporary mode of demythologizing the composer is represented by the rise of psychoanalytic biography, finding its high-water-mark in Maynard Solomon's 1977 *Beethoven*; here the great composer becomes a sympathetic object of powerful psychological forces.[59] Finally, the last decade has witnessed attempts not only to debunk the Beethoven paradigm but to indict it as perniciously masculinist. This latter trend constitutes a more proactive way to get beyond the myth, or "get down off the beanstalk," in Susan McClary's memorable phrase.[60]

The case of Beethoven and his reception offers a distinctly profiled history of the trajectory of canon formation and deformation in the modern Western world. Though admittedly somewhat arbitrary, our parsing of the history of Beethoven reception into four separate stages has at the least allowed us to capture some of the shape-shifting ways of the canonized figure: first, Beethoven points to the future as a preternaturally empowered subject; then he becomes a suprasubjective, almost godlike, redeemer; then an objective, essentialized dispenser of natural law, pointing, if anywhere, to the past; and lastly he is rendered a mere product, or symptom, of a now suspect bourgeois culture.

Of course, strong traces of each earlier stage still inform the succeeding stages, and running through them all is the undiminished viability of Beethoven's music – whether as the ultimate "music of the subject" (or, according to Adorno's view of his late style, the ultimate critique of that music), the ultimate realization of the Viennese Classical Style, the ultimate embodiment of the German artistic spirit, the ultimate exemplar of

Victorian musical soundness, or the ultimate music of masculinist power. Even now, after a century seemingly intent on annihilating all formerly comforting illusions of greatness and transcendent authority offered by the leading figures in our history, we have not yet managed to put the Beethoven myth behind us. For Beethoven continues to require that we grapple with him, continues to ask much of us, to call us out. This, more than anything, is why we cannot let him go: his music remains a sounding provocation to what we are pleased to think of as our better selves.

17 Beethoven at large: reception in literature, the arts, philosophy, and politics

DAVID B. DENNIS

Amid the enormous collection of Beethoven-inspired lyric in the Beethoven-Haus archives of Bonn stands a thick folder overflowing with poems "on single sheets," in other words never published. Hand-written or carefully typed, these verses were submitted by their authors themselves, often after visits to the Geburtshausmuseum. Such amateur but heartfelt works remind us that the majority of artistic responses to Beethoven come from men and women whose names remain unfamiliar to the world of high letters; they might reveal more about how his music and life-story move general listeners than all "expert" disputations. Above all the collection symbolizes a compulsion widely felt by persons who encounter this composer, his music, or simply memorabilia and places associated with him: Beethoven lovers tend to react to his art in active, often creative fashions, not passively. Such is the intense, ongoing influence that he and his works have on Western and even world cultures, both inside and outside musical life.

The history of Beethoven's impact on the Western music tradition, discussed in this volume by Margaret Notley and Scott Burnham, contains myriad examples of his incomparable effect on nineteenth- and twentieth-century musicians. Here we will explore how his life and music also motivate endeavors in non-musical areas, including literature, the visual arts, philosophy, politics, even religion. Beethoven has been idolized by persons of all walks of life, and many nationalities, as a "role model" or an "educator." His triumphs over deafness and loneliness fixed his reputation as a paradigm of the "artist." Inspired by this heroic image and the élan of his most popular works, musicians, writers, visual artists, politicians, and a host of others have attempted to imitate aspects of his personality, and convince others to do likewise.

That Beethoven's was a complex character partly explains the diversity of ways listeners set him into their cultural and ideological horizons. Combing through records of his inconsistent, even volatile nature, interpreters have found evidence to support associating the composer and his music with almost every modern current of thought and behavior. The goal of this chapter is not to critique the manner in which listeners understand Beethoven: whether it is Beethoven's "actual" person and music or

legends about them that affect how individuals write, design, philoso-
phize, govern, or worship is not the point. But while reviewing productive
responses triggered by his music, it is important to keep in mind the
difference between Beethoven the hero and "Beethoven Hero."[1]

Early literary reactions to Beethoven included critiques of his compositions – and person – as "complicated," even "bizarre": Mozartian detrac-
tors warned that his "new style" had the potential to ignite a blaze that
could consume all music rules. By the beginning of the nineteenth
century, however, the mere mention of Beethoven's name aroused
notions of "genius" among the avant garde of musical taste.[2] Reasons for
this revision of the critical framework, which transformed judgment of
Beethoven as a Great Man into an "article of superstition," remain the
subject of debate.[3] Some propose a broad explanation linking contemporary revolutions in science, society, and politics to new ways of listening
which rendered "modern" audience members more amenable to
Beethoven's turbulent manipulation of musical forms.[4]

Within the broad strokes of this framework, a peculiar sort of individual is commonly identified as having first practiced the "modern" way of
listening and provoked others to idealize above all the "rush" of
Beethoven's creations. Scholars generally agree that common perceptions
of Beethoven were strikingly – and permanently – colored by his young
contemporaries, the Romantics. E. T. A. Hoffmann and Bettina Brentano
urged listeners to interact emotionally with music, Beethoven's in particular, seeking and expressing soulful responses instead of merely being
entertained. Doing so, they helped overcome initial resistance to the vigor
of these compositions and launched the tradition of exploring parallels
between Beethoven's works and other artistic forms of expression.[5]

Romantics underscored Beethoven's self-description as a *Tondichter*
or "poet of tones" in order to associate him with their own goal of synthe-
sizing the arts. This epithet functioned as a beacon summoning interpreters to mine his music for poetical ideas.[6] Most poetic allusion to
Beethoven, however, aims at revealing the secrets behind his unique creative prowess. Leading Romantics such as Clemens Brentano and Friedrich
de la Motte-Fouqué pictured Beethoven as a conjurer commanding
spirits from whom he received musical ideas, extending associations with
magical idealism to the extreme.[7] In 1813 Brentano may have been the
first to suggest that his loss of hearing could be considered an advantage,
comparing the deaf composer to a blind seer:

> Without senses, the same as God
> Knowing and writing only himself.[8]

Franz Grillparzer, who had the honor of eulogizing Beethoven at his Vienna funeral, portrayed the composer as outcast and ignored, doomed to suffer alone, but – like a fairy-tale wizard – in possession of magnificent powers:

> An enchanter, tired of the world and life,
> Sealed his magic in an impregnable chest,
> Threw the key into the sea, and died.
> Little men gave it all they had, in vain!
> No tool opened the stubborn lock.
> The magic slept like its master.[9]

In his fantastic characterization of 1831 Ernst Ortlepp portrayed Beethoven as a sorrowful Werther wandering through sublime scenes like those Caspar David Friedrich painted:

> There stands a loner
> In the mid of night,
> On the rocky cliffs.
> Beneath him thunders
> The waterfall;
> Beyond, the old castle
> Shimmers supernaturally.[10]

Nikolaus Lenau's "Beethoven's Bust" (1855) countered the usual equation of Beethoven and turbulence with all-too-rare allusions to the composer's gentler side:

> Shhh! Still softer!
> Hear the songs
> Picked up from nature's spirit,
> Which it whispers
> In the first dreams of a beautiful child.[11]

To the vital tradition of Beethoven reception in France,[12] Charles Baudelaire contributed his own "evil flower." *La Musique* (1857), dedicated to Beethoven, carried romantic natural imagery to the very end, where Baudelaire made his usual decadent shift into pessimistic self-analysis:

> Music often takes me like a sea . . .
> a raging storm on the great deep my cradle,
> and dead calm the looking-glass of my despair![13]

Across the Atlantic, Walt Whitman modeled verse on Beethoven's pulsing compositions: "Hasting, urging, restless, – no flagging, not even in the 'thoughts' or meditations – to be perceived with the same perception that enjoys music – free and luxuriant – as in Beethoven's."[14] The American bard expressed his love for Beethoven's Septet op. 20 explicitly – like "nature laughing on a hillside in sunshine"[15] – but it is in the structure of his lines, long and expansive, pressing forth themes conceived on a grand scale, that one senses the most telling indications of Beethoven's influence on Whitman's art.[16] Rarer than efforts to betoken the composer's genius are such attempts to produce poetry that somehow follows the rhythms and formal developments of his music. T. S. Eliot revealed intriguing musical concepts behind his own "Four Quartets" (1942) presumably inspired by Beethoven's late works:[17] "I think that a poet may gain much from the study of music . . . It is in the concert room rather than in the opera house that the germ of a poem may be quickened."[18]

Alongside poetic invocations of Beethovenian vitality, novels and short stories tend to address the composer in more direct ways, either through passing references in tales not otherwise focused on him or through characters modeled on his personality and life story.[19] Wolfgang Robert Griepenkerl's novella *Das Musikfest oder Die Beethovenianer* (1841) stands out because it represents the extent to which references to Beethoven can carry narrative forth in a story which is not primarily about him. The entire work, about conflict between conservatives and "Beethovenians" over a festival intended to promote his music, was contrived to let characters voice opinions of the composer. Some attack him as mad and dangerous, others worship him as a liberalizing force somehow associated with the European revolutions of 1830. Every conversation leads to Beethoven, whether among orchestra members, salon guests, or lovers. This panoply of Beethoven allusions signifies every extreme in early reception, especially politicization of the composer by *Vormärz* (c. 1830–48) leftists and rightists.

Better known to English speakers are references to Beethoven in E. M. Forster's *A Room with a View* (1908) and *Howard's End* (1910). Both instances – when Lucy Honeychurch disturbs her friends by playing the Piano Sonata op. 111 on a rainy day in Florence[20] and when Helen Schlegel listens to "the most sublime noise that has ever penetrated into the ear of man" – register the ongoing influence of Romanticism on literary allusion to Beethoven. For Forster's Helen, the last movement of the Fifth Symphony "started with a goblin walking quietly over the universe, from end to end. Others followed him . . . Panic and emptiness! Panic and emptiness! . . . Beethoven took hold of the goblins and made them do what he wanted . . . But the goblins were there. They could return. He had said so bravely, and that is why one can trust Beethoven when he says other things."[21]

This image of a superhuman tamer of spirits also predominates in stories that depict Beethoven himself or feature characters based on him. The earliest fictionalized portraits, Johann Peter Lyser's *Ludwig van Beethoven* (1834), Elise Polko's *Ludwig van Beethoven* (1852), and Wolfgang Müller von Königswinter's *Furioso* (1861), highlight the composer's youth. Many elements of these portrayals – ill treatment by his father, shyness, a sense that the world does not understand him, roaming in free nature, disdain for money, and especially the desire for creative force instead of love – were standard in other novels of the period wherein Romantics fantasized about wholly fictional artists.[22] Regardless of their origin, these characteristics mark bellelettristic depictions through the twentieth century. Although he never made a concrete reference to the composer in his own novels, Victor Hugo sketched the main lines of Beethoven representation: "crippled body, flying soul," producing music like a "deep mirror in a cloud" that reflects everything his listeners desire; in it "the dreamer will recognize his dream, the sailor his storm ... and the wolf his forests."[23]

Important examples of characters based on the composer are Romain Rolland's Jean Christophe and Thomas Mann's Adrian Leverkühn. Writing when his countrymen were still stinging from their defeat in the Franco-Prussian War, Rolland identified Beethoven as a hero who could inspire Frenchmen to shake off their malaise. Answering Charles Péguy's call for "saints and heroes in a godless time," Rolland presented the composer as a holy martyr who sublimated pain through creative acts.[24] "Blessed is the misfortune that has come upon thee! Blessed the sealing of thine ears!"[25] wrote Rolland, since it was by overcoming the terror of deafness that Beethoven showed a path to self-redemption: "poor, sick, alone – and yet a victor!"[26] Rolland produced several books and essays to popularize his reading of Beethoven – indeed, to found a Beethoven cult in France, in spite (and even denial) of his hero's Germanic origins. His masterwork was *Jean Christophe* (1904–12), an epic about an artist whose youth was directly based on the composer's, especially in the sense of obstacles overcome.

Thomas Mann incorporated into *Doktor Faustus* (1947) every sort of literary response to Beethoven: reference to specific works, direct portrayal of the composer, and association of the real with an imagined artist, Adrian Leverkühn. The best-known Beethoven components of this novelistic critique of National Socialism appear in two lectures given by the stuttering music teacher, Wendell Kretschmar. The first is an analysis of Beethoven's Piano Sonata op. 111, which Kretschmar represents as the culmination – and terminus – of sonata form. In the context of general Beethoven reception, however, the second major reference – in Kretschmar's lecture on fugue – is more important: this wartime portrait tied the composer to Mann's desperate assessment of German culture, in light of its crimes against humanity and humanism, as demonic:

> It was in high summer of the year 1819, at the time when Beethoven was working on the *Missa solemnis* . . . He worked in his room on the Credo, the Credo with the fugue – [two visitors] heard him through the closed door. The deaf man sang, he yelled and stamped above the Credo – it was so moving and terrifying that the blood froze in their veins as they listened. But as in their great concern they were about to retreat, the door was jerked open and Beethoven stood there – in what guise? The very most frightful! With clothing disheveled, his features so distorted as to strike terror to the beholders; the eyes dazed, absent, listening all at once; he had stared at them, they got the impression that he had come out of a life-and-death struggle with all the opposing hosts of counterpoint.[27]

By depicting him as afflicted, Mann blended Beethoven's genius with that of his main character, Leverkühn, who was ravaged by the effects of syphilis and an imagined pact with the devil. To be sure, Mann's Beethoven stood only half way down the ladder toward dementia: Leverkühn's reactionary modernism would complete the fall and herald Germany's return to its barbaric roots. Yet, by spotlighting an anecdote of Beethoven *in extremis* Mann linked him to the notion that genius entails mental imbalance. Through this selective use of biographical detail, *Doktor Faustus* drew Beethoven into the post-Auschwitz context, marked by obsession with the satanic side of Western society and art.

As in poetry, narratives modeled on the music of Beethoven instead of just touching upon his life are less common. One novel written with a specific Beethoven work in mind is Anthony Burgess's *Napoleon Symphony* (1974). "What I have in front of me when I am working is the score of the *Eroica*. I will make the various sections of the novel correspond to the various sections of the symphony, so that if I take, say, eight bars of Beethoven, it's roughly equivalent to three pages of my own work."[28] To do this, he filled his story with the thoughts and actions of Napoleon Bonaparte, starting with two brusque pinches on the cheeks of his bride (suggesting, with much irony, Beethoven's opening E♭ chords), including battles at Rivoli, Acre, Marengo, Borodino, the Berzina River, and Waterloo, and ending with death-rattle fantasies on St. Helena. It is in repeated images, phrases, and even whole paragraphs that readers sense Burgess's "musical" form. "The novel," he declared, "is based on the life of Napoleon, but the life is so organized that it fits into a symphonic pattern, so that you don't worry too much about chronology. You worry about themes and trying to contrive an allegro movement, a scherzo, and a set of variations for a finale. In other words, following exactly . . . the pattern of Beethoven's *Eroica*."[29]

Burgess's abstract approach notwithstanding, popularizing and explaining Beethoven are the motives behind most literary references. Nowhere is this tendency stronger than in the array of plays and films portraying Beethoven.[30] Judging from the critical response to a recent theatrical portrait, Bernard Rose's film *The Immortal Beloved* (1994), it is the potential to suggest the personal significance of individual compositions that most fascinates dramatists and their audiences: hence the large number of plots centered on his failed loves, his struggle over nephew Karl, and his deafness – often combined with dream sequences in which the composer converses with muses about the emotional content of his works.[31] Though never fully realized, and often descending into kitsch, a "total experience" of Beethoven's daily life and creative process seems their common goal.

Evocations in poems, stories, novels, and dramas afford authors and readers alike means to identify with the person they believe responsible for the pleasures and meanings they derive from Beethoven's music. However, literary treatment alone does not satisfy the impulse to relate with this composer: thus the urge to represent him in all the visual media. The ubiquitousness of Beethoven imagery in nineteenth- and twentieth-century fine arts, and its even wider presence in commercial bric-a-brac, has had the ironic effect of making his physical appearance more familiar than his music. Beethoven portraits, illustrations, and cartoons in infinite variety have been used to promote anything remotely related to the Western music tradition (and much that is not). Thus the "sign" of this composer's mien in particular has come to "signify" serious Western music in general. However, the commercialization of Beethoven's physiognomy in the second half of the twentieth century overshadows a long tradition of fashioning his likeness for reasons other than marketing. Through every phase of modern art history, painters and sculptors have conveyed their regard for this musician as a source of inspiration across artistic boundaries.[32]

Portraits done during Beethoven's life, often in a Romantic vein, established a number of constants in the visual representation of this genius. Unruly hair, tensed brow, frowning mouth, gaze directed elsewhere: some of these traits have become visual clichés used to portray and imitate "modern artists" as a whole.[33] After Beethoven's death, his image underwent the worst forms of Biedermeier trivialization, the most widely distributed were pictures of "Beethoven by the Brook," ostensibly composing his Sixth Symphony.[34] But it was in mid-century that attempts to capture his "titanic" presence in stone, bronze, and paint began in earnest. Fulfilling Robert Schumann's call for a "Monument for Beethoven" and at the same time confirming his fears about how "Philistines" would manage the matter,[35] cities associated with Beethoven's life commissioned statues through the century.[36] Taken together, these monuments embody the conflicting motives of depicting the composer "as he really appeared" while simultaneously idealizing him: strategies include cleansing him of dermatological imperfections, restraining his hair within classical proportions, and draping toga-like garments on him.[37]

One of the most successful placements of Beethoven on a pedestal is Kaspar Clemens Zumbusch's Vienna monument (1880). Scowling downward, the composer is as imposing as Michelangelo's *Moses* (though in nineteenth-century dress). The apotheotic effect of this bronze is achieved by allegorical figures surrounding the subject: Prometheus and Nike symbolize the dichotomous nature of his creativity, nine *putti* play the "roles" of his symphonies, an eagle is awestruck by his presence.[38] Taking this iconographical strategy to fin-de-siècle extremes, Max Klinger devoted seventeen years to gathering materials and sculpting symbols for his *gesamt*-representation of Beethoven-as-hero, first exhibited at the 1902 Vienna Secession. Perceiving the composer in Nietzschean terms, Klinger enthroned him on a craggy block of purple marble suggesting Zarathustra's aerie, the heights of which even eagles strain to reach. Stripped almost bare, the composer overwhelms his feathered visitor with utter concentration, jaw taut and fists clenched. Yet it is again associated imagery, on the jewel-encrusted throne, that communicates Klinger's far-reaching conception of the composer. His blend of purple, black, and white marbles; bronze, gold, and ivory; opals, agate, and jasper; classical, pagan, and Christian imagery presents Beethoven as encompassing the whole of Western tradition[39] – in Nietzsche's words, one whose "gaze has become strong enough to make out the bottom of the dark well of being and . . . the distant constellations of future civilizations."[40]

Likewise obsessed with Beethoven, French sculptor Antoine Bourdelle produced over forty-five versions of him in various media between 1887 and 1929.[41] Bourdelle left many of his busts with rough and ragged surfaces suggesting primal forces in the composer's character: like Michelangelo's bound slaves, Bourdelle's Beethovens emerge from earth's stony veins (see Plates 1 and 2). But the most telling aspect of this artist's renderings of Beethoven's visage is their sheer number. Never convinced that he had captured the face definitely, Bourdelle returned to it again and again, each time discovering a new Beethoven, ever more distorted by his sufferings – or by the sculptor's recognition that no single perspective could signal the totality of the man.

Perhaps the most popular of Beethoven-related paintings in its own time was Lionello Balestrieri's *Beethoven: Kreutzer Sonata* (Plate 3). Its moving romanticization of the *La Bohème* milieu may explain much of the acclaim this picture enjoyed at the 1900 World Exposition in Paris.[42] But Balestrieri's decision to depict men and women in postures of transfixion while listening to Beethoven's sonata for violin and piano (with the composer's presence suggested only via a mask on the wall) also seems to have touched a popular chord. Liberated from the need to monumentalize the earthbound source of these experiences, images suggesting their spiritual impact may best convey the transcendentalism of Beethoven's master-works. This is nowhere more true than in the friezes Gustav Klimt designed to complement Klinger's sculpture at the 1902 Vienna Secession exhibition. Fashioned in Klimt's suggestive style intimating psycho-sexual drives then being postulated by Sigmund Freud, each of the three panels proposes psychological correlates for portions of Beethoven's Ninth Symphony (see Plates 4–7). Implying that Beethoven struggled to avoid traps of sensual desire and sublimated libido into art, Klimt's imagery raised the ire of some who condemned the friezes as pornographic.[43] It also tempted Beethoven reception into terms of sexuality that were to become central to scholarship in the second half of the century then dawning.[44]

Devotees who consider Beethoven's creative force in metaphysical terms have also drawn him into Western philosophical discourse. Pianist and critic Edward Dannreuther produced in 1876 a florid example of philosophizing about the composer: "The serious study of Beethoven's music is assuredly as powerful an auxiliary in the cause of culture as the study of philology. The spirit of Beethoven is as humanizing as the spirit of Sophocles. To read a string quartet, even taken in the light of a bracing intellectual exercise, seems on a par with reading a Platonic dialogue. Nay, one may affirm more than this – Beethoven is, in the best sense of the word, an ethical, a religious teacher."[45] Sure to make today's formalists wince, Dannreuther's argument is nonetheless part of an important current of reception among general listeners and major philosophers.

Hegel did not make direct reference to Beethoven, even in his extensive writings about music aesthetics. But on the basis that the composer owned a volume or two of Hegel's works, and sometimes simply because of their contemporaneity, interpreters have sought to establish that the two men ordered experience and ideas similarly. One view holds that Beethoven's inner existence progressed according to Hegelian patterns: "Beethoven's life, like Hegel's conception of reality, is a Becoming that advances only through negation and contradiction. His life was a flux, a manifestation of Hegel's *Unruhe*; but its goal was rest, at a point where man, having become aware of the dialectical process within him, has

Plate 1 Antoine Bourdelle, *Beethoven with Short Hair*, 1890

Plate 2 Antoine Bourdelle, *Head of Beethoven, as a Capital*, 1924

Plate 3 Lionello Balestrieri, *Beethoven: Kreutzer Sonata*, 1900

Plate 4 Gustav Klimt, *Frieze for the Beethoven Exhibition 1902*, left panel, detail: *The Sufferings of Weak Humanity, Knight, Ambition, Pity*

Plate 5 Gustav Klimt, *Frieze for the Beethoven Exhibition 1902*, central panel, detail: *The Hostile Powers*

Plate 6 Gustav Klimt, *Frieze for the Beethoven Exhibition 1902*, central panel, detail: *Typhon, Lewdness, Lust, and Excess*

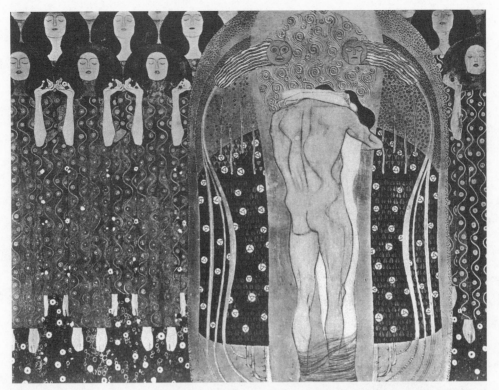

Plate 7 Gustav Klimt, *Frieze for the Beethoven Exhibition 1902*, right panel, detail: *This Kiss for the Whole World*

become truly free."[46] Related to this dialectical analysis of Beethoven's spiritual evolution are idealistic interpretations of his music. Granted that Haydn, Mozart, and other eighteenth-century composers contributed to the development of the "sonata principle," Beethoven's manipulation of this form earns highest standing among Hegelians: "It is he who pursues most relentlessly the dialectic of becoming, driving his thematic complexes through from what they are not but seem to be, to what they are but appear not to be."[47]

Among philosophers who did discuss Beethoven and his music, Nietzsche, Theodor Adorno, and Ernst Bloch stand out. They genuinely incorporated ideas about the composer into their thought. As a young man, Nietzsche set forth in poetry the awe he felt before this sublime creator:

> I look upon you mutely,
> Wishing to ask your eyes,
> Why, you miraculous man,
> Does my pulse beat stormily
> When you pass through the forest of my soul?[48]

The philosopher felt a strong affinity with Beethoven, recognizing that both suffered and gained from solitude: "There will always be demi-gods who can endure life and live victoriously under such terrible conditions; and if you want to hear their lonely song, listen to the music of Beethoven."[49] It was only with Beethoven, in Nietzsche's view, that music "began to discover the language of pathos, of passionate desire, of the dramatic events which take place in the depths of man . . . Beethoven was the first to let music speak a new language, the hitherto forbidden language of passion."[50] Moved by the *Sternenzelt* (starry canopy) depicted in the Ninth's finale, Nietzsche allowed that one could employ the symphony heuristically to apprehend the philosophy of Dionysus: "Transform Beethoven's Ode to Joy into a painting; let your imagination conceive the multitudes bowing to the dust, awestruck – then you will approach the Dionysian. Now the slave is a free man, now all the rigid, hostile barriers that necessity, caprice, or 'impudent convention' have fixed between man and man are broken."[51]

Adorno advocated a musical sociology in which the "inner syntax" of musical language correlates with social conditions and cultural patterns (whether composers are conscious of this or not).[52] After his apprenticeship in Classicism, works of Beethoven's "second style period" signaled to Adorno bourgeois-humanist hope that a "whole" man might emerge from the ruins of the *ancien régime*: "If we listen to Beethoven and do not hear anything of the revolutionary bourgeoisie – not the echo of its

302 David B. Dennis

slogans, the need to realize them, the cry for that totality in which reason and freedom are to have their warrant – we understand Beethoven no better than does one who cannot follow the purely musical content of his pieces."[53] But this optimistic moment was premature, according to Adorno: by resolving oppositions between theme (individual) and form (society) at the recapitulation of his middle works in sonata style, the composer suggested an artificial teleology just as Hegel did when he averred that the Prussian state of his time embodied the highest stage of historical evolution. To Adorno, unresolved tensions in the *Missa solemnis*, the late quartets, and the last sonatas better signify the outcome of the revolutionary period. Dismayed by conditions after the Congress of Vienna, Adorno's late Beethoven shed light on the true state of affairs in the post-Enlightenment world, where, detached from nature and dominated by technology, individuals would remain alienated – indeed, be rendered "inhuman."[54]

Unlike Adorno and other members of the intellectual left, Bloch celebrated music not because of perceived social content, but because "it derives its energy from the anticipatory presence, from intimations of the 'not yet' . . . completely beyond the scope of the empirically verifiable."[55] In very Romantic terms, Bloch described a way out of the modern impasse which he sensed in Beethoven's works especially: upon hearing them "everything false and stifling melts away. The leadenness disperses, and the distortions vanish . . . 'How elated we feel at the thought of you, infinite one!' . . . Our soul bubbles up to the stars in the initial rough, tempestuous, eloquent sea of this music. Beethoven is Lucifer's benign offspring, the demon that leads to the ultimate things." Bloch's search for a "musical initiation into the truth of Utopia" finds "the first fully comprehensive light" in Beethoven's opera: "Every future storming of the Bastille is implicitly expressed in *Fidelio* . . . Here and nowhere else . . . music becomes a rosy dawn, militant-religious, the dawning of a new day so audible that it seems more than simply a hope."[56]

Though primarily philosophical, the political implications of both Adorno's analyses and Bloch's visions place them in a parallel tradition in which Beethoven and his compositions have been dogmatized and used as powerful symbols for manifold ideologies. Ludicrous as some such claims seem, politicization of Beethoven is not a matter of simple projection. He was a political man in many senses: by the end of his life he talked about politics to such an extent that some friends no longer wanted to dine with him, either because they were tired of hearing his outbursts or afraid he would be overheard by secret agents.[57] However, lacking a systematically worked-out ideology in an era of shifting alliances, the composer expressed contradictory opinions at various points in his life that could be used by almost every European political movement. Politicizing Beethoven has not always required projecting doctrine onto his works, but often merely selecting indications that he would have associated with one group or another, then arguing that these stand for "our" Beethoven and that other aspects of his biography are irrelevant or misleading.[58]

This process has occurred across the modern political spectrum – particularly but not exclusively in Germany – and includes efforts to demonstrate that Beethoven was everything from a proto-communist to a forerunner of fascism. Romantic interpretations of the composer as revolutionary emerged by the time of the uprisings in 1848–49. After 1870 supporters of German empire endorsed aggressively nationalistic assessments while Marxists portrayed him in socialistic terms. This conflict came to a head in the first decade of the twentieth century, when the workers' movement competed against volkish critics to claim Beethoven's legacy, while liberals assigned it to elite culture. During the First World War, Germans resisted enemy assertions that they had "forfeited the right" to enjoy his music. Every political group active in the Weimar Republic "fought tooth and nail to demonstrate that he belonged exclusively to their circle."[59] Nazis imposed an image of Beethoven as an aesthetic Führer, volkish and militaristic, though small pockets of "resistance" perceived his music as a symbol of humanitarian ideals. After the Second World War, German reception mirrored the division of the nation: notions of the composer as social revolutionary reigned in East Germany while commercialization and a de-ideologizing view of Beethoven as "all-too-human" operated in the popular culture of the West.[60]

Political responses that highlight the aggressive aspects of his character and music – overlooking the more tranquil qualities of both[61] – have been countered by voices beatifying the composer. Over the last two centuries, secularization of European society has been accompanied by a counter tendency to sanctify the arts, especially music. Romantics rejected the relegation of instrumental expression to minor aesthetic rank during the Enlightenment, affording music a sacred function by which man might transcend the quotidian and approach the infinite.[62] Beethoven's art was a focal point in this world view. Bettina Brentano glorified it in an 1810 letter to Goethe: "I believe in a divine magic that is an element of spiritual nature; and this magic, Beethoven exercises in his art. All he could tell you about is pure magic; no motive, no orientation is not the expression of a superior existence."[63]

For some, Beethoven becomes even more than a purveyor of sacred messages, himself a deity. "A second time Jesus, with his pains, ascended Calvary," exclaimed Georges Pioch at the start of the twentieth century: "A musician, it is true; but a prophet as well; I am tempted to say – a Messiah. For his work is and will be the most immeasurable of all gospels."[64] In this cult of personality, Beethoven's manuscripts serve as holy texts; above all, the Ninth Symphony captivates moderns in search of secure precepts in a world of shifting mores.[65] Karl Rafael Henning discovered in 1888 a set of Beethovenian commandments, each put forth in a movement of the Ninth:

> I. Man's life should be a noble struggle for *Virtù*, despite all the powers of fate. II. Man can with discretion enjoy the delights of life but not become too caught up with them. III. Man should be submissive even before the loss of whatever love he finds on earth. IV. Above the stars lives a loving father who calls us his children and who wants us all to reach out the hand of reconciliation to one another in brotherly love. This is the greatest happiness.[66]

It is at this level of reverence that the startling popularity of Beethoven's Ninth Symphony in Japan seems to function. Since the Second World War it has become tradition to perform the *Daiku* (Big Ninth) every December throughout the country. Most remarkable about this rite is that when the choral finale arrives all sing along, audience and performers alike. The annual concert at Osaka in 1989 featured a chorus of ten thousand; sports stadiums are regularly filled for these rituals.[67] The zenith of this custom occurred during the Opening Ceremonies of the 1998 Winter Olympics in Nagano, Japan. Led by conductor Seiji Ozawa, professional singers and inhabitants of local logging towns performed the Ninth Symphony in a ritual which did bring the world community together. Fin-de-millennium communications technology enabled choirs in major cities around the globe to simultaneously add their voices to this celebration of the Olympic and Beethovenian spirits. This Western composer's life and music have clearly become touchstones in world culture.

Reception history studies the ways musical ideas interact with human experience and aspiration: via interpretations and reinterpretations by listeners. Most important is that this dialectic takes place mainly after the composer's work is done, as compositions are performed through time and people engage with them more closely. It is worthwhile to consider the meanings that Beethoven and his works obtain once performed, for it is these that impact mentalities and societies, inspiring men and women to craft poems, write novels, sculpt monuments, paint friezes, order concepts, make political decisions, go into battle, worship, and embrace. What might Beethoven himself have thought about all this? Perhaps

Nietzsche's estimate is best:

> He would probably be silent for a long while, uncertain whether he should raise his hand to curse or bless, but perhaps say at last: "Well, well! That is neither I nor not-I, but a third thing – it seems to me, too, something right, if not just the right thing. But you must know yourselves what to do, since in any case it is you who have to listen. As our Schiller says, '*The living man is right.*' So have it your own way, and let me go down again."[68]

Notes

1 Some thoughts on biography and a chronology of Beethoven's life and music

1 Tri-partite periodizations were grounded in century-old partitions of life cycles and history; the latter was particularly influential in the nineteenth century, when historical perspectives were very strong. See James Webster, "The Concept of Beethoven's Early Period in the Context of Periodizations in General," BF 3 (1994), 1–29.

2 Joseph Kerman, *The New Grove Beethoven* (New York, 1983), 89.

3 See Kerman, ibid., who also suggests sub-division of later periods.

4 Maynard Solomon, *Beethoven Essays* (Cambridge, MA, 1988), 121.

5 The University of Connecticut hosted a conference in March 1993 entitled "Beethoven in Vienna 1792–1803: The First Style Period." Selected papers were published in BF 3 and 4. A conference on the middle period, "Beethoven in Vienna: the Second Style Period, 1803–1812," was organized by the Historical Keyboard Society of Wisconsin in Milwaukee in April 1994. In October 1996 the late style was discussed at a conference at Harvard University, "International Beethoven Conference: Rethinking Beethoven's Late Period: Sources, Aesthetics, and Interpretation, Nov. 1996"; selected papers from this conference will appear in forthcoming volumes of BF.

6 Sources: Thayer–Forbes; Joseph Kerman and Alan Tyson, *The New Grove Beethoven*, "Worklist," 158–92; *The Beethoven Compendium*, ed. Barry Cooper, "Calendar of Beethoven's Life, Works and Related Events" (London, 1991), 12–36; personal communications from Maynard Solomon.

2 Beethoven at work: musical activist and thinker

1 After the death of his mother in 1787, Beethoven assumed increasing responsibility for his family and in 1789 began to receive half of the salary of his father, a court musician who suffered from drunkenness. Although he never returned to Bonn, his ties to his native city were kept alive through his continuing association with his brothers Caspar Anton Carl (1774–1815) and Nikolaus Johann (1776–1848), who moved to Vienna (Nikolaus Johann eventually settled in Linz), and a good number of close friends, some of whom, like Stephan von Breuning, settled in Vienna. A valuable but dated study of Beethoven's early life is Ludwig Schiedermair, *Der junge Beethoven* (Leipzig, 1925).

2 See Tia DeNora, *Beethoven and the Construction of Genius: Musical Politics in Vienna, 1792–1803* (Berkeley, 1995), 37–60. DeNora provides the most up-to-date picture of Beethoven's activity in his first decade in Vienna, but her argument that his success, indeed his greatness, was largely a consequence of his and his patrons' skill at cultural politics has been very controversial.

3 Letter to Breitkopf & Härtel, August 1812. BG II, no. 591; Anderson I, no. 380.

4 See Thayer–Forbes, 840, and Maynard Solomon, *Beethoven* (New York, 1977), 273.

5 Wegeler–Ries, 19.

6 Beethoven compared the "greatest pianoforte players [who] were also the greatest composers" to the "pianists of today, who prance up and down the keyboard with passages which they have practised – putsch, putsch, putsch; – what does that mean? Nothing!" See Thayer–Forbes, 599, cited from Tomaschek's autobiography, *Libussa* (Prague, 1846), 359 ff.

7 Article in *London Musical Miscellany*, 1852; Cited in Thayer–Forbes, 185.

8 See *The Beethoven Compendium*, ed. Barry Cooper (London, 1991), 134.

9 See *Beethoven: His Life, Work and World*, ed. H. C. Robbins Landon (London, 1992), 149–50.

10 See the commentary in Thayer–Forbes, 908, based on a review in AmZ 26 (1824), 438.

11 The conversation books, in the edition by K. H. Köhler, G. Herre, and D. Beck (*Ludwig van Beethovens Konversationshefte* [Leipzig, 1968–93]), are an indispensable primary source, but must be used with caution and imagination! They represent only one side of the conversation, there are gaps and illegibilities; moreover, after Beethoven's death Anton Schindler doctored the conversation books and destroyed many of them; see Dagmar Beck and Grita Herre, "Anton Schindlers fingierte Eintragungen in den Konversationsheften," in *Zu Beethoven: Aufsätze und Annotationen*, ed. Harry Goldschmidt (Berlin, 1979), 11–89. Caution is also recommended in reading the reminiscences (many of which were written years after

Beethoven's death) and biographies; some contain deliberate and major falsifications, for example an early biography by Anton Schindler (first published 1840; Eng. trans., 1841; and reissued in translation fairly recently [*Beethoven as I Knew Him*, ed. D. W. MacArdle, London, 1966]), which remained highly influential into the twentieth century. On the unreliability of Schindler, who went so far as to claim friendship with Beethoven many years prior to their actual acquaintance, see Maynard Solomon's introduction to Gerhard von Breuning, *Memories of Beethoven,* tr. Henry Mins and Maynard Solomon, ed. Solomon (Cambridge, 1995), 1–16. Gerhard, the son of Stephan von Breuning, spent much time with Beethoven in his last years. Solomon argues for the credibility of his memoirs, which were first published under the name *Aus dem Schwarzspanierhause* (Vienna, 1874).

12 Cited in Thayer–Forbes, 371, translation revised. Seyfried published these remarks in his appendix to his highly flawed edition of *Ludwig van Beethovens Studien im Generalbass, Contrapunkt und in der Compositionslehre,* 2nd edn. (Leipzig, 1853), 16–17.

13 See Gülke, "Zum Verhältnis von Intention und Realisierung bei Beethoven," in *Musikkonzepte 8: Beethoven: Das Problem der Interpretation,* ed. Heinz-Klaus Metzger and Rainer Riehn (Munich, 1979), 34–53; citations on p. 39.

14 Thayer–Forbes, 371.

15 A persistent image of Beethoven, particularly in the last decade of his life, is that of an isolated, alienated individual, in an "intellectual environment [that] was shockingly inferior," whose daily life, "was one of dull mediocrity." Visitors "tell him how famous he is, he receives them with gracious condescension; in spirit he withdraws from them," and accepts their praise as a "lonely man rather than by the greatest artist." Citations from Paul Bekker, *Beethoven* (Berlin, 1912); Eng. trans. by M. N. Bozman (London and Toronto, 1927), 55. This view, colored by romantic notions of the suffering genius, is not entirely wrong, but perhaps too strongly and one-sidedly asserted; Breuning understood Beethoven's greatness but he could also testify to his simpler humanity.

16 Breuning, *Memories,* 74.

17 The publishers (themselves often enough an enemy!) Tobias Haslinger and Anton Steiner were respectively the "Little Adjutant" and the "Lieutenant General," Diabelli, the Provost Marshal; Beethoven's nickname "Falstafferl" for the violinist Ignaz Schuppanzigh is not inconsistent with this conceit. See Solomon (*Beethoven,* 258–61), who describes a "devoted,

but faintly sycophantic" group of non-aristocratic friends and notes the conspicuous absence of women, in sharp contrast to the significant role played in his life by women, most of whom were aristocrats, in the first two decades of his career in Vienna.

18 See Thayer–Forbes, 1108–10 for a list of his quarters.

19 See Anne-Louise Coldicott, *The Beethoven Compendium,* ed. Cooper, 135.

20 December 1811, in a letter from Xaver Schnyder von Wartensee, a young Swiss musician visiting Vienna, to Hans Georg Nägeli in Zurich. Cited from *Letters to Beethoven and Other Correspondence,* tr. and ed. Theodore Albrecht, 3 vols. (Lincoln, NB, 1996), I, no. 157.

21 Czerny wrote about Beethoven's piano playing and pedagogy in several sources; among them are *On the Proper Performance of All Beethoven's Works for the Piano* (London, 1846) and *Complete Theoretical and Practical Piano Forte School,* op. 500, 3 vols. (London, 1839–42). Both are translations of German editions issued shortly earlier. On Brunsvik see Thayer–Forbes, 235.

22 There is a voluminous literature on Beethoven's pianism. Three recent studies are: George Barth, *The Pianist as Orator: Beethoven and the Transformation of Keyboard Style* (Ithaca, 1992); Kenneth Drake, *The Sonatas of Beethoven as he Played and Taught Them* (Bloomington, 1981); and William Newman, *Beethoven on Beethoven: Playing His Piano Music His Way* (New York, 1988).

23 Cited in Wegeler–Ries, 82–83. Ries acknowledged that Beethoven's kindness to him stemmed from his friendship with Ries's father Johann, Beethoven's violin teacher in Bonn. Not all of Beethoven's students were treated so gently!

24 Thayer–Forbes, 294; the citation is from an article by Ries in 1824 in the English musical journal *The Harmonicon.* In 1817 Beethoven recommended Aloys Förster as a teacher to the visiting English musician Cipriani Potter.

25 On the relationship between Beethoven and Haydn, see James Webster", The Falling-Out between Haydn and Beethoven: The Evidence of the Sources," in *Beethoven Essays: Studies in Honor of Elliot Forbes,* ed. Lewis Lockwood and Phyllis Benjamin (Cambridge, MA, 1984), 3–45. On Beethoven's musical studies see Richard Kramer, "Notes to Beethoven's Education," JAMS 28 (1975), 72–101.

26 Kramer, "Notes," 73.

27 See Alfred Mann, "Beethoven's Contrapuntal Studies with Haydn," MQ 56 (1970), 711–26. Kramer argues that Haydn was a conscientious teacher, contrary to Beethoven's

claim that he learned nothing from him and his other Viennese teachers ("Notes," 91).

28 In the years following 1813 he composed forty canons (see Barry Cooper, *Beethoven and the Creative Process* [Oxford, 1990], 25) and sometime in the years 1809–15 he copied a canon by William Byrd from Mattheson.

29 BG VI, no. 1686, 1 July 1823; Anderson III, no. 1203. My translation.

30 BG V, nos. 2107, 2201, and 2203; Anderson II, nos.1473 and 1532 (BG 2201 not in A.).

31 Anton Diabelli wrote to Beethoven in August 1816 advising him on the project. No publisher is named. Sieghard Brandenburg doubts Schindler's assertion that Hoffmeister in Leipzig was the interested publisher; see BG III, no. 960 and note 1 (p. 285) and *Letters,* ed. Albrecht, II, no. 230. In 1803 Beethoven had expressed interest in a complete edition of his extant works, "to be made under my supervision and after a severe revision." The project also did not come to fruition. See Cooper, *Creative Process,* 173.

32 See Alexander Ringer, "Beethoven and the London Pianoforte School," MQ 56 (1970), 742–58.

33 In a letter to Ries in July 1823 about a collection of piano pieces published by T. Boosey in London, "Allegri di Bravura &c Dagli Sequenti Compositori Beethoven, Hummel, Moscheles, Ries, &c." BG V, no. 1703; Anderson III, no. 1209.

34 Cited from "Erinnerungen aus meinem Leben," as translated in *Beethoven: Letters, Journals and Conversations,* tr. and ed. Michael Hamburger (New York, 1951), 54–55.

35 See Maynard Solomon's translation of the diary, in "Beethoven's Tagebuch," in his *Essays,* 233–95. Citation on p. 258, entry no. 43. The translation includes a detailed commentary on the entries. Solomon notes that this entry records the "earliest documentary evidence of his high regard for Gluck." In the diary, Beethoven could unequivocally acknowledge his debt to Haydn. Publicly, however, his remarks were mixed; see Webster, "The Falling-Out," and in the transmission through reminiscences, more negative than positive evidence emerges.

36 In a letter to Breitkopf & Härtel of October 1810; BG IV, no. 474; Anderson I, no. 281.

37 See Elaine Sisman and Michael Tusa (this volume, pp. 52 and 208) and, for example, Bathia Churgin, "Beethoven and Mozart's Requiem: A New Connection," JM 5 (1987), 457–77; Lewis Lockwood, "Beethoven before 1800: The Mozart Legacy," BF 3 (1994), 39–52; Birgit Lodes, "When I try, now and then, to give musical form to my turbulent feelings": The Human and the Divine in the Gloria of

Beethoven's *Missa solemnis,*" BF 6 (1998), 163, fn. 44; and JTW, 34 and 36.

38 From a conversation with Cipriani Potter, Thayer–Forbes, 683.

39 Ibid., 683. Beethoven admired the playing of John Cramer. Tomaschek (*Libussa*) reports on a conversation of 1814, in which Beethoven ridiculed Meyerbeer's early opera *Die beiden Kalifen* and criticized his percussion playing in a recent performance of *Wellington's Victory.*

40 BG V, no. 1716; Anderson III, no. 1213. Beethoven, who knew that Spohr disliked Rossini, had critical words for Spohr's music (that he did not share with Spohr); in turn Spohr (and Weber too) were opposed to much of Beethoven's music. (See Spohr's commentary on the Fifth Symphony in *Beethoven: Symphony No. 5 in C minor,* ed. Elliot Forbes [New York, 1971], 186–87, and Weber's reviews in *Carl Maria von Weber: Writings on Music,* tr. Martin Cooper, ed. John Warrack [Cambridge, 1981].)

41 BG IV, no. 1318; Anderson II, no. 955. The letter describes how Beethoven used Rudolf's music library in Vienna in order to get ideas for the mass he was composing for the Archduke's inauguration as Archbishop of Olmütz. Beethoven first expresses the hope that he will be able to work quickly and then turns to aesthetic matters: "The chief purpose is *rapid execution* united to a *better unification of art* [*bessere Kunstvereinigung*], wherein *practical considerations,* however, may of necessity admit certain exceptions; in which connexion, the older composers render us double service, since there is generally real artistic value in their works (among them, of course, only the *German Händel* and *Sebastian Bach* possessed genius)." Translation adapted from Anderson, whose translation of "Kunstvereinigung" as "understanding of the arts" is mistaken and misleading.

42 This is a very skeletal summary of a protracted period of very complicated negotiations about the Mass and other works in lieu of or in addition to its sale. The most detailed account is in Thayer–Forbes, 768–70 and 785–94, and Solomon, *Beethoven,* 271–72. In the pertinent correspondence Beethoven referred several times to the "Jew" Schlesinger, a publisher of some of his music; these are among the few instances of anti-Semitic remarks documented for Beethoven.

43 Letter to Zelter, Feb. 1823, BG V, no. 1563; Zelter asked Beethoven to provide an arrangement of the mass that could be performed without instruments; Beethoven did not do so. Letter to Ries, BG V, no. 1580; Anderson III, no. 1143.

44 BG II, no. 496; Anderson I, no. 320. My translation.

45 BG II, no. 408; Anderson I, no. 228. Translation by Anderson modified.

46 Solomon, *Beethoven*, 28.

47 Xenophon, Horace, Homer, Plato, and Aristotle were among the classical authors Beethoven favored. Beethoven practiced German–Italian translation in 1812, see Solomon, *Essays*, 251.

48 See Brandenburg's introduction to BG I, LXVI. Beethoven "would rather write ten thousand notes than one letter of the alphabet," as he confided in a letter in 1820 to Nikolaus Simrock in Bonn; BG IV, no. 1418; Anderson II, no. 1037.

49 Citations from Solomon, *Beethoven*, 36–38. On page 37, Solomon writes: "Beethoven's was, of course, a popularized conception of Kant – one which had no room for Kant's epistemology or his exploration of the faculties of knowledge. Beethoven had no training or aptitude for discussion of the distinctions between the world of phenomena and the world of 'noumena'; the Kantian idea of time and space as a priori forms of perception was beyond the grasp and probably beyond the interest of the teen-age composer who had never gone past grade school . . ."

50 BG I, no. 65; Anderson I, no. 51.

51 BG II, no. 685; Anderson I, no. 376. Translation by Anderson modified.

52 See Arnold Schmitz, *Das Romantische Beethovenbild: Darstellung und Kritik* (Berlin, 1927), 51–53.

53 See William Kinderman, *Beethoven* (Berkeley and Los Angeles, 1995), 1–15. Citation from the previously cited letter to Rudolph in 1819.

54 Solomon also stresses the personal, biographic impulses, which make the work a "search for order" by Beethoven (*Essays*, 3–34). Beethoven in 1809 wanted to compose incidental music to Schiller's *William Tell* but was assigned Goethe's *Egmont*; at this time Schiller's plays had begun to dominate the repertory of the Theater an der Wien after having been banned by the censor. Beethoven often cited passages from Schiller or referred to him in correspondence and in the conversation books and the diary.

55 See Sisman, "Pathos and the Pathétique: Rhetorical Stance in Beethoven's C-Minor Sonata, Op. 13," BF 3 (1994), 81–106; citation, p. 94. In contemporary writing on music the symphony was usually considered the genre most capable of expressing the sublime; Beethoven's attribution of pathos to this sonata, one of only several programmatic or descriptive subtitles in his instrumental music, is consistent with his attempt to achieve – in some works – a grander sonata style and an aesthetic status

analogous to the symphony. See Glenn Stanley, "Genre Aesthetics and Function: Beethoven's Piano Sonatas in Their Cultural Context," BF 6 (1998), 1–30.

56 Cf. the diary entry of 1813: "The best way not to think of your woes is to keep busy," in Solomon, *Essays*, 248.

57 Cited from Solomon, *Beethoven*, 117. In deconstructing the Testament Solomon notes a discrepancy between the "real pathos" of some passages and the "stilted, even literary formulations emphasizing his adherence to virtue," for which reason Solomon "remains unpersuaded by the references to suicide" (p. 118). Solomon suggests that the Testament was meant to be read after his future death, and concludes that it was a symbolic "leave-taking," in which he "enacted his own death," and "recreated himself in a new guise, self-sufficient and heroic" (p. 121).

58 "Vom Adel" (1792); see Schmitz, *Das Romantische Beethovenbild*, 64.

59 Citation from E. T. A. Hoffmann's review of the Fifth Symphony (AmZ, 1810), cited in *E. T. A. Hoffmann's Musical Writings*, tr. Martyn Clarke, ed. David Charlton (Cambridge, 1989), 238. The remark on simplicity was written c. 1805 in the Mendelssohn 15 sketchbook, p. 291, and refers to music for piano; that about beauty is recorded in the diary around the time that Beethoven was composing patriotic works for performance at the Congress of Vienna.

60 See Winton Dean, "Beethoven and Opera," in *The Beethoven Reader*, ed. Denis Arnold and Nigel Fortune (New York, 1971), 381–82. Dean's discussion of *Fidelio* has well-deserved classic status.

61 See my review of Scott Burnham's *Beethoven Hero* (Princeton, 1995) in JAMS 50 (1997), 64–83.

62 See Kinderman, *Beethoven*, 336. The incident is related by Breuning, *Memories of Beethoven*, 102.

63 Solomon sees in the diaries Beethoven's attempts to resolve a "central conflict – between his longings for human contact and his devotion to art . . . repeatedly Beethoven exhorts himself to break his isolation; he expresses his desire to take meals with friends, to share his griefs with others, and to hold fast to the threads of social and familial kinship" (*Essays*, 236–37).

64 On Beethoven's preoccupation with a star-filled heaven and a brief discussion of other Christian literature that he read, see Birgit Lodes, *Das Gloria in Beethovens Missa Solemnis* (Tutzing, 1997), 113–19. Among the writings are *Golden Grains of Wisdom and Virtue* and *A Little Bible for the Sick and the Dying* (both published in 1819 in Graz) by the future

Regensburg Bishop Johann Michael Sailer. Sometime after 1811 Beethoven, who was fiercely critical of the Catholic Church as an institution, acquired Christoph Christian Sturm's Christian-pantheistic *Reflections of the Works of God in Nature*; the chapter "The Immeasurability of the Starry Heavens" (*Unermeßlichkeit des Sternenhimmels*), from which the following excerpt is taken, is one of several underlined passages in a book to which he repeatedly turned: "King of heaven, Lord of the Stars, Father of the Spirits and Mankind! If only my thoughts could fill the vault of the heavens, so that I might always be aware of your greatness! If I could only elevate myself to those infinite realms, where you have revealed your greatness so much more than on this earth. If I could only pass from star to star, as I now go from flower to flower, until I reach your sanctuary, where you rule with ineffable majesty! But my wishes are in vain, as long as I am a pilgrim here on earth. Only when my spirit is freed from the bonds of its coarse body, will I perceive the greatness and beauty of these heavenly realms. Until then, as long as I live here, I will summon all humanity to praise your greatness." Translation of excerpt in Lodes, *Das Gloria*, 119, n. 151.

65 Solomon, *Essays*, 229.

66 Ibid.

67 Diary entry, 1813, translation by author; cf. Solomon, *Essays*, 248, entry 7c. German original: "Leben gleicht der Töne Beben / Und der Mensch dem Saitenspiel."

68 The remark on self-discovery – the aesthetic and psychological core of his entire admonition – is, for Beethoven, unusually eloquent and deserves direct citation; "ja ehe, wenn man sich so selbst mitten in der Kunst erblickt, [verursacht es] ein großes Vergnügen." BG V, no. 1686, Anderson III, nos. 1203 and 1204.

3 The compositional act: sketches and autographs

1 Thayer–Forbes, 372.

2 London, British Library, Add. MS 41631.

3 See *Ludwig van Beethoven: Autograph Miscellany from circa 1786 to 1799*, ed. Joseph Kerman, 2 vols. (London, 1970). For more on Beethoven's early sketches up to 1798, see Douglas Johnson, *Beethoven's Early Sketches in the "Fischhof Miscellany": Berlin Autograph 28*, 2 vols. (Ann Arbor, 1980).

4 See JTW.

5 See Barry Cooper, *Beethoven and the Creative Process* (Oxford, 1990), 217–18.

6 See JTW 461–508.

7 See Nicholas Cook, "Beethoven's Unfinished

Piano Concerto: A Case of Double Vision?", JAMS 42 (1989), 338–74.

8 See, for example, Sieghard Brandenburg, "Die Quellen zur Entstehungsgeschichte von Beethovens Streichquartett Es-dur op. 127," BJ 10 (1978–81), 221–76, where the author's description of the autograph of op. 127 refers (p. 268) to "the removal of leaves and correspondingly the new writing of individual bars and sections on inserted leaves."

9 See JTW. Several of the sketchbook descriptions and reconstructions owe much to the work of Sieghard Brandenburg.

10 *Ein Skizzenbuch von Beethoven* (Leipzig, 1865); *Ein Skizzenbuch von Beethoven aus dem Jahre 1803* (Leipzig, 1880); *Beethoveniana* (Leipzig, 1872); *Zweite Beethoveniana* (Leipzig, 1887); all reprinted in 2 vols. (New York, 1970).

11 The most extended general account is in Cooper, *Creative Process*, 104–74.

12 A synopsis sketch for the finale of the *Eroica* is given in N 1880, 50. See also Cooper, *Creative Process*, 106–07.

13 See Robert Winter, *Compositional Origins of Beethoven's String Quartet in C sharp minor, op. 131* (Ann Arbor, 1982).

14 See, for example, Lewis Lockwood, "The Autograph of the First Movement of Beethoven's Sonata for Violoncello and Pianoforte, Opus 69," *The Music Forum* 2 (1970), 1–109.

15 Taken from BG IV, 278.

16 See Barry Cooper, "The Revised Version of Beethoven's Fourth Piano Concerto," in *Performing Beethoven*, ed. Robin Stowell (Cambridge, 1994), 23–48. An alternative hypothesis that the insertions were intended for a chamber version of the work seems far less plausible.

17 See Charles Timbrell, "Notes on the Sources of Beethoven's Opus 111," ML 58 (1977), 204–15.

18 See Willy Hess, *Beethovens Oper Fidelio und ihre drei Fassungen* (Zurich, 1953).

19 See Alan Tyson, "The Problem of Beethoven's 'First' *Leonore* Overture," JAMS 28 (1975), 292–334.

20 Carl Czerny, *On the Proper Performance of all Beethoven's Works for the Piano*, ed. Paul Badura-Skoda (Vienna, 1970), 11.

21 The Beethoven-Haus is slowly bringing out a complete edition of the sketchbooks, and there are plans to publish some of them elsewhere too.

4 "The spirit of Mozart from Haydn's hands": Beethoven's musical inheritance

1 Charles Rosen, *The Classical Style: Haydn, Mozart, Beethoven* (New York, 1971), 19.

2 Commentators are strikingly divided on which older composer exerted more influence on Beethoven, with models for specific works acting as contested ground, as we will see.

3 Musicians and music-lovers in Vienna are listed by these categories in Johann Ferdinand Ritter von Schönfeld, *Jahrbuch der Tonkunst von Wien und Prag 1796*, facs. ed. Otto Biba (Munich and Salzburg, 1976); chaps. 1–3 tr. Kathrine Talbot in *Haydn and His World*, ed. Elaine Sisman (Princeton, 1997), 289–320.

4 Letter of 28 December 1782; Mozart, *Briefe und Aufzeichnungen*, ed. Wilhelm Bauer, Otto Erich Deutsch, and Joseph Eibl, 7 vols. (Kassel, 1962–75), III, no. 715.

5 A little-known pianist named Stainer von Felsburg performed a sonata, probably op. 90, in February 1816; see Glenn Stanley, "Genre Aesthetics and Function: Beethoven's Piano Sonatas in Their Cultural Context," BF 6 (1998), 2.

6 On the sometimes problematic nature of the public–private dichotomy, see Mary Hunter, "Haydn's London Piano Trios and His Salomon String Quartets: Public vs. Private?" in *Haydn and His World*, 103–30.

7 On rhetoric in this period, see Elaine R. Sisman, *Haydn and the Classical Variation* (Cambridge, MA, 1993), chap. 2; and *Mozart: The "Jupiter" Symphony*, (Cambridge, 1993), chaps. 2 and 8. On topics, see Leonard Ratner, *Classic Music: Expression, Form, and Style* (New York, 1980); Wye J. Allanbrook, *Rhythmic Gesture in Mozart: Le Nozze di Figaro and Don Giovanni* (Chicago, 1983); V. Kofi Agawu, *Playing with Signs: A Semiotic Interpretation of Classic Music* (Princeton, 1991); Robert Hatten, *Musical Meaning in Beethoven: Markedness, Correlation, and Interpretation* (Bloomington, 1994); Harold Powers, "Reading Mozart's Music: Sound and Syntax, Text and Topic," *Current Musicology* 59 (1995), 5–44.

8 Neal Zaslaw, *Mozart's Symphonies: Context, Performance Practice, Reception* (Oxford, 1989), 417–18.

9 Johann Abraham Peter Schulz, "Symphonie," in Johann Georg Sulzer, *Allgemeine Theorie der schönen Künste*, 4 vols. in 2 (Leipzig, 1771–74), tr. Thomas Christensen in *Aesthetics and Musical Composition in the German Enlightenment: Selected Writings of Johann Georg Sulzer and Heinrich Christoph Koch*, ed. Nancy Kovaleff Baker and Thomas Christensen (Cambridge, 1995), 106. The idea of the grand style of rhetoric as a musical topic of this era is discussed in my *Mozart: The "Jupiter" Symphony*, 9–10 and 47–48.

10 See Elaine R. Sisman, "Genre, Gesture, and Meaning in Mozart's 'Prague' Symphony," in *Mozart Studies 2*, ed. Cliff Eisen (Oxford, 1997), 27–84.

11 Ibid., 73–80.

12 Georg August Griesinger, *Biographische Notizen über Joseph Haydn* (Leipzig, 1810), tr. in *Haydn: Two Contemporary Portraits*, ed. Vernon Gotwals (Madison, 1963), 61.

13 Hatten, *Musical Meaning in Beethoven*, chap. 4, even claims that the entire sonata op. 101 represents the pastoral as an "expressive genre."

14 The D minor slow movement of the F major quartet op. 18 no. 1, said by Beethoven to describe "the last sighs" of Romeo and Juliet in the Tomb Scene, may also be part of this complex. On the "pathetic accent," see my "Pathos and the *Pathétique*: Rhetorical Stance in Beethoven's C-minor Sonata, op. 13," BF 3 (1994), 81–105, at 91, 98, and n. 81.

15 Thayer–Forbes, 115.

16 In "Mozart and the Nature of Musical Genius," a paper read at the symposium "Mozart's Nature, Mozart's World" at the Museum of Fine Arts in Boston (February 1991), Mark Evan Bonds described the change over the course of the eighteenth century from "having genius," a trait that could be cultivated, to "being a genius," an intrinsic quality of the self.

17 Tia DeNora, *Beethoven and the Construction of Musical Genius: Musical Politics in Vienna, 1792–1803* (Berkeley, 1995), 87; significantly, DeNora uses Landon's translation of the relevant passage (in *Beethoven: A Documentary Study* [New York, 1970], 59), which makes it seem a literal playing-out of the "Haydn's hands narrative": "[who] has put himself in the hands of our immortal Haydn in order to be initiated into the holy secrets of the art of music." In fact the original uses the verb "sich übergeben," or "committed/entrusted himself" to Haydn, which avoids the precise imagery of the "hands of" Haydn. In fact the same verb is used in the subsequent sentence, when Haydn, "during his absence" (presumably in London) "entrusted" his student to Albrechtsberger.

18 The nonentities include Clement, a violinist-composer (forty-three lines); Häring, a violinist who leads musical amateurs ("these geniuses") on the violin (forty lines); Kreybig, conductor of the Hofkapelle and a "genius on the violin" (thirty-nine); and Raphael, a composer and fortepianist who "works at the official statistical office" and is a "true musical genius" (twenty-seven). See Schönfeld, *Jahrbuch der Tonkunst von Wien und Prag* 1796, chap. 2.

19 Edward Young, *Conjectures on Original Composition* (London, 1759), quoted in Elaine

Sisman, "Haydn, Shakespeare, and the Rules of Originality," in *Haydn and His World*, 3–56, at 10.

20 Gotthold Ephraim Lessing, *Hamburgische Dramaturgie* (Hamburg, 1769), ed. Otto Mann (Stuttgart, 1958), 191–92. The rhetorical tone here is strikingly like that of the beginning of Beethoven's "Heiligenstadt Testament": "O you men who think or say that I am malevolent, stubborn, or misanthropic, how greatly do you wrong me. You do not know the secret cause that makes me seem that way to you." Translation in Maynard Solomon, *Beethoven* (New York, 1977), 116.

21 Griesinger, *Biographische Notizen*, 114, in *Haydn*, ed. Gotwals, 61.

22 Translated in H. C. Robbins Landon, *Haydn: Chronicle and Works*, vol. IV: *The Years of "The Creation," 1796–1800* (Bloomington and London, 1977), 339.

23 Anderson I, no. 9: "I should never have written down this kind of piece, had I not already noticed fairly often how some people in Vienna after hearing me extemporize of an evening would note down on the following day several peculiarities of my style and palm them off with pride as their own."

24 Douglas Johnson, "1794–1795: Decisive Years in Beethoven's Early Development," in BS III, 1–28; Bathia Churgin, "Beethoven and Mozart's Requiem: A New Connection," JM 5 (1987), 457–77; Roger Kamien, "The Slow Introduction of Mozart's Symphony no. 38 in D, K. 504 ('Prague'): A Possible Model for the Slow Introduction of Beethoven's Symphony no. 2 in D, op. 36," *Israel Studies in Musicology* 5 (1990), 113–30; Elaine R. Sisman, "Tradition and Transformation in the Alternating Variations of Haydn and Beethoven," Acta 62 (1990), 152–82; Carl Schachter, "Mozart's Last and Beethoven's First: Echoes of K. 551 in the First Movement of Opus 21," in *Mozart Studies*, ed. Cliff Eisen (Oxford, 1991), 227–51; Jeremy Yudkin, "Beethoven's Mozart Quartet," JAMS 45 (1992), 30–74; Lewis Lockwood, "Beethoven before 1800: The Mozart Legacy," BF 3 (1994), 39–52, and literature cited in its n. 15, p. 46; Adena Portowitz, "Innovation and Tradition in the Classic Concerto: Mozart's K. 453 (1784) as a Model for Beethoven's Fourth Concerto (1805–06)," *The Beethoven Journal* 12 (1997), 65–72.

25 See the literature cited in James Webster, "Traditional Elements in Beethoven's Middle-Period Quartets," in *Beethoven, Performers, and Critics: The International Beethoven Congress Detroit, 1977*, ed. Robert Winter and Bruce Carr (Detroit, 1980), 94–133, at notes 8, 10, 11.

26 For example, Johnson proposes Haydn's Symphony no. 95 as the model for Beethoven's C minor Piano Trio op. 1 no. 3 (in "1794–1795: Decisive Years," 18–22), while Basil Smallman writes that the first movement "reflects the spirit more of Mozart than of Haydn, particularly the former's C minor piano sonata, K 457" (*The Piano Trio: Its History, Technique, and Repertoire* [Oxford, 1990], 51).

27 He copied out parts of Mozart's String Quartets in G major K. 387 and A major K. 464 in 1799–1800 in preparation for writing his op. 18 quartets; he copied out parts of Haydn's *Schöpfungsmesse* when commissioned to write the Mass in C in 1807; and he copied out fugal works by Marpurg and J. S. Bach in 1817–18 when writing the "Hammerklavier" Sonata.

28 Douglas Johnson dates the copy of op. 20 no. 1 to 1794 on the basis of the handwriting; see *Beethoven's Early Sketches in the "Fischhof Miscellany," Berlin Autograph 28* (Ann Arbor, 1980), 102; Thayer–Forbes, 166–68, places op. 3 in 1793–94; Kurt Dorfmüller asserts 1794 in *Beiträge zur Beethoven Bibliographie* (Munich, 1978), 293.

29 Johnson believes that Beethoven's sketches for a C major symphony in 1795–96 "owed a good deal to methods he had observed in Haydn's first set of London symphonies, especially the one in C major (no. 97)"; *Beethoven's Early Sketches*, 464.

30 See H. C. Robbins Landon, *The Symphonies of Joseph Haydn* (London, 1955), 227; A. Peter Brown, "The Trumpet Overture and Sinfonia in Vienna (1715–1822): Rise, Decline and Reformulation," in *Music in Eighteenth-Century Austria*, ed. David Wyn Jones (Cambridge, 1996), 13–69.

31 Webster mentions this "tradition" in "Traditional Elements in Beethoven's Middle-Period String Quartets," 105.

32 Cited in n. 13 above.

33 On the rhetorical character of the "doubting" passage, see my *Mozart: the "Jupiter" Symphony*, 49.

34 Michael Tusa, "Beethoven's 'C-Minor Mood': Some Thoughts on the Structural Implications of Key Choice," BF 2 (1993), 1–27, esp. 7–9; Joseph Kerman, "Beethoven's Minority," in *Write All These Down: Essays on Music* (Berkeley and Los Angeles, 1994), 217–37, esp. 225–26.

35 Thayer–Forbes, 209. Tusa argues that the evidence of Beethoven's works of the 1790s suggests that he must have known it well before the parts were published in 1800; "Beethoven's 'C-minor Mood,'" 8n.

36 Tusa, "Beethoven's 'C-minor Mood,'" 24–25.

37 On the importance of the properties of keys

in this period, see Rita Steblin, *A History of Key Characteristics in the Eighteenth and Early Nineteenth Centuries* (1981; rpt. Rochester, NY, 1996).

38 For a list of works that use themes resembling the slow movement of Symphony no. 88, see Georg Feder, "Stilelemente Haydns in Beethovens Werken," in *Bericht über den internationalen musikwissenschaftlichen Kongress Bonn 1970*, ed. Carl Dahlhaus et al. (Kassel, 1971), 65.

39 On difficulty, especially in contrapuntal styles in this period, see my "Genre, Gesture, and Meaning in Mozart's 'Prague' Symphony," 47–56.

40 This segment of the present chapter is based on chapter 8 of my book *Haydn and the Classical Variation*. On Beethoven's independent sets of variations, see Glenn Stanley, "Beethoven's 'wirklich gantz neue Manier' and the Path to It: Beethoven's Variations for Piano, 1783–1802," BF 3 (1994), 53–79.

41 Cicero, *Orator*, trans. H. M. Hubbell, Loeb Classical Library 342 (Cambridge, MA, 1938), xiv.43, p. 339.

42 Themes with different structures usually came from popular arias or other vocal originals.

43 Heinrich Christoph Koch, *Musikalisches Lexikon* (Frankfurt am Main, 1802), s.v. "Variazionen, Variazioni."

44 C[hristian] F[riedrich] Michaelis, "Ueber die musikalische Wiederholung und Veränderung," AmZ 13 (1803), cols. 197–200. Michaelis was Beethoven's exact contemporary (1770–1834). A short biography appears in *Music and Aesthetics in the Eighteenth and Early Nineteenth Centuries*, ed. Peter le Huray and James Day (Cambridge, 1981), 286.

45 Joseph Kerman, *The Beethoven Quartets* (New York, 1966), 62.

46 Ibid., 61.

5 Phrase, period, theme

1 AmZ 15 (1813), trans. from Stefan Kunze (ed.), *Ludwig van Beethoven: Die Werke im Spiegel seiner Zeit* (Laaber, 1987), 25.

2 AmZ 14 (1812), trans. Robin Wallace in *Beethoven's Critics: Aesthetic Dilemmas and Resolutions during the Composer's Lifetime* (Cambridge, 1986), 24.

3 Gustav Jenner, *Johannes Brahms als Mensch, Lehrer und Künstler: Studien und Erlebnisse* (Marburg, 1905), 60, tr. Carl Schachter in "The First Movement of Brahms's Second Symphony: The Opening Theme and Its Consequences," *Music Analysis* 2 (1983), 55.

4 For the organization and some of the terminology of this introduction, I am indebted to William Rothstein, *Phrase Rhythm in Tonal Music* (New York, 1989), 16–101.

5 See Joel Lester, *Compositional Theory in the Eighteenth Century* (Cambridge, MA, 1992), 164 and 286.

6 Johann Philipp Kirnberger, *The Art of Strict Musical Composition*, tr. David Beach and Jürgen Thym (New Haven and London, 1982), 114.

7 Rothstein, *Phrase Rhythm*, 15.

8 Carl Czerny, Appendix (c. 1832–34) to Anton Reicha, *Course of Musical Composition*, tr. A. Merrick, ed. J. Bishop (London, [1854]), reprinted in Ian Bent, *Music Analysis in the Nineteenth Century*, vol. I: *Fugue, Form and Style* (Cambridge, 1994), 195. Quite frequently, a rising scale is elaborated at the beginning of scherzo movements, as in those of the String Quartet in F major op. 18 no. 1, the First Symphony, the Piano Trio in B♭ major op. 97, and the String Quartet in E♭ major op. 127.

9 In the autograph manuscript of the Scherzo of the Ninth Symphony (mm. 177–238), Beethoven even wrote the numbers "1 2 3 1 2 3" under the score at the beginning of the *ritmo di tre battute* passage. These numbers indicate that the passage is organized in groups of nine bars. For a discussion of hypermeter and the *ritmo di tre battute* passage, see Rothstein, *Phrase Rhythm*, 8–10, and 38–39.

10 Ibid., 26. For a recent discussion of themes combining features of a period and sentence, see William Caplin, "Hybrid Themes: Toward a Refinement in the Classification of Classical Theme Types," BF 3 (1994), 151–66.

11 For an interesting discussion of blurred phrase boundaries in late Beethoven, see Edward Cone, "Beethoven's Experiments in Composition: The Late Bagatelles," BS II, 93–94.

12 Heinrich Christoph Koch, *Introductory Essay on Composition*, tr. and ed. Nancy Kovaleff Baker (New Haven and London, 1983), 54–55.

13 Ibid., 55.

14 The chromatic succession E♭–E♮–F plays a prominent role throughout the movement, most obviously as an upbeat figure at the beginning of the coda (mm. 66–69). Analogous chromatic lead-ins are also found in m. 4 of two other early slow movements in A♭ major, those of the Piano Trio in E♭ major op. 1 no. 1 and the Piano Sonata in C minor op. 10 no. 1.

15 Beethoven uses the same technique of repetition in the Cavatina of the String Quartet in B♭ major op. 130, as Lewis Lockwood observes in *Beethoven: Studies in the Creative Process* (Cambridge, 1992), 215.

16 Heinrich Schenker, *Beethovens fünfte Sinfonie* (Universal Edition, 1925), 42.

17 For a discussion of unison texture in Classical music, see Janet M. Levy, "Texture as a Sign in Classic and Early Romantic Music," JAMS 35 (1982), 507–31.

18 See the translation of Hoffmann's review of the Fifth Symphony in *Beethoven: Symphony no. 5 in C minor*, ed. Elliot Forbes (New York, 1971), 153.

19 See the opening bars of Fig. 6 of Schenker's analysis of the first movement in *Beethoven: Symphony no. 5*, ed. Forbes, 180.

20 This motivic connection is discussed in John Rothgeb, "Thematic Content: A Schenkerian View," *Aspects of Schenkerian Theory*, ed. David Beach (New Haven and London, 1983), 56.

21 See Lockwood, *Beethoven: Studies in the Creative Process*, 200–02.

22 For a highly stimulating discussion of Beethoven's rhythm, see William Rothstein, "Beethoven with and without 'Kunstgespräng': Metrical Ambiguity Reconsidered," BF 4 (1995), 165–94.

23 Schindler–MacArdle, 485.

24 Ibid., 417.

25 Quoted from *Beethoven: Symphony no. 5*, ed. Forbes, 156.

26 Ibid., 156.

27 Carl Czerny, *School of Practical Composition: Complete Treatise on the Composition of All Kinds of Music*, tr. John Bishop, 3 vols. (New York, 1979), I, 19.

28 Rhythmic acceleration in Mozart's music is examined in Edward Lowinsky, "On Mozart's Rhythm," in *The Creative World of Mozart*, ed. Paul Henry Lang (New York, 1963), 31–55.

29 Rosen, *The Classical Style: Haydn, Mozart, Beethoven* (New York, 1971), 64.

30 See the facsimile of the autograph, *Ludwig van Beethoven: Sonata quasi una fantasia "Mondschein," op. 27, no. 2*, ed. Keisei Sakka (Tokyo, 1970), 25.

31 For discussions of this procedure in the second movements of the Piano Sonata in E major op. 14 no. 1 and the Piano Sonata in E♭ major op. 27 no. 1, see Carl Schachter, "Rhythm and Linear Analysis: Durational Reduction," *Music Forum* 5 (1980), 220–22; and "Rhythm and Linear Analysis: Aspects of Meter," *Music Forum* 6/1 (1981), 52–53.

32 The term "shadow meter" was introduced by Frank Samarotto in a paper, "Strange Dimensions: Regularity and Irregularity in Deep Levels of Rhythmic Reduction," delivered at the Second International Schenker Symposium (1992). Several examples of this procedure are analyzed in Rothstein,

"Beethoven with and without 'Kunstgespräng'."

33 Donald Francis Tovey, *A Companion to Beethoven's Pianoforte Sonatas*, (London, 1931), 105.

34 Rothstein, "Beethoven with and without 'Kunstgespräng'," 174.

35 Ibid., p. 174. I am indebted to William Rothstein (personal communication) for the observation about the suspended fourths in the alto of mm. 1 and 5.

36 James Webster, *Haydn's "Farewell" Symphony and the Idea of Classical Style* (Cambridge, 1991), 127. For Webster's stimulating discussion of destabilizing opening gestures in Haydn's music, see pp. 127–33.

37 I have borrowed this felicitous phrase from Patrick McCreless, "Schenker and Chromatic Tonicization: A Reappraisal," in *Schenker Studies*, ed. Hedi Siegel (Cambridge, 1990), 131.

38 See, for example, Edward Aldwell and Carl Schachter, *Harmony and Voice Leading*, 2nd. edn. (New York, 1989), 572–74; Charles Burkhart, "Schenker's Motivic Parallelisms," *Journal of Music Theory* 22 (1978), 145–75; Roger Kamien, "Aspects of the Recapitulation in Beethoven Piano Sonatas," *The Music Forum* 4 (New York, 1976), 195–235; Joseph Kerman, *The Beethoven Quartets* (New York, 1966), 93–103; and Rosen, *The Classical Style*, 120–23 and 130–31.

39 Rosen, *The Classical Style*, 129.

40 The following selective list of non-tonic opening harmonies does not include instances in slow introductions or themes following slow introductions: V: Piano Trio in G major op. 1 no. 2, Scherzo; V without third of chord: Ninth Symphony, first movement; V⁷: String Quartet in D major op. 18 no. 3, first movement, Piano Sonata in A major op. 101, first movement; V⁹: Piano Concerto no. 3 in C minor, finale; Piano Trio in E♭ major op. 1 no. 1, Scherzo; II₅⁶ (IV with added sixth): Piano Sonata in E♭ major op. 31 no. 3, first movement; IV: Sonata for Piano and Cello in G minor op. 5 no. 2, finale, Piano Concerto no. 4 in G major op. 58, finale; VI: String Quartet in E minor op. 59 no. 2, finale; diminished seventh: String Quartet in F minor op. 95, third movement; augmented sixth: Piano Sonata in F♯ major op. 78, finale, Sonata for Piano and Violin in G major op. 96, Scherzo; V⁷ of II: String Quartet in B♭ major op. 130, finale.

41 For more detailed discussions of this theme see Roger Kamien, "Aspects of the Recapitulation," 228–33; and Janet Schmalfeldt, "Form as the Process of Becoming: The Beethoven-Hegelian Tradition and the 'Tempest' Sonata," BF 4 (1995), 56–71, which considers the entire exposition.

42 Czerny, *School of Practical Composition*, I, 35.

43 See Bathia Churgin, "Harmonic and Tonal Instability in the Second Key Area of Classic Sonata Form," in *Convention in Eighteenth- and Nineteenth Century Music: Essays in Honor of Leonard G. Ratner*, ed. Wye J. Allanbrook, Janet M. Levy, and William P. Mahrt (Stuyvesant, NY, 1992), 23–57.

44 For a discussion of auxiliary cadences see Heinrich Schenker, *Free Composition*, tr. and ed. Ernst Oster (New York, 1979), 88–89. The auxiliary cadence often corresponds with the "expanded cadential progression" as described in William E. Caplin, "The 'Expanded Cadential Progression': A Category for the Analysis of Classical Form," *Journal of Musicological Research* 7(1987), 215–57.

6 "The sense of an ending": goal-directedness in Beethoven's music

1 Anton Webern, *The Path to the New Music*, ed. Willi Reich (Bryn Mawr, PA, 1963), 51.

2 Heinrich Schenker, *Free Composition (Der freie Satz)*, tr. and ed. Ernst Oster, 2 vols. (New York and London, 1979), I, 129.

3 This expression, and my title, mimics Frank Kermode, *The Sense of an Ending: Studies in the Theory of Fiction* (Oxford, 1967).

4 Taken from Don Fowler, "Second Thoughts on Closure," in *Classical Closure: Reading the End in Greek and Latin Literature*, ed. Deborah H. Roberts, Francis M. Dunn, and Don Fowler (Princeton, 1997), 3. Fowler is here quoting his own earlier study, "First Thoughts on Closure: Problems and Prospects," *Materiale e discussione per l'analisi dei testi classici* 22 (1989), 75–122. The bibliography (pp. 275–302) to *Classical Closure* provides a wide-ranging list of sources for the study of closure, including several specifically musical studies: Carolyn Abbate, *Unsung Voices: Opera and Musical Narrative in the Nineteenth Century* (Princeton, 1991); Kofi Agawu, "Concepts of Closure and Chopin's Opus 28," *Music Theory Spectrum* 9 (1987), 275–301; *Playing With Signs: A Semiotic Interpretation of Classic Music* (Princeton, 1991); Catherine Clément, *Opera, or the Undoing of Women*, tr. Betsy Wing (Minneapolis, 1988); Robert G. Hopkins, *Closure and Mahler's Music: The Role of Secondary Parameters* (Philadelphia, 1990); Paul Robinson, "A Deconstructive Postscript: Reading Libretti and Misreading Opera," in *Reading Opera*, ed. Arthur Groos and Roger Parker (Princeton, 1988), 328–46. To these may be added Peter Cahn, "Aspekte der Schlußgestaltung in Beethovens Instrumentalwerken," AfMW 39 (1982), 19–31;

Joseph Kerman, "Notes on Beethoven's Codas," BS III, 141–60; Lewis Lockwood, "Beethoven and the Problem of Closure: Some Examples from the Middle-Period Chamber Music," in *Beiträge zu Beethovens Kammermusik: Symposion Bonn 1984*, ed. Sieghard Brandenburg and Helmut Loos (Munich, 1987), 254–72; George Edwards, "The Nonsense of an Ending: Closure in Haydn's String Quartets," MQ 75 (1991), 227–54; Hermann Danuser, "Musical Manifestations of the End in Wagner and in Post-Wagnerian *Weltanschauungsmusik*," 19CM 18 (1994), 64–82; and Maynard Solomon, "Beethoven's Ninth Symphony: The Sense of an Ending," in *Probleme der symphonischen Tradition im 19. Jahrhundert: Internationales musikwissenschaftliches Colloquium Bonn 1989*, ed. Siegfried Kross (Tutzing, 1990), 145–56.

5 Fowler, "Second Thoughts on Closure," 4.

6 Scott Burnham, *Beethoven Hero* (Princeton, 1995), xiii. It is because closure – and especially the role of the coda – has been frequently examined in relation to Beethoven's "heroic" works that I concentrate here on the early and late periods.

7 Ibid., 142.

8 Op. 2, published in 1796, were Beethoven's first piano sonatas to bear an opus number; however, the three "Kurfürsten" Sonatas WoO 47 had also been published, in 1783.

9 There is an implicit resolution $d\flat^3$–c^3 in mm. 54–55, but c^3 cannot be sounded because of the parallel fifths that would result with the bass progression $g\flat$–f.

10 Eighth Symphony, 1st mvt., m. 190; "Appassionata," 1st mvt., m. 135. The first movement of the "Razumovsky" String Quartet in F op. 59 no. 1 extends this strategy even to the beginning of the exposition. Both there and at the recapitulation, the opening theme is heard over $^6_4$ harmony; only in the coda is it presented with conventional root-position support. Compare Kerman's suggestion ("Notes on Beethoven's Codas," p. 149) of "a general principle behind Beethoven's codas at this period of his life … Again and again there seems to be some kind of instability, discontinuity, or thrust in the first theme which is removed in the coda."

11 William Kinderman, *Beethoven* (Oxford, 1995), 34, hears in the progression $a\flat^2$–g^2–f^2–e^2–f^2 an expanded reference to the turn figure of m. 2.

12 The concept of "gap-fill" has been developed extensively in the work of Leonard B. Meyer: see particularly his *Explaining Music: Essays and Explorations* (Berkeley, Los Angeles, and London: 1973). Also relevant to the present

analysis is Ernst Oster, "Register and the Large-Scale Connection," in *Readings in Schenker Analysis and Other Approaches*, ed. Maury Yeston (New Haven and London, 1977), 54–71.

13 Naturally, this is a somewhat drastically reductive definition of a classical variation set; for broader discussion see Elaine R. Sisman, *Haydn and the Classical Variation* (Cambridge, MA, and London, 1993); and Esther Cavett-Dunsby, *Mozart's Variations Reconsidered: Four Case Studies (K. 613, K. 501 and the Finales of K. 421 [417b] and K. 491)* (New York and London, 1989).

14 On the early variation sets see Glenn Stanley, "The 'wirklich gantz neue Manier' and the Path to It: Beethoven's Variations for Piano, 1783–1802," BF 3 (1994), 53–79.

15 This, and the concomitant exploration of fugue in the late works, may be explained partly in terms of his seeking to find alternatives to sonata form in the large-scale instrumental genres. Variation technique, or *structure* (as opposed to *form*) might even inflect sonata form: for example, the exposition and recapitulation of the slow movement in the "Hammerklavier" Sonata stand to one another in the relation of "theme" to "variation." Conversely, many late variation movements are inflected by sonata-form dynamic, as discussed below.

16 For a translation, by Derrick Puffett and Alfred Clayton, of Schenker's analysis of this movement, see Heinrich Schenker, *The Masterwork in Music: A Yearbook, Volume III (1930)*, ed. William Drabkin (Cambridge, 1997), 51–59. Schenker's analysis is discussed in Esther Cavett-Dunsby, "Schenker's Analysis of the 'Eroica' Finale," *Theory and Practice* 11 (1989), 43–51, and in Nicholas Marston, "Notes to an Heroic Analysis: A Translation of Schenker's Unpublished Study of Beethoven's Piano Variations, op. 35," in *Nineteenth-Century Piano Music: Essays in Performance and Analysis*, ed. David Witten (New York and London, 1997), 20–24.

17 On the variation movements in the late quartets, see William Kinderman, "Tonality and Form in the Variation Movements of Beethoven's Late Quartets," in *Beiträge zu Beethovens Kammermusik: Symposion Bonn 1984*, ed. Sieghard Brandenburg and Helmut Loos (Munich, 1987), 135–51.

18 See Nicholas Marston, "Beethoven's 'Anti-Organicism'? The Origins of the Slow Movement of the Ninth Symphony," in *Studies in the History of Music, 3: The Creative Process* [ed. Ronald Broude] (New York, 1993), 169–200.

19 Further on the variation movement in

op. 109, see Nicholas Marston, *Beethoven's Piano Sonata in E, op. 109* (Oxford, 1995), 81–96 and 184–251.

20 The return to Tempo 1 and the tonic key at m. 33 in the slow movement of op. 135 may also be taken to articulate a reprise-variation; but the transfer here of the thematic melody to the bass differentiates this case from those mentioned above.

21 As is well known, Beethoven's most daring departure from the tonal conventions of the genre is to be found in the Variations op. 34, where the variations articulate a series of keys related by descending thirds: F(theme) – D – Bb – G – Eb – C min–maj – F. The completion of a V–I cadence coupled with the reprise-character of variation 6 once again engenders clear parallels with sonata-form procedure. Also noteworthy is the extended coda, which in this case is appropriately *non*-modulating, serving rather to reconfirm the regained tonic.

22 For a translation of Schenker's unpublished analysis of op. 35 see Marston, "Notes to an Heroic Analysis," 24–52. On op. 120, see William Kinderman, *Beethoven's Diabelli Variations* (Oxford, 1987); my review of Kinderman's book ("In the Beginning," 19CM 12 [1988], 87–89) is germane to the present study in that it enlarges upon Kinderman's claim (p. 129) that "the close of the Diabelli Variations is ambiguous, and pregnant with implications"; see also my comments on the end of the op. 74 finale in "Analysing Variations: The Finale of Beethoven's String Quartet op. 74," *Music Analysis* 8 (1989), 318. Op. 120 and op. 74 each challenge the sense of their ending, and in a similar way.

23 For further detail see Marston, *Beethoven's Piano Sonata in E, op. 109*.

24 In 1793 Koch noted of the symphony that while "the character of magnificence and grandeur" was appropriate to the first movement, that of "gaiety" was necessary in the finale: see Heinrich Christoph Koch, *Introductory Essay on Composition*, tr. Nancy Kovaleff Baker (New Haven and London, 1983), 197–98. That variation and rondo were perceived as less "demanding" than sonata-form structures was not simply a matter of morphological features but also of thematic material: rondo and variation themes were typically more self-contained, simpler in structure, and lighter in tone than sonata themes.

25 What is suggested here of the symphonic finale is frequently also true of the first-movement exposition: Haydn's second-group and codetta material is generally "lighter" in tone than that of the first group.

26 Beethoven's strategy in the Fifth Symphony has inspired a vast literature, headed by E. T. A. Hoffmann's celebrated 1810 review: see *Ludwig van Beethoven: die Werke im Spiegel seiner Zeit*, ed. Stefan Kunze (Laaber, 1987), 100–12, and *E. T. A. Hoffmann's Musical Writings*, tr. Martyn Clarke, ed. David Charlton (Cambridge, 1989), 234–51. (Hoffmann's discussion [Charlton edn., p. 250] of the unsettling effect of the closing bars of the finale is interesting in the present context.) The "sense of an ending" created by the finale is due, of course, to much more than the modal shift from minor to major: the militaristic, celebratory quality of the metrically four-square main theme stands in complete contrast to the nervous, obsessive motivic construction of the first movement; the C major of the finale is foreshadowed within the second movement (see mm. 30–38 and their repetitions); and the more immediate minor–major shift is rehearsed *within* the finale with the reappearance of material from the Scherzo, leading to the resumption of the main finale theme, in mm. 153–207.

27 See Maynard Solomon, "The Ninth Symphony: A Search for Order," 19CM 10 (1986), 3–23; repr. in Maynard Solomon, *Beethoven Essays* (Cambridge, MA, and London, 1988), 3–32.

28 Consider also the descending *third* e^2–d^2–$c\sharp^2$ in m. 6 of the first movement: this progression does succeed in shifting the dominant, but upward (via E♯) to vi, rather than to I via $V^{8–7}$ voice leading.

29 Beethoven's choice of the dominant minor (e) rather than the relative major (C) as the key of the second group in this movement is bound up with the need to withhold an affirmative statement of C major until the finale.

30 Richard Kramer, "Between Cavatina and *Overtura*: Opus 130 and the Voices of Narrative," BF 1 (1992), 178.

31 Op. 131 "is neither, strictly speaking, one long movement nor a succession of independent movements": Robert Winter, "Plans for the Structure of the String Quartet in C Sharp Minor, op. 131," BS II, 134. Winter, however, doubts the seriousness of the numbering, which originated with Beethoven's corrections to the surviving *Stichvorlage* of op. 131: see Robert Winter, "Compositional Origins of Beethoven's String Quartet in C♯ Minor, op. 131" (Ph.D. diss., University of Chicago, 1978), 137–39.

32 Beethoven's only other multimovement work in C♯ minor – the "Moonlight" Sonata, composed a quarter of a century before op. 131 – also reserves a sonata-form movement for its finale, and seems to toy with thematic transformation: does not the repeated $g\sharp^2$ which is the goal of the ascending arpeggios at the beginning of the first subject in the finale allude to the repeated $g\sharp^1$ in the characteristic dotted rhythm of the first movement?

33 Joseph Kerman, *The Beethoven Quartets* (London, 1967), 303–49.

34 Ivan Mahaim, *Naissance et renaissance des derniers quatuors de Beethoven*, 2 vols. (Paris, 1964); Klaus Kropfinger, "Das gespaltene Werk: Beethovens Streichquartett op. 130/133," in *Beiträge zu Beethovens Kammermusik: Symposion Bonn 1984*, ed. Sieghard Brandenburg and Helmut Loos (Munich, 1987), 328. On Mahaim's interpretation and the substitute finale see Kerman, *The Beethoven Quartets*, 367–74; also the review-article by Ora Frishberg Saloman, "Origins, Performances, and Reception History of Beethoven's Late Quartets," MQ 80 (1996), 525–40, with a response by Klaus Kropfinger, "What Remained Unresolved [was unerledigt blieb]," ibid., 541–47; and Barbara R. Barry, "Recycling the End of the 'Leibquartett': Models, Meaning, and Propriety in Beethoven's Quartet in B-flat major Opus 130," JM 13 (1995), 355–76. See also John Daverio, this volume pp. 162–64.

35 Kropfinger, "Das gespaltene Werk," 315. Certainly, Beethoven's sketches often reveal a strong concern for the ending of a work or movement at an early stage of composition. The genesis of the *Eroica* symphony represents a special case; but for the argument that "its finale … was the basic springboard, the essential invariant concept to which the remaining movements of the symphony were then adapted," see Lewis Lockwood, "The Earliest Sketches for the *Eroica* Symphony," in Lewis Lockwood, *Beethoven: Studies in the Creative Process* (Cambridge, MA, and London, 1992), 136.

36 Barry Cooper, *Beethoven and the Creative Process* (Oxford, 1991), 209, 214.

37 Joseph Kerman, "Beethoven Sketchbooks in the British Museum," *Proceedings of the Royal Musical Association* 93 (1966–67), 83; *The Beethoven Quartets*, 269–70. See also Kramer, "Between Cavatina and *Overtura*," 187: "To seek the composer's intention is to obscure what ought to be the real task: to seek the meaning of the work."

38 Kerman, *The Beethoven Quartets*, 288, 294, 282.

39 Kramer, "Between Cavatina and *Overtura*," 172–73.

40 Ibid., 181, n. 20, referring to the work of Helga Lühning, "Die Cavatina in der italienischen Oper um 1800," *Analecta Musicologica* 21 (Laaber, 1982), 333–69.

41 Kramer, "Between Cavatina and *Overtura*," 176 and Example 6.

42 Rudolph Reti, *The Thematic Process in Music* (London and New York, 1951); Ludwig Misch, "Two B Flat Major Themes," in *Beethoven Studies*, tr. G. I. C. de Courcy (Norman, OK, 1953), esp. 26: "the harmonic progression of the first movement shapes the course of the entire tonal structure of the B flat Major Quartet"; Kerman, *The Beethoven Quartets*, esp. 303–25.

43 Kerman, *The Beethoven Quartets*, 319.

44 Ibid., 322. Compare the earlier remarks on the same page in which the sense of an ending in the *Grosse Fuge* is located in its serving to confirm, rather than resolve, "the previous dynamic of disruption."

45 Susan McClary, "Sexual Politics in Classical Music," in *Feminine Endings: Music, Gender, and Sexuality* (Minneapolis and Oxford, 1991), 61, 62.

46 Abbate, *Unsung Voices*, 56.

47 Kerman, *The Beethoven Quartets*, 367.

48 Kristin M. Knittel, "From Chaos to History: The Reception of Beethoven's Late Quartets" (Ph.D. diss., Princeton University, 1992), 221.

49 Kerman, *The Beethoven Quartets*, 370, 322.

50 On the interpretation of op. 130 *als Ganzes* see the essay by Kropfinger in *Beethoven: Interpretationen seiner Werke*, ed. Albrecht Riethmüller, Carl Dahlhaus, and Alexander L. Ringer (Laaber, 1994), 299–316; also 338–47 for essays on op. 133 and its four-hand piano arrangement, op. 134.

51 Kerman, *The Beethoven Quartets*, 374.

52 Walter Riezler, *Beethoven*, trans. G. D. H. Pidcock (London, 1938), 239. Kropfinger, too, speaks of two different "wholes" in his essay on op. 130 in *Beethoven: Interpretationen seiner Werke*, esp. 314–16.

53 For an introduction to this issue, see Deborah H. Roberts, "Afterword: Ending and Aftermath, Ancient and Modern," in *Classical Closure*, ed. Roberts, Dunn, and Fowler, 251–73. Although she mentions (p. 266) the possibility that a reader "may have access to an aftermath the author had in mind but never wrote," Roberts does not mention the recent penchant among contemporary authors for writing "fictional" sequels to popular classic novels.

54 Commentators have frequently observed various points of connection not only between the new finale and the *Grosse Fuge*, but between the new finale and the earlier movements of op. 130. Most obvious, perhaps, is the relationship of the circle-of-fifths underpinning of the opening theme of the new finale (G–C–F–B♭) to that of the *Overtura* in the fugue: see Kerman, *The Beethoven Quartets*, 372–73; Kropfinger, "Das gespaltene Werk," 323, and *Beethoven:*

Interpretationen seiner Werke, esp. 314 for the suggestion that the newly composed finale might be understood as a "commentary less on the replaced fugal finale than on the fact of the exchange"; Misch, "Two B Flat Major Themes," 28: "the theme of the subsequent finale was derived from the totality of the B flat major quartet, like a new germ cell from a living organism." See also the essay on op. 130 by Michael Steinberg in *The Beethoven Quartet Companion*, ed. Robert Winter and Robert Martin (Berkeley, Los Angeles, and London, 1994), 244 (Ex. 20).

55 Despite its chronological priority, the separation of the *Grosse Fuge* from op. 130 and its publication with an individual, higher, opus number contribute to a sense of its functioning as an aftermath, an ending beyond the ending. Meanwhile, compact disc technology, if not live performance, allows the listener to programme *either* finale as an "aftermath" to the other.

56 See Gerhard von Breuning, *Memories of Beethoven: From the House of the Black-Robed Spaniards*, ed. Maynard Solomon (Cambridge, 1992), 101–2.

57 Roberts, "Afterword," 273.

7 The piano music: concertos, sonatas, variations, small forms

1 Recent discussions of this issue include Glenn Stanley, "Genre Aesthetics and Function: Beethoven's Piano Sonatas in Their Cultural Context," BF 6 (1998), 1–29; and Lydia Goehr, *The Imaginary Museum of Musical Works: An Essay in the Philosophy of Music* (Oxford, 1992), esp. chap. 8, 205–42. Goehr regards the "work-concept" as coming into being only around 1800, whereby "For the first time [extemporization] was seen to stand in strict opposition to composition 'proper'" (p. 234). Notwithstanding Beethoven's sensitivity to alteration of his musical texts, such a perceived opposition between improvisation and composition conflicts sharply with his own practice and convictions, as reflected for instance in his statement to Tomaschek from 1814, cited on p. 106 above.

2 Thayer–Forbes, 115.

3 For a recent study of Bach's impact on Beethoven, see my article "Bachian Affinities in Beethoven," in *Bach Perspectives* vol. III, ed. Michael Marissen (Lincoln, NB and London, 1998), 81–108.

4 An analysis of the social ramifications of Beethoven's challenging keyboard style is offered by Tia DeNora in *Beethoven and the Construction of Genius: Musical Politics in Vienna, 1792–1803* (Berkeley and Los Angeles, 1995).

5 On Beethoven's musical rhetoric, see Mark Evan Bonds, *Wordless Rhetoric: Musical Form and the Metaphor of the Oration* (Cambridge, MA, 1991), esp. 177–91; George Barth, *The Pianist as Orator: Beethoven and the Transformation of Keyboard Style* (Ithaca and London, 1992); and Elaine Sisman, "Pathos and the *Pathétique*: Rhetorical Stance in Beethoven's C-Minor Sonata, op. 13," BF 3 (1994), 81–105.

6 Cited in Alfred Einstein, *Mozart: His Character, His Work* (New York, 1962; first pub. 1945), 243.

7 See Thayer–Forbes, 351. Sketches for the original version of the "Waldstein" Sonata (with the *Andante favori*) are found in the "Eroica" Sketchbook (Landsberg 6) and date from the last weeks of 1803; sketches for the replacement slow movement are lacking, but that movement was presumably composed in the spring of 1804.

8 Thayer–Forbes, 599; the source is Tomaschek's autobiography, *Libussa* (Prague, 1846), 359ff.

9 For a discussion of the aesthetics of sonata form, see Carl Dahlhaus, *Ludwig van Beethoven: Approaches to his Music*, tr. Mary Whittall (Oxford, 1991), esp. chaps. 5–8, 91–165, and Stanley, "Genre Aesthetics."

10 A probing discussion of aesthetic significance in Beethoven is contained in Robert Hatten, *Musical Meaning in Beethoven: Markedness, Correlation, and Interpretation* (Bloomington, 1994).

11 See Mies, *Die Krise der Konzertkadenz bei Beethoven* (Bonn, 1970), esp. 52–53. Mies cites Gustav Nottebohm's comment "that of all the quartets the one in C♯ minor makes in its form the strongest impression of an improvisation" (p. 52).

12 Thayer–Forbes, 275.

13 See Block, "Organic Relations in Beethoven's Early Piano Concerti and the 'Spirit of Mozart,'" in *Beethoven's Compositional Process*, ed. William Kinderman (Lincoln, NB and London, 1991), 55–81, esp. 73. Charles Rosen points out motivic connections between the first and last movements of Mozart's D minor concerto in *The Classical Style* (New York, expanded edn. 1997), 235, remarking that "for the first time the first and last movements of a concerto are so strikingly and openly related." Beethoven's involvement with Mozart's concerto is confirmed by his surviving cadenzas for the work, WoO 58.

14 Douglas Johnson has drawn attention to this relation in "1794–95: Decisive Years in Beethoven's Early Development," in BS III, 16.

15 Alfred Brendel, in his discussion of the passage in *Music Sounded Out* (London, 1990), 24, imagines questions that this chord might suggest to the audience, including: "'Are we really coming to an end?,' 'Wouldn't you like the cadenza to be over?,' 'What a ridiculous frenzy!,' 'Heavens, didn't we forget the trill?,' 'As it didn't work before, why should it work now?,' or simply 'Am I fooling you well?'"

16 See *Ludwig van Beethoven. Klavierkonzert Nr. 3 in c, op. 37, Studienpartitur* ed. Hans-Werner Küthen (Kassel, London, New York, 1987), preface, v.

17 An ongoing discussion concerning the Orpheus "programme" in the Andante con moto of Beethoven's Fourth Concerto is contained in Owen Jander, "Beethoven's 'Orpheus in Hades,'" 19CM 8 (1984), 195–212; Edward T. Cone, "Beethoven's Orpheus – or Jander's?", 19CM 8 (1984), 283–86; Joseph Kerman, "Representing a Relationship: Notes on a Beethoven Concerto," *Representations* 39 (1992), 80–101; and most recently Jander, "Orpheus Revisited: A Ten-Year Retrospect on the Andante con moto of Beethoven's Fourth Piano Concerto," 19CM 19 (1995), 31–49.

18 This process is a particularly important feature of Beethoven's style, to which Alfred Brendel has drawn special attention in his essays "Form and Psychology in Beethoven's Piano Sonatas" and "The Process of Foreshortening in the First Movement of Beethoven's Sonata op. 2, no. 1," in *Musical Thoughts and Afterthoughts* (Princeton, 1976). Also see Erwin Ratz, *Einführung in die musikalische Formenlehre* (Vienna, 1968), 23–24.

19 Beethoven also utilized the four-movement design in the subsequent Sonata in E♭ major op. 7 and in the Sonata in D major op. 10 no. 3, and contemplated a four-movement plan for the C minor Sonata op. 10 no. 1, while sketching that work (see William Drabkin, "Early Beethoven," in *Eighteenth-Century Keyboard Music*, ed. Robert L. Marshall [New York, 1994], 402, n. 10). He returned to the four-movement plan in opp. 22, 26, 31 no. 3, and 106.

20 A detailed discussion of this movement is contained in my article "Beethoven's High Comic Style in Piano Sonatas of the 1790s, or Beethoven, Uncle Toby, and the 'Muckcart-driver,'" BF 5 (1996), 123–27.

21 For a detailed discussion of this relationship, see William Kinderman, *Beethoven* (Oxford, 1995), 20–27.

22 *A Companion to Beethoven's Pianoforte Sonatas* (London, 1931), 169.

23 "Structuralism and Musical Plot," *Music Theory Spectrum* 19 (1997), 13–34, esp. 22–31 (quotation from 31).

24 Thayer–Forbes, 668.
25 Cited by Martin Zenck, *Die Bach-Rezeption des Späten Beethoven: Zum Verhältnis von Musikhistoriographie und Rezeptions-geschichtsschreibung der "Klassik"* (Stuttgart, 1986), 152.
26 See Schindler–MacArdle, 210.
27 Cited in Maynard Solomon, *Beethoven* (New York, 1977), 300.
28 The importance of descending third relations in the "Hammerklavier" Sonata is discussed in detail by Rosen in *The Classical Style*, 407–34. See also Ratz, *Einführung in die musikalische Formenlehre*, 201–41.
29 For detailed analysis, see my studies "Integration and Narrative Design in Beethoven's Piano Sonata in A♭ major Opus 110," BF 1 (1992), 111–45, esp. 120–21; and the essays on these sonatas in *Beethoven: Interpretation seiner Werke*, ed. Albrecht Riethmuller, Carl Dahlhaus, and Alexander L. Ringer (Laaber, 1994), II, 162–81.
30 A recent discussion of the early variations for piano is offered by Glenn Stanley in "The 'wirklich gantz neue Manier' and the Path to It: Beethoven's Variations for Piano, 1783–1802," BF 3 (1994), 53–79.
31 Cf. Lewis Lockwood, "The Compositional Genesis of the Eroica Finale," in *Beethoven's Compositional Process*, ed. William Kinderman (Lincoln, NB and London, 1991), 82–101, esp. 84–85; reprinted in Lockwood's *Beethoven: Studies in the Creative Process* (Cambridge, MA, and London, 1992).
32 A discussion and full transcription of the 1819 draft is offered in my book *Beethoven's Diabelli Variations* (Oxford, 1987); the 1999 rprt. includes my CD of the work with Hyperion Records.
33 Hans von Bülow, notes in his edition of op. 120 (*Ludwig van Beethoven: Variations for the Pianoforte*, vol. II [New York, 1898], 43).
34 Brendel, *Musical Thoughts and Afterthoughts*, 14.
35 This situation parallels that of Mozart, who similarly left only one completed fantasy for solo piano: the Fantasy in C minor K. 475, in addition to incomplete works, such as the Fantasy in D minor K. 397/385g.
36 See N II, 508–11.
37 Cf. William Meredith, "The Origins of Beethoven's op. 109," *The Musical Times* 126 (1985), 713–16; and Nicholas Marston, *Beethoven's Piano Sonata in E, op. 109* (Oxford, 1995), 30–37.
38 The first five apparently have an earlier origin, and Gustav Nottebohm proposed on the basis of sketches that nos. 2–5 dated from the period 1800–04. Nos. 7–11 were sketched by

Beethoven in the summer or fall of 1820 and first published as nos. 28–32 in Friedrich Starke's *Wiener Piano-Forte-Schule* in 1821. No. 6 was sketched on a leaf containing work on the Credo of the *Missa solemnis* and probably dates from 1820. No. 7 bears similarity to the third and tenth "Diabelli" variations, and no. 8 also shows a motivic relationship to the third "Diabelli" variation.
39 The beginning of this Allemande, which dates from about 1800, was re-barred and incorporated into the middle section of the second movement of the quartet.
40 Wilfrid Mellers, *Beethoven and the Voice of God* (New York, 1983), 412. An insightful discussion of paradoxical aspects of op. 126 no. 6 is offered by Sylvia Imeson in her book *"The time gives it proofe": Paradox in the Late Music of Beethoven* (New York, 1996), 5, 29–32.

8 Beethoven's chamber music with piano: seeking unity in mixed sonorities
1 The signal exceptions are the sonatas for cembalo and violin of J. S. Bach, BWV 1014–1019: here co-equal keyboard parts are written out in full, rather than in figured bass, and the reinforcement of the bass line by a gamba is referred to in the title as *se piace*, or optional.
2 William S. Newman, *The Sonata in the Classic Era* (Durham, NC, 1963), 98–105.
3 Charles Rosen, *The Classical Style* (New York, 1972), 351–65.
4 E.g. see the finales of Mozart's Piano Trio in B♭ K. 502 or his Piano Quartet in G minor, Haydn's Piano Trio in E♭ Hob. XV:29 and Beethoven's Quintet for Piano and Winds op. 16.
5 Maynard Solomon, *Beethoven* (New York, 1979), 98; see also Derek Melville, "Beethoven's Pianos," in *The Beethoven Companion*, ed. Denis Arnold and Nigel Fortune (London, 1971), 41–67.
6 However, the implementation of these changes was probably a slower process, involving as it did either the purchase of a new instrument or a rather delicate operation on an older one. The new bows, on the other hand, were quickly accepted by violinists as superior. This may well argue against the use of the old style bows for "authentic" performances of late eighteenth-century music. The current fashion of so-called "transitional" bows is also deceptive, as the name implies a much more orderly development process than was the case. In fact, there was a considerable lack of uniformity among bows produced during both Baroque and Classical periods, and even well

into the nineteenth century. See Robin Stowell, *Violin Technique and Performance Practice in the Late 18th and Early 19th Centuries* (Cambridge, 1985), 11–31.

7 Lewis Lockwood, "Beethoven's Early Works for Violoncello and Contemporary Violoncello Technique," in *Beethoven-Kolloquium 1977: Dokumentation und Aufführungspraxis*, ed. R. Klein, (Kassel, 1978), 180.

8 Boris Schwarz, "Beethoven and the French Violin School," MQ 44 (1958), 431–47.

9 Solomon, *Beethoven*, 47.

10 This refers to the mature works starting with K. 301. There are also several juvenile works in the accompanied keyboard sonata style.

11 For a flamboyant example of this, see m. 388 of the Trio op. 70 no. 1, mvt. 3.

12 Nigel Fortune, "The Chamber Music with Piano," in *The Beethoven Companion,* ed. Arnold and Fortune, 202.

13 As if to make amends to the piano for his unconventional first theme, Beethoven offers the piano plenty of virtuoso writing, and a second theme that is kept exclusively to the piano until the recapitulation. Incidentally, in places where a *forte* statement brings all the instruments together, pianos of this period produce a fine jangling effect, clearly intentional on Beethoven's part, which is mostly lost with the rounder sound of a modern instrument.

14 Such writing is not only typical of Mozart, but also remarkably similar to the Adagio of the violin sonata K. 481 (also an A♭ major movement in an E♭ major work), although in this comparison it is Mozart who is harmonically the more daring.

15 Solomon, *Beethoven*, 73–77; Solomon suggests that there are more subtle and internal reasons why a rift with Haydn may have suited Beethoven at that point, so that the issue of the C minor trio may have been little more than a convenient pretext.

16 See, for example, an unusual thematic use of the lowest string of the cello, an octave below the piano left hand, to achieve a hushed and woolly sonority (m. 390, 3rd movement).

17 This is not to say that the cello part of op. 5 no. 2 is uninteresting; only that it relies more upon safer and less innovative uses of alto and tenor range thematic statements and sustained bass notes; moreover, some particularly subtle and beautiful moments, such as the transition to the recapitulation in the first movement, do not rely upon the cello at all.

18 Joseph Kerman, *The Beethoven Quartets* (New York, 1966), 6.

19 D. F. Tovey, *Beethoven* (London, 1944), 89: "If Beethoven's early works had been mostly in the style of [the solo piano sonata] op. 2, no. 3 or the Violoncello Sonata in F, op. 5, no. 1, and he had died before producing anything more characteristic, it would have been possible to argue that here was an ambitious composer who evidently aspired to be greater than either Mozart or Haydn, but who already showed the tendency to inflation that leads through the style of Hummel to the degenerate styles of the virtuoso pianoforte-writers." Comments on cadenzas later in the same article.

20 Lockwood, "Beethoven's Early Works for Violoncello," 176–77.

21 Fortune, "The Chamber Music with Piano," 216.

22 He does parody an Alberti accompaniment in the first movement of op. 12 no. 3, mm. 29–43, but the articulations in the violin part make it clear that he has in mind a texture more sparkling and distinctive than the unobtrusive Alberti blanket.

23 Solomon, *Beethoven*, 99–100.

24 Interestingly, Niecks describes this work in such different terms – "an idyll, so sweet and lovely is its character" – that it is hard to imagine he is referring to the same music: Frederich Niecks, "Beethoven's Sonatas for Piano and Violin", *Monthly Musical Record* nos. 236, 237 (London, 1890) in *The Beethoven Companion,* ed. Thomas Scherman and Louis Biancolli (Garden City, 1972), 180.

25 Schwarz, "Beethoven and the French Violin School," 431–47.

26 In addition to French school influences on violin figurations, the Triple Concerto has a passage (coda of the first movement, mm. 498–506) which adds triplets in successive instruments to existing trills in a manner so similar to an excerpt from Viotti's Twenty-Fourth Concerto (Andante sostenuto, mm. 57–61) that the resemblance is probably not coincidental.

27 Hector Berlioz, *Voyages en Allemagne et en Italie* (Paris, 1844) cited in Schwarz, "Beethoven and the French Violin School," 431–47.

28 Lewis Lockwood, "The Autograph of the First Movement of the Sonata for Violoncello and Pianoforte, Opus 69," in *Beethoven Essays: Studies in Honor of Elliott Forbes*, ed. Lewis Lockwood and Phyllis Benjamin (Cambridge, MA, 1984).

29 Tyson also discusses changes made between sketchbook and autograph. See: Alan Tyson, "Stages in the Composition of Beethoven's Piano Trio op. 70, no. 1," *Proceedings of the Royal Musical Association* 97 (1970–71), 1–19.

30 Solomon, *Beethoven*, 98.

31 Note that these are fundamentally different from the op. 5 cadenzas that Tovey found

objectionable: although technically extremely difficult, they cannot be construed as virtuoso displays; rather, they are brief improvisatory and developmental commentaries.

32 Alfred Brendel, *Musical Thoughts and Afterthoughts* (Princeton, 1976), 154–61.

33 If one considers the basic beat to be the quarter note, as I think proper here, the tempo is so slow as to be far below the range of normal metronomes.

34 Schwarz, "Beethoven and the French Violin School," 441.

35 Alfred Brendel, *Music Sounded Out* (London, 1990), 62.

36 Fortune, "The Chamber Music with Piano," 221.

9 Manner, tone, and tendency in Beethoven's chamber music for strings

1 Walter Benjamin, "The Image of Proust" (1929), in *Illuminations: Essays and Reflections*, ed. Hannah Arendt, tr. Harry Zohn (New York, 1969), 201.

2 See his letter of 13 July 1802 to Breitkopf & Härtel, in Anderson I, no. 59.

3 Beethoven's (not always deftly executed) arrangement of the Piano Trio op. 1 no. 3 for string quintet was perhaps stimulated by his displeasure with an overly literal reworking, probably by a Herr Kaufmann. See Alan Tyson, "The Authors of the op. 104 String Quintet," in BS I, 158–61. On the arrangement of op. 14 no. 1 for string quartet, see Helga Lühning, "Beethoven als Bearbeiter eigener Werke," in *Münchener Beethoven-Studien* (Munich and Salzburg, 1992), 124–27; and Eberhard Enss, *Beethoven als Bearbeiter eigener Werke* (Taunusstein, 1988), 69–82.

4 AmZ 22 (15 November 1820), 784.

5 Chopin, however, reported to his friend Joseph Nowakowski in April 1832 that the Paris Conservatoire Orchestra made a sensation with a performance of one of Beethoven's quartets using a string section of fifty players. See Robert Winter, "Performing the Beethoven Quartets in Their First Century," in *The Beethoven Quartet Companion*, ed. Robert Winter and Robert Martin (Berkeley and Los Angeles, 1994), 43.

6 Gustav Schilling, *Encyclopädie der gesamten musikalischen Wissenschaften oder Universal-Lexicon der Tonkunst* (Stuttgart, 1835–42), V, 591.

7 Carl Czerny, *School of Practical Composition* op. 600, tr. John Bishop, 3 vols. (London, c. 1848), II, 2–23. Czerny notes that the addition of another viola to the standard quartet group may influence "the invention of ideas, melodies, chords and figures" (p. 17).

8 Beethoven's sketches for a C major quintet (WoO 62), probably dating from September through November 1826, point to the neo-classical idiom of the F major String Quartet op. 135 and the new finale for op. 130. See Martin Staehelin, "Another Approach to Beethoven's Last Quartet Oeuvre: The Unfinished String Quintet of 1826/27," in *The String Quartets of Haydn, Mozart, and Beethoven: Studies of the Autograph Manuscripts*, ed. Christoph Wolff (Cambridge, MA, 1980), 309–16.

9 On this point, see James Webster, "Traditional Elements in Beethoven's Middle-Period String Quartets," in *Beethoven, Performers, and Critics*, ed. Robert Winter and Bruce Carr (Detroit, 1980), 102.

10 Deryck Cooke, however, goes too far in tracing practically all the principal motivic ideas of the late quartets to the opening of op. 127, in whose upper-voice melody he also finds the four-note pattern embedded. See "The Unity of Beethoven's Late Quartets," *Music Review* 24 (1963), 30–49. Although the importance of this cell in the late quartets cannot be denied, Dahlhaus rightly observes that it is less a fixed motive than an abstract sequence of intervals from which Beethoven creates a "magic of association." See Dahlhaus, *Ludwig van Beethoven: Approaches to his Music*, tr. Mary Whittall (Oxford, 1991; orig. pub. *Ludwig van Beethoven und seine Zeit*, Laaber, 1987), 227–29. Beethoven's pattern can be traced to two sources: the B–A–C–H motive, which heads off the humorous canon "Kühl, nicht lau," dated 3 September 1825, and the family of fugue subjects built around the interval of a diminished seventh (see, e.g., the Kyrie of Mozart's *Requiem* K. 626, and the finale of Haydn's F minor Quartet op. 20 no. 4). For a discussion of the canon as a thematic repository for Beethoven's late quartets, see Emil Platen, "Über Bach, Kuhlau und die thematisch-motivische Einheit der letzten Quartette Beethovens," in *Beiträge zu Beethovens Kammermusik: Symposion Bonn 1984*, ed. Sieghard Brandenburg and Helmut Loos (Munich, 1987), 152–64. The themes of Mozart's Kyrie and Haydn's F minor quartet fugue came up in a conversation between Beethoven and Karl Holz in mid-July 1825, at the very time when Beethoven was working on op. 132. See CB VIII, 19. A close relative of these motivic configurations appears in sketches, probably dating from August 1824, for a projected sonata for piano four-hands. See William Kinderman, *Beethoven* (Berkeley, 1995), 295–96.

11 On the evidence provided by the sketches for the interdependence of the late quartets, see:

323 Notes to pages 149–52

Sieghard Brandenburg, "Die Quellen zur Entstehungsgeschichte von Beethovens Streichquartett Es-dur op. 127," BJ 10 (1978–81), 127–74; "The Autograph of Beethoven's Quartet in A minor Opus 132: The Structure of the Manuscript and its Relevance for the Study of the Genesis of the Work," in *The String Quartets of Haydn, Mozart, and Beethoven*, ed. Wolff, 283–85, 292–93; and Kinderman, *Beethoven*, 323.

12 See Ludwig Finscher, *Studien zur Geschichte des Streichquartetts I: Die Entstehung des klassischen Streichquartetts. Von den Vorformen zur Grundlegung durch Joseph Haydn* (Kassel, 1974), 279–99. Finscher's main sources include: Johann Friedrich Reichardt, Preface to *Vermischte Musikalien* (1773); Heinrich Christoph Koch, *Versuch einer Anweisung zur Composition* (1793) and *Musikalisches Lexikon* (1802); Giuseppe Carpani, *Le Haydine* (1812); Carl Maria von Weber's review of F. E. Fesca's quartets in AmZ 20 (1818), cols. 589–90; and Gustav Schilling, *Versuch einer Philosophie des Schönen in der Musik oder Aesthetik der Tonkunst* (1838). Similar points of view are expressed in August F. C. Kollmann, *An Essay on Practical Musical Composition* (London, 1799), 14; Schilling, *Encyclopädie*, vol. V, 591–92; and Czerny, *School of Practical Composition*, II, 6–7.

13 Review of op. 127 in *Berliner allgemeine musikalische Zeitung* 4 (1827), 25–27; see *Ludwig van Beethoven–Die Werke im Spiegel seiner Zeit–Gesammelte Konzertberichte und Rezensionen bis 1830*, ed. Stefan Kunze (Laaber, 1987), 556.

14 See Finscher, *Studien zur Geschichte des Streichquartetts*, 299; and Robert Winter, "Performing the Beethoven Quartets in Their First Century," in *The Beethoven Quartet Companion*, ed. Winter and Martin, 53–54.

15 See August Wilhelm Schlegel, *Lectures on Dramatic Art and Literature*, tr. John Black (London, 1914), 17–28.

16 *Fragmente zur Litteratur [sic] und Poesie*, no. 851, in *Kritische Friedrich Schlegel Ausgabe [KFSA]*, ed. Ernst Behler, Jean-Jacques Anstett, and Hans Eichner (Munich, Paderborn, Vienna, 1958–), XVI, 157.

17 Johann Wolfgang von Goethe, *Essays on Art and Literature*, ed. John Gearey, tr. Ellen von Nardroff and Ernest H. von Nardroff, *Collected Works*, III (Princeton, 1994), 71–73.

18 Schlegel specifically equates "tendency" and formal incompletion in *Fragmente zur Litteratur und Poesie*, nos. 411, 918, and 960; see *KFSA* XVI, 119, 163, 165–66. For a commentary on his association of manner, tendency, and tone with the novel, see Peter Szondi, "Friedrich Schlegel's Theory of Poetical Genres: A

Reconstruction from the Posthumous Fragments," in *On Textual Understanding and Other Essays*, tr. Harvey Mendelsohn (Minneapolis, 1986), 90.

19 See Otto Erich Deutsch, *Schubert: Die Dokumente seines Lebens; Franz Schubert: Neue Ausgabe sämtlicher Werke*, Series 8, Supplement, V (Kassel, 1964), 45.

20 Hermann Hirschbach, "Ueber Beethoven's letzte Streichquartette," *Neue Zeitschrift für Musik* [NZfM] 11 (1839), 6. Hirschbach claims that these works relate to the quartets of Haydn and Mozart as "a magnificent novella [does] to its old Italian and Spanish forebears."

21 On Beethoven's reading of Schlegel's translations, see his letter of May 1810 to Therese Malfatti, in Anderson I, no. 258. On his knowledge of Schlegel's *Vorlesungen*, see Leon Botstein, "The Patrons and Publics of the Quartets: Music, Culture, and Society in Beethoven's Vienna," in *The Beethoven Quartet Companion*, ed. Winter and Martin, 102. The published *Vorlesungen* appear in an entry from late September 1824 in a list of books representing "the most outstanding works in their respective fields." CB VI, 363.

22 Entry of early February 1823, in CB II, 348. Some of Beethoven's associates voiced less than complimentary opinions of the leading guru of early Romanticism. In a conversation of December 1819, Carl Joseph Bernhard claimed that Friedrich Schlegel did nothing but "eat, drink, and read the Bible"; CB I, 169.

23 Wilhelm von Lenz's tripartition of Beethoven's output into early, middle, and late phases has proven to be remarkably resilient despite many attempts to supplant it. As James Webster has argued, this scheme concords with views of temporal organization that are deeply embedded in our culture. See Wilhelm von Lenz, *Beethoven et ses trois styles* (St. Petersburg, 1852); and James Webster, "The Concept of Beethoven's 'Early' Period in the Context of Periodization in General," BF 3 (1994), 1. Beethoven's principal chamber works for strings can be easily mapped onto the traditional periodization. Indeed, they fall within three discrete timespans, each between two and five years long. The String Trios op. 8 and op. 9 nos. 1–3, the String Quartets op. 18, and the String Quintet op. 29 date between 1796 and 1801. The Quartets op. 59 nos. 1–3, op. 74, and op. 95 were composed in the five years from 1806 to 1811. The intensely productive period between June 1824 and November 1826 saw the completion of the Quartets opp. 127, 132, 130, 131, and 135. It would be unfruitful, however, to hold too rigidly to this tripartition. The Quintet op. 29,

for instance, belongs chronologically with the early works, but, as I argue below, conceptually with the middle-period quartets.

24 Roland Barthes draws this distinction in "Writing Degree Zero," though he couches it in terms of the difference between "language" (i.e. style in the broad sense) and "style" (i.e. what I am calling "manner"). See Roland Barthes, *A Barthes Reader*, ed. Susan Sontag (New York, 1983), 31–33.

25 Anderson I, no. 63.

26 Among many studies, see Douglas Johnson, "1794–1795: Decisive Years in Beethoven's Early Development," in BS III, 16–17; and Lewis Lockwood, "Beethoven before 1800: The Mozart Legacy," BF 3 (1994), 45.

27 By Joseph Kerman's count, the motive occurs no less than 104 times in the course of 313 bars. Its presence was even more pronounced in the earlier, and somewhat longer, "Amenda" version of the quartet, where it appears 130 times. See Joseph Kerman, *The Beethoven Quartets* (New York, 1966), 32.

28 See Finscher, *Studien zur Geschichte des Streichquartetts I*, 298; and Lockwood, "Beethoven before 1800," 45. For accounts of the points of contact between Mozart's K. 464 and Beethoven's op. 18 no. 5, see Kerman, *The Beethoven Quartets*, 58–63; and Jeremy Yudkin, "Beethoven's 'Mozart' Quartet," JAMS 45 (1992), 30–74.

29 Beethoven's earliest surviving attempts at fugal writing for the quartet medium (Preludes and Fugues, Hess 29–31) date from 1794–95, during his period of contrapuntal study with Johann Albrechtsberger.

30 See Webster, "Traditional Elements," 94–133 for a thorough exposition of this view.

31 See O. G. Sonneck, *Beethoven: Impressions of Contemporaries* (New York, 1926), 31.

32 Kollmann, *An Essay on Practical Musical Composition*, 19. Cf. the commentary in Michael Broyles, "The Two Instrumental Styles of Classicism," JAMS 36 (1983), 226–27. As Broyles also points out, Daniel Gottlob Türk's *Klavierschule* of 1789 even mentions "symphonies" for keyboard instruments.

33 See Winter, "Performing the Beethoven Quartets," 35–36. Schuppanzigh's quartet concerts lasted for only three seasons.

34 Dahlhaus makes a similar point in his analysis of the first movement of op. 59 no. 3. See *Ludwig van Beethoven*, 176–77.

35 For a critical review of the many attempts to account for the movement's form, and a consideration of its ultimate shape in light of Beethoven's revisions of the autograph (like the first movement of the quartet, the Allegretto was originally to have included a massive repeat of its development and recapitulation), see

Lewis Lockwood, "A Problem of Form: the 'Scherzo' of Beethoven's String Quartet in F major op. 59, no. 1," BF 2 (1993), 85–95.

36 For Carl Dahlhaus, lyricism and a more relaxed approach to development characterize the works conceived between Beethoven's heroic, middle phase and his esoteric late period, i.e. op. 74 through op. 97. See *Ludwig van Beethoven*, 203–08. Arguably the elements of what Dahlhaus calls a "transitional" phase were already in place when Beethoven completed the op. 29 quintet in 1801.

37 See AmZ 13 (1811), col. 351; and Elaine R. Sisman, *Haydn and the Classical Variation* (Cambridge, MA, and London, 1993), 242–46.

38 Review of op. 131, AmZ 30 (1828), in Kunze, *Ludwig van Beethoven – Die Werke im Spiegel seiner Zeit*, 572. An essay on Beethoven's late music in *The Penny Magazine* (11 January 1840) carried the same notion to extremes in suggesting that Beethoven's late quartets "are not genuine; that is . . . they have been put together by some enterprising publisher from detached scraps of manuscript found among Beethoven's papers." See Elsie and Denis Arnold, "The View of Posterity: An Anthology," in *The Beethoven Reader*, ed. Denis Arnold and Nigel Fortune (New York, 1971), 504.

39 Theodor Adorno articulated this position in his 1959 essay "Alienated Masterpiece: The *Missa Solemnis*," tr. Duncan Smith, *Telos* 9 (1976–77), 113–24. For a close reading of Beethoven's opp. 127, 130, and 132 grounded in Adorno's thought, see Daniel K. L. Chua, *The "Galitzin" Quartets of Beethoven: opp. 127, 132, 130* (Princeton, 1995).

40 Kerman, *The Beethoven Quartets*, 171.

41 Ibid., 181.

42 See Kinsky-Halm, 397. Beethoven explained his comment in a letter to Schott of 19 August 1826: "You said in your letter that it [op. 131] should be an original quartet. I felt rather hurt; so as a joke I wrote beside the address that it was a bit of patchwork. But it is really *brand new . . .*", Anderson III, no. 1498.

43 See Ludwig van Beethoven, *Supplemente zur Gesamtausgabe*, ed. Willy Hess VIII (Wiesbaden: Breitkopf & Härtel, 1964), 18 and 37; and *Ludwig van Beethoven's Werke*, Series 25 (Leipzig: Breitkopf & Härtel, 1887), 368.

44 Kerman, *The Beethoven Quartets*, 201–02.

45 Review of Anton Bohrer, Piano Trio op. 47, in *NZfM* 5 (1836), 16. Schumann seems to have sensed, if only instinctively, the subtle logic behind Beethoven's interweaving of supremely simple musical ideas with passages of daunting complexity.

46 In Hirschbach's view, this was especially true of opp. 127, 120, 131, and 135. See *NZfM* 11 (1839), 13–14, 49–50.

47 Ibid., 49–50.

48 In his review of the quartet for an 1829 issue of the *Berliner allgemeine musikalische Zeitung*, A. B. Marx related this infamous passage to what he considered to be the *Grundidee* ("basic idea") of the quartet: "the melancholy reminiscence of a bygone and more beautiful time." For Marx, the good humor of the movement is unmasked as a "forced gaiety" approaching "wildness" and "desolation" at the point where the ostinato spins out of control. See Kunze, *Ludwig van Beethoven – Die Werke im Spiegel seiner Zeit*, 595.

49 Klaus Kropfinger has argued most vigorously for this view on the basis of his study of the sketches for op. 130; see his "Das gespaltene Werk–Beethovens Streichquartett op. 130/133," in *Beiträge zu Beethovens Kammermusik: Symposion Bonn 1984*, ed. Sieghard Brandenburg and Helmut Loos (Munich, 1987), 315; and "What Remained Unresolved [Was unerledigt blieb]," MQ 80 (1996), 541–47. Cf. also Kinderman, *Beethoven*, 303–04; and Richard Kramer, "Between Cavatina and Overture: Opus 130 and the Voices of Narrative," BF 1 (1992), 185–89.

50 Stefan Kunze, "Beethovens Spätwerk und seine Aufnahme bei den Zeitgenossen," in *Beiträge zu Beethovens Kammermusik: Symposion Bonn 1984*, 71. The reviewer of the first performance of op. 130 on 21 March 1826 was not alone in finding the *Grosse Fuge* "incomprehensible, like Chinese." See AmZ 28 (1826), 311.

51 See Barbara R. Barry, "Recycling the End of the 'Leibquartett': Models, Meaning, and Propriety in Beethoven's Quartet in B-Flat major Opus 130," JM 13 (1995), 355–76; and Maynard Solomon, "Beethoven's Ninth Symphony: The Sense of an Ending," *Critical Inquiry* 17 (1991), 290–91.

52 Kerman, *The Beethoven Quartets*, 370.

53 For an account of the *Grosse Fuge* as a kind of neo-Baroque *Kunstbuch*, see Warren Kirkendale, "The 'Great Fugue' op. 133: Beethoven's 'Art of Fugue,'" Acta 35 (1963), 14–24.

54 See Kramer, "Between Cavatina and Overture," 172.

55 For a discussion of the importance of the fantasia tradition in Beethoven's earlier chamber music, see Lewis Lockwood, "The Problem of Closure: Some Examples from the Middle-Period Chamber Music," in Lockwood, *Beethoven: Studies in the Creative Process* (Cambridge, MA, and London, 1992), 188. On the *Grosse Fuge* as symphonic poem, see Philip Radcliffe, *Beethoven's String Quartets* (New York, 1968), 138.

56 Friedrich Schlegel argued for a similar "relativization" of the classical poetic genres –

epos, lyric poem, and drama – in the modern literary genre *par excellence*, the novel. See Szondi, "Friedrich Schlegel's Theory of Poetical Genres," 91–93.

57 This was not the only time that Beethoven had second thoughts about the effects of a large movement within a quartet. At one point he contemplated vast repeats of the development and recapitulation (or "seconda parte," to use Beethoven's term) in the first and second movements of op. 59 no. 1, but ultimately rejected this idea. See Lewis Lockwood, "Process versus Limits: A View of the Quartet in F major Opus 59 no. 1," in *Beethoven: Studies in the Creative Process*, 205–08; and "A Problem of Form," in *Beethoven: Studies in the Creative Process*, 90–95. Lockwood also notes that large-scale repeats were added to–and later deleted from–the finale of the same quartet.

10 Sound and structure in Beethoven's orchestral music

It should be noted that my perspective on the subject of this chapter derives primarily from experiences performing the orchestral works in concert.

1 Paul Bekker, *Die Sinfonie von Beethoven bis Mahler* (Berlin, 1918), 10–20, 56–57. See the argument on this notion that stresses, as does Bekker's, the formal and structural role played by the orchestral apparatus: in Peter Gülke, "Zur Bestimmung des Sinfonischen bei Beethoven," *Deutsches Jahrbuch der Musikwissenschaft* (1970), 67–95.

2 See Siegfried Oechsle, *Die Symphonie nach Beethoven: Studien zu Schubert, Schumann, Mendelssohn und Gade* (Kassel, 1992), 18, 25, 27, 30.

3. Johann Georg Sulzer, *General Theory of the Fine Arts* (1771–74), tr. and ed. Thomas Christensen, in *Aesthetics and the Art of Musical Composition in the German Enlightenment*, ed. Nancy K. Baker and Thomas Christensen (Cambridge, 1995), 101, 106–07.

4 E. T. A. Hoffmann, "Review of Spohr's First Symphony" (AmZ 13 [1811]), in *E. T. A. Hoffmann's Musical Writings*. tr. Martyn Clarke, ed. David Charlton (Cambridge, 1989), 272.

5 "Beethoven's Instrumental Music" (in *Kreisleriana*) and "Review of Beethoven's Fifth Symphony," in *E. T. A. Hoffmann's Musical Writings*, 97–100, 238.

6 For Nägeli and the opinions of Fink, Hand, and Schumann see Oechsle, *Die Symphonie*, 31–44.

7 Hoffmann, "Spohr's First Symphony," 285.

8 Carl Dahlhaus, *Ludwig van Beethoven: Approaches to his Music*, tr. Mary Whittall (Oxford, 1991), 50–51, 76–81.

9 Dahlhaus, "Symphonie und Symphonischer Stil um 1850," in *Jahrbuch des Staatlichen Instituts für Musikforschung Preussischer Kulturbesitz 1983/84* (Merseburg, 1984), 43–50.

10 See Bekker, *Sinfonie*, 51.

11 Dahlhaus, *Die Musiktheorie im 18. und 19. Jahrhundert. Zweiter Teil: Deutschland* (Darmstadt, 1989), 234–38.

12 See Felix Weingartner, *Die Symphonie nach Beethoven* (Leipzig, 1909), 2–3.

13 It is interesting to note that many early twentieth-century musical modernists approved of Mahler's re-scoring of Beethoven. See Egon Wellesz's admiring comments on Mahler's changes in the scoring of no. 9 in Egon Wellesz, *Die neue Instrumentation*, 2nd edn., 2 vols. (Berlin, 1928), II, 18–22.

14 A statistical analysis of the repertoire of the Vienna, Boston, Leipzig, and New York orchestras from their inceptions further confirms the relative significance of each of the nine symphonies and the various overtures. In the period 1881–1949 the Boston Symphony Orchestra performed no. 5, 49 times; no. 3, 45 times; no. 7, 42 times; no. 6, 35 times; no. 8, 33 times; no. 4, 34 times; no. 1, 27 times; and no. 2, 26 times. No. 9 was done 33 times in part or entirely. The Vienna Philharmonic between 1842 and 1910 performed no. 5, 35 times; no. 7, 33 times; no. 3, 28 times; no. 8, 25 times; no. 4, 20 times; no. 6, 19 times; no. 2, 14 times; no. 1, 10 times; and no. 9, 24 times. The New York Philharmonic from 1842 to 1930 performed no. 5, 101 times; no. 3, 82 times; No. 7, 68 times; no. 6, 46 times; no. 8, 45 times; no. 4, 32 times; no. 2, 20 times; no. 1, 16 times; and no. 9, 31 times. Finally, at the Leipzig Gewandhaus from 1881 to 1915, no. 5 was performed 34 times; no. 7, 32 times; no. 3, 31 times; no. 8, 25 times; no. 2, 15 times; nos. 1 and 6, 10 times each; and no. 9, 34 times. The sources for these data are M. A. DeWolfe Howe, *The Boston Symphony Orchestra 1881–1931* (Boston, 1931); H. Earle Johnson, *Symphony Hall, Boston* (New York, 1979/1950); Richard von Perger, *Fünfzig Jahre Wiener Philharmoniker 1860–1910* (Vienna, 1910); Henry Krehbiel, James Huneker, and John Erskine, *Early Histories of the New York Philharmonic* (New York, 1979); Howard Shanet, *Philharmonic: A History of New York's Orchestra* (New York, 1975); and *Die Gewandhaus Konzerte zu Leipzig 1781–1981*, ed. Johannes Forner, 2 vols. (Leipzig, 1981).

15 It experienced a serious decline in popularity after 1945 in part as a result of a modernist prejudice on behalf of formalist aesthetics. See Owen Jander, "The Prophetic Conversation in Beethoven's 'Scene by the Brook,'" MQ 77/3 (1993), 508–59; also Mahler's comments on no. 6 in Natalie Bauer-Lechner,

Recollections of Gustav Mahler (Cambridge, 1980), 44–45, 113–14.

16 Its programmatic content, whether connected to Napoleon or Prometheus (in light of the self-quotation in the last movement), has never been held against it. See Dahlhaus, *Ludwig van Beethoven*, 19–29.

17 See Elisabeth Eleanor Bauer, *Wie Beethoven auf den Sockel kam: Die Entstehung eines musikalischen Mythos* (Stuttgart, 1992), 261ff; and Mark Evan Bonds, *After Beethoven: Imperatives of Originality in the Symphony* (Cambridge, MA, 1996), passim, on the role of the Ninth Symphony. For further reading see Andreas Eichhorn, *Beethovens Neunte Symphonie: Die Geschichte ihrer Aufführung und Rezeption* (Kassel, 1993); Nicholas Cook, *Beethoven: Symphony no. 9* (Cambridge, 1993); and David Benjamin Levy, *Beethoven: The Ninth Symphony* (New York, 1995). See also Berlioz's comments on no. 9 cited in Katharine Ellis, *Music Criticism in Nineteenth Century France* (Cambridge, 1995), 104–12, and Karl Goldmark's recollection of Gottfried Preyer's derision of no. 9 in the 1840s at the Vienna Conservatory as a mark of Beethoven's madness in *Notes from the Life of a Viennese Composer* (New York, 1927), 46–48.

18 See Albrecht Riethmüller's essay in *Beethoven: Interpretationen seiner Werke*, ed. Albrecht Riethmüller, Carl Dahlhaus, and Alexander L. Ringer, 2 vols. (Laaber, 1994), II, 34–45.

19 For the most recent basic and detailed information on the nine symphonies see the entries in *Beethoven: Interpretationen*, ed. Riethmüller, Dahlhaus, Ringer. Also see the analyses contained in Donald F. Tovey, *Essays in Musical Analysis: Symphonies and Other Orchestral Works* (New York, 1989), and Gerhart von Westerman, *Knauers Konzertführer*, 3rd edn., with an introduction by Wilhelm Furtwängler (Munich, 1951).

20 Alban Berg, cited in the 1918 manifesto of the Society for Private Musical Performances in Willi Reich, *Alban Berg* (New York, 1965), 49.

21 See Peter Gülke, "Zur Bestimmung," and "The Orchestra as Medium of Realization," MQ 80/2 (1996), 269–75.

22 I am accepting here the traditional nineteenth-century estimate of the novelty of Beethoven's sound. It should be said that late Haydn possesses more than a few striking precedents, not only in *The Seasons*, but in the late symphonies, no. 103 in E♭ foremost among them.

23 See Hector Berlioz–Richard Strauss, *Treatise on Instrumentation* (Huntington LI, n.d.), 177. See also Adam Carse, *The History of Orchestration* (New York, 1925; rpt. 1964),

232–34; and Louis A. Coerne, *The Evolution of Modern Orchestration* (New York, 1908), 53–57.
24 Kent Kennan and Donald Grantham, *The Technique of Orchestration* (Englewood Cliffs, NJ, 1990), 80.
25 C. M. Widor, *Die Technik des modernen Orchesters* (Leipzig, 1904), 30. Widor criticizes Beethoven's scoring for clarinets in a passage in *Egmont*, citing insufficient support for a dissonance in a chord through the use of a single clarinet.
26 Ibid., 48.
27 Ibid., 253.
28 H. Riemann, *Handbuch der Orchestrierung* (Berlin, 1921), 29–36.

11 Beethoven's songs and vocal style
1 Published in AmZ 12 (July 1810).
2 W. H. Wackenroder, *Werke und Briefe* (Heidelberg, 1967), 255. As quoted in Carl Dahlhaus, *Ludwig van Beethoven: Approaches to his Music,* tr. Mary Whittall (Oxford, 1995), 67. Tieck contributed four essays to Wackenroder's *Phantasien über die Kunst* of 1789–99.
3 As translated by Linda Siegel in her *Music in German Romantic Literature* (Novato, CA, 1983), 131.
4 Ibid., 97.
5 See the preface to J. P. A. Schulz's *Lieder im Volkston* of 1782, as quoted by Jack Stein, *Poem and Music in the German Lied from Gluck to Hugo Wolf* (Cambridge, MA, 1971), 28.
6 See Achim von Arnim's *On Folksongs* of 1805, as translated by Siegel, *Music in German Romantic Literature*, 202.
7 Ibid., 43.
8 A comment from the poet and composer C. F. D. Schubart, as quoted in Margaret Mahony Stoljar, *Poetry and Song in Late Eighteenth-century Germany* (London, 1985), 32.
9 See Siegel, *Music in German Romantic Literature*, 43.
10 See Stoljar, *Poetry and Song*, 149.
11 Christopher Reynolds discusses Beethoven's ways of representing ideas via techniques of concealment in "The Representational Impulse in Late Beethoven, I: An die ferne Geliebte," Acta 60 (1988), 43–61. See p. 56 in particular.
12 Friedrich Schiller, *Über naive und sentimentalische Dichtung* (Stuttgart, 1978), 75–77.
13 Ibid., 36.
14 See Douglas Johnson, "1794–1795: Decisive Years in Beethoven's Early Development," BS III, 22–24.
15 Robert Winter, "The Sketches for the 'Ode to Joy,'" in *Beethoven, Performers, and Critics: The International Beethoven Congress, Detroit, 1977,* ed. Winter and Bruce Carr (Detroit, 1980), 184.

16 Ibid., p. 201. See also Maynard Solomon, "Beethoven and Schiller," in *Beethoven, Performers, and Critics,* p. 170.
17 Winter, "The Sketches to the 'Ode to Joy,'" 207.
18 See Joseph Kerman, "Voice," *The Beethoven Quartets* (New York, 1966), 191–222.
19 Richard Wagner, "Opera and Drama," tr. William Ashton Ellis, *Richard Wagner's Prose Works* (London, 1893), II, 290.
20 See Ludwig Misch, "The Upper Pitches of the Voices more through the Instruments," in *Beethoven Studies,* tr. G. I. C. de Courcy (Norman, OK, 1953), 167–69.
21 See *Beethoven: Letters, Journals and Conversations,* ed. Michael Hamburger (London, 1951), 193 and 237.
22 Joseph Kerman, "*An die ferne Geliebte,*" BS I, 154.
23 Ibid., 134.
24 See Barry Cooper, *Beethoven's Folksong Settings: Chronology, Sources, Style* (Oxford, 1994), 198.
25 Ibid., 69–92.
26 See Solomon, *Essays,* 256.
27 Cooper, *Beethoven's Folksong Settings,* 76.
28 Ibid., 203–05.
29 *Beethoven,* ed. Hamburger, 212.
30 See Lorraine Gorrell, *The Nineteenth-century German Lied* (Portland, Oregon, 1993), 97.
31 See Helga Lühning, "Gattungen des Liedes," in *Beiträge zu Beethovens Kammermusik,* ed. Sieghard Brandenburg (Munich, 1987), 191–204, for a full discussion of the overlapping of genres in Beethoven's songs.
32 See Elizabeth Norman McKay, *Franz Schubert: A Biography* (Oxford, 1996), 48.
33 According to Denis Matthews (*Beethoven* [London, 1985], 208), these arias were written for Joseph Lux, a *buffo* singer at the Bonn court.
34 *Beethoven,* ed. Hamburger, 223.
35 See William Kinderman, *Beethoven* (Berkeley, 1995), 139–40.
36 See Stein, *Poem and Music in the German Lied,* 53–54.
37 Dahlhaus, *Ludwig van Beethoven,* 3.
38 Kinderman, *Beethoven,* 147.
39 Schiller, *Über naive und sentimentalische Dichtung,* 4–5.

12 Beethoven's essay in opera: historical, text-critical, and interpretative issues in *Fidelio*
1 At least that is what one normally infers from Beethoven's comment, "Well, I have quickly had an old French libretto adapted and am now beginning to work on it . . ." in his letter to Friedrich Rochlitz of 4 January 1804. Cited after Anderson I, no. 87a. For the original German see BG I, no. 176.

2 The precise chronology of composition over this span of twenty-three months – documented by sketches in the so-called "Eroica" Sketchbook (Kraków, Biblioteka Jagiellonska, Beethoven aut. Landsberg 6) and "Leonore" Sketchbook (SBB, Beethoven Autograph Mendelssohn 15) – is difficult to ascertain and has led to conflicting hypotheses. For opposed interpretations of the evidence see: (1) Alan Tyson, "Das Leonoreskizzenbuch (Mendelssohn 15): Probleme der Rekonstruktion und der Chronologie," BJ 9 (1973/77), 469–99; and (2) Theodore Albrecht, "Beethoven's *Leonore*: A New Compositional Chronology Based on May–August, 1804 Entries in Sketchbook Mendelssohn 15," JM 7 (1989), 165–90. The title *Fidelio* was chosen by the theater authorities over Beethoven's preferred title, *Leonore*, probably to avoid confusion with Ferdinando Paer's *Leonora*, an Italian adaptation of the same story first performed in Dresden on 3 October 1804.

3 For the circumstances of the first performances from the perspective of contemporary observers see Thayer–Forbes I, 386–87, and TDR II, 488–91.

4 A few arias from the opera were performed at a private subscription concert in March 1807 arranged by Beethoven's patron Prince Franz Joseph Maximilian Lobkowitz. See BG I, no. 251, note 4.

5 Early efforts include Otto Jahn's piano–vocal score of the 1806 version, which indicated variants from the first version as well (Leipzig, c. 1853), and Erich Prieger's two publications of his reconstruction of the 1805 version, a piano–vocal score (Leipzig, 1905) and a full score, 2 vols. (Leipzig, 1908 and 1910). The most widely available reconstruction is Willy Hess's edition (in large part a photographic reproduction of Prieger's score) in *Beethoven. Leonore. Oper in drei Aufzügen. Partitur der Urfassung vom Jahre 1805*, vols. XI–XII of *Beethoven. Supplemente zur Gesamtausgabe* (Wiesbaden, 1967). For recent literature on the textual problems of the 1805 version see: Clemens Brenneis, "Beethoven's 'Introduzione del IIdo Atto' und die 'Leonore' von 1805," *Beiträge zur Musikwissenschaft* 32 (1990), 181–203; Michael C. Tusa, "The Unknown Florestan: The 1805 Version of 'In des Lebens Frühlingstagen,'" JAMS 46 (1993), 175–221; and Helga Lühning, "Auf der Suche nach der verlorenen Arie des Florestan," in *Festschrift Christoph-Hellmut Mahling zum 65. Geburtstag*, ed. Axel Beer, Kristina Pfarr, and Wolfgang Ruf, Mainzer Studien zur Musikwissenschaft 37, 2 vols. (Tutzing, 1997), I, 771–94.

6 Oldrich Pulkert, "Die Partitur der zweiten Fassung von Beethovens Oper 'Leonore' im Musikarchiv des Nationaltheaters in Prag,' in *Bericht über den internationalen Beethoven-Kongress 20. bis 23. März 1977 in Berlin*, ed. Harry Goldschmidt, Karl-Heinz Köhler, and Konrad Niemann (Leipzig, 1978), 247–57. See also Lühning, "Auf der Suche nach der verlorenen Arie des Florestan," 779–87. Lühning is currently editing the 1806 version for the complete critical edition of Beethoven's works published by Beethoven-Haus and G. Henle.

7 See Alan Tyson, "The Problem of Beethoven's 'First' *Leonore* Overture," JAMS 28 (1975), 292–334.

8 Treitschke's letters to the theater directors in Darmstadt and Karlsruhe of 20 August 1814 and 10 September 1814, respectively, describe the retention or omission of Leonore's aria as "gleich thunlich" ("equally feasible"). BG III, nos. 731 and 736. See also Manfred Schuler, "Unveröffentlichte Briefe von Ludwig van Beethoven und Georg Friedrich Treitschke. Zur dritten Fassung des 'Fidelio,'" *Die Musikforschung* 35 (1982), 53–62.

9 See Helga Lühning, "Beethovens langer Weg zum 'Fidelio,'" in *Opernkomposition als Prozess*, ed. Werner Breig, Musikwissenschaftliche Arbeiten, 29 (Kassel, 1996), 65–90, especially 82–83. An undated letter from Beethoven to Treitschke from the summer of 1814 (Anderson I, no. 483; BG III, no. 725) reveals that Beethoven contemplated publishing the opera in full score, but Treitschke evidently persuaded the composer that it would be financially more advantageous to sell manuscript copies of the score to the theaters, the normal practice for German opera at the time.

10 See, for instance, the entry in his diary: "Die Oper Fidelio 1814 statt März bis 15ten May neu geschrieben und verbessert" ("The opera *Fidelio* 1814, instead of March, newly written and improved by 15 May"). Cited after Maynard Solomon, "Beethoven's Tagebuch of 1812–1818," in BS III, 224.

11 In addition to the music performed at the three productions there survive two pre-premiere versions of Marzelline's aria, an earlier version of the grave-digging duet, and an incomplete early version of Leonore's aria. For the early versions of Marzelline's aria see *Gesänge mit Orchester*, ed. Willy Hess, vol. II of the *Supplemente zur Gesamtausgabe* (Wiesbaden, 1960), 35–56. For the early versions of Leonore's aria and of the grave-digging duet see *Leonore*, ed. Hess, vol. XII of the *Supplemente zur Gesamtausgabe*, 555–86.

12 A modern edition of Bouilly's libretto is available in Willy Hess, *Das Fidelio-Buch* (Winterthur, 1986), 327–63.

13 Jean-Nicolas Bouilly, *Mes récapitulations* (Paris, 1837); quoted after David Galliver, "*Fidelio* – Fact or Fantasy," *Studies in Music* 15 (1981), 84.

14 For a review of the evidence see Galliver, "*Fidelio* – Fact or Fantasy," 82–92. Further, as David Charlton has shown, scenes of imprisonment and liberation in earlier *opéras-comiques* provided him with numerous models for the treatment of such a topic. See his "The French Theatrical Origins of *Fidelio*," in *Ludwig van Beethoven: Fidelio*, [ed.] Paul Robinson (Cambridge, 1996), 51–67.

15 For a recent discussion of the theme of freedom in *Fidelio* see Paul Robinson, "Fidelio and the French Revolution," in *Ludwig van Beethoven: Fidelio*, 68–100.

16 See Alan Tyson, "Beethoven's Heroic Phase," *Musical Times* 110 (1969), 139–41.

17 Gerhard von Breuning recalled Beethoven's answer to the question as to why he had never written a second opera: "I wished to write another opera but I found no suitable text-book for it. I must have a text which stimulates me; it must be something moral, elevating. Texts which Mozart could compose I would never have been able to set to music. I never have been able to get into the mood for setting lewd texts. I have received many text-books, but as I have said, none which I would wish to have." Quoted after *Beethoven: Impressions of His Contemporaries*, ed. Oscar G. Sonneck (New York, 1926), 206–07.

18 See, for instance, the paraphrase of Kant's *Critique of Practical Reason* that Beethoven copied into one of his conversation books in early 1820: "das moralische / Gesez in unß /, u. der gestirnte / Him[m]el über unß" Kant!!!" CB I, 235.

19 A modern edition of Sonnleithner's libretto is printed by Adolf Sandberger in his *Ausgewählte Aufsätze zur Musikgeschichte*, 2 vols. (Munich, 1921–24), II, 325–65. See also *Ludwig van Beethoven: alle vertonten und musikalisch bearbeiteten Texte*, ed. Kurt Schürmann (Münster, 1980), 27–75.

20 God is not altogether absent in Bouilly's libretto, but it is significant that references to "Dieu" (God) in the published French libretto (e.g. Florestan's Recitative and Romance) become the classical "Dieux" (gods) in Gaveaux's score. Anti-religious sentiment may also help account for the fact that the second solo ascribed to Leonore in Bouilly's libretto, the prayerful *Air* "O toi, mon unique espérance" with its explicit references to the Judaeo-Christian Deity ("Dieu"), was not set by Gaveaux (or at least not included in the published score of 1798).

21 In the memorable formulation by Harry Goldschmidt, "Jacobinian harshness" has been tempered in a "Josephinian" manner; see his "Die Ur-*Leonore*," in *Beethoven. Werkeinführungen* (Leipzig, 1975), 262. In the event the opera was initially rejected by the censors, who probably feared that audiences would understand Pizarro as a negative symbol of the state. To allay their doubts Sonnleithner reminded them, however, that the action had been set in the sixteenth century and that Pizarro's evil actions are a matter of personal revenge; what is more, the Empress herself considered the story one of her favorites. See Thayer–Forbes, 385–86.

22 David Charlton's explication of the ideology of Bouilly's libretto as a critique of the excesses of the Reign of Terror and thus a typical product of the so-called Thermidorian reaction is persuasive; see Charlton, "The French Theatrical Origins," 64–67. But whether Beethoven in 1804–05 understood Bouilly's libretto in this manner is unclear. Certainly the image of Florestan's imprisonment could bring to mind the Bastille and, by association, the idea of revolution against *royal* abuse; hence the censors' concerns about the 1805 libretto.

23 The piece in question, formerly thought to be the March in B♭ (1806/5), is now known to be a piece (WoO 2b) formerly attributed to the incidental music to Christoph Kuffner's tragedy *Tarpeja*. See Brenneis, "Beethoven's 'Introduzione del IIdo Atto,'" 193–200. The fact that the title page of the published 1805 libretto describes the work as "Eine Oper in zwey Aufzügen" further suggests that the division into three acts took place fairly close to the time of the premiere.

24 In his letter of 2 June 1806 to his sister, Eleonore von Breuning, Breuning described the goal of the revisions as to make the action "lebhafter und schneller"; see Wegeler–Ries, 62–63. For a critical edition of the libretto of 1806 see *Leonore. Oper in zwei Aufzügen von Ludwig van Beethoven: Das Libretto der Aufführung von 1806*, ed. Helga Lühning (Bonn, 1996).

25 However, Breuning possibly did prepare a new text for Rocco's aria, since a manuscript score with an alternative text ("Von dem Schlüssel hört erzählen") survives; see Hess, *Das Fidelio-Buch*, 231–32, as well as *Beethoven. Dramatische Werke*, III [= *Supplemente zur Gesamtausgabe*, XIII] (Wiesbaden, 1970), 137 and xxxvi. But the piece was not published in the 1806 libretto, and it was not included in the 1810 piano–vocal score.

26 Martin Ruhnke, "Die Librettisten des *Fidelio*," in *Anna Amalie Abert zum 65.*

Geburtstag. Opernstudien, ed. Klaus Hortschansky (Tutzing, 1975), 131. Another detail of the 1806 libretto that enhances Leonore's symbolic function is the fact that it is she rather than Marzelline (as had been the case in 1805) who releases the prisoners for their daily exercise in the prison garden, thereby reverting to a detail present in Bouilly's libretto that Sonnleithner had changed.

27 See, for instance, Breuning's detailed description of Marzelline's response to Rocco's praise of "Fidelio" in the dialogue leading up to the famous Canon: "Marzelline (welche während dem Lobe, das Rocco Leonoren ertheilte, die größte Theilname hat blicken lassen, und sie mit immer zunehmenden Bewegung liebevoll betrachtet hat . . .)."

28 Whereas Act 2 of the 1805 version starts with the same courtyard setting as the end of Act 1, the corresponding point in the 1806 version (Act 1, scene 4) moves the action to another, more austere, part of the fortress for Pizarro's first appearance.

29 A note in a sketch for a revision of the Marzelline–"Fidelio" duet (SBB, Mendelssohn 15, p. 344), one of the few known sketches for the 1806 version, suggests Beethoven's lead in this textual revision: "hier für Fidelio ein anderer Text, der mit ihr einstimmt . . ." See N II, 454.

30 For Treitschke's reminiscences of the 1814 collaboration with Beethoven see "*Die Zauberflöte. Der Dorfbarbier. Fidelio*. Beitrag zur musikalischen Kunstgeschichte," in *Orpheus. Musikalisches Taschenbuch für das Jahr 1841*, 239–64, especially 259–64. Like all such memoirs published many years after the fact they must be treated with a certain skepticism.

31 As noted above, Beethoven and Treitschke at first had no plans to reinstate Rocco's "gold aria."

32 Heinrich W. Schwab correctly notes, however, that the placement of the duet at the very start of the opera actually increases the audience's sense of stylistic disruption, since it raises expectations that the work will have a light, comical air about it. See "*Fidelio (Leonore)*, op. 72," in *Beethoven. Interpretationen seiner Werke*, ed. Albrecht Riethmüller, Carl Dahlhaus, and Alexander L. Ringer, 2 vols. (Laaber, 1994), I, 548.

33 For a defense of the aria's original ending (or rather, the ending of 1806) on the grounds that it presents a more truthful picture of Florestan see Romain Rolland, *Beethoven the Creator. The Great Creative Epochs. I: From the Eroica to the Appassionata*, tr. Ernest Newman (New York, 1929), 238.

34 In the manuscript libretto that Treitschke prepared for Beethoven (Bonn, Beethoven-Haus, NE 85) the text of Leonore's soliloquy differs significantly from that which Beethoven ultimately set. See Lühning, "Beethovens langer Weg," 69–71.

35 As Ruhnke ("Die Librettiten des *Fidelio*," 134) observes, the *exceptional* nature of their release corresponds better to the awe-filled music with which the prisoners emerge into the open air.

36 Treitschke, "*Die Zauberflöte. Der Dorfbarbier. Fidelio*," 260.

37 For example, see Winton Dean, "Beethoven and Opera," in *The Beethoven Reader*, ed. Denis Arnold and Nigel Fortune (New York, 1971), 366–67.

38 On this problem see Carl Dahlhaus, *Ludwig van Beethoven: Approaches to His Music*, tr. Mary Whittall (Oxford, 1991), 182.

39 For a more extended treatment of Beethoven's compositional approach in *Fidelio*, see my "Music as Drama: Structure, Style, and Process in *Fidelio*," in *Ludwig van Beethoven: Fidelio*, ed. Robinson, 101–31.

40 Schwab, "*Fidelio (Leonore)*, op. 72," 558–59.

41 According to the admittedly unreliable Anton Schindler, Beethoven especially admired *Die Zauberflöte* for the way that Mozart had therein united all of the musical genres from the *Lied* to the chorale and fugue. Schindler (1860), II, 164–65.

42 For a listing of surviving passages from Mozart's works copied in Beethoven's hand see Bathia Churgin, "Beethoven and Mozart's Requiem: A New Connection," JM 5 (1987), 475–76.

43 Philip Gossett, "The Arias of Marzelline: Beethoven as a Composer of Opera," BJ 10 (1978/81), 141–83, especially 172–74. See also my "Beethoven and Opera: The Sketches for the Grave-Digging Duet in *Leonore*," BF 5 (1996), 52–53.

44 As he expressed himself in the letter to Rochlitz of 4 January 1804, "I have finally broken with Schikaneder, whose empire has really been entirely eclipsed by *the light* of the brilliant and attractive French operas . . ." (original emphasis). Anderson I, no. 87a; BG I, no. 176.

45 For the stylistic evidence of Beethoven's dependence on Bouilly see Dean, "Beethoven and Opera," 343–44, and Rainer Cadenbach, "Die 'Leonore' des Pierre Gaveaux – Ein Modell für Beethovens 'Fidelio'?" in *Collegium Musicologicum: Festschrift Emil Platen zum sechzigsten Geburtstag*, ed. Martella Gutiérrez-Denhoff (Bonn, 1986), 100–21.

46 On the Cherubini excerpts, taken from the Act 1 Trio and Finale, see Alan Tyson, "Das

Leonoreskizzenbuch (Mendelssohn 15)," 490. It seems significant that two of the items added by Sonnleithner to Bouilly, the new conclusion of Act 2 (Act 1 of 1806 and 1814) and the great quartet in Act 3 (or Act 2), point to Cherubinian models. With respect to the former, Pizarro's ranting entrance and *Aria con coro* are quite reminiscent of the treatment accorded the villain Dourlinski at the end of Act 2 of *Lodoiska*. And the latter may well have been inspired by the *Morceau d'ensemble et chœur* no. 7 in *Les deux journées*, a frenzied confrontation that, like the original version of the quartet, ends on an unresolved dissonance to signify the lack of dramatic resolution.

47 In the 1805 libretto Leonore's aria occupies the same position as the strophic *romance* "Qu'il ma fallu depuis deux ans" in Bouilly's libretto; moreover, Sonnleithner's first version of the text, transmitted in the printed libretto of 1805, matches the two-stanza structure of the French poem. At some point prior to the premiere, however, Sonnleithner revised the text to facilitate a more typically Italianate structure for the soliloquy. See N II, 447, and Lühning, "Beethovens langer Weg," 67–69. The verses added in this second version, the prayerful quatrain "Komm Hoffnung, laß den letzten Stern," were perhaps inspired by the second solo for Leonore in Bouilly's libretto, the *Air* "O toi, mon unique espérance," a piece that, as mentioned above, does not occur in Gaveaux's published score.

48 See Wolfgang Osthoff, "Beethovens 'Leonoren'-Arien," in *Gesellschaft für Musikforschung. Bericht über den internationalen musikwissenschaftlichen Kongreß Bonn 1970*, ed. Carl Dahlhaus, Hans Joachim Marx, Magda Marx-Weber, and Günther Massenkeil (Kassel, 1973), 191–99.

49 For a discussion of the surviving sketches for the original version of the aria see Tusa, "The Unknown Florestan," 183–94, and Lühning "Auf der Suche nach der verlorenen Arie des Florestan," 787–94.

50 On the problem of "leitmotivic" thinking in Beethoven's opera see Dahlhaus, *Ludwig van Beethoven*, 188–93.

51 A stage instruction added by Treitschke in 1814 has a guard appear atop the wall at this point.

52 In the following discussion of the Trio, the measure numbers refer to Hess's edition of the 1805 version.

53 Dahlhaus, *Ludwig van Beethoven*, 190–93.

54 Peter Gülke, "Kompositorisch genau kalkulierte Unmöglichkeit: Marzelline und Jacquino singen ein Anti-Duett," *Österreichische Musikzeitschrift* 44 (1989), 346–49.

55 For a more detailed discussion of the duet along these lines see my "Beethoven and Opera: The Sketches for the Grave-Digging Duet in *Leonore*," 1–63.

56 For a more extended discussion see Tusa, "Music as Drama: Structure, Style, and Process in *Fidelio*," 127–30.

57 For detailed comparisons of the three versions from the perspective of Alfred Lorenz's theories on musical form see Hess, *Das Fidelio-Buch*, especially 113–225; this material appeared earlier in his *Beethovens Oper Fidelio und ihre drei Fassungen* (Zurich, 1953). Hess's comparisons and conclusions do, however, require some adjustments in the light of the literature cited above in notes 5, 6, and 7.

58 As is well known, this beautiful section of the finale is based upon a movement ("Da stiegen die Menschen ans Licht") from Beethoven's early Cantata on the Death of Emperor Joseph II WoO 87, of 1790.

59 Early reviews noted that the tenor sang badly off-pitch. See Tusa, "The Unknown Florestan," 210–11. Cuts in the 1806 version the Act 2 Trio "Euch werde Lohn" also tend to leave Florestan less exposed.

60 See below, note 67.

61 Hess's score of the 1805 version – basically a photographic reprint of Prieger's – includes a contrabassoon in the duet, but Hess himself notes that the contrabassoon part was added in 1806; see his critical report in the *Supplemente zur Gesamtausgabe*, XIII, xl.

62 The new overture was not ready for the premiere in 1814, at which performance Beethoven substituted one of his older overtures, possibly the one to *The Ruins of Athens*. See Alan Tyson, "Yet Another 'Leonore' Overture?" ML 58 (1977), 201.

63 This revision is anticipated by the piano–vocal score of the 1806 version prepared by Beethoven's student Carl Czerny (Leipzig, 1810), in which Beethoven may have felt that the piece, removed from its theatrical context, required a full cadence for musical closure.

64 Anderson I, no. 481. Sieghard Brandenburg has recently dated the letter prior to 5 April 1814; see BG III, no. 709.

65 The result is frequently, as Winton Dean observes in his classic essay on the opera, an asymmetrical approach to phrase structure that signals a composer on the cusp of his late style. See "Beethoven and Opera," 367.

66 Gossett, "The Arias of Marzelline," 181–82.

67 According to Schindler, Frau Milder-Hauptmann explained to him in 1836 that she had refused to perform the aria in 1814 unless Beethoven rewrote it. Schindler (1860), I, 135–36.

68 For other instances where the declamation of 1814 seems significantly improved see Pizarro's aria (the word "morden" at m. 39), the prisoners' chorus in the Act 1 finale (the phrase "eine Gruft" at mm. 38–39 and the word "frei" at m. 86), and the Adagio of Florestan's aria (the phrase "Wahrheit wagt' ich kühn zu sagen" at mm. 61–62).

69 For comparisons of the various versions see Helga Lühning, "B oder H? Über Beethovens Revisionen des Quartetts 'Er sterbe,'" in 35. *Beethovenfest Bonn: Das Buch zum Programm* (Bonn, 1997), especially 75–82, and Schwab, "*Fidelio* (*Leonore*), op. 72," 555–58. In this respect the substitution of B♭ for B♮ at m. 92 (a feature already adumbrated in the 1810 piano–vocal score), seems a rare *lessening* of dramatic impact in the 1814 version.

70 See above, note 17. For a summary of Beethoven's abortive operatic plans see Dean, "Beethoven and Opera," 381–86.

71 "Opern und alles seyn lassen nur für deine Weise schreiben . . ." Solomon, "Beethoven's Tagebuch of 1812–1818," 253.

13 Probing the sacred genres: Beethoven's religious songs, oratorio, and masses

1 See Maynard Solomon, "The Quest for Faith," in his *Beethoven Essays* (Cambridge, MA, 1988), 216–29 and 348–51 (notes to the chapter); and Siegfried Kross, "Beethoven und die rheinisch-katholische Aufklärung," in his *Beethoven: Mensch seiner Zeit* (Bonn, 1980), 9–35.

2 His own copy (Reutlingen 1811 edition; today SBB, Mus. ms. Beethoven autogr. 40,2) contains numerous annotations.

3 Günther Massenkeil, "6 Klavierlieder op. 48," in *Beethoven: Interpretationen seiner Werke*, ed. Albrecht Riethmüller, Carl Dahlhaus, and Alexander Ringer (Laaber, 1994), I, 343ff.

4 See Max Friedlaender, *Das deutsche Lied im 18. Jahrhundert: Quellen und Studien*, 2 vols. (repr. Hildesheim, 1962), II, 55–57, 494 (statistics), and 527 (supplement).

5 See Helga Lühning, *Beethoven Werke. Gesamtausgabe, Abt. XII Bd. 1: Beethoven. Lieder und Gesänge mit Klavierbegleitung. Kritischer Bericht* (Munich, 1990), 24f.

6 See, for example, op. 48 no. 4, mm. 19ff.; *Adelaide* op. 46, mm. 32ff.; "Abendlied unterm gestirnten Himmel" WoO 150, mm. 10ff. and 44f.; Ninth Symphony, Finale, e.g. at the words, "über Sternen muß er wohnen" (Adagio ma non troppo, ma divoto); various passages in the *Missa solemnis*, where the text suggests the human apprehension of God. The musical idea is transformed from word-painting, especially in the earlier works, to a symbol for the

incomprehensible surmounting of the human horizon (above all, in the late works); see Lodes, *Das Gloria in Beethovens Missa solemnis* (Tutzing, 1997), 113–21.

7 Theodore Albrecht argues that Beethoven had already begun the composition in October 1802. See "The Fortnight Fallacy: A Revised Chronology for Beethoven's *Christ on the Mount of Olives*, op. 85, and the Wielhorsky Sketchbook," *Journal of Musicological Research* 11 (1991), 263–84. Beethoven himself emphasized the short gestation period several times in letters.

8 Beethoven presumably had a decisive part in developing the libretto with Franz Xaver Huber.

9 Barry Cooper, "Beethoven's Oratorio and the Heiligenstadt Testament," *The Beethoven Journal* 10 (1995), 20.

10 According to Josef Blöchlinger, Beethoven expressed the view around 1819 that "Christ is nothing but a crucified Jew" (Theodor von Frimmel, *Beethoven-Studien*, 2 vols. [Munich and Leipzig, 1905–06], II, 117); Beethoven's conversation with his nephew at the beginning of September 1823 can be interpreted similarly (CB IV, 102).

11 Sieghard Brandenburg, "Beethovens Oratorium *Christus am Ölberg*. Ein unbequemes Werk," in *Beiträge zur Geschichte des Oratoriums seit Händel: Festschrift Günther Massenkeil zum 60. Geburtstag*, ed. Rainer Cadenbach and Helmut Loos (Bonn, 1986), 215f.

12 For a detailed account, see Alan Tyson, "The 1803 Version of Beethoven's *Christus am Oelberge*," MQ 56 (1970), 551–84.

13 The third and fourth lines must be "Schlagt links den Weg nur ein. Er muß ganz nahe sein" (Beethoven to Breitkopf & Härtel on 28 January 1812; BG II, no. 545; Anderson I, no. 345).

14 AmZ 14 (1812); in *Ludwig van Beethoven: Die Werke im Spiegel seiner Zeit*, ed. Stefan Kunze (Laaber, 1987), 234.

15 Ibid., 240; from AmZ 14 (1812).

16 Ibid., 237–39; from *Berliner allgemeine musikalische Zeitung* 4 (1828).

17 Jeremiah Walker R. McGrann, *Beethoven's Mass in C, Opus 86: Genesis and Compositional Background*, 2 vols. (Ph.D. diss., Harvard University, 1991; Ann Arbor, 1993), 205–14.

18 Johann Harich, "Beethoven in Eisenstadt," in *Joseph Haydn und seine Zeit: Festschrift anläßlich der 150. Wiederkehr des Todestages von Joseph Haydn, Bürgenländische Heimatblätter* 21/2 (1959), 179.

19 See Birgit Lodes, "'Von Herzen – möge es wieder – zu Herzen gehn!' Zur Widmung von Beethovens *Missa solemnis*," in *Altes im Neuen: Festschrift Theodor Göllner zum 65. Geburtstag*,

ed. Bernd Edelmann and Manfred Hermann Schmid (Tutzing, 1995), 295–306.

20 For an account of the genesis see Robert Winter, "Reconstructing Riddles: The Sources for Beethoven's *Missa Solemnis*," in *Beethoven Essays: Studies in Honor of Elliot Forbes*, ed. Lewis Lockwood and Phyllis Benjamin (Cambridge, MA, 1984), 217–50.

21 Compare letters from 13 November 1821 to Schlesinger, 5 June 1822 to Peters, and 10 March 1824 to Schott and H. A. Probst.

22 Letter to Breitkopf & Härtel: BG II, no. 484; Anderson I, no. 294. Translation modified from Anderson.

23 See Andreas Friesenhagen, *Die Messen Ludwig van Beethovens: Studien zur Vertonung des liturgischen Textes zwischen Rhetorik und Dramatisierung* (Cologne, 1996), 107–21.

24 In his review of the C major Mass, E. T. A. Hoffmann criticized this "utterly strange modulation": "The reviewer cannot exactly recommend imitating this modulation"; AmZ 15 (1813), quoted from *Ludwig van Beethoven*, ed. Kunze, 257.

25 Rudolf Stephan, "Messe C-Dur op. 86," in *Beethoven: Interpretationen*, ed. Riethmüller, Dahlhaus, and Ringer, II, 6.

26 Reviewer in the AmZ 17 (1815); quoted from *Ludwig van Beethoven*, ed. Kunze, 249.

27 Beethoven to J. A. Streicher on 19 September 1824; BG V, no. 1875; Anderson III, no. 1307. Translation modified from Anderson.

28 For a lucid discussion of the formal and symphonic dimensions of the Kyrie (and all other movements) of the *Missa solemnis* see William Drabkin, *Beethoven: Missa solemnis* (Cambridge, 1991).

29 See Warren Kirkendale, "New Roads to Old Ideas in Beethoven's *Missa solemnis*," MQ 56 (1970), 666ff.

30 See Thrasybulos Georgiades, "Zu den Satzschlüssen der Missa Solemnis," in *Gesellschaft für Musikforschung. Bericht über den internationalen musikwissenschaftlichen Kongreß Bonn 1970*, ed. Carl Dahlhaus, Hans Joachim Marx, Magda Marx-Weber, and Günther Massenkeil (Kassel, 1973), 37–42.

31 For the Gloria, see Birgit Lodes, "'When I try, now and then, to give musical form to my turbulent feelings': The Human and the Divine in the Gloria of Beethoven's *Missa solemnis*," in BF 6 (1998), 143–79; for the Credo and Benedictus, see William Kinderman, "Beethoven's Symbol for the Deity in the Missa Solemnis and the Ninth Symphony," 19CM 9 (1985), 102–08.

32 The juxtaposition of contrasting images is already remarkable in the Credo of the C major Mass (unlike, for example, Haydn's "Nelson" Mass [Hob. HXII:11] and *Missa in tempore belli* [Hob. HXII:9], the opening section, mm. 1–130, is not held together by either continuous instrumental motion or unified dynamics); compare, as well, the powerfully expressive, often "dramatic" setting of individual statements (e.g. "et expecto," mm. 268ff.), which usually arises from the declamation of the text (see also "genitum, non factum," mm. 68–71).

33 Carl Dahlhaus, *Ludwig van Beethoven: Approaches to his Music*, tr. Mary Whittall (Oxford, 1991), 201.

34 A possible source of inspiration was the "Pie Jesu" from Luigi Cherubini's C minor Requiem, a work which Beethoven treasured; see Birgit Lodes, "Requiem in der Zeit der schönen Tode," in *Messe und Motette*, Handbuch der musikalischen Gattungen 9, ed. Horst Leuchtmann and Siegfried Mauser (Laaber, 1998), 297.

35 Theodor Göllner, "'Et incarnatus est' in Beethovens Missa solemnis," *Annuario musical* 43 (1988), 189–99.

36 Drabkin, *Beethoven: Missa solemnis*, 100; Walter Riezler, *Beethoven* (London, 1938), 190.

37 McGrann, *Mass in C*, 409–13.

38 See Beethoven's note above the Dona section (mm. 96ff.), "Bitte um innern und äußern Frieden" ("Prayer for inner and outward peace"), which in the sketches (Artaria 201, 79) and the autograph (leaf 11) still reads: "Dona nobis pacem representing *inner and outer peace*"; from William Drabkin, "The Sketches and Autographs for the Later Movements of Beethoven's *Missa solemnis*," BF 2 (1993), 129.

39 Drabkin, *Beethoven: Missa solemnis*, 93f.

40 The source is a German edition (Landshut, 1831), a translation of the French tenth edition. I am grateful to Professor Friedrich W. Riedel for having drawn my attention to this work.

41 Similarly Thomas a Kempis, *Nachfolge Christi*, Book 3, Chapters 23 ("Four things produce great joy"), 25 ("What constitutes lasting peace of mind and true progress"), and 42 ("Do not build your peace on people"). Beethoven owned the book in a Reutlingen edition.

42 Lombez, *Ueber den innern Frieden*, 355f.

43 Ibid., 355.

44 That the conception of the *Missa solemnis* is relevant for the understanding of other late works can only be suggested here: Beethoven interrupted composition on it after he had already worked out most of the Agnus (except for the conclusion) in order to compose his final two piano sonatas, opp. 110 and 111. See William Drabkin, "The Agnus Dei of Beethoven's *Missa Solemnis*: The Growth of Its

Form," in *Beethoven's Compositional Process*, ed. William Kinderman (Lincoln, NB and London, 1991), 156. The fugue subject in op. 110 is closely connected in its motivic material with the fugue subject of the Gloria and the "pacem" theme of the Agnus in the *Missa solemnis*. By interlocking the powerfully expressive slow movement and the fugue Beethoven seems to want to convey the message of the Agnus in purely instrumental music: the solitary sorrowful human of the Adagio ma non troppo finally finds hymn-like transcendence in (inner and outer) peace.

45 This is documented in Beethoven's autograph copy of the text for the Mass Ordinary (SBB, Mus. Ms autogr. 35,25). The German translation entered next to the Latin text comes from Ignaz Aurelius Fessler, *Ansichten von Religion und Kirchentum*, 3 vols. (Berlin, 1805), II, 404–49. For the translation of individual words, Beethoven drew on the Latin–German dictionary by Immanuel Johann Gerhard Schmeller (SBB, Mus. Ms autogr. 40,8), which was also in his possession.

46 German original: "Ist das ästhet. Problem der M.s. das der Nivellierung aufs Allgemein-Menschliche?" See Fragment 298 (1957) from Theodor W. Adorno, *Beethoven: Philosophie der Musik. Fragmente und Texte*, ed. Rolf Tiedemann (Frankfurt am Main, 1993), 203. More on the topic appeared in his radio talk written the same year, "Verfremdetes Hauptwerk – Zur *Missa Solemnis*," in ibid., 204–22, especially 214–16.

47 In addition to the studies by the two authors already cited, see William Kinderman, "Beethoven's Compositional Models for the Choral Finale of the Ninth Symphony," in *Beethoven's Compositional Process*, 160–88.

14 "With a Beethoven-like sublimity": Beethoven in the works of other composers

I would like to thank Richard Boursy for his comments on this chapter.

1 Charles Ives, *Essays Before a Sonata and Other Writings*, ed. Howard Boatwright (New York, 1961), 36.

2 Richard Wagner, *My Life*, tr. Andrew Gray, ed. Mary Whittall (New York, 1983), 35–36. For Wagner's reception of Beethoven, see Klaus Kropfinger, *Wagner and Beethoven*, tr. Peter Palmer (Cambridge, 1991).

3 Leo Treitler, "History, Criticism, and Beethoven's Ninth Symphony," 19CM 3 (1980), 195.

4 The Ninth's choral finale has assumed a more central position in subsequent music

history than its opening. Exploiting Beethoven's prestige, Wagner construed the introduction of voices as pointing toward the music drama as the "symphony" of the future. Expanding on a point originally made by Friedrich Chrysander in an early review, several recent authors have interpreted the reference to the "Ode to Joy" and subsequent events in the finale of Brahms's First Symphony as a detailed refutation of Wagner's claim and a deliberate validation of the purely instrumental symphony. See, for example, Mark Evan Bonds, *After Beethoven: Imperatives of Originality in the Symphony* (Cambridge, MA, 1996), 138–74. Beethoven's Ninth also inspired a wide variety of choral symphonies, including Mendelssohn's *Lobgesang*, Franz Liszt's *Faust* Symphony, and Gustav Mahler's Eighth (among others).

5 Theodor W. Adorno, *Alban Berg: Master of the Smallest Link*, tr. Juliane Brand and Christopher Hailey (Cambridge, 1991), 110; Robert P. Morgan, "The Eternal Return: Retrograde and Circular Form in Berg," in *Alban Berg: Historical and Analytical Perspectives*, ed. David Gable and Robert P. Morgan (Oxford, 1991), 147–49.

6 See, for example, Adorno, *Alban Berg*, 76.

7 Natalie Bauer-Lechner, *Recollections of Gustav Mahler*, tr. Dika Newlin, ed. Peter Franklin (London, 1980), 157–58.

8 Ibid.

9 For a recent treatment of the Sixth Symphony, see Richard Will, "Time, Morality, and Humanity in Beethoven's *Pastoral* Symphony," JAMS 50 (1997), 271–329.

10 Along with various inanimate phenomena, Knecht's heading does mention a whistling shepherd and the "sweet voice" of a shepherdess, but it presents the entire scene as viewed from the outside. As is well known, Beethoven entered the words "Mehr Ausdruck der Empfindung als Malerei" ("More expression of feeling than tone-painting") in his autograph for the symphony. This touches on an important issue in German aesthetics at the time: whether music is an imitative or expressive art. See Walter Serauky, *Die musikalische Nachahmungsästhetik in Zeitraum von 1700 bis 1850* (Münster-in-Westfalen, 1929).

11 Richard Wagner, "Beethoven," *Gesammelte Schriften und Dichtungen*, 3rd edn., 10 vols. (Leipzig, 1897), IX, 61–126. See also Carl Dahlhaus, *The Idea of Absolute Music*, tr. Roger Lustig (Chicago, 1989), 132–33.

12 D. Kern Holoman, "Berlioz," in *The Nineteenth-Century Symphony*, ed. D. Kern Holoman (New York, 1997), 109 and 136 n. 6;

Judith Silber Ballan, "Marxian Programmatic Music: A Stage in Mendelssohn's Musical Development," in *Mendelssohn Studies,* ed. R. Larry Todd (Cambridge, 1992), 149–61; R. Larry Todd, *Mendelssohn: The Hebrides and Other Overtures* (Cambridge, 1993), 70–71.

13 *Memoirs of Hector Berlioz, Member of the French Institute, Including His Travels in Italy, Germany, Russia and England, 1803–1865,* tr. and ed. David Cairns (New York, 1969), 104.

14 Hector Berlioz, *A Critical Study of Beethoven's Nine Symphonies,* tr. Edwin Evans (London, 1958), 19.

15 See the related discussion in Aaron Copland, "Berlioz Today," reprinted in *Fantastic Symphony,* ed. Edward T. Cone (New York, 1971), 298 and 300.

16 Nicholas Temperley, "The *Symphonie fantastique* and Its Program," MQ 57 (1971), 597.

17 See the letter from Mendelssohn to his mother of 15 March 1931; quoted in *Fantastic Symphony,* ed. Cone, 282.

18 Friedhelm Krummacher, *Mendelssohn – Der Komponist: Studien zur Kammermusik für Streicher* (Munich, 1978), 87–88.

19 A number of writers have pointed out the resemblances, including Joscelyn Godwin, "Early Mendelssohn and Late Beethoven," ML 55 (1974), 280–84; Philip Radcliffe, *Mendelssohn,* 2nd edn. (London, 1976), 93–94; Krummacher, *Mendelssohn – der Komponist,* 192 and 218; Wulf Konold, *Felix Mendelssohn Bartholdy und seine Zeit* (Regensburg, 1984), 111–38; Charles Rosen, *The Romantic Generation* (Cambridge, MA, 1995), 574–80.

20 *Bref till Adolf Fredrik Lindblad från Mendelssohn, Dohrn, Almqvist, Atterbom, Geiger, Fredrika Bremer, C. W. Bottiger och Andra* (Stockholm, 1913), 19–20, quoted in Krummacher, *Mendelssohn – der Komponist,* 72.

21 *Bref till Lindblad från Mendelssohn,* 20; quoted in Krummacher, *Mendelssohn – der Komponist,* 87.

22 Igor Stravinsky, *Poetics of Music in the Form of Six Lessons,* tr. Arthur Knodel and Ingolf Dahl (New York, 1947), 79.

23 Wagner, "Zukunftsmusik," *Gesammelte Schriften,* VII, 127.

24 See, for example, Carl Dahlhaus, *Nineteenth-Century Music,* tr. J. Bradford Robinson (Berkeley and Los Angeles, 1989), 255–57.

25 See, for example, Margaret Notley, "Discourse and Allusion: The Chamber Music of Brahms," in *Nineteenth-Century Chamber Music,* ed. Stephen E. Hefling (New York, 1998), 253–54.

26 Arnold Schoenberg, "Brahms the Progressive," *Style and Idea,* tr. Leo Black, ed. Leonard Stein (Berkeley and Los Angeles, 1975), 398–441. Schoenberg discusses motivic features of Beethoven's op. 95 at 423–24.

27 Erwin Stein, "Das gedankliche Prinzip in Beethovens Musik und seine Auswirkung bei Schönberg," *Musikblätter des Anbruch* 9 (1927), 117–21. On the rejection of Beethoven by many other composers in the 1920s, see Hans Heinrich Eggebrecht, *Zur Geschichte der Beethoven-Rezeption* (Laaber, 1994), 13–33.

28 Stein, "Das gedankliche Prinzip," 117–19.

29 From Schoenberg's own analysis of his quartets, reprinted in *Schoenberg, Berg, Webern: The String Quartets, A Documentary Study,* ed. Ursula von Rauchhaupt (Hamburg, 1971), 42 and 36. See also Fred Steiner, "A History of the First Complete Recording of the Schoenberg String Quartets," *Journal of the Arnold Schoenberg Institute* 2 (1977–78), 132, where Schoenberg cites Liszt's Piano Sonata and symphonies by Bruckner and Mahler, along with op. 131 again.

30 *Schoenberg, Berg, Webern,* ed. Rauchhaupt 36 and 39.

31 This scheme summarizes Schoenberg's analysis in ibid., 39–42. Although Schoenberg stresses Beethoven's C♯ minor quartet as an influence, a connection with Liszt's Piano Sonata is more obvious.

32 Robert P. Morgan, "Coda as Culmination: The First Movement of the 'Eroica' Symphony," in *Music Theory and the Exploration of the Past,* ed. Christopher Hatch and David W. Bernstein (Chicago, 1993), 360.

33 On this feature in the *Eroica* first movement, see Lewis Lockwood, "'Eroica' Perspectives: Strategy and Design in the First Movement," in BS II, 96–99; see, as well, Schoenberg, "Heart and Brain in Music," in *Style and Idea,* 64–66.

34 That the whole-tone formations function as quasi-dominants becomes patent in this passage, which culminates in the dominant of C♯ minor.

35 Pierre Boulez, for example, cited this fugue and that in the "Hammerklavier" Sonata as "rare examples of counterpoint 'rebelling' against the increasing claims of harmonic functions." See *Orientations,* tr. Martin Cooper, ed. Jean-Jacques Nattiez (Cambridge, MA, 1986), 255. And see the remarks by Stravinsky below.

36 Stein, "Das gedankliche Prinzip," 119.

37 Stephen Walsh, *The Music of Stravinsky* (Oxford, 1988), 130.

38 Igor Stravinsky and Robert Craft, *Dialogues and a Diary* (London, 1968), 124.

39 Stravinsky and Craft, *Dialogues,* 43. I am

grateful to Richard Wilson for suggesting that I
look at this concerto and lending me a score.
40 Leonard B. Meyer, *Style and Music: Theory,
History, and Ideology* (Philadelphia, 1989), 304.
41 Review, "Stravinsky's Late Beethoven," from
New York Herald Tribune of 23 March 1944;
reprinted in Virgil Thomson, *The Musical Scene*
(New York, 1945), 100–01.
42 Ibid.
43 Eric Walter White, *Stravinsky: The Composer
and His Works* (London and Boston, 1979), 391.
In a talk after the first performance of the
Concerto for Two Pianos, Stravinsky referred to
the work as in three movements, indicating that
for him the third and fourth constituted one
movement. White reprints this talk in his
Appendix A as item 6, 581–85.
44 For a discussion of Brahms's preoccupation
with "logic" in music, see Margaret Notley,
"Brahms as Liberal: Genre, Style, and Politics in
Late Nineteenth-Century Vienna," 19CM 17
(1993), 113–15.
45 Nicholas Marston, "Schumann's Monument
to Beethoven," 19CM 14 (1991), 248 n. 4.
46 Rosen, *The Romantic Generation*, 103.
47 Nicholas Marston, *Schumann: Fantasie,
op. 17* (Cambridge, 1992), 1–22.
48 Ibid.
49 Ibid.
50 Elizabeth Wilson quotes a conversation
between Shostakovich and Druzhinin in
Shostakovich: A Life Remembered (London,
1994), 470.
51 Birgit Lodes reevaluates the evidence for
this position in "Richard Strauss' Skizzen zu
den 'Metamorphosen' und ihre Beziehung zu
'Trauer um München,'" *Die Musikforschung* 47
(1994), 234–52. I am also grateful to Bryan
Gilliam for our conversation about this
composition.
52 Timothy L. Jackson, "The Metamorphosis of
the *Metamorphosen*: New Analytical and
Source-Critical Discoveries," in *Richard Strauss:
New Perspectives on the Composer and His Work*,
ed. Bryan Gilliam (Durham, NC, 1992), 195.
53 For an account of the complex chronology,
see Geoffrey Block, *Ives: Concord Sonata: Piano
Sonata no. 2 ("Concord, Mass., 1840–1860")*
(Cambridge, 1996), 29–30.
54 Ives, *Essays Before a Sonata*, xxv.
55 Ibid., 36.
56 Thus, Mozart's C minor piano sonata is
often anachronistically termed "Beethovenian,"
as in Alfred Einstein, *Mozart: His Character, His
Work*, tr. Arthur Mendel and Nathan Broder
(New York, 1945), 247. For Schubert's reception
of Beethoven, see Edward T. Cone, "Schubert's
Beethoven," MQ 56 (1970), 779–93.
57 Peter Heyworth, "The First Fifty Years," in

Pierre Boulez: A Symposium, ed. William Glock
(London and New York, 1986), 12.
58 Charles Rosen, "The Piano Music," in
Boulez: A Symposium, 91, asserts that "the use of
op. 106 signifies an aspiration to the sublime in
the academic sense" and notes the well-known
reference to Beethoven's sonata at the
beginning of Brahms's C major piano sonata
(his op. 1!).
59 Pierre Boulez, *Conversations with Célestin
Deliège* (London, 1973), 41.
60 The Beethovenian scherzo has more
frequently been discussed for its impact on
subsequent composers.
61 See, for example, Glenn Watkins, *Soundings:
Music in the Twentieth Century* (New York,
1988), 408–10.
62 See, for example, Steven D. Block, "George
Rochberg: Progressive or Master Forger?"
Perspectives of New Music 20 (1981–82), 407–09.

15 Beethoven's music in performance: historical perspectives

1 A provocative commentator on this
development has been Richard Taruskin, most
notably in a pair of essays, "The New Antiquity"
and "Resisting the Ninth," which appeared
originally in 1987 and 1989 respectively and
have recently been reprinted in revised form in
Taruskin's collection *Text and Act: Essays on
Music and Performance* (New York and Oxford,
1995), 202–24 and 235–61.
2 A representative sampling of the types of
work currently being pursued in this area can
be found in *The Practice of Performance: Studies
in Musical Interpretation*, ed. John Rink
(Cambridge, 1995).
3 I shall not attempt to deal here with
Beethoven's vocal or choral works: important as
they are within his oeuvre, they are mostly
peripheral to the main historical trends in
performing his music, which have been driven
by his pre-eminence as an instrumental
composer. There is, not surprisingly, a large
literature on performance practice in
Beethoven. The most recent volume on the
subject is *Performing Beethoven*, ed. Robin
Stowell, Cambridge Studies in Performance
Practice 4 (Cambridge, 1994). Perhaps the most
detailed study to focus on one particular area of
the composer's output is William S. Newman,
*Beethoven on Beethoven: Playing His Piano
Music His Way* (New York and London, 1988). A
useful summary of the main issues involved is
provided by Anne-Louise Coldicott in *The
Beethoven Compendium*, ed. Barry Cooper
(London, 1991), 280–89.
4 Beethoven was also a competent violinist,
and in his youth played viola in the court

orchestra at Bonn. See Clive Brown, "Ferdinand David's Editions of Beethoven," in *Performing Beethoven*, ed. Stowell, 117–18.

5 These were first published by A. Diabelli, Vienna, in (?)1842, and have been reprinted in a modern facsimile edition, edited by Paul Badura-Skoda, as *Über den richtigen Vortrag der sämtlichen Beethoven'schen Klavierwerke: Czerny's "Erinnerungen an Beethoven" sowie das 2. and 3. Kapitel des IV. Bandes der "Vollständigen theoretisch-practischen Pianoforte-Schule op. 500."* (Vienna, 1963).

6 Polish pianist Theodor Leschetizky (1830–1915) was one of the most influential teachers of the nineteenth century.

7 A searching recent examination of Czerny's writings on and editions of Beethoven is George Barth, *The Pianist as Orator: Beethoven and the Transformation of Keyboard Style* (Ithaca and London, 1992), especially chap. 3. Another important figure in the early performance history of Beethoven's music was pianist and composer Ignaz Moscheles; although only briefly associated with Beethoven, in his edition of the piano sonatas published during the 1830s he claimed to supply metronome markings that reproduced exactly Beethoven's own tempi. The notion of an authentic performing legacy no doubt conferred an air of legitimacy to the many "traditional" modifications and accretions to Beethoven's scores in performance that became established in the course of the nineteenth century.

8 One should not, however, lay too great a stress on the deafness issue. Despite the fact that it obviously left Beethoven unable to cope with such questions as orchestral balance in an actual performance, the virtual sound-world in his mind's ear seems to have remained astonishingly vivid throughout his life: witness the daringly imaginative textures of the late quartets. Hungarian violinist Joseph Böhm, who in 1825 rehearsed the Quartet op. 127 under Beethoven's supervision, recalled his great sensitivity to visual indications such as bow movements, "from which he was able to judge the smallest fluctuations in tempo and rhythm"; quoted in Thayer–Forbes, 941.

9 Barry Cooper has recently suggested that even dealing with the most apparently solid state of his music, the work as notated, Beethoven could take a fluid approach, with several divergent sources offering equally valid versions of a work, sometimes occasioned by alterations made for particular performances: see "Beethoven's Revisions to his Fourth Piano Concerto," in *Performing Beethoven*, ed. Stowell, 33.

10 I exclude from this category present-day performances using period instruments and/or playing styles.

11 Although Beethoven can hardly have relished the exact parity of the 15 strings and 15 wind employed in the first performance of the *Eroica* symphony in Prince Lobkowitz's palace: see Eva Badura-Skoda, "Performance Conventions in Beethoven's Early Works," in *Beethoven, Performers, and Critics: The International Beethoven Congress, Detroit, 1977*, ed. Robert Winter and Bruce Carr (Detroit, 1980), 73.

12 For a more detailed account of orchestral and general concert conditions see Mary Sue Morrow, *Concert Life in Haydn's Vienna: Aspects of a Developing Musical and Social Institution*, Sociology of Music 7 (Stuyvesant, NY, 1989). Although the issue is of only marginal interest for the present discussion, it should be noted that Viennese musical life was not limited by the simple dichotomy of public versus private but embraced many shades in between, affecting audience makeup, performance personnel, venue etc.

13 BG III, no. 903; Anderson II, no. 560.

14 See Philip Whitmore, *Unpremeditated Art: The Cadenza in the Classical Keyboard Concerto* (Oxford, 1991), 201. Beethoven may have felt that whereas in a cadenza the performer's contribution was clearly set apart from the rest of the work, embellishments of the kind added by Czerny were to the average listener indistinguishable from the composer's original text.

15 For a broad view of Beethoven's place in the composer-performer culture of his day see Glenn Stanley, "Genre Aesthetics and Function: Beethoven's Piano Sonatas in their Cultural Context," BF 6 (1998), 1–29. On Beethoven as pianist (and teacher) see the useful summary in Newman, *Beethoven on Beethoven*, 76–82; even after deafness began to undermine his playing – from around 1809 he performed only occasionally in public – he was renowned for his improvisations. Indeed, he preferred improvisation to playing his published sonatas and other works, the performance of which he entrusted instead to pupils such as Czerny and Ries.

16 And impulsiveness had its dangers, even for Beethoven. As early as c. 1799–1800, before deafness began to affect Beethoven's playing, fellow virtuoso J. B. Cramer reported that, "one day he would play [a composition] with great spirit and expression, but the next day it would sound moody and often muddled to the point of unclarity"; this is recorded by Anton Schindler in Schindler–MacArdle, 413, and quoted in Newman, *Beethoven on Beethoven*,

80. Such impressions were not untypical: on this issue the often unreliable Schindler is supported by other sources.

17 As was the practice of the time, in both situations Beethoven directed in conjunction with the principal violinist, a dual control that in Beethoven's case was essential given his deficiencies as a conductor.

18 For a digest of the most famous reports of Beethoven's conducting see Elliot W. Galkin, *A History of Orchestral Conducting: In Theory and Practice* (New York, 1988), 543–49.

19 See Schindler–MacArdle, 423n.

20 Letter to the publisher Schott, dating from the second half of December 1826, in which Beethoven promised to send metronome marks for the Ninth Symphony (BG VI, no. 2244; Anderson II, no. 1545).

21 On Beethoven's early involvement with the metronome – or chronometer, as it was then called – see Thayer–Forbes, 686–88. A useful summary of the principal issues and scholarship concerning Beethoven and the metronome can be found in Newman, *Beethoven on Beethoven*, 83–99. Beethoven had intended to provide metronome marks for the last five string quartets, but died before he could do so. Except for the "Hammerklavier," Beethoven supplied no markings for the piano sonatas. Czerny attempted to make good this omission by publishing metronome marks for all the sonatas after Beethoven's death, claiming to be reproducing "authentic" tempi stemming from the composer; but since he produced several different sets during his lifetime, in some cases diverging quite significantly from one another, this claim is rendered highly dubious: see Barth, *The Pianist as Orator*, 61–62.

22 See Taruskin, "The New Antiquity," 218.

23 See Thayer–Forbes, 687–88.

24 Of those close to Beethoven, Czerny offers the most detailed observations and suggestions on tempo flexibility, although their exact significance and degree of comprehensiveness is not always clear: see Barth, *Pianist as Orator*, chap. 3. Sandra P. Rosenblum, who also discusses Czerny at some length, suggests that Beethoven's use of tempo flexibility set his practice apart from that of Haydn and Mozart, who preferred mostly strict tempi, and that it became gradually more important to both his music and his playing as time went by: see *Performance Practices in Classic Piano Music: Their Principles and Applications* (Bloomington and Indianapolis, 1988), 383–92. While much of the surviving evidence on tempo relates to piano music, it seems clear from the testimony of Schindler, corroborated by more reliable sources such as Ignaz Moscheles, that tempo flexibility should also apply, *mutatis mutandis*, to other media. In his life of the composer Schindler even included an annotated score example, taken from the Larghetto of the Second Symphony, to illustrate this point in relation to orchestral music (*The Life of Beethoven*, ed. Ignaz Moscheles, 2 vols. [London, 1841], II, 142–44); he implies that his tempo modifications and other directions stem from conversations with the composer about this particular movement (he does not claim to have heard Beethoven conduct the work, however, as Richard Taruskin erroneously states in "Resisting the Ninth," 256). In the realm of the string quartet, we have contemporary reports of Schuppanzigh's quartet which suggest that the group used considerable tempo modification in playing Beethoven's works for this medium, several of which they introduced. It must be said that in the orchestral domain, Beethoven's desire for tempo flexibility would have posed challenges of ensemble that surely exceeded the capabilities of the kinds of groups with which he typically worked, and of his own conducting; thus a description of Beethoven's conducting by Ignaz von Seyfried, music director of the Theater an der Wien, in which he talks of the composer demanding "an effective *tempo rubato*" when conducting (see Thayer–Forbes, 371), seems more likely to represent what Beethoven sought to achieve rather than what the orchestra actually produced.

25 See Barth, *Pianist as Orator*; in addition, conductor Nikolaus Harnoncourt has carried his ideas on rhetoric in eighteenth-century music into the realm of Beethoven's orchestral works, in performances and recordings with the Chamber Orchestra of Europe in particular.

26 E. T. A. Hoffmann, "Der echte Künstler lebt nur in dem Werke," in "Beethovens Instrumentalmusik," *Musikalische Novellen und Aufsätze*, I, ed. E. Istel (Regensburg, 1919), 69; quoted in Lydia Goehr, *The Imaginary Museum of Musical Works: An Essay in the Philosophy of Music* (Oxford, 1992), 1, in the author's translation.

27 Although this particular phrase is Lydia Goehr's, the idea of a musical museum goes back to Liszt, writing in 1835: see *Imaginary Museum of Musical Works*, 205.

28 The main focus here will be on orchestral music; for chamber music see Robert Winter, "Performing the Beethoven Quartets in Their First Century," in *The Beethoven Quartet Companion*, ed. Robert Winter and Robert Martin (Berkeley and Los Angeles, 1994), 29–57; on piano music see William S. Newman,

The Sonata since Beethoven: The Third and Final Volume of a History of the Sonata Idea (Chapel Hill, NC, 1969). As Newman makes clear, the sonata, long associated with the private domain, moved more slowly than other genres into the glare of fully public performance. A phenomenon which has received little attention, and which is beyond the scope of the present study, is the emergence during the nineteenth century of what might be termed, by analogy with the work-concept, the "oeuvre-concept." The fact that all three dominant areas of Beethoven's output could be taken to chart in its entirety a progress from youthful genius to aging seer has always seemed attractive, but it was of special relevance for an age fascinated not only by Beethoven's life, but by the whole concept of biography as a model for music historiography. As possible evidence for a developing desire to hear individual works within a musico-biographical context, it is interesting to note, for instance, that entire cycles of Beethoven's piano sonatas were already being performed by the early 1860s, and on both sides of the Atlantic: see Newman, *The Sonata since Beethoven*, 13 and 736.

29 The most thorough recent study of this concept is Goehr, *Imaginary Museum of Musical Works*; the centrality of Beethoven to its crystallization is argued by Goehr in a chapter revealingly entitled "After 1800: The Beethoven Paradigm." See also Carl Dahlhaus, *Nineteenth Century Music*, tr. J. Bradford Robinson (Berkeley and Los Angeles:, 1989), 8–12 and 138.

30 See William S. Newman, "Liszt's Interpreting of Beethoven's Piano Sonatas," MQ 58/2 (1972), 193–94. Newman notes that Liszt played only ten of the sonatas in public more than once: the "Moonlight," "Tempest," and "Appassionata" Sonatas; opp. 26 and 90; and the last five. In the middle years of his career, as Kapellmeister at Weimar, he became also a significant conductor of Beethoven.

31 Ibid.

32 See Newman, *The Sonata since Beethoven*, 56–60.

33 Newman, "Liszt's Interpreting of Beethoven's Piano Sonatas," 196–97. An obvious creative space for Liszt the composer-performer existed in the concerto cadenza; yet, curiously, the only Beethoven concerto he played was the "Emperor," which does not contain an *ad libitum* cadenza.

34 For examples of such practices in the orchestral arena see David Pickett, "A Comparative Survey of Rescorings in Beethoven's Symphonies," in *Performing Beethoven*, ed. Stowell, 205–06.

35 And perhaps a potential projection, too, of listeners' own identification with the heroic self-actualization played out in the music, to invoke the view of Beethoven's art set out in Scott Burnham's *Beethoven Hero* (Princeton, 1995).

36 "Address to the Members of the Academy of Fine Arts of the Institute," in *A Travers Chants* (Paris, 1862), cited in *Mozart, Weber, and Wagner, with Various Essays on Musical Subjects*, tr. Edwin Evans (London, 1918), 101–02; cited in José Bowen, "Mendelssohn, Berlioz, and Wagner as Conductors: the Origins of the Ideal of 'Fidelity to the Composer,'" *Performance Practice Review* 6/1 (1993), 82.

37 For a detailed discussion of these issues see Bowen, "The Conductor and the Score: The Relationship Between Interpreter and Text in the Generation of Mendelssohn, Berlioz and Wagner" (Ph.D. diss., Stanford University, 1993).

38 Wagner's most extended discussion of conducting appears in the essay "Über das Dirigieren," published first in installments in the *Neue Zeitschrift für Musik* from November 1869 to January 1870, and then widely reprinted and translated.

39 Wagner's principal example of a Beethoven orchestral movement that demands tempo modification is the first movement of the *Eroica* symphony; he implies that the tempo must slacken for both the second subject and the E minor theme in the development. Although the essay is on conducting, his most detailed illustrative examples are in fact taken from chamber works, the "Kreutzer" sonata and the String Quartet op. 131, both cases involving transition from one mood to another.

40 See Nicholas Cook, *Beethoven: Symphony no. 9* (Cambridge, 1993), 56.

41 Ibid., 52–56, from which the music example here is adapted. Cook notes that Wagner's alteration was employed even by the literalist Toscanini, who also extended the flute transposition back a bar; and that Mahler went even further in rewriting this passage, removing altogether punctuating trumpet and timpani parts.

42 See Pickett, "Rescoring in Beethoven's Symphonies," 213. In the context of such widespread retouchings, the perpetuation of textual errors in nineteenth-century orchestral scores and parts of Beethoven may seem less surprising than it otherwise would; indeed, many of these errors have survived up to the present day, and in the case of the symphonies, only now are comprehensively critical editions beginning to appear. A collected – although not fully complete – edition of Beethoven's works

was published by Breitkopf & Härtel in the mid-1860s (earlier attempts at a collected edition had proved abortive), but this was not a critical edition in the modern sense, and editions of Beethoven based on a comparative evaluation of primary sources had to wait until the twentieth century.

43 It even affected the string quartets, traditionally a bastion of "classical" Beethoven: see Leon Botstein, "The Patrons and Publics of the Quartets: Music, Culture, and Society in Beethoven's Vienna," in *The Beethoven Quartet Companion*, ed. Winter and Martin, 77–109.

44 The cause is well known, of course: Cosima von Bülow, née Liszt, left her husband for Wagner in 1869.

45 See New Grove, s.v. "Bülow, Hans (Guido) von," by John Warrack, 452.

46 Bülow was responsible for the sonatas from op. 53 on, as well as the *Pathétique* and "Moonlight" Sonatas, and opp. 26, 27 no. 1, and 31 no. 3. On this edition and others see William S. Newman, "A Chronological Checklist of Collected Editions of Beethoven's Solo Piano Sonatas Since His Own Day," *Notes* 33 (1976–7), 503–30.

47 *On Conducting*, tr. Ernest Newman (New York, 1934), 28. Weingartner's essay appeared originally in 1895.

48 See Joseph Horowitz, *Understanding Toscanini: How He Became an American Culture God and Created a New Audience for Old Music* (New York, 1987), 87; also Pickett, "Rescoring in Beethoven's Symphonies," 221.

49 See Robert Philip, *Early Recordings and Musical Style: Changing Tastes in Instrumental Performance, 1900–1950* (Cambridge, 1992), chap. 1. Philip points out that tempo modification of this era – which he believes must reflect the essentials of much nineteenth-century practice – included dramatic speeding up, something now hardly ever encountered, as well as slowing down, and that this generated a more extreme range of tempi than is typical of current performance practice, which emerged gradually after 1945. Furthermore, such approaches applied to solo and chamber music as well as orchestral music. Philip has written in more detail on Beethoven in "Traditional Habits of Performance in Beethoven Recordings," in *Performing Beethoven*, ed. Stowell, 195–204.

50 "The New Antiquity," 223.

51 The first major Beethoven recording, and a landmark for recording history in terms of the combined eminence of both work and conductor, was the 1913 account of the Fifth Symphony by Artur Nikisch and the Berlin Philharmonic Orchestra (HMV D89–92, reissued on CD as Symposium 1087).

52 This is certainly the case in his November 1952 recording with the Vienna Philharmonic (EMI 1C149–53 434 M), where the tempo reaches c. ♩=136 in the transition, but has slowed to c. ♩=118 by the end of the second subject group.

53 Quoted in Horowitz, *Understanding Toscanini*, 102.

54 Nicholas Cook, "The Conductor and the Theorist: Furtwängler, Schenker and the First Movement of Beethoven's Ninth Symphony," in *The Practice of Performance*, ed. Rink, 105–25.

55 HMV DB2955–60.

56 *The Recordings of Beethoven: As Viewed by the Critics From High Fidelity* (Great Barrington, MA, 1971).

57 It should be added that the greater freedom always implied by solo performance in comparison with ensemble playing has ensured that Beethoven's piano music continues to receive a relatively wide range of interpretations, particularly in the area of tempo; see, for instance, the analyses of selected recorded performances presented in Joanna Goldstein, *A Beethoven Enigma: Performance Practice and the Piano Sonata, Opus 111*, American University Studies, Series XX, Fine Arts, vol. II (New York, 1988), chaps. 5–8.

58 Issued in 1994 on Archiv 439 904–2.

59 See Taruskin, "Last Thoughts First," *Text and Act*, 31–37.

16 The four ages of Beethoven: critical reception and the canonic composer

1 Franz Grillparzer, *Sämtliche Werke, Dritter Band: Ausgewählte Briefe, Gespräche, Berichte* (Munich, 1964), 882.

2 Ibid., 884–85.

3 Friedrich Rochlitz, AmZ 29 (1827), 227.

4 Robin Wallace, *Beethoven's Critics: Aesthetic Dilemmas and Resolutions during the Composer's Lifetime* (Cambridge, 1986), 5.

5 Wilhelm von Lenz, *Beethoven et ses trois styles* (1852; repr. New York, 1980); Aléxandre Oulibicheff, *Beethoven, ses critiques, ses glossateurs* (Paris, 1857).

6 For an engaging and insightful cultural analysis of contemporaneous views of Beethoven's compositional idiosyncrasies, see Tia DeNora, *Beethoven and the Construction of Genius: Musical Politics in Vienna, 1792–1803* (Berkeley, 1995), esp. 129–37.

7 As Richard Taruskin has it: "The history of music in the nineteenth century could be written in terms of the encroachment of the sublime upon the domain of the beautiful." Richard Taruskin, "Resisting the Ninth," 19CM 12 (1989), 249.

8 *E. T. A. Hoffmann's Musical Writings: Kreisleriana, The Poet and the Composer, Music Criticism*, tr. Martyn Clarke, ed. David Charlton (Cambridge, 1989), 236. Hoffmann's review of the Fifth Symphony originally appeared in the AmZ, 4 July and 11 July 1810.

9 Ibid., 237–38.

10 As Hoffmann writes, specifically regarding the Fifth Symphony: "It unfolds Beethoven's romanticism, rising in a climax right to the end, more than any other of his works, and irresistibly sweeps the listener into the wonderful spirit-realm of the infinite." Ibid., 239.

11 For a more detailed discussion of the notion of "beau désordre" as it arises in Hoffmann's Beethoven criticism, see my review of Charlton's edition *of E. T. A. Hoffmann's Musical Writings* in 19CM 14 (1990), 286–96.

12 This is a central tenet of Karl Philip Moritz's aesthetics of the unified artwork. See Klaus-Dieter Dobat, *Musik als romantische Illusion: Eine Untersuchung zur Bedeutung der Musikvorstellung E. T. A. Hoffmanns für sein literarisches Werk* (Tübingen, 1984), 63.

13 On Marx and the cultural milieu of Berlin, see my introduction to A. B. Marx, *Musical Form in the Age of Beethoven* (Cambridge, 1997).

14 For a compelling and influential examination of the work concept in Western musical thought and its association with Beethoven, see Lydia Goehr, *The Imaginary Museum of Musical Works: An Essay in the Philosophy of Music* (Oxford, 1992).

15 For a highly detailed argument in support of the overwhelming – and hitherto underplayed – importance of Marx for the canonization of Beethoven, see Elisabeth Eleonore Bauer, *Wie Beethoven auf den Sockel kam: Die Entstehung eines musikalischen Mythos* (Stuttgart, 1992).

16 "... so gilt es nun heute an diesem Musiker Beethoven nachzuweisen, daß durch ihn, da er denn in der reinsten Sprache aller Völker redet, der deutsche Geist den Menschengeist von tiefer Schmach erlöste." *Richard Wagner, Dichtungen und Schriften. Jubiläumsausgabe*, ed. Dieter Borchmeyer, 10 vols. (Frankfurt am Main, 1983), IX, 63.

17 See David B. Dennis, *Beethoven in German Politics, 1870–1989* (New Haven, 1996), 32ff.

18 Wagner, *Beethoven*, 38

19 Ibid., 49.

20 Ibid., 64.

21 Ibid., 71–72. And see K. M. Knittel, "Wagner, Deafness, and the Reception of Beethoven's Late Style," JAMS 51 (1998), 49–82.

22 At one point, Wagner curiously adulterates these bardic strains with some more naturalistic observations about the physical structure of Beethoven's skull, born of a recent exhumation; he reckons the skull's unusual thickness to be a form of biological protection for the overly sensitive brain within. *Beethoven*, 69.

23 Ibid., 66.

24 Ibid., 83.

25 Ibid., 66.

26 "Ihm ist das Gefällige versagt; dafür ist sein wahrhaftes Dichten und Tun innig und erhaben." Ibid., 109.

27 "Während die deutschen Waffen siegreich nach dem Zentrum der französischen Zivilisation vordringen, regt sich bei uns plötzlich das Schamgefühl über unsere Abhängigkeit von dieser Zivilisation, und tritt als Aufforderung zur Ablegung der Pariser Modetrachten vor die Öffentlichkeit." Ibid., 96.

28 Ibid., 109.

29 Ibid., 76–78.

30 Nor should we forget how important op. 131 was for the development of Wagner's own musical style. See William Kinderman, "Review Article: Wagner's Beethoven," BF 3 (1994), 175.

31 Arnold Schmitz, *Das romantische Beethovenbild: Darstellung und Kritik* (Bonn, 1927), 178.

32 Ibid., 178–79.

33 August Halm, *Beethoven* (Berlin, 1927), 64–65.

34 See Dennis, *Beethoven in German Politics*, 115–25.

35 For a valuable discussion of the concept of "objective Geist" in Halm's work, see Lee Rothfarb, "Beethoven's Formal Dynamics: August Halm's Phenomenological Perspective," BF 5 (1996), 69–70.

36 Halm, *Beethoven*, 328.

37 Ibid., 332–34.

38 Ibid., 325.

39 Ibid., 329.

40 "Was aber Beethoven gelang, so vollkommen gelang, daß wir die Idee fast mit Händen greifen können, das ist die Musik der Phasen, der Verwandlungen, der Zeiten und Lebensalter, die dennoch eine untrennbare, eine grandiose Einheit bildet: eine Errungenschaft in der Geschichte des Musik-Geistes, die an Wert durch keine andere überwogen wird." Halm, *Beethoven*, 336.

41 "Wir erkennen darum das Motiv Beethovens als den Keim der Sonate, dessen Explosivkraft die Bahn des Werkes aus sich herausschleudert – ohne Zutat – nur durch Variation seines eigenen Inhalts." Walter Engelsmann, "Die Sonatenform Beethovens: Das Gesetz," *Die Musik* 17/6 (March 1925), 431.

I am grateful to Roger Lustig, who introduced me to Engelsmann's essay.

42 "Wer alle übrigen Werke als im gleichen Sinn gewachsen zu erkennen vermag, wird mit mir das Gesetz bilden können: JEDE SONATE BEETHOVENS IST IN ALLEN IHREN SÄTZEN, TEILEN UND THEMEN AUS EINEM EINZIGEN KOPFTHEMA ODER KOPFMOTIV ENTWICKELT." Ibid.

43 For a more detailed version of this claim see my *Beethoven Hero* (Princeton, 1995), 89–102.

44 Donald Francis Tovey, *A Companion to Beethoven's Piano Sonatas* (London, 1931), 3.

45 Ibid., 8.

46 Tovey, "Some Aspects of Beethoven's Art Forms," in *The Mainstream of Music and Other Essays* (New York, 1949), 294.

47 Joseph Kerman, "Tovey's Beethoven," *Write All These Down: Essays on Music* (Berkeley, 1994), 155–72.

48 Guido Adler, "Beethovens Charakter," in *Beethoven-Almanach der Deutschen Musikbücherei auf das Jahr 1927*, ed. Gustav Bosse (Regensburg, 1927), 80.

49 Ibid., 92.

50 Hermann Abert, *Zu Beethovens Persönlichkeit und Kunst* (Leipzig, 1927), 15–20. This essay was initially published in the *Jahrbuch der Musikbibliothek Peters für 1925*, and was reprinted in a special edition to commemorate 26 March 1927, the hundredth anniversary of Beethoven's death.

51 Abert, *Zu Beethovens Persönlichkeit*, 23.

52 Adler, "Beethovens Charakter," 77. See also Abert, *Zu Beethovens Persönlichkeit*, 11.

53 Adler, "Beethovens Charakter," 87.

54 Abert, *Zu Beethovens Persönlichkeit*, 25.

55 Hans Heinrich Eggebrecht, *Zur Geschichte der Beethoven-Rezeption: Beethoven 1970* (Mainz, 1972), 7.

56 Ulrich Schmitt, *Revolution im Konzertsaal: Zur Beethoven-Rezeption im 19. Jahrhundert* (Mainz, 1990); Martin Geck and Peter Schleuning, *"Geschrieben auf Bonaparte": Beethoven's "Eroica": Revolution, Reaktion, Rezeption* (Reinbek bei Hamburg, 1989); Dennis, *Beethoven in German Politics*; DeNora, *Beethoven and the Construction of Genius*; Burnham, *Beethoven Hero*.

57 William Kinderman, *Beethoven* (Berkeley, 1995); Thomas Sipe, *Beethoven: Symphony No. 3, "Eroica"* (Cambridge, 1998); Maynard Solomon, "Beethoven and Schiller," in *Beethoven Essays* (Cambridge, MA, 1988), 205–15.

58 See particularly Rose Rosengard Subotnik, "Adorno's Diagnosis of Beethoven's Late Style: Early Symptom of a Fatal Condition," JAMS 29 (1976), 242–75.

59 Maynard Solomon, *Beethoven* (New York, 1977). For the other studies mentioned in this paragraph, see note 56, including as well Andreas Eichhorn, *Beethovens Neunte Symphonie. Die Geschichte ihrer Aufführung und Rezeption* (Kassel, 1993).

60 Susan McClary, *Feminine Endings: Music, Gender, and Sexuality* (Minneapolis and Oxford, 1991), 112.

17 Beethoven at large: reception in literature, the arts, philosophy, and politics

1 See Scott Burnham, *Beethoven Hero* (Princeton, 1995).

2 See Robin Wallace, *Beethoven's Critics: Aesthetic Dilemmas and Resolutions During the Composer's Lifetime* (Cambridge, 1986), 10–16, and Tia DeNora, *Beethoven and the Construction of Genius: Musical Politics in Vienna, 1792–1803* (Berkeley, 1995), 161, 180.

3 See DeNora, *Beethoven and the Construction of Genius*, passim, and the critical response to this book, including Charles Rosen, "Did Beethoven Have All the Luck?" *The New York Review of Books* (14 November 1996), 57–61, and Nicholas Vazsonyi, book review, *German Studies Review* (October 1997), 436–38.

4 See Ulrich Schmitt, *Revolution im Konzertsaal: Zur Beethoven-Rezeption im 19. Jahrhundert* (Mainz, 1990).

5 See Arnold Schmitz, *Das romantische Beethovenbild: Darstellung und Kritik* (Berlin, 1927).

6 The Beethoven-Haus Archive catalogue lists over four hundred entries under the heading "Beethoven in Literature: Poems." See Wallace, *Beethoven's Critics*, 80–82.

7 See Schmitz, *Das romantische Beethovenbild*, 4 and Friedrich de la Motte-Fouqué, *An Beethoven* (1827), in *Erstes poetisches Beethoven-Album: Zur Erinnerung an den grossen Tondichter und an dessen Säcularfeier, 17 Dezember 1870*, ed. Hermann Josef Landau, (Prague, 1872), 187.

8 Clemens Brentano, "Beethovens Musik" (1813), in *Die Propyläen*, December 1920.

9 Franz Grillparzer, "Klara Wieck und Beethoven. F-Moll-Sonate" (c. 1830), in *Beethoven-Almanach der Deutschen Musikbücherei auf das Jahr 1927*, ed. Gustav Bosse (Regensburg, 1927), 54.

10 Ernst Ortlepp, "Haydn, Mozart und Beethoven," in *Gedichte von Ernst Ortlepp* (Leipzig, 1831), 31.

11 Nikolaus Lenau, "Beethovens Büste" (1855), in Landau, *Beethoven-Album*, 107.

12 See Leo Schrade, *Beethoven in France: The Development of an Idea* (New Haven, 1942).

13 Charles Baudelaire, *La Musique: Beethoven,* in *Les Fleurs du Mal,* tr. Richard Howard (Boston, 1983), 71.

14 Cited in Charmenz S. Lenhart, *Musical Influence on American Poetry* (Athens, GA, 1956), 173.

15 Walt Whitman, "Beethoven's Septet," in *The Works of Walt Whitman,* vol. II, ed. Malcom Cowley (New York, 1968), 158.

16 See Donna Beckage, "Beethoven in Western Literature" (Ph.D. diss. University of California, Riverside, 1977), 255.

17 Ibid., 257–63.

18 T. S. Eliot, "The Music of Poetry," in Eliot, *On Poetry and Poets* (New York, 1957), 32.

19 The Beethoven-Haus Archive catalogue lists over two hundred entries under the heading "Novels and Short Stories." Deserving more attention than is possible here are Honoré de Balzac's *Le peau de chagrin* (1831), *La recherche de l'absolue* (1834), *Le lys dans la vallée* (1836), *César Birotteau* (1837), *Béatrix* (1839), and *Ursele Miroet* (1842), Georges Sand's *Lettres d'un voyager* (1834), George Bernard Shaw's *Love among Artists* (1881), Leo Tolstoy's *The Kreutzer Sonata* (1889), Marcel Proust's *La recherche du temps perdu* (1913–28), André Gide's *La symphonie pastorale* (1918), Antonio Fogazzaro's *Piccolo mondo moderno* (1930), André Malraux's *L'espoir* (1937), Aldous Huxley's *Eyeless in Gaza* (1936) and *Two or Three Graces* (1949), Virginia Woolf's *The Voyage Out* (1949), Günter Grass's *The Tin Drum* (1959), and Milan Kundera's *The Unbearable Lightness of Being* (1984) – to mention only a few by some celebrated authors. See Beckage, "Beethoven in Western Literature," passim.

20 E. M. Forster, *A Room With A View* (Norfolk, CT, 1922), 53–54.

21 E. M. Forster, *Howards End* (London, 1947), 32–36.

22 See Sieghard Brandenburg, "Künstlerroman und Biographie: Zur Entstehung des Beethoven-Mythos im 19. Jahrhundert," in *Beethoven und die Nachwelt: Materialien zur Wirkungsgeschichte Beethovens,* ed. Helmut Loos (Bonn, 1986), 65–80, and Egon Voss, "Das Beethoven-Bild der Beethoven-Belletristik: Zu einigen Beethoven-Erzählungen des 19. Jahrhunderts," in *Beethoven und die Nachwelt,* ed. Loos, 81–94.

23 Victor Hugo, *William Shakespeare,* cited in Schrade, *Beethoven in France,* 57, 257 n. 15.

24 See ibid., 68–71, 145–52, 156.

25 Romain Rolland, *Beethoven the Creator,* tr. Ernest Newman (New York, 1964), 10.

26 Romain Rolland, *La vie de Beethoven* (Paris, 1903), 78.

27 Thomas Mann, *Doktor Faustus: The Life of the German Composer Adrian Leverkühn as Told by a Friend,* tr. H. T. Lowe-Porter (New York, 1992), 58.

28 Charles T. Bunting, "An Interview in New York with Anthony Burgess," *Studies in the Novel* 5 (1973), 505.

29 Ibid.

30 The Beethoven-Haus Archive catalogue lists over forty entries under the heading "Dramas."

31 See Donald F. Sloane, "A Multiple-choice Quiz on the Historical Accuracy of Bernard Rose's *Immortal Beloved,*" *The Beethoven Journal* 10/1 (Spring 1995), 30–39.

32 The Beethoven-Haus Archive catalogue lists almost one thousand entries under the heading "Illustrations, Portraits, and Monuments."

33 Contemporary efforts ranged from pencil sketches by Louis Letronne (1814), August von Klöber (1818), and Josef Daniel Böhm (1819–20) to formal portraits by Willibrord Josef Mähler (1804 and 1815), Franz Klein (1812), Ferdinand Schimon (1818–19), Joseph Karl Stieler (1819), and Ferdinand Georg Waldmüller (1823). See Alessandra Comini, *The Changing Image of Beethoven: A Study in Mythmaking* (New York, 1987), passim.

34 Ibid., 86.

35 See Robert Schumann, "Monument für Beethoven," in *Gesammelte Schriften über Musik und Musiker,* ed. Martin Kreisig, 5th edn., 2 vols. (Leipzig, 1914), I, 134.

36 Monuments were erected in Bonn (1845), Heiligenstadt (1863), Vienna (1880), and Berlin (1903).

37 Comini, *The Changing Image,* passim.

38 Ibid., 348–52, 385–87.

39 Ibid., 403–15.

40 *The Complete Works of Friedrich Nietzsche,* vol. VI: *Human, All Too Human,* Part I, tr. Helen Zimmern (1909–11; rpt. New York, 1964), I, 265.

41 Comini, *The Changing Image,* 338.

42 Ibid., 398.

43 See Jean-Paul Bouillon, *Klimt: Beethoven* (New York, 1987), passim, and Comini, *The Changing Image,* 399–403.

44 See, for instance, Richard Sterba and Editha Sterba, *Beethoven and His Nephew: A Psychological Study of Their Relationship* (New York, 1937) and Maynard Solomon, *Beethoven* (New York, 1977). Beyond the scope of this essay on creative responses to Beethoven, biographical representations also follow the contours of modern Western intellectual development. For critical insight into the history of writing Beethoven biographies, see Maynard Solomon, "Thoughts on Biography," in *Beethoven Essays* (Cambridge, MA and London, 1988), 101–15.

45 Edward Dannreuther, "Beethoven and his

Works: A Study," *Macmillan's Magazine* 34 no. 201 (July 1876), 194.

46 Wilfrid Mellers, *Beethoven and the Voice of God* (New York, 1983), 21–22.

47 Christopher Ballantine, *Music and Its Social Meanings* (New York, 1984), 33. See also Janet Schmalfeldt, "Form as the Process of Becoming: The Beethoven-Hegelian Tradition and the Tempest Sonata," BF 4 (1995), 37–71, and Scott Burnham, "Criticism, Faith, and the *Idee*: A. B. Marx's Early Reception of Beethoven," 19CM (Spring 1990), 183–92.

48 Friedrich W. Nietzsche, "Beethovens Tod" (1863), in *Jungendschriften, 1861–1864*, vol. II, *Friedrich Nietzsches Werke: Historisch-kritische Gesamtausgabe* (Munich, 1934), 322–25.

49 Friedrich W. Nietzsche, "Schopenhauer as Educator," in *Untimely Meditations*, tr. R. J. Hollingdale (Cambridge, 1983), 140.

50 Friedrich W. Nietzsche, "Richard Wagner in Bayreuth," in *Untimely Meditations*, 240–41.

51 Friedrich W. Nietzsche, *The Birth of Tragedy*, tr. Walter Kaufmann (New York, 1967), 37.

52 See Theodor W. Adorno, *Beethoven: Philosophie der Musik* (Frankfurt, 1993).

53 Theodor W. Adorno, "Theses on the Sociology of Art," tr. Brian Trench, *Working Papers in Cultural Studies* 2 (Spring 1972), 62.

54 See Rose Rosengard Subotnik, "Adorno's Diagnosis of Beethoven's Late Style: Early Symptom of a Fatal Condition," in Subotnik, *Developing Variations: Style and Ideology in Western Music* (Minneapolis, 1991), 15–41, John Deathridge, "Fragments of a Single Hidden Music: Adorno's Lifelong Struggle to Write a Fully Fledged Interpretation of Beethoven," *Times Literary Supplement*, 15 September 1995, and Colin Sample, "Adorno on the Musical Language of Beethoven," MQ 78/2, (Summer 1994), 385–86.

55 Cited in David Drew, "Introduction From the Other Side: Reflections on the Bloch Centenary," introduction to Ernst Bloch, *Essays on the Philosophy of Music*, tr. Peter Palmer (Cambridge, 1985), xxv.

56 Bloch, *Essays*, 31, 240, 243.

57 Freiherr Kübeck von Kübau refused to keep company with Beethoven because his constant politicizing bored him. See Karl Nef, "Beethovens Beziehungen zur Politik," *Zeitschrift für Musik* 5 (May 1925).

58 David B. Dennis, *Beethoven in German Politics, 1870–1989* (New Haven and London, 1996), 22–31.

59 Julius Nitsche, "Jonny neben Beethoven: Errinerung an eine Jahrhundertfeier in wirrer Zeit," *Völkischer Beobachter* (Berlin), 26 March 1937.

60 See Dennis, *Beethoven in German Politics*, passim.

61 See Carl Dahlhaus, *Nineteenth-Century Music*, tr. J. Bradford Robinson (Berkeley, 1989), 76.

62 See Willem Erauw, "Musica morale, miracolo musicale: Le développement du mythe de Beethoven en Italie du nord au dix-neuvième siècle," *Bulletin de l'Institute Historique Belge de Rome*, 66 (1996), 171.

63 Bettina Brentano, Letter to Goethe, 10 May 1810, in *Movements, Currents, Trends: Aspects of European Thought in the Nineteenth and Twentieth Centuries*, ed. Eugen Weber, (Lexington, MA, 1922), 127.

64 Georges Pioch, "Beethoven," in *Portraits d'hier* (1909), cited in Schrade, *Beethoven in France*, 193.

65 See Ruth A. Solie, "Beethoven as Secular Humanist: Ideology and the Ninth Symphony in Nineteenth-Century Criticism," in *Explorations in Music, the Arts, and Ideas: Essays in Honor of Leonard B. Meyer*, ed. Eugene Narmour and Ruth A. Solie (Stuyvesant, NY, 1988), 36.

66 Karl Rafael Hennig, *Beethoven's neunte Symphonie* (Leipzig, 1888), cited in Solie, "Beethoven as Secular Humanist," 22.

67 Andrew Horvat, "Beethoven Mania Touches the Right Chords," *Far Eastern Economic Review*, 4 January 1990, 16–17, and Yano Jun'ichi, "Why is Beethoven's Ninth so well loved in Japan?" *Japan Quarterly* 12 (1982), 477.

68 *The Complete Works of Friedrich Nietzsche*, vol. VI: *Human, All-too-Human*, Part II, tr. Paul V. Cohn (1909–11; rpt. New York, 1964), 68.

Selected further reading

Primary sources

Letters, conversation books, diaries

Beethoven: Letters, Journals and Conversations, ed.and tr. Michael Hamburger (New York, 1951)

Letters to Beethoven and Other Correspondence, ed. and tr. Theodore Albrecht, 3 vols. (Lincoln, NB, 1996)

The Letters of Beethoven, ed. and tr. Emily Anderson, 3 vols. (London, 1961, rpt. 1985)

Ludwig van Beethoven: Briefwechsel Gesamtausgabe, ed. Sieghard Brandenburg, 8 vols. (Munich, 1997–98)

Ludwig van Beethovens Konversationshefte, ed., Karl-Heinz Köhler, Gritta Herre, and Dagmar Beck, 10 vols. (Leipzig, 1968–93)

Beck, Dagmar and Herre, Gritta, "Anton Schindlers fingierte Eintragungen in den Konversationsheften," in *Zu Beethoven: Aufsätze und Annotationen*, ed. Harry Goldschmidt (Berlin, 1979), 11–89

Busch-Weise, Dagmar von, "Beethovens Jugendtagebuch," *Studien zur Musikwissenschaft*, 25 (1962), 68–88

Kerst, Friedrich, *Beethoven, the Man and the Artist, as Revealed in his Own Words*, tr. Henry Edward Krehbiel (New York, 1964)

Kerst, Friedrich, ed., *Die Erinnerungen an Beethoven*, 2 vols. (Stuttgart, 1913)

Leitzmann, A., ed., *Ludwig van Beethoven, Berichte der Zeitgenossen, Briefe und persönliche Aufzeichnungen* (Leipzig, 1921)

Schmidt-Görg, Joseph, ed., *Des Bonner Bäckermeisters Gottfried Fischer Aufzeichnungen über Beethovens Jugend* (Bonn and Munich, 1971)

Solomon, Maynard, "Beethoven's Tagebuch of 1812–1818," in BS III, ed. Alan Tyson (Cambridge, 1982), pp. 193–288; rev. version in Solomon, *Beethoven Essays*, (Cambridge, 1988), 233–95; see also M. Solomon, *Beethovens Tagebuch* (Bonn, 1990)

Stadlen, Peter, "Schindler's Beethoven Forgeries," *The Musical Times*, 118 (1977), 549–52

"Schindler and the Conversation Books," *Soundings*, 7 (1978), 2–18

Editions of autograph scores and sketches exclusive of fragments, single leaves, and short gatherings (n.e. indicates that the name of the editor was not included in the publication)

Piano Concerto no. 2 in B♭ op. 19

'*Concerto per il piano-forte, opera . . .' Piano Concerto No. 2 in B♭ Major, op. 19. Facsimile of the Autograph Score and Autograph Piano Part in the Possession of the*

Staatsbibliothek, Berlin and the Beethoven-Haus, Bonn, ed. Michael C. Tusa (New York, forthcoming)

Piano Sonata in A♭ op. 26

As-dur Sonate Op. 26. Facsimile, ed. Erich Prieger (Bonn, 1895)

Piano Sonata in C♯ minor op. 27 no. 2

1. *Sonata op. 27, no.2: popularly known as Moonlight sonata: with three manuscripts notes of the master*, ed. Heinrich Schenker (Vienna, c. 1921)

2. *Ludwig van Beethoven: Faksimile des Autographs und der Original-Ausgabe 1802 der Sonate quasi una fantasia "Mondschein" op. 27 no. 2*, ed Keisei Sakka (Tokyo, 1970)

Piano Sonata in D op. 28

Piano Sonata, Op. 28. Facsimile of the Autograph, Sketches, and First Edition, ed. Martha Frohlich, 2 vols. (Bonn, 1996)

Violin Sonata in G op. 30 no. 3

Violin sonata in G major, op. 30, no. 3: facsimile of the autograph manuscript in the British Library, Add. MS 37767, ed. Alan Tyson (London, 1980)

Romances for Violin and Orchestra in G and F opp. 40 and 50

Zwei Romanzen fur Violine und Orchester op. 40 und 50. Faksimile-Ausgabe der autographen Partituren mit Klavierauszug, ed. Willy Hess (Winthertur, 1990)

Piano Sonata in C op. 53

Klaviersonate in C-dur, op. 53. Faksimilie-Ausgabe des im Beethoven-Haus Bonn befindlichen Autographs. ed. Martin Staehelin (Bonn 1984); reprint with a new introduction of edition of 1955, ed. Joseph Schmidt-Görg (Bonn 1955)

Symphony no. 3 in E♭ op. 55

Symphonie Nr. 3, Es-dur, op. 55: "Eroica". Partitur-Manuskript (Beethovens Handexemplar): vollständige Faksimile-Ausgabe im Originalformat – Orchesterstimmen der Uraufführung und früher zeitgenössischer Aufführungen: verkleinerte Reproduktion, ed. Otto Biba (Vienna, c. 1993)

Piano Sonata in F minor op. 57

1. *Sonate appassionata (en fa mineur, opus 57)* (Paris, 1927)

2. *Klaviersonate F-moll Opus 57. Faksimile der Urschrift* (Leipzig, 1971)

String Quartet in F op. 59 no. 1

String Quartet Opus 59 No. 1. First "Razumovsky" Quartet, ed. Alan Tyson (London, 1980)

String Quartet in E minor op. 59 no. 2

Beethoven: String Quartet Op. 59 No. 2. Second "Razumovsky" Quartet, in E Minor, facsimile of the autograph score, ed. Alan Tyson (London, 1980)

Violin Concerto in D op. 61

Konzert für Violine und Orchester, D-dur, Opus 61, ed. Franz Grasberger (Graz, 1979)

Symphony no. 5 in C minor op. 67

Fünfte Symphonie: nach der Handschrift im Besitz der Preußischen Staatsbibliothek, ed. Georg Schünemann (Berlin, 1942)

Cello Sonata in A op. 69: first movement

1. *Sonata for Violoncello and Pianoforte: Opus. 69, First Movement. Facsimile of the Autograph*, ed. Lewis Lockwood (New York, 1970)

2. *Sonate für Violoncello und Klavier op. 69. Das Autograph des ersten Satzes – Erste*

Fassung des ersten Satzes. Rekonstruktion von Sieghard Brandenburg, ed. Sieghard
   Brandenburg (Bonn, 1992)

**Fidelio op. 72: recitative and aria "Gott, welch Dunkel hier. In des Lebens
Frühlingstagen"**
*Fidelio: "Gott, welch Dunkel hier. In des Lebens Frühlingstagen."Faksimile nach dem
   Autograph aus dem Nachlaß des Komponisten in der Deutschen Staatsbibliothek
   Berlin*, ed. Karl-Heinz Köhler (Leipzig, 1976)

Piano Sonata in F♯ op. 78
Das Autograph der Klaviersonate in Fis-dur (Munich, 1923)

Piano Sonata in E minor op. 90
Klaviersonate e-moll op. 90, ed. Michael Ladenburger (Berlin, 1993)

Violin Sonata in G op. 96
*Sonate fur Klavier und Violine, G-dur, opus 96: Faksimile nach dem im Eigentum der
   Pierpont Morgan Library, New York, befindlichen Autograph*, ed. Martin Staehelin
   (Munich, 1977)

Song Cycle *An die ferne Geliebte* op. 98
*An die ferne Geliebte, Liederkreis von Alois Jeitteles, Opus 98. Faksimile nach dem im
   Besitz des Bonner Beethovenhauses befindlichen Original* (Munich, 1970)

Piano Sonata in A op. 101
Klaviersonate in A-dur, opus 101, ed. Sieghard Brandenburg (Munich, 1999)

Piano Sonata in E op. 109
Piano sonata, op. 109. Facsimile of the holograph in the Library of Congress, ed.
   Oswald Jonas (New York, 1965)

Piano Sonata in A♭ op. 110
Klaviersonate, As-dur, op. 110. Faksimile nach dem Autograph, ed. Karl Michael
   Komma (Stuttgart, c. 1967)

Piano Sonata in C minor op. 111
1. *Klaviersonate C-Moll, Opus 111: im Faksimile der Urschrift* (Leipzig, 1952; reprint
   of *Klaviersonate in C-Moll Op. 111*, Munich, 1922)
2. *Piano Sonata No. 32 in C Minor, Op. 111. Reproduction of the Autograph . . .*, ed.
   Eric Simon (New York, 1968; reprint of Leipzig, 1952)
3. Facsimile in Molteni, Angela. *Ludwig van Beethoven: la vita, le opere* (Milan, 1989)

Missa solemnis op. 123: Kyrie
*Missa solemnis, opus 123: Kyrie. Faksimile nach dem Autograph. Das Kyrie der Missa
   solemnis; Geschichte und Gestalt der Handschrift*, ed. Wilhelm Virneisel (Tutzing,
   1965)

Symphony no. 9 in D minor op. 125
*Sinfonie mit Schluss-Chor über Schillers Ode: An die Freude, fur grosses Orchester, 4
   Solo und 4 Chor-Stimmen. 125tes Werk* (Leipzig, 1924; photographic reprint,
   1975)

Six Bagatelles for Piano op. 126
*Sechs Bagatellen für Klavier, Op. 126. Faksimile der Handschriften und der
   Originalausgabe mit einem Kommentar*, ed. Sieghard Brandenburg, 2 vols.
   (Bonn, 1984)

Concerto cadenzas
Sämtliche Kadenzen. Faksimile Ausgabe, ed. Willy Hess (Zurich, 1979)

Four Settings of "Nur wer die Sehnsucht kennt" WoO 134

1. *"Nur wer die Sehnsucht kennt." Lied in vier Fassungen (WoO 134) nach einem Gedicht von Johann Wolfgang von Goethe von Ludwig van Beethoven. Faksimile des Autographs mit einer Studie*, ed. Helga Lühning (Bonn, 1986)
2. *Vier Kompositionen aus den Jahren 1807–08: Nur wer die Sehnsucht kennt (WoO 134): aus Johann Wolfgang von Goethes Wilhelm Meister. Faksimile-Wiedergabe nach dem im Besitz des Bonner Beethoven-Hauses befindlichen Autograph (Sammlung H. C. Bodmer) im Jahre des 200. Geburtstages des Komponisten*, ed. Paul Mies (Bonn, 1970)

Sketchbooks and miscellanies (n.e. indicates that the name of the editor was not included in the publication)

"Kafka": *Ludwig van Beethoven: Autograph Miscellany from circa 1786 to 1799: British Museum Additional Manuscript 29801, ff. 39–162*, ed. Joseph Kerman, 2 vols. with commentary and transcription (London, 1970)

"Fischhof": *Beethoven's Early Sketches in the "Fischhof Miscellany": Berlin Autograph 28*, ed. Douglas Johnson, 2 vols. with commentary and transcription (Ann Arbor, 1980)

"Grasnick 2": *Ein Skizzenbuch zu Streichquartetten aus Op. 18: SV 46*, ed. Wilhelm Virneisel, 2 vols. with commentary and transcription (Bonn, 1972–74)

"Autograph 19e": *A Sketchbook from the Summer of 1800. Sketches for the String Quartets, op. 18, Nos. 1, 2 and 6, the Piano Sonata Op. 22, and for Various Other Works*, ed. Richard Kramer, 2 vols. with commentary and transcription (Bonn, 1996)

"Landsberg 7": *Ein Notierungsbuch von Beethoven, aus dem Besitze der Preussischen Staatsbibliothek zu Berlin*, ed. Karl Lothar Mikulicz (Leipzig, 1927; rpt. Hildesheim, 1972)

"Kessler": *Kesslersches Skizzenbuch. Vollständiges Faksimile des Autographs mit einem Nachwort und einem Register von Sieghard Brandenburg*, ed. Sieghard Brandenburg, 2 vols. with commentary and transcription (Bonn, 1976/78)

"Wielhorsky": *Kniga eskizov Beethovena za 1802–1803 gody*, ed. Natan Fisman, 3 vols. with commentary and transcription (Moscow, 1962)

"Pastoral Symphony Sketchbook": *Beethoven. Ein Skizzenbuch zur Pastoralsymphonie Op. 68 und zu den Trios Op. 70, 1 und 2*, ed. Dagmar Weise, 2 vols. with commentary, transcription, and three folios in facsimile (Bonn, 1961)

"Grasnick 3": *Ein Skizzenbuch zur Chorfantasie op. 80 und zu anderen Werken*, ed. Dagmar Weise, 1 vol. with commentary, transcription, and three folios in facsimile (Bonn, 1957)

"Landsberg 5": *Ludwig van Beethoven: Ein Skizzenbuch aus dem Jahre 1809 Landsberg 5*, ed. Clemens Brenneis, 2 vols. with commentary and transcription (Bonn, 1992/1993)

"Wittgenstein": *Ein Skizzenbuch zu den Diabelli-Variationen und zur Missa solemnis SV 154. Faksimile*, ed. Joseph Schmidt-Görg, 2 vols. with commentary and transcription (Bonn, 1968/1972)

"Engelmann": *Skizzenbuch. Recueil thématique de L. v. Beethoven. Autograph*
    contentant 37 pages de musique . . ., facsimile only (Leipzig, 1913)
Three Pocket Sketchbooks to the Missa solemnis, ed. Joseph Schmidt-Görg
1. Bonn Bh 107: *Ein Skizzenbuch aus den Jahren 1819/20, SV 81. Faksimile,* 2 vols.
    with commentary and transcription (Bonn, 1952/68)
2. Bonn Bh 108: *Ein Skizzenbuch zum Credo, SV 82. Faksimile,* 2 vols. with
    commentary and transcription (Bonn, 1968/70)
3. Bonn Bh 109: *Ein Skizzenbuch zum Benedictus und zum Agnus Dei, SV 83.*
    Faksimile, 2 vols. with commentary and transcription (Bonn, 1968/70)
"Moscow"
1. "Ein Moskauer Skizzenbuch von Beethoven," *Musikalische Bildung,* 1–2 (1927),
    9–58 (facsimile), 75–91 (commentary)
2. *Ludwig van Beethoven: Moscow Sketchbook from 1825,* ed. Elena Vyaskova
    (Moscow, 1995)

Literature on autograph sources (for catalogues see p. 350)
Johnson, Douglas, Tyson, Alan, and Winter, Robert, eds., *The Beethoven Sketchbooks:*
    History, Reconstruction, Inventory (Oxford, 1985)
Kramer, Richard, "The Sketch Itself," in *Beethoven's Compositional Process,* ed.
    William Kinderman (Lincoln, NB, 1991)
Lockwood, Lewis, "On Beethoven's Sketches and Autographs: Some Problems of
    Definition and Interpretation," Acta 42 (1970), 32–47
    "The Beethoven Sketchbooks and the General State of Sketch Research," in
    Beethoven's Compositional Process, ed. William Kinderman (Lincoln, NB, 1991)
Marston, Nicholas, "Beethoven's Sketches and the Interpretative Process," BF 1
    (1992), 225–42
Mies, Paul, *Die Bedeutung der Skizzen Beethovens zur Erkenntnis seines Stiles*
    (Leipzig, 1925); tr. Doris L. Mackinnon as *Beethoven's Sketches* (New York, 1929,
    rpt. 1974)
Nottebohm, Gustav, *Ein Skizzenbuch von Beethoven* (Leipzig, 1865); tr. Jonathan
    Katz in *Two Beethoven Sketchbooks* (London, 1979), 3–43
    Ein Skizzenbuch von Beethoven aus dem Jahre 1803 (Leipzig, 1880); tr. Jonathan
    Katz in *Two Beethoven Sketchbooks* (London, 1979), 47–125
    Beethoveniana (Leipzig and Winterhur, 1872)
    Zweite Beethoveniana. Nachgelassene Aufsätze (Leipzig, 1887)
Schmidt, Hans, "Die Beethoven Handschriften des Beethovenhauses in Bonn."
    Beethoven-Jahrbuch, 7 (1971), 1–443; addenda and corrigenda in BJ 8
    (1971–72), 207–20
    "Verzeichnis der Skizzen Beethovens," BJ 6 (1969), 7–128
Taub, Robert, "The Autograph of the First Movement of Beethoven's Piano Trio Op.
    70 No. 1," Doctor of Musical Arts Thesis (The Juilliard School, 1981)
Tyson, Alan, *The Authentic English Editions of Beethoven* (London, 1963)
Unverricht, Hubert, *Die Eigenschriften und die Originalausgaben von Werken*
    Beethovens in ihrer Bedeutung fur die moderne Textkritik (Basel, 1960)
Westphal, Kurt, *Vom Einfall zur Symphonie: Einblick in Beethovens Schaffensweise*
    (Berlin, 1965)

Catalogues and bibliographical sources

Albrecht, Otto Erich, "Beethoven Autographs in the United States," in *Beiträge zur Beethoven-Bibliographie*, ed. Kurt Dorfmüller (Munich, 1978), 1–11

Albrecht, Theodore, *Beethoven: A Guide to Research* (New York, 1992)

Bartlitz, Evaline, *Die Beethoven-Sammlung in der Musikabteilung der Deutschen Staatsbibliothek: Verzeichnis* (Berlin, 1970)

Dorfmüller, Kurt, ed., *Beiträge zur Beethoven Bibliographie* (Munich, 1978)

Fishman, Nathan, "Verzeichnis aller in der UdSSR ermittelten und registrierten Beethoven-Autographe. Stand: 1. Januar 1980," *Zu Beethoven* 3, ed. Harry Goldschmidt (Berlin, 1988), 113–40

Fuchs, Ingrid, ed., *Musikautographe Ludwig van Beethovens in öffentliche Wiener Sammlungen* (Tutzing, forthcoming)

Hess, Willy, *Verzeichnis der nicht in der Gesamtausgabe veröffentlichten Werke Ludwig van Beethovens* (Wiesbaden, 1957)

Kerman, Joseph, "Beethoven Sketchbooks in the British Museum," *Proceedings of the Royal Musical Association* 93 (1966–67), 77–96

Kinsky, George, *Das Werk Beethovens: Thematisch-bibliographisches Verzeichnis seiner sämtlichen vollendeten Kompositionen*, compl. and ed. Hans Halm (Munich and Duisburg, 1955)

Klein, Hans-Günter, *Ludwig van Beethoven: Autographe und Abschriften*, Staatsbibliothek Preussischer Kulturbesitz, Kataloge der Musikabteilung, ed. Rudolf Elvers, 1st series, *Handschriften*, 2 (Berlin, 1975)

Newman, William S., "A Chronological Checklist of Collected Editions of Beethoven's Solo Piano Sonatas Since His Own Day," *Notes* 33 (1976–7), 503–30

Schmidt, Hans, "Verzeichnis der Skizzen Beethovens," BJ 6 (1969), 7–128
  "Die Beethoven Handschriften des Beethovenhauses in Bonn," BJ 7 (1971), vii–xxiv and 1–443; addenda and corrigenda in BJ 8 (1971–2), 207–20

Schürmann, Kurt, ed., *Ludwig van Beethoven: alle vertonten und musikalisch bearbeiteten Texte* (Münster, 1980)

Slezak, Friedrich, *Beethovens Wiener Originalverleger* (Vienna, 1987)

Tyson, Alan, *The Authentic English Editions of Beethoven* (London, 1963)

Unger, Max, ed., *Eine Schweizer Beethovensammlung. Katalog* (Zurich, 1939)

Year books, conference reports, collections of essays

Beethoven Essays: Studies in Honor of Elliot Forbes, ed. Lewis Lockwood, and Phyllis Benjamin (Cambridge, MA, 1984)

Beethoven Forum, ed. Lewis Lockwood et al., vols. 1–7 (Lincoln, 1992–99)

Beethoven. Interpretationen seiner Werke, ed. Albrecht Riethmüller, Carl Dahlhaus, and Alexander L. Ringer, 2 vols. (Laaber, 1994)

Beethovenjahrbuch, ed. Theodor Frimmel, vols. 1–2 (Munich and Leipzig, 1908–09)

Neues Beethoven Jahrbuch, ed. Adolf Sandberger, vols. 1–10 (Augsburg, 1924–42)

Beethoven Jahrbuch. Zweite Reihe, ed. Joseph Schmidt-Görg et al., vols. 1–10 (Bonn, 1953–80)

Beethoven-Studien, ed. Erich Schenk (Vienna, 1970)

Beethoven Studies, ed. Alan Tyson, vol. I (New York, 1973; London, 1974); vol. II
  (Oxford, 1977); vol. III (Cambridge, 1982)
Beethoven Symposion Wien 1970, ed. Erich Schenk (Vienna, 1971)
Bericht über den Internationalen Musikwissenschaftlichen Kongress Bonn 1970, ed.
  Carl Dahlhaus, et al. (Kassel, 1971)
Bericht über den Internationalen Beethoven-Kongress 20.–23. März 1977 in Berlin, ed.
  Harry Goldschmidt, Karl-Heinz Köhler, and Konrad Niemann (Leipzig, 1978)
Musikkonzepte 8: Beethoven: Das Problem der Interpretation, ed. Heinz-Klaus
  Metzger and Rainer Riehn (Munich, 1979)
Ludwig van Beethoven, ed. Ludwig Finscher (Darmstadt, 1983)
The Beethoven Compendium, ed. Barry Cooper (London, 1991)
The Beethoven Journal, ed. William Meredith, vols. 1–13 (San Jose, 1986–98). (Early
  volumes published as the *Beethoven Newsletter*)
The Beethoven Reader, ed. Denis Arnold, and Nigel Fortune (New York, 1971)
The Creative World of Beethoven, ed. Paul Henry Lang (New York, 1971); rpt. of MQ
  66 (1970), 515–793
The Beethoven Companion, ed. Thomas Scherman, and Louis Biancolli (Garden
  City, 1972)
Zu Beethoven: Aufsätze und Annotationen, ed. Harry Goldschmidt (Berlin, 1979)
Zu Beethoven 2: Aufsätze und Dokumente, ed. Harry Goldschmidt (Berlin, 1984)
Zu Beethoven 3: Aufsätze und Dokumente, ed. Harry Goldschmidt (Berlin, 1988)

Biographies, life-and-works studies
Abert, Hermann, *Zu Beethovens Persönlichkeit und Kunst* (Leipzig, 1927)
Adler, Guido, "Beethovens Charakter," in *Beethoven-Almanach der Deutschen
  Musikbücherei auf das Jahr 1927*, ed. Gustav Bosse (Regensburg, 1927)
Bankl, Hans, and Jesserer, Hans. *Die Krankheiten Ludwig van Beethovens:
  Pathographie seines Lebens und Pathologie seiner Leiden* (Vienna, 1987)
Bekker, Paul, *Beethoven* (Berlin, 1912); tr. Mildred M. Bozman (London and
  Toronto, 1990)
Brandenburg, Sieghard, and Gutiérrez-Denhoff, Martella, eds., *Beethoven und
  Böhmen: Beiträge zu Biographie und Wirkungsgeschichte Beethovens* (Bonn,
  1988)
Breuning, Gerhard von, *Memories of Beethoven: From the House of the Black-Robed
  Spaniards*, ed. Maynard Solomon, tr. Henry Mins and Maynard Solomon
  (Cambridge, MA, 1992), first publ. as *Aus dem Schwarzspanierhause* (Vienna,
  1874)
Cooper, Martin Du Pre, *Beethoven: The Last Decade 1817–1827* (Oxford, 1970)
Dahlhaus, Carl, *Ludwig van Beethoven und seine Zeit* (Laaber, 1987)
  Nineteenth-Century Music, tr. J. Bradford Robinson (Berkeley, 1989)
Dannreuther, Edward, "Beethoven and his Works: A Study," *Macmillan's Magazine*,
  vol. 34, no. 201 (July 1876)
DeNora, Tia, *Beethoven and the Construction of Genius: Musical Politics in Vienna,
  1792–1803* (Berkeley, 1995)
  "Deconstructing Periodization: Sociological Methods and Historical
  Ethnography in Late Eighteenth-Century Vienna," BF 4 (1995), 1–15

Forbes, Elliot, rev. and ed., *Thayer's Life of Beethoven*, 2 vols. (Princeton, NJ, 1964)

Frimmel, Theodor von, *Beethoven-Studien* (Munich and Leipzig, 1905–06)
Beethoven-Handbuch, 2 vols. (Leipzig, 1926)

Goldschmidt, Harry, *Um die Unsterbliche Geliebte: Eine Bestandsaufnahme* (Leipzig, 1977)

Halm, August, *Beethoven* (Berlin, 1927)

Hanson, Alice Marie, *Musical Life in Biedermeier Vienna* (Cambridge, 1985)

Hess, Willy, *Beethoven-Studien* (Bonn, 1972)

Johnson, Douglas, "Music for Prague and Berlin: Beethoven's Concert Tour of 1796," in *Beethoven, Performers, and Critics: The International Beethoven Congress*, ed. Robert Winter and Bruce Carr (Detroit, 1980), 24–40
"1794–1795: Decisive Years in Beethoven's Early Development," in BS III, ed. Alan Tyson (Cambridge, 1982), 1–28

Kagan, Susan, *Archduke Rudolph, Beethoven's Patron, Pupil, and Friend: His Life and Music* (Stuyvesant, NY, 1988)

Kerman, Joseph, and Tyson, Alan, *The New Grove Beethoven* (London, 1983)

Kerst, Friedrich, *Beethoven, the Man and the Artist, as Revealed in his Own Words*, tr. Henry Edward Krehbiel (New York, 1964)

Kerst, Friedrich, ed., *Die Erinnerungen an Beethoven*, 2 vols. (Stuttgart, 1913)

Kinderman, William, *Beethoven* (Berkeley, 1995)

Knight, Frida, *Beethoven and the Age of Revolution* (London, 1973)

Knittel, K. M., "Imitation, Individuality, and Illness: Behind Beethoven's 'Three Styles,'" BF 4 (1995), 17–36

Kramer, Richard, "Notes to Beethoven's Education," JAMS 28 (1975), 72–101

Kross, Siegfried, *Beethoven: Mensch seiner Zeit* (Bonn, 1980)

Landon, H. C. Robbins, *Beethoven: A Documentary Study* (London, 1970; abridged edn., 1974)
Beethoven: His Life, Work and World (London, 1992)

Lühning, Helga, and Brandenburg, Sieghard, eds., *Beethoven: Zwischen Revolution und Restauration* (Bonn, 1989)

Mann, Alfred, "Beethoven's Contrapuntal Studies with Haydn," MQ 56 (1970), 711–26

Marx, Adolf Bernhard, *Ludwig van Beethoven: Leben und Schaffen* (Berlin, 1859)

Matthews, Denis, *Beethoven* (London, 1985)

Mellers, Wilfrid, *Beethoven and the Voice of God* (New York, 1983)

Moore, Julia V., "Beethoven and Musical Economics" (Ph.D. diss., University of Illinois, Champaign-Urbana, 1987)

Moscheles, Ignaz, ed., *The Life of Beethoven*, 2 vols. (London, 1841)

Newman, Ernest, *The Unconscious Beethoven* (London, 1927; rev. edn., 2/1969)

Nohl, Ludwig, *Beethovens Leben*, 3 vols. (Vienna, 1864; Leipzig, 1867 and 1877)
Beethoven, Liszt, Wagner (Vienna, 1874)

Oulibicheff, Aléxandre, *Beethoven, ses critiques, ses glossateurs* (Paris, 1857)

Riezler, Walter, *Beethoven*, tr. George Douglas H. Pidcock (London, 1938)

Rolland, Romain, *La vie de Beethoven* (1903)
Beethoven: Les grandes époques créatrices, 5 vols. (Paris, 1928–57; translations of vols. I and II, New York, 1929, 1931)
Beethoven the Creator, tr. Ernest Newman (New York, 1964)

Schiedermair, Ludwig, *Der junge Beethoven* (Leipzig, 1925)

Schindler, Anton, *Biographie von Ludwig van Beethoven* (Münster, 1840); tr. as *The Life of Beethoven*, ed. Ignaz Moscheles, 2 vols. (London, 1841); 2nd edn. with supplementary chapter "Beethoven in Paris" (Münster, 1845); 3rd edn., 2 vols. (Münster, 1860); tr. C. S. Jolly as *Beethoven as I Knew Him*, ed. D. W. MacArdle (London, 1966)

Schmidt-Görg, Joseph, *Beethoven: Die Geschichte seiner Familie* (Bonn, 1964)

Schmidt-Görg, Joseph, and Schmidt, Hans, *Ludwig van Beethoven* (Bonn and Hamburg, 1970)

Schrade, Leo, *Beethoven in France* (New Haven, 1942)

Smolle, Kurt, *Wohnstätten Ludwig van Beethovens von 1792 bis zu seinem Tod* (Bonn, 1970)

Solomon, Maynard, *Beethoven* (New York, 1977; 2nd edn. 1998)

   Beethoven Essays (Cambridge, MA, 1988), 205–15

Sonneck, Oskar G., *Beethoven: Impressions of Contemporaries* (New York, 1926)

Sorsby, Maurice, "Beethoven's Deafness," *Journal of Laryngology and Otology* 45 (1930), 529–44

Sterba, Richard, and Sterba, Editha, *Beethoven and His Nephew: A Psychological Study of Their Relationship* (New York, 1937)

Tellenbach, Marie-Elisabeth, *Beethoven und seine "unsterbliche Geliebte," Josephine Brunswick* (Zurich, 1983)

Tovey, Donald Francis, *Beethoven* (London, 1944)

Tyson, Alan, "Ferdinand Ries (1784–1838): The History of his Contribution to Beethoven Biography," 19CM 7 (1984), 209–21

Webster, James, "The Falling-Out between Haydn and Beethoven: The Evidence of the Sources," in *Beethoven Essays: Studies in Honor of Elliot Forbes*, ed. Lewis Lockwood and Phyllis Benjamin (Cambridge, MA, 1984), 3–45

   "The Concept of Beethoven's 'Early' Period in the Context of Periodizations in General," BF 3 (1994), 1–27

Wegeler, Franz Gerhard, and Ries, Ferdinand, *Biographische Notizen über Ludwig van Beethoven* (Koblenz, 1838); 2nd edn. with "Nachtrag" by Wegeler (Koblenz, 1845); rev. A. Kalischer (Berlin, 1906); tr. Frederick Noonan as *Remembering Beethoven* (Arlington, 1987)

Wolf, Stefan, *Beethovens Neffenkonflikt* (Munich, 1995)

The music: style and structure, genre studies, and individual works, including sketch studies

Agawu, Kofi, *Playing with Signs: A Semiotic Interpretation of Classic Music* (Princeton, 1991)

Broyles, Michael E., *Beethoven: The Emergence and Evolution of Beethoven's Heroic Style* (New York, 1987)

Cooper, Barry, *Beethoven and the Creative Process* (Oxford, 1990)

Dahlhaus, Carl, *Ludwig van Beethoven, Approaches to his Music*, tr. Mary Whittall (Oxford, 1991)

Enss, Eberhard, *Beethoven als Bearbeiter eigener Werke* (Taunusstein, 1988)

Hatten, Robert, *Musical Meaning in Beethoven: Markedness, Correlation, and Interpretation* (Bloomington, 1994)

Imeson, Sylvia, *"The time gives it proof." Paradox in the Late Music of Beethoven* (New York, 1996)

Kolisch, Rudolf, "Tempo and Character in Beethoven's Music," MQ 77 (1993), 90–131

Lenz, Wilhelm von, *Beethoven et ses trois styles* (Paris, 1852, rpt. New York, 1980)

Lockwood, Lewis, "Beethoven before 1800: The Mozart Legacy," BF 3 (1994), 39–52

　　Beethoven: Studies in the Creative Process (Cambridge, MA, 1992)

Lühning, Helga, "Beethoven als Bearbeiter eigener Werke," in *Münchener Beethoven-Studien* (Munich, 1992), 117–27

Metzger, Heinz-Klaus, and Riehn, Rainer, ed., *Musikkonzepte 8: Beethoven: Das Problem der Interpretation* (Munich, 1979)

Misch, Ludwig, *Die Faktoren der Einheit in der Mehrsätzigkeit der Werke Beethovens* (Munich and Duisburg, 1958)

Ratner, Leonard, *Classic Music: Expression, Form, and Style* (New York, 1980)

Reti, Rudolph, *The Thematic Process in Music* (New York, 1951)

Rosen, Charles, *The Classical Style: Haydn, Mozart, Beethoven*, rev. exp. edn. (New York, 1997)

Rothfarb, Lee A., "Beethoven's Formal Dynamics: August Halm's Phenomenological Perspective," BF 5 (1996), 65–84

Rothstein, William, "Beethoven with and without *Kunstgespräng*: Metrical Ambiguity Reconsidered," BF 4 (1995), 165–93

Schmitz, Arnold, *Beethovens 'zwei Prinzipe'* (Berlin, 1923)

Schwarz, Boris, "Beethoven and the French Violin School," MQ 44 (1958), 431–47

Sisman, Elaine R., "Tradition and Transformation in the Alternating Variations of Haydn and Beethoven," Acta 62 (1990), 152–82

Stadlen, Peter, "Beethoven and the Metronome," *Soundings* 9 (1982), 38–73

Tovey, Donald F., *Beethoven* (London, 1944; rpt. 1965)

Piano music

Barford, Philip, "The Piano Music – II," in *The Beethoven Companion*, ed. Denis Arnold and Nigel Fortune (London, 1971), 126–93

Barth, George, *The Pianist as Orator, Beethoven and the Transformation of Keyboard Style* (Ithaca, 1992)

Cone, Edward, "Beethoven's Experiments in Composition: The Late Bagatelles," in BS II, ed. Alan Tyson (London, 1977), 84–105

Cook, Nicholas, "Beethoven's Unfinished Piano Concerto: A Case of Double Vision?" JAMS 42 (1989), 338–74

Drake, Kenneth, *The Sonatas of Beethoven as he Played and Taught Them* (Bloomington, 1981)

Fischer, Edwin, *Beethoven's Pianoforte Sonatas*, tr. Stanley Godman (London, 1959)

Frohlich, Martha, *Beethoven's Appassionata Sonata* (Oxford, 1991)

Jeffrey, Brian, ed., *Ludwig van Beethoven: The 32 Piano Sonatas in Reprints of the First and Early Editions* (London, 1989)

Kinderman, William, *Beethoven's Diabelli Variations* (Oxford, 1987)

"Integration and Narrative Design in Beethoven's Piano Sonata in A♭ Major, Opus 110," BF 1 (1992), 111–45

"Beethoven's High Comic Style in Piano Sonatas of the 1790s, or Beethoven, Uncle Toby, and the 'Muckcart-driver,' " BF 5 (1996), 119–38

Kramer, Lawrence, "Beethoven's Two-Movement Piano Sonatas and the Utopia of Romantic Esthetics," in L. Kramer, *Music as Cultural Practice 1880–1900* (Berkeley, 1990)

"Primitive Encounters: Beethoven's 'Tempest' Sonata, Musical Meaning, and Enlightenment Anthropology," BF 6 (1998), 31–66

Macdonald, Hugh, "Fantasy and Order in Beethoven's Phantasie op. 77," in *Modern Musical Scholarship*, ed. Edward Olleson (Stocksfield, 1980), 141–50

Marshall, Robert L., ed., *Eighteenth-Century Keyboard Music* (New York, 1994)

Marston, Nicholas, "Approaching the Sketches for Beethoven's 'Hammerklavier' Sonata," JAMS 44 (1991), 404–50

Beethoven's Piano Sonata in E, Op. 109 (Oxford, 1995)

"From A to B: The History of an Idea in the 'Hammerklavier' Sonata," BF 6 (1998), 97–128

Münster, Arnold, *Studien zu Beethoven's Diabelli-Variationen* (Munich, 1982)

Newman, William, *Beethoven on Beethoven: Playing His Piano Music His Way* (New York, 1988)

Reti, Rudolph, *Thematic Patterns in Sonatas of Beethoven* (London, 1967)

Ringer, Alexander, "Beethoven and the London Pianoforte School," MQ 56 (1970), 742–58, rpt. in *The Creative World of Beethoven*, ed. Paul H. Lang (New York, 1971)

Schmalfeldt, Janet, "Form as the Process of Becoming: The Beethoven-Hegelian Tradition and the 'Tempest' Sonata," BF 4 (1995), 37–71

Sipe, Thomas, "Beethoven, Shakespeare, and the 'Appassionata,' " BF 4 (1995), 73–96

Sisman, Elaine R., "Pathos and the *Pathétique:* Rhetorical Stance in Beethoven's C-Minor Sonata, Op. 13," BF 3 (1994), 81–105

"After the Heroic Style: *Fantasia* and the 'Characteristic' Sonatas of 1809," BF 6 (1998), 67–96

Stanley, Glenn, "The 'wirklich gantz neue Manier' and the Path to It: Beethoven's Variations for Piano, 1783–1802," BF 3 (1994), 53–79

"Genre Aesthetics and Function: Beethoven's Piano Sonatas in Their Cultural Context," BF 6 (1998), 1–29

Tovey, Donald Francis, *A Companion to Beethoven's Pianoforte Sonatas* (London, 1931)

Tyson, Alan, "The First Edition of Beethoven's Op. 119 Bagatelles," MQ 44 (1963), 331–38

Music for small ensemble

Bockholdt, Rudolf, and Weber-Bockholdt, Petra, eds., *Beethovens Klavier-Trios: Symposion München 1990* (Munich, 1992)

Brandenburg, Sieghard, "The Historical Background to the Heiliger Dankgesang in Beethoven's A minor Quartet op. 132," in BS III, ed. Alan Tyson (Cambridge, 1982), 161–91

Brandenburg, Sieghard, and Loos, Helmut, eds., *Beiträge zu Beethovens Kammermusik: Symposion Bonn 1984* (Munich, 1987)

Chua, Daniel K. L., *The "Galitzin" Quartets of Beethoven: Opp. 127, 132, 130* (Princeton, 1995)

Cooke, Deryck, "The Unity of Beethoven's Late Quartets," *Music Review* 24 (1963), 30–49

Finscher, Ludwig, *Studien zur Geschichte des Streichquartetts II: Die Entstehung des klassischen Streichquartetts. Von den Vorformen zur Grundlegung durch Joseph Haydn* (Kassel, 1974)

Fortune, Nigel, "The Chamber Music with Piano," in *The Beethoven Companion*, ed. Denis Arnold and Nigel Fortune (London, 1971)

Jander, Owen, "The 'Kreutzer' Sonata as Dialogue," *Early Music* 16 (1988), 34–49

Kerman, Joseph, *The Beethoven Quartets* (Oxford, 1976)

Kinderman, William, "Tonality and Form in the Variation Movements of Beethoven's Late Quartets," in *Beiträge zu Beethovens Kammermusik: Symposium Bonn 1984*, ed. Sieghard Brandenburg and Helmut Loos (Munich, 1987) 135–51

Kirkendale, Warren, "The 'Great Fugue' Op. 133: Beethoven's Art of Fugue," Acta 35 (1963), 14–24

Kramer, Richard, '"Das Organische der Fuge': On the Autograph of Beethoven's String Quartet in F major, op. 59, no. 1," in *The String Quartets of Haydn, Mozart, and Beethoven*, ed. Christoph Wolff (Cambridge, 1980), 223–65
  "Between Cavatina and Overture: Opus 130 and the Voices of Narrative," BF 1 (1992), 165–89

Kropfinger, Klaus, "Das gespaltene Werk: Beethovens Streichquartett op. 130/133," *Beiträge zu Beethovens Kammermusik: Symposion Bonn 1984*, ed. Sieghard Brandenburg and Helmut Loos (Munich, 1987), 296–335

Levy, Janet M., *Beethoven's Compositional Choices: The Two Versions of op. 18, no. 1, First Movement* (Philadelphia, 1982)

Lockwood, Lewis, "The Autograph of the First Movement of Beethoven's Sonata for Violoncello and Pianoforte, op. 69," *The Music Forum* 2 (1970), 1–109
  "Beethoven's Early Works for Violoncello and Contemporary Violoncello Technique," in *Beethoven-Kolloquium 1977: Autographe und Aufführungspraxis*, ed. Rudolf Klein (Kassel, 1978), 174–82
  "A Problem of Form: The 'Scherzo' of Beethoven's String Quartet in F Major, Op. 59, No. 1," BF 2 (1993), 85–95

Mahaim, Ivan, *Naissance et renaissance des derniers quatuors de Beethoven*, 2 vols. (Paris, 1964)

Mitchell, William J., "Beethoven's La Malinconia from the String Quartet, op. 18, no. 6," *The Music Forum* 3 (1973), 269–80

Obelkevich, Mary R., "The Growth of a Musical Idea – Beethoven's Op. 96," *Current Musicology* 11 (1971), 91–114

Radcliffe, Philip, *Beethoven's String Quartets* (London, 1965, New York, 1968)

Ratner, Leonard, *The Beethoven String Quartets: Compositional Strategies and Rhetoric* (Sandford, 1995)

Reynolds, Christopher, "Ends and Means in the Second Finale to Beethoven's Op.

30, no. 1," in *Beethoven Essays: Studies in Honor of Elliot Forbes*, ed. Lewis Lockwood and Phyllis Benjamin (Cambridge, MA, 1984), pp. 127–45

Simpson, R., "The Chamber Music for Strings," in *The Beethoven Companion*, ed. Denis Arnold and Nigel Fortune (London, 1971), pp. 241–78

Staehelin, Martin, "Another Approach to Beethoven's Last String Quartet Oeuvre: The Unfinished String Quintet of 1826/27," in *The String Quartets of Haydn, Mozart, and Beethoven: Studies of the Autograph Manuscripts*, ed. Christoph Wolff (Cambridge, 1980), 302–23

Wallace, Robin, "Background and Expression in the First Movement of Beethoven's Op. 132," JM 7 (1989), 3–20

Webster, James, "Traditional Elements in Beethoven's Middle-Period String Quartets," in *Beethoven, Performers, and Critics: The International Beethoven Congress Detroit 1977*, ed. Robert Winter and Bruno Carr (Detroit, 1980), 94–133

Winter, Robert, *Compositional Origins of Beethoven's String Quartet in C sharp minor, Op. 131* (Ph.D. diss., University of Chicago, 1978; Ann Arbor, 1982)

Winter, Robert and Martin, Robert, eds., *The Beethoven Quartet Companion* (Berkeley, 1994)

Symphonies and concertos

Berlioz, Hector, *A Critical Study of Beethoven's Nine Symphonies*, tr. Edwin Evans (London, 1958)

Brandenburg, Sieghard, "Die Skizzen zur Neunten Symphonie," in *Zu Beethoven 2: Aufsätze und Annotationen*, ed. Harry Goldschmidt (Berlin, 1984), 88–129

Cavett-Dunsby, Esther, "Schenker's Analysis of the 'Eroica' Finale," *Theory and Practice* 11 (1989), 43–51

Cook, Nicholas, "Beethoven's Unfinished Piano Concerto: A Case of Double Vision?" JAMS, 42 (1989), 338–74
  Beethoven Symphony No. 9 (Cambridge, 1993)

Floros, Constantin, *Beethovens Eroica und Prometheus-Musik* (Wilhelmshaven, 1978)

Forbes, Elliot, ed., *Ludwig van Beethoven: Symphony No. 5 in C minor* (New York, 1971)

Frogley, Alain, "Beethoven's Struggle for Simplicity in the Sketches for the Third Movement of the Pastoral Symphony," BF 4 (1995), 99–134

Geck, Martin and Schleuning, Peter, *"Geschrieben auf Bonaparte": Beethoven's "Eroica" – Revolution, Reaktion, Rezeption* (Hamburg, 1989)

Gossett, Philip, "Beethoven's Sixth Symphony: Sketches for the First Movement," JAMS 27 (1974), 248–84

Gülke, Peter, "Zur Bestimmung des Sinfonischen bei Beethoven," in *Deutsches Jahrbuch der Musikwissenschaft* (1970), 67–95
  Zur Neuausgabe der 5. Sinfonie von Ludwig van Beethoven: Werk und Edition (Leipzig, 1978)

Hinton, Stephen, "Not *Which* Tones? The Crux of Beethoven's Ninth," 19CM 22 (1998), 61–77

Hopkins, Antony, *The Nine Symphonies of Beethoven* (London, 1981)

Jander, Owen, "Orpheus Revisited: A Ten-Year Retrospect on the Andante con moto of Beethoven's Fourth Piano Concerto," 19CM 19 (1995), 31–49

Jones, David Wyn, *Beethoven: Pastoral Symphony* (Cambridge, 1996)

Kerman, Joseph, "Representing a Relationship: Notes on a Beethoven Concerto," *Representations* 39 (1992), 80–101

Kinderman, William, "Beethoven's Symbol for the Deity in the *Missa solemnis* and the Ninth Symphony, 19CM 9 (1985), 102–18

Konold, Wulff, *Ludwig van Beethoven: Violin-Konzert D-Dur, op. 61, Werkmonographie mit Partitur* (Mainz, 1986)

Kramer, Lawrence, "The Harem Threshold: Turkish Music and Greek Love in Beethoven's 'Ode to Joy,'" *19th-Century Music* 22 (1998), 78–90

Levy, David, *Beethoven. The Ninth Symphony* (New York, 1995)

Lockwood, Lewis, " 'Eroica' Perspectives: Strategy and Design in the First Movement," in BS II, ed. Alan Tyson (Cambridge, 1982), 85–105

Marston, Nicholas, "Beethoven's 'Anti-Organicism'? The Origins of the Slow Movement of the Ninth Symphony," in *Studies in the History of Music 3: The Creative Process*, ed. Ronald Broude (New York, 1993), 169–200

Meredith, William, "Forming the New from the Old: Beethoven's Use of Variation in the Fifth Symphony," in *Beethoven's Compositional Process* (Lincoln, NB, 1991), 101–21

Plantinga, Leon, *Beethoven's Concertos* (New York, 1998)

Sanders, Ernest, "The Sonata-Form Finale of Beethoven's Ninth Symphony," 19CM 22 (1998), 54–60

Schachter, Carl, "Mozart's Last and Beethoven's First: Echoes of K. 551 in the First Movement of Opus 21," in *Mozart Studies*, ed. Cliff Eisen (Oxford, 1991) 227–51

Schenker, Heinrich, *Beethovens Neunte Sinfonie* (Vienna, 1912; rpt. 1969)
Beethovens Fünfte Sinfonie (Vienna, 1925; rpt. 1969)
Beethoven's Ninth Symphony: A Portrayal of its Musical Content, with Running Commentary on Performance and Literature as well, tr. and ed. John Rothgeb (New Haven, 1992)

Schneider, Hans, *Ludwig van Beethoven: 8. Sinfonie F-Dur, op. 93* (Mainz, 1989)

Sipe, Thomas, *Beethoven: Symphony No. 3, "Eroica"* (Cambridge, 1998)

Solie, Ruth, "Beethoven as Secular Humanist: Ideology and the Ninth Symphony in Nineteenth-century Criticism," in *Explorations in Music, the Arts and Ideas: Essays in Honor of Leonard B. Meyer*, ed. E. Narmour and R. Solie (New York, 1988)

Solomon, Maynard, "Beethoven's Ninth Symphony: A Search for Order," 19CM 10 (1986), 3–23

Taruskin, Richard, "Resisting the Ninth," 19CM 12 (1989), 241–56

Treitler, Leo, "History, Criticism, and Beethoven's Ninth Symphony," 19CM 3 (1979–80), 193–210

Tusa, Michael, "*Noch einmal:* Form and Content in the Finale of Beethoven's Ninth Symphony," BF 7 (1999), 113–37

Walz, Matthias, "Kontrastierende Werkpaare in Beethovens Symphonien," AfMW 46 (1989), 271–93

Webster, James, "The Form of the Finale of Beethoven's Ninth Symphony," BF 1 (1992), 25–62

Whiting, Steven Moore, "'Hört ihr wohl': Zu Funktion und Programm von Beethovens Chorfantasie," AfMW 45 (1988), 132–47

Will, Richard, "Time, Morality, and Humanity in Beethoven's Pastoral Symphony," JAMS 50 (1997), 271–329

Opera and songs

Cadenbach, Rainer, "Die 'Leonore' des Pierre Gaveaux – Ein Modell für Beethovens 'Fidelio'?" in *Collegium Musicologicum: Festschrift Emil Platen zum Sechzigsten Geburtstag*, ed. Martella Gutiérrez-Denhoff (Bonn, 1986), 100–21

Charlton, David, "The French Theatrical Origins of *Fidelio*," in *Ludwig van Beethoven: "Fidelio,"* ed. Paul Robinson (Cambridge, 1996), 51–67

Cooper, Barry, *Beethoven's Folksong Settings: Chronology, Sources, Style* (Oxford, 1994)

Dean, Winton, "Beethoven and Opera," in *The Beethoven Reader*, ed. Denis Arnold and Nigel Fortune (New York, 1971), 381–82

Hess, Willy, *Beethovens Oper Fidelio und ihre drei Fassungen* (Zurich, 1953)

Kerman, Joseph, "An die ferne Geliebte," in BS I, ed. Alan Tyson (New York, 1973), 123–57

Lühning, Helga, "Beethovens langer Weg zum 'Fidelio,'" in *Opernkomposition als Prozess*, ed. Werner Breig, Musikwissenschaftliche Arbeiten 29 (Kassel, 1996), 65–90

Reynolds, Christopher, "The Representational Impulse in Late Beethoven, I: *An die ferne Geliebte*," Acta 60 (1988), 43–61

"Florestan Reading *Fidelio*," BF 4 (1995), 135–64

Robinson, Paul, "*Fidelio* and the French Revolution," in *Ludwig van Beethoven: "Fidelio,"* ed. Paul Robinson (Cambridge, 1996), 68–100

Tusa, Michael C., "Beethoven and Opera: The Grave-digging Duet in *Leonore* (1805)," BF 5 (1996), 1–63

"Music as Drama: Structure, Style, and Process in *Fidelio*," in *Ludwig van Beethoven: "Fidelio,"* ed. Paul Robinson (Cambridge, 1996), 101–31

Masses and sacred music

Adorno, Theodor, "Alienated Masterpiece: The Missa Solemnis," tr. Duncan Smith, *Telos* 9 (1976–77), 113–24

Brandenburg, Sieghard, "Beethovens Oratorium *Christus am Ölberge*. Ein unbequemes Werk," in *Beiträge zur Geschichte des Oratoriums seit Händel: Festschrift Günther Massenkeil zum 60. Geburtstag*, ed. Rainer Cadenbach and Helmut Loos (Bonn, 1986), 203–20

Churgin, Bathia, "Beethoven and Mozart's Requiem: A New Connection," JM 5
      (1987), 457–77
Drabkin, William, *Beethoven: Missa solemnis* (Cambridge, 1991)
   "The Sketches and Autographs for the Later Movements of Beethoven's *Missa
      solemnis*," BF 2 (1993), 97–132
Fiske, Roger, *Beethoven's Missa Solemnis* (London, 1979)
Friesenhagen, Andreas, *Die Messen Ludwig van Beethovens: Studien zur Vertonung
      des liturgischen Textes zwischen Rhetorik und Dramatisierung* (Cologne, 1996)
Kirkendale, Warren, "New Roads to Old Ideas in Beethoven's Missa solemnis," MQ
      56 (1970), 665–701
Lodes, Birgit, *Das Gloria in Beethovens Missa Solemnis* (Tutzing, 1997)
   "'When I try, now and then, to give musical form to my turbulent feelings': The
      Human and the Divine in the Gloria of Beethoven's *Missa solemnis*," BF 6
      (1998), 143–79
McGrann, Jeremiah Walker R., *Beethoven's Mass in C, Opus 86: Genesis and
      Compositional Background*, 2 vols. (Ph.D. diss., Harvard University, 1991; Ann
      Arbor, 1993)
Treitler, Leo, "'To Worship that Celestial Sound': Motives for Analysis," JM 1 (1982),
      153–70
Tyson, Alan, "The 1803 Version of Beethoven's *Christus am Oelberge*," MQ 56
      (1970), 551–84
Winter, Robert, "Reconstructing Riddles: The Sources for Beethoven's Missa
      Solemnis," in *Beethoven Essays: Studies in Honor of Elliot Forbes*, ed. Lewis
      Lockwood and Phyllis Benjamin (Cambridge, 1984), 217–50
Zickenheiner, Otto, *Untersuchungen zur Credo-Fuge der Missa Solemnis von Ludwig
      van Beethoven* (Munich, 1984)

Reception

Adorno, Theodor W., *Beethoven: Philosophie der Musik. Fragmente und Texte*, ed.
      Rolf Tiedemann (Frankfurt, 1993)
Bauer, Elisabeth Eleanor, *Wie Beethoven auf den Sockel kam. Die Entstehung eines
      musikalischen Mythos* (Stuttgart, 1992)
Beckage, Donna, "Beethoven in Western Literature" (Ph.D. diss., University of
      California, Riverside, 1977)
Bonds, Mark Evan, *After Beethoven. Imperatives of Originality in the Symphony*
      (Cambridge, MA, 1996)
Burnham, Scott, "Criticism, Faith, and the Idee: A. B. Marx's Early Reception of
      Beethoven," 19CM 14 (1990), 183–92.
   "On the Programmatic Reception of Beethoven's *Eroica* Symphony," BF 1 (1992),
      1–24
   Beethoven Hero (Princeton, 1995)
Cadenbach, Rainer, ed., *Mythos Beethoven* (Laaber, 1986)
Comini, Alessandra, *The Changing Image of Beethoven: A Study in Mythmaking*
      (New York, 1987)
Dennis, David B., *Beethoven in German Politics, 1870–1989* (New Haven, 1996)

Eggebrecht, Hans Heinrich, *Zur Geschichte der Beethoven-Rezeption* (Mainz, 1972; Laaber, 1994)

Eichhorn, Andreas, *Beethovens Neunte Symphonie. Die Geschichte ihrer Aufführung und Rezeption* (Kassel, 1993)

Hinton, Stephen, "Adorno's Unfinished *Beethoven*," BF 5 (1996), 139–53

Knittel, Kristen Marta, "From Chaos to History: The Reception of Beethoven's Late Quartets" (Ph.D. diss., Princeton University, 1992)

Kropfinger, Klaus, *Wagner and Beethoven*, tr. Peter Palmer (Cambridge, 1991)

Kunze, Stefan, ed., *Ludwig van Beethoven: Die Werke im Spiegel seiner Zeit. Gesammelte Konzertberichte und Rezensionen bis 1830* (Laaber, 1987)

Loos, Helmut, ed., *Beethoven und die Nachwelt: Materialien zur Wirkungsgeschichte Beethovens* (Bonn, 1986)

Newman, William S., "The Beethoven Mystique in Romantic Art, Literature and Music," MQ 69 (1983), 345–87

Saloman, Ora Frishberg, "Origins, Performances, and Reception History of Beethoven's Late Quartets," MQ 80 (1996), 525–40

Schering, Arnold, "Einleitung. Zur Geschichte und Aesthetik der Beethovendeutung," in Schering, *Beethoven und die Dichtung* (Berlin, 1936), 13–120

Schmitz, Arnold, *Das Romantische Beethovenbild: Darstellung und Kritik* (Berlin, 1927)

Schrade, Leo, *Beethoven in France: The Development of an Idea* (New Haven, 1942)

Treitler, Leo, "History, Criticism, and Beethoven's Ninth Symphony," 19CM 3 (1980), 193–210

Wallace, Robin, *Beethoven's Critics: Aesthetic Dilemmas and Resolutions during the Composer's Lifetime* (Cambridge, 1986)

Zenck, Martin, *Die Bach-Rezeption des Späten Beethoven: Zum Verhältnis von Musikhistoriographie und Rezeptionsgeschichtsschreibung der "Klassik"* (Stuttgart, 1986)

Performance practice

Badura-Skoda, Eva, "Performance Conventions in Beethoven's Early Works," in *Beethoven, Performers, and Critics: The International Beethoven Congress*, ed. Robert Winter and Bruce Carr (Detroit, 1980), 52–75

Badura-Skoda, Paul, ed., *Über den richtigen Vortrag der sämtlichen Beethoven'schen Klavierwerke: Czerny's "Erinnerungen an Beethoven" sowie das 2. und 3. Kapitel des IV. Bandes der "Vollständigen theoretisch-practischen Pianoforte-Schule op. 500"* (Vienna, 1963)

Brown, Clive, "The Orchestra in Beethoven's Vienna," *Early Music* 16 (1988), 4–20
  "Historical Performance, Metronome Marks and Tempo in Beethoven's Symphonies," *Early Music* 19 (1991), 247–58

Czerny, Carl, *On the Proper Performance of All Beethoven's Works for the Piano*, ed. Paul Badura-Skoda (Vienna, 1970)

Del Mar, Norman, *Conducting Beethoven*, 2 vols. (New York, 1992)

Eichhorn, Andreas, *Beethovens Neunte Symphonie: Die Geschichte ihrer Aufführung und Rezeption* (Kassel, 1993)

Goldstein, Joanna, *A Beethoven Enigma: Performance Practice and the Piano Sonata, Opus 111* (New York, 1988)

Newman, William S., "Liszt's Interpreting of Beethoven's Piano Sonatas," MQ 58 (1972), 185–209

Stowell, Robin, ed., *Performing Beethoven*, Cambridge Studies in Performance Practice 4 (Cambridge, 1994)

Winter, Robert and Carr, Bruce, eds., *Beethoven, Performers, and Critics: The International Beethoven Congress* (Detroit, 1980)

General index

Abert, Hermann, 286–87
Adler, Guido, 286–87
  Dämonie, 287
Adorno, Theodor W., 235, 240, 289, 290,
  301–02, 324n.39
Albrecht, Theodor, 332n.7
Albrechtsberger, Johann Georg, 8, 20,
  311n.17, 324n.29
Allgemeine musikalische Zeitung, 11, 16, 52,
  274, 276
Amenda, Karl, 9, 153
Aristotle, 25, 309n.47
Arnim, Achim von, 186
Arnim, Antonie Brentano von, 11
Arnim, Bettina Brentano von, 11, 341n.13
  (*see also under* Brentano)
Arnim, Franz von Brentano, 11
Artaria, Domenico (publisher), 23, 162,
  201

Bach, Carl Philipp Emanuel, 20, 21, 22, 25, 46,
  52, 82, 125, 218–19
  *Versuch über die wahre Art, das Clavier zu
  spielen*, 20, 21
Bach, Johann Sebastian, 22, 25, 52, 119, 120,
  124, 283, 308n.41, 312n.27
  B minor Mass, 22
  Clavierübung, 124
  "Goldberg" Variations, 91
  Well-Tempered Clavier, 20, 105
Badura-Skoda, Paul, 270
Baillot, Pierre, 137
Balestrieri, Lionello, 300
  Beethoven: Kreutzer Sonata, 300
Bartók, Béla, 253–54
  String Quartet no. 1, 254
  Third Piano Concerto, 253
Baudelaire, Charles, 294
  La Musique, 294
Bauer-Lechner, Natalie, 240
Beethoven, Caspar Carl (brother), 4, 11, 12,
  23, 306n.1
Beethoven, Johann van (father), 7
Beethoven, Johanna (sister-in-law), 12, 13
Beethoven, Karl (nephew), 4, 10, 11, 12, 13,
  15, 19, 21, 23, 30, 298, 332n.10

Beethoven, Maria Magdalena (mother), 7
Beethoven, Nikolaus Johann (brother), 7, 10,
  19, 23, 306n.1
Bekker, Paul, 5, 165, 166, 167, 168, 171, 176
  Beethoven, 5
Berg, Alban, 171, 240
  Three Orchestral Pieces op. 6, 240
Berliner allgemeine musikalische Zeitung, 150,
  223, 276–77
Berlioz, Hector, 241–42, 243, 244, 262,
  263–64
  Symphonie fantastique, 242
Bernstein, Leonard, 18, 270
Bismarck, Otto von, Prince, 278
Bloch, Ernst, 301, 302
Block, Geoffrey, 108
Böhm, Joseph, 337n.8, 343n.33
Bonds, Mark Evan, 311n.16
Boosey, T. (publisher), 308n.33
Botstein, Leon, 7
Bouilly, Jean-Nicolas, 200, 202–05, 206, 209,
  329nn.20, 22, 331nn.46, 47
  Léonore, ou L'amour conjugal, 200, 202
Boulez, Pierre, 253, 335n.35
  Second Piano Sonata, 253
Bourdelle, Antoine, 299
Brahms, Johannes, 64, 141, 168, 240, 245,
  250
  First Piano Concerto, 240
  First Symphony, 334n.4
  Piano Sonata in C major, op. 1, 336n.58
  String Quartet in C minor, op. 51, no. 1,
  245
Brandenburg, Sieghard, 25, 222
Breitkopf & Härtel, 22, 25, 107, 224, 332n.13,
  340n.42
Brendel, Alfred, 123, 141, 142, 145, 319nn.15,
  18
Brentano, Antonie, 4
Brentano, Bettina, 198, 293, 303
Brentano, Clemens, 293
Breuning, Eleonore von, 52, 329n.24
Breuning, Gerhard von, 19, 329n.17
Breuning, Stephan von, 21, 200, 204–06,
  306n.1, 307nn.11, 15
Bridgetower, George, 10, 138

Index of Beethoven's compositions and sketches